Advocating Dignity

Pennsylvania Studies in Human Rights

Bert B. Lockwood Jr., Series Editor

A complete list of books in the series is available from the publisher.

Advocating Dignity

Human Rights Mobilizations in
Global Politics

Jean H. Quataert

PENN

University of Pennsylvania Press

Philadelphia

Published by
University of Pennsylvania Press
Philadelphia, Pennsylvania 19104-4112

Printed in the United States of America on acid-free paper

10   9   8   7   6   5   4   3   2   1

Library of Congress Cataloging-in-Publication Data

Quataert, Jean H. (Jean Helen), 1945–
    Advocating dignity : human rights mobilizations in global politics / Jean H. Quataert.
        p. cm. — (Pennsylvania studies in human rights)
    Includes bibliographical references and index.
    ISBN 978-0-8122-4163-1 (alk. paper)
    1. Human rights.   2. Citizenship.   3. Ethnic conflict.   I. Title.
JC571.Q465   2009
    323—dc22

                                                                          2009004277

To Donald, and our shared commitments

Contents

Illustrations

Figures

Maps

Preface

The origin of this book in some ways reflects my own intellectual biography as a German historian. It follows from my earlier study of the medical philanthropic associations run by patriotic women in the territories of Germany during the long nineteenth century. In the 1860s, when many Central European states signed the Geneva Conventions, these associations became part of the state and, after the wars of unification, the national German Red Cross. These ties drew me to the International Red Cross and Crescent movement and its wartime humanitarian relief services and also, for the first time, to international law. I had to grapple with many problems at the heart of this project on human rights: for example, the place of norms in power politics, of rights traditions in state-building, and of the role of history-writing in the struggle for a more just and peaceful world order. My readings on the International Committee of the Red Cross also pushed my interests beyond German borders and into a world of transnational networks and connections.

To place this book solely in the context of scholarly research, however, misses much of its passion. As a historian, I always have been deeply committed to teaching and writing about a past that is vital to the present. I tell my students that history is one of the great humanistic disciplines because it continuously speaks to the concerns and issues of each new generation. This book, I hope, practices what I preach. Based on my years as a working historian, this book reflects my conviction that historical perspectives are necessary for critical understanding of present-day challenges. As a historical inquiry, the book explores the emergence and development of human rights thinking and organizing and their impact on the course of global and domestic politics since 1945. And it does so partly by drawing on the voices, perspectives, and activities of the many courageous individuals and groups who took up the struggle for human rights in specific local, transnational, and international contexts.

Much is at stake in writing about human rights advocacy. The topic captures many ethical visions of a different future premised on human dignity: of global justice, equality, and nondiscrimination; of individual and group empowerment; and of meeting basic human and security needs in the face of armed struggle, environmental degradation, famines, and poverty. Their advocacy brought these principles to the intersection of clashing community, state, and global power interests. A major challenge has been to find the right voice for this book—to balance my own personal values and strong commitment to international human rights and humanitarian laws and norms with the need to offer historically precise accounts of the compromises and impediments that have affected the history. I have not shied away from confronting the limitations of human rights work, which had its own biases and uneven application. It was as flawed and imperfect as the human beings who originally created and then defended it from their own understandings, interests, and values. In confronting these conflicting pulls, I hope I have struck the right tone.

In writing this book, I have drawn widely from many fields of inquiry, including legal studies, philosophy, international relations theory, and political science, as well as women's and gender history. In addition, I have read broadly in the literature written by the activists themselves, from prominent U.N. staff to the founders of mainstream international nongovernmental organizations to those running refugee camps and providing humanitarian relief during times of war and civil strife to the people involved in the day-to-day campaigns for justice and equity. Each writes from his or her passionate and particular point of view.

As a project with a global reach for both specialists and the interested public, the book makes extensive use of secondary literature. It is not a traditional historical monograph rooted in archival materials but nonetheless uses primary sources. I have consulted a number of archives, notably for the background contexts, working in the repositories of the international socialist movement (the International Institute of Social History, Amsterdam) and also the archives and historical libraries of international feminism, namely The Women's Library (the Fawcett Library) in London and the International Information Centre and Archives for the Women's Movement in Amsterdam. In this age of the World Wide Web, furthermore, archival sources are available online, including extensive records of the African National Congress, the domestic organization at the center of the international antiapartheid movement. Also available online is the full range of official U.N. documents, reflecting over sixty years of operation. Use of such Web-based materials is necessary for a contemporary project such as mine; as I learned from the Binghamton University Library reference staff, even the U.S. government now publishes many of its lower-level official reports only on the Web.

I owe a large debt of gratitude to many colleagues, friends, and students, and I am pleased to offer my thanks for their help at various stages of this project. Moving into the global terrain has its pitfalls for any historian trained and practiced in a national frame. Complementing the writing of this book, I have taught human rights since 1945 at Binghamton University, testing many of the book's ideas and hypotheses. My students have been receptive, appropriately skeptical, and challenging. I also have asked area specialists to read parts of the manuscript at various phases of writing and have received invaluable critiques from them. I want to thank, specifically, Nancy Appelbaum, Joel Benin, Herbert Bix, Fa-ti Fan, Zackary Lockman, Tiffany Patterson, Charles D. Smith, and John Stoner. With their help, I have negotiated very complicated and contested historiographies; the final interpretations, of course, are my own. I also benefited from bibliographical suggestions from Herbert S. Lewis and Jon Abbink, Ethiopian scholars. My recent acquisition of a new family brought me a number of lawyer relatives whom I have consulted about matters of domestic and international law. Felicia Sarner and David Webber have given me easy access to important U.S. case law and tried to streamline my writing style with an eye to the legal brief, although probably in vain! Shelley Rose, an emerging scholar of German history, read my chapter on gender and, with Thomas M. Sliva, helped me with the figures. Kevin Heard prepared the maps. I am grateful for their contributions. I also want to thank the two readers for this book for the generosity with which they shared their knowledge of the debates and literature as they engaged my book.

My husband, Donald, as usual, has been a marvelous sounding board and gentle critic, helping me deal—uncharacteristically for a nineteenth-century historian—with the shifting contemporary contexts since 9/11, which necessarily affect the interpretation of the recent past. At just the right moment, he said I needed to stop writing and draw conclusions from a present, which for me, then, became fixed, even as the struggles for human rights principles and laws continue to evolve and develop in the face of the ongoing flow of time.

Map 1. The global human rights arena: The Americas.

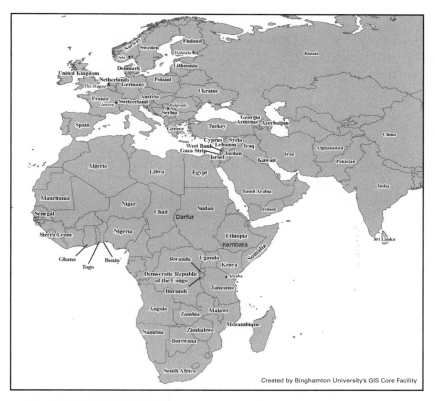

Map 2. The global human rights arena: Eurasia, Africa, and Australia.

Introduction
The New Moral Order: Between Human Dignity and Territorial Sovereignty

> All human beings are born free and equal in dignity and rights.
> —Article 1, The Universal Declaration of Human Rights (1948)

The human rights system emerged in 1945 as a victor's response to the tragedies and atrocities of World War II, a global war that began with the Japanese invasion of China in 1937 and took its devastating toll on human life and property until the summer of 1945. The war was "total war" unrestrained by law—a war that obliterated the distinctions between soldiers and civilians; destroyed whole towns, villages, and cities; and produced the ghastly death camps of the Nazi Holocaust. Nazi and Axis policies included the mass deportations of people; abuses of prisoners of war; extensive reliance on slave labor; and, for the Japanese, the widespread use of women as sex slaves for their imperial army. From the seventy-two belligerent states at war, eighty million to one hundred million soldiers were called to arms; thirty-two million soldiers died in the war; and an unprecedented number of noncombatants also perished. Eleven million people were slaughtered in prisons and extermination camps and more than twenty million civilians are estimated to have died in the Soviet Union alone. The sheer scale of war in Europe and Asia laid bare the vulnerability of human beings to the unbridled exercise of state and military power.[1]

Capitalizing on the widespread belief that the war had destroyed the foundations of the old state and imperial order, a converging resolve elevated rights principles and guarantees to a new prominence in international relations. Although the Allied leaders were careful to keep their own military actions and political records hidden from public scrutiny, they prepared the way for a significant departure in the calculations of interests in global politics. Using treaty law that is binding on the ratifying states, they extended the jurisdiction of international law to protect the fundamental human rights of all people, everywhere. Breaking with legal precedent, they made rights guarantees part of a universal treaty system and inserted human rights oversight into the agenda of the fledgling United Nations, the intergovernmental body established in October 1945 to promote international peace, security, and cooperation. Human rights criteria now entered the evolving debates about the nature and extent of security for people and states.

These actions inaugurated the first human rights system in world history. Armed with the full weight of what history had just revealed about the human capacity for evil, this system commanded great moral authority, which its authors were able to translate in a few years into three components: (1) a permanent U.N. committee structure of oversight and norm-setting, (2) authority to codify new international human rights and criminal law and make it binding on the ratifying states, and (3) a willingness to respond to—if not yet mobilize—international public opinion that was becoming invested in halting grave injustices and abuses abroad. It is not surprising, then, that John P. Humphrey, the Canadian jurist and prominent architect of the U.N. human rights project, described so vividly the atmosphere of "optimistic excitement" in these early years of human rights history. In his own words, the undertaking to remake the law was "nothing short of revolutionary."[2]

Left unqualified, Humphrey's claim captured only one side of the very complex process of international reconstruction after 1945. Many pressing international problems required concerted attention; among them were decisions of military occupation, the fate of refugees from the war and of peoples newly displaced in the Middle East and South Asia, and world financial reform. The challenges also included the colonial independence movements and, not least, the growing antagonism between the United States and the Soviet Union over power and principles. Although the framers of the United Nations wanted to avoid the failures of past efforts at establishing collective security, they approached these issues with the same "realist" principles that had been the basis of international relations for centuries: territorial sovereignty, national security, and balance of power. Not surprisingly, the institutional and normative advances in rights protection were inserted into this international system of power and state calculations of interests. From the start, then, a forceful and time-honored defense of sovereign authority checked the revolutionary potential in human rights formulations. Article 2 (7) of the Charter of the United Nations was clear on the point. It said, "Nothing contained in the present Charter shall authorize the United Nations to intervene in matters which are essentially within the domestic jurisdiction of any state." As boldly stated in the article, internationalism stopped at the territorial borders of the state; sovereignty demanded that the domestic jurisdiction of each state was exempt from the full force of international law.

From its origins in the fervor of postwar reconstruction, the human rights system was caught in a set of contradictions. As Humphrey rightly understood, in matters of law it broke with earlier international legal traditions that had made the state the sole unit of action and analysis. For the first time in history, a collective embrace of human rights in the U.N. Charter gave individual persons in and of themselves legal rights in the international arena. In addition, assigning responsibility for humanitarian and human rights issues to permanent U.N. organs meant continuous attention to this vital new arena of international politics. However, the human rights system was not given its own effective enforcement mechanisms. Rather, it was inserted into the state system of the United Nations, which simultaneously proclaimed universal human rights and defended territorial immunity from the intrusion of international legal norms. In the face of these conflicting pressures, the fate of the human rights system was not at all clear at its inception.

Competing in the arena of global politics, human rights consciousness defied the odds. Slowly gathering momentum for more than half a century, it has fashioned its own culture and institutional forms, which have a global—if uneven—reach. Human rights values are visible in the proliferation of nongovernmental organizations (NGOs) committed to all manner of rights advocacy, in the development of effective and novel transnational mobilization strategies to win the public over to human rights causes, and in the day-to-day grassroots work in support of victims on the ground, often at great personal and political cost. By the last third of the twentieth century, the language of human rights had become an increasingly effective medium by which to press a moral claim. The British ethicist Mary Midgley has called this change of consciousness "radical" and an "immense enlargement of our moral scene." In her view, it is sustained from below, reflecting widespread and popular understandings of what comprises the fundamental basis of justice and fair play. The legitimacy of human rights language has arisen from its practical uses by people caught in real life-threatening situations. As Midgley sees it, human rights values have become the language of resistance in the streets. Although Midgley glosses over a number of vexing problems, not the least of which is an identification of "the people" at hand able to use the concept's normative powers, she is correct to anchor the human rights movement in popular sentiments and to stress its novelty. "New wine always needs new bottles," she writes.[3]

Human Dignity and Territorial Sovereignty

As Midgley underscores, human rights values are demanding attention as a collective vision, establishing high ethical standards of behavior and accountability for individuals and nations. Since 1945, however, the development of human rights norms, laws, and institutions has not resolved the inherent contradictions present in the initial phases of postwar implementation. The system remains caught between two normative poles of international thought and action: morality and sovereignty.[4] In their purest forms, neither norm can properly explain the system's actual work and impact.

Human rights express the nobler parts of the human endeavor—efforts to safeguard liberties, promote social well-being, and ensure mutual tolerance and respect as necessary ingredients for human dignity. They are, however, not the sum total of morality. Rights neither exhaust nor supplant moral systems that are rooted in religion, the charitable imperative, or popular ideas about the common good. Indeed, they coexist and at times even compete with other moral systems. Human rights visions, however, help illuminate the murky world of good and evil, justice and injustice, and they bring these judgments purposefully into the international arena. To be sure, the language of rights speaks of a straightforward moral compass to guide individual behavior and official state actions according to shared ethical standards and judgments. But rights are not self-evident, self-policing, or ethically monolithic; they are historical constructs rooted in struggle and are even at odds with one another. They must be defended time and time again in each particular historical context. The gains are only as strong as their defenders. Continuously contested by calculations of power and self-interest, the cause of right *alone* cannot ensure a fair and an equitable outcome.[5]

Those responsible for the postwar order in 1945 returned to the state model for the organization of the international community. Territorial sovereignty remains its normative cornerstone. Even though the Charter of the United Nations adopted the voice of "we, the peoples," membership is state-based and new states derive their legitimacy partly from their adherence to the purposes of the United Nations. Sovereign power affirms state authority against other competing claimants in the nation, particularly with its monopoly over the use of force; it also represents the basis of international relations, organized around the fictive notion of an equality of autonomous sovereign states operating in the international arena. Of course, power and wealth have never been apportioned equally. The norms of sovereignty in fact can translate into unbridled territorial authority. This means, for example, that strong states, great powers, and superpowers can advance their perceived national interests with relative impunity under the guise of sovereign prerogatives; for weaker states, sovereignty becomes the shield behind which to defend the integrity of the state against any outside interference.

But sovereignty is not static. Since the Age of Democratic Revolutions in the late eighteenth century, it has been embodied, too, in the sovereign people, the ultimate source of political legitimacy in liberal state doctrine and, subsequently by its corollary, self-determination as the legitimate basis for nation-state building and colonial independence movements. Even as they acknowledge the sovereign territorial state as the bedrock of "civilized" international relations, postmodern theorists recently have begun to address the "projects of exclusion" that constitute the people in a territory and to probe the competing and fragmented nature of sovereign power to dispense violence and justice.[6]

More to the point, in the human rights era since 1945 the norms and laws of international rights have come to represent an alternative non-territorial source of sovereignty that limits state actions. First, international human rights law often asks for substantive changes in domestic legislation and administrative practices. A good example is Australia when, in 1975, it adhered to the most important international law banning racial discrimination, the International Convention on the Elimination of All Forms of Racial Discrimination (1965, in force 1969). By then, to be sure, sentiment in the country had turned away from its whites-only immigration policy, but ratification of the convention required domestic passage of the first national nondiscrimination legislation.[7] Second, in its ability to defend people at risk, the human rights system has its own forms of normative power that can bring the full force of public outrage to a crisis-ridden situation. Increasingly, it also has recourse to the whole apparatus of international criminal law, with its powers to indict, arrest, try, and punish war criminals and others accused of flagrant human rights abuses. The system is arrayed with and, at times, against the states, which continue to pursue their own calculations of economic and political interests and security needs. The playing field is hardly equal. States, after all, have a variety of concrete and tangible forms of power, most notably, of course, military weapons. In this clash of appreciably distinct worlds, wrongs can go unpunished and justice can be denied.

This book offers a detailed historical account of the emergence, development, and impact of human rights advocacy networks in their concrete daily operations in the uncertain terrain *between* the absolutes of moral right and sovereign power. It sees these human rights movements as vital, although underrated, ingredients of international political developments since 1945. A topic on their own terms, human rights movements overlap and intersect with the international community, a concept that is loosely applied but properly designates the decision-makers in nation-states in the international arena as well as in intergovernmental organizations and agencies and in treaty-based committees.

This book is framed by two formative efforts to universalize human rights values between 1945 and 2005. At stake for human rights after 1945 was the universality, at least in principle, of human rights guarantees irrespective of geographic location or nationality. Human rights norms and values were to be a common benchmark to make political and social practices compatible with the inherent dignity and worth of every person. At stake by 2005 was the universal applicability of the rules of international criminal and human rights laws for all people, from state leaders to soldiers to other individuals, irrespective of their membership in strong and powerful or small and weak states. Neither leadership nor great power status can exempt any individual from the force of the law. If the proclamation of principles was the precondition for the growing efforts to apply international human rights and criminal law universally, there is nothing predetermined about the outcomes. They are cumulative products of many historical struggles from below reinforced by novel transnational linkages in international society. This book argues that the human rights system is best understood not abstractly, in terms of what human rights do and mean in theory, but concretely, through its specific historical operations confronting the many obstacles of power and privilege arrayed against it. The movements for human rights over the past sixty years are indeed the founding texts of human rights history.

Human Rights Advocacy from Below: Transnational Perspectives

The sentiment on a bumper sticker that was popular in 1990s America contains an important insight that applies to the evolution of the human rights system after 1945: "Act locally and think globally." As it prescribes, the human rights movement has become global because its many struggles are local. That is, human rights mobilizations have become a part of the very fabric of struggle for change on the local level. The human rights vocabulary contained in the international declarations and conventions has helped reconfigure these ongoing local conflicts. In turn, the confrontations with human tragedies on the ground have broadened the normative and legal definitions of what constitutes specific human rights violations and abuses. In its historical development, the human rights system was fed by the interdependency of local events, national responses, and international attention. These struggles on the ground offer new ways to think about the interpenetration of local, national, and international spheres of activities in practice. As a global movement, the human rights system has invented mechanisms to move ideas, strategies, and structures across national and cultural frontiers, which historically have impeded broad-based change. It is this linkage of peoples and groups in civil societies to others across national borders that makes the movement *transnational* in the international arena.[8]

Over the past sixty years, the transnational nature of human rights ideals in various modes of translation has spread across territorial borders and into many different communities and cultures. The translations have fueled furious opposition, which often is as much about fears of the uneven processes of global economic integration and Western hegemony as it is about the universal claims of human rights. Thus, the history of human rights movements is intricately connected to the changing international debates and conflicts over war and peace, the uses and abuses of power, profits versus sustainable growth, and cultural autonomy in the context of universal claims. Human rights history, however, speaks to a globalization from below.

"Transnational" is not only a descriptive term. It is a dynamic analytical tool that simultaneously keeps in focus local contexts and international settings. It is a perspective that moves seamlessly from local through national and regional to international arenas and back again, all the while addressing the transnational responses to local situations, on the one hand, and crediting the grassroots pressures on regional and international decision-making in matters of law and policy, on the other. Human rights consciousness has shaped a new form of global politics, which is sustained by all manner of local struggles. Human rights advocacy over the past sixty years has been able to mobilize and sustain a growing public involvement in human rights causes even more broadly conceived. Advocacy has become transnational due to the increased ability of local activists and organizations to develop horizontal ties to like-minded people across borders and vertical links to national and international organizations and agencies. The formal system of institutions and treaty lawmaking centering on the United Nations is continuously reinvigorated and strengthened by its ties to local individuals, organizations, and groups engaged in day-to-day rights advocacy. The daily work, in turn, is supported by the ongoing activities from above.

There is nothing academic about this point. It derives in part from the way activists themselves have written about their own work from the bottom up. For D. J. Ravindran, an Indian lawyer, adult educator, and activist, human rights values came to permeate the substance of his efforts to defend against injustices on the local level. Involved in local organizing, Ravindran increasingly drew inspiration from international human rights norms, which refashioned his values and strategies, giving rise to a new consciousness of self and his connections to others. "Human rights activism itself," he wrote, "is premised on the concept of the inherent dignity of individuals."[9]

Ravindran had not started out as a human rights activist. As he put it, "I have never been a direct victim of any major human rights violation. In the 1970s, as a student, I was influenced by the radicalism of that decade. I, like many others of that generation, was concerned about ensuring social justice." After considerable work among the poor, Ravindran became convinced of the importance of listening more closely to those he was organizing and he turned to education. "The adult education program was aimed at enabling [the] rural poor to examine their situation and to transform it. I had moved from working for political change in which political ideals mattered, to participatory approaches to social change in which people mattered." The organizers in Ravindran's group confronted many hurdles. As he explained it, women literacy workers faced violence by men who opposed their leadership; a staff member was tortured for demanding higher wages for agricultural workers; caste inequalities led to other antagonisms. Human rights norms helped make sense of these tragic situations. "My exposure to [the] international human rights system changed my perspective on these problems. Now I see them as violations."

Ravindran began to spread the word about rights—to organize a series of workshops for local activists who already were aiding tribal peoples and the rural poor. He set up his meetings around the same practices of mutual exchange that he had developed earlier in order to tap into and validate local knowledge and experience. Through these dialogues, the participants came to a new appreciation of human dignity as fundamental to any movement for social change. This realization proved transformative. Ravindran described the changes that followed. The organizers started to see their own work "in a new light," he noted. "They felt that the repression faced by them from local vested interests was not just a problem; it was an assault on their dignity and freedom. They believed that they were not only fighting for the rights of tribals, but also to ensure respect for their own rights." Through this collective process of exchange, reflection, and growth, Ravindran with others had come to understand a powerful psychological mechanism that sustains local activism and supports a wider identification as a human rights community. Advocacy seeks to protect the dignity of the victims of human rights abuses; it also affirms the dignity of the activists themselves. In grassroots mobilization, Ravindran wrote, "We enhance our own dignity." In turn, this new insight helped make human rights violations anywhere "an affront" to the dignity of every person.[10] Advocacy pushed individual perspectives beyond the specific local and territorial borders.

A Social Historian in the Field

Much of the academic literature on human rights is written from the perspective of political scientists concerned with international relations theory and practice and also with international law. Nearly uniformly, the authors adopt a perspective from above, examining the major institutional components of the international world order and the ideas that guide them. Very little of the analysis is set in a historical context. The "realists" among them—reflecting and reinforcing state practices based on perceived rational interests—deny that moral calculations or international law play any causative role in the operations of the system.[11] In this literature, however, "realists" are challenged by "constructivists," whose position is defended most prominently by Jack Donnelly, a political scientist working in political theory and international relations. Donnelly argues that rights are moral claims that "construct" human nature and, consequently, shape state practices to ensure all human beings a life of dignity. According to Donnelly, these claims have been set down in the Universal Declaration of Human Rights; adopted by the General Assembly of the United Nations in 1948; and, with overlapping consensus, now are adhered to by all nation-states around the globe. Donnelly proposes a "universal declaration model" as a vital prism through which to examine major themes of international politics from passage of multilateral agreements to foreign policy decision-making to advancing democracy and economic development. Indeed, this model offers possibilities for bringing state policies into alignment with moral imperatives.[12]

From the perspective of international law, Richard Falk stakes out a more critical position about the possibility of social justice under the constraints of geopolitical interests and, more recently, of neoliberal economic pressures. But he, too, takes human rights norms and laws seriously, advancing a "progressivist" argument about the ongoing evolution of international law in response to the shifting character of international politics. Thus, Falk also represents an interpretive school of thought among legal scholars vitally concerned with the means and ends of international politics.[13] Both approaches, however, still examine international relations from above and give short shrift to specific human agency. Donnelly's adherence to a model-based analysis works against a dynamic assessment of the efforts of different historical movements to make the model's values operative. Falk sees legal advances as products of struggles, to be sure, but is drawn to big political ideas, such as the shifting understandings of self-determination rather than the specific historical contexts for these changes. Complementing these schools of interpretation, the field of political science has contributed valuable case studies of responses to people in crisis in a particular locality. Here, authors in the main test theory, examining in detail the role of norms in the calculations of international politics, for example. These are case-specific studies, however, and not typically reconnected to the ongoing structural developments of the human rights system since 1945.[14]

Only recently have historians joined the debates on the role of human rights in international politics. Some have made very challenging interventions into the political science literature, reassessing, from a historical vantage point, the dominant realist model of international relations. Akira Iriye, for example, argues for the centrality of international organizations—both intergovernmental agencies such as the United Nations or its affiliate group the United Nations Educational, Scientific and Cultural Organization (UNESCO) and international NGOs—in the making of the post-1945 world. In the context of the Cold War, he shifts attention from great power politics to international cooperation, as a range of state and nonstate actors developed institutional connections that testified to a growing consciousness of a global community with shared agendas and interests. He catalogs the remarkable rise in the numbers of transnational networks since 1945, which, in his analysis, capture the newly emerging consciousness of a "wider world over and above the separate states and national societies." Among his prime examples are international organizations devoted to human rights causes.[15] Iriye's work marks an important step in rewriting the *history* of postwar international relations as a grid of transnational cooperative activities transcending Cold War divisions. However refreshing a perspective, his approach remains at too general an analytical level. Thus, it is insufficient to examine the specific meanings and emotions that are at stake in a particular struggle for rights. And it cannot assess the constraints imposed on the work of transnational human rights advocacy networks by the clash of Cold War ideologies.

Other historians have explored the genealogy of human rights. To date, much of this literature reproduces one or the other of two easily conflated fallacies. The first regards all historical expressions of rights and moral principles as forerunners of human rights and, in fact, elides them all together. The second understands human rights to be a "revival" or "rebirth" of natural rights philosophy and law characteristic of the European Enlightenment in the eighteenth century. Although interrelated, they pose different challenges for the requirement of historical precision. The slippage has meant, however, that many authors, including political scientists offering a snapshot of the historical emergence of human rights, simply use "natural rights" and "human rights" interchangeably.

Typical of the first approach is the collection of documents titled *The Human Rights Reader,* which, in tracing the origins of human rights, for example, includes biblical principles, texts drawn from Buddhism and the Koran, as well as the Magna Carta. It is important to acknowledge the multiple moral traditions that have established ethical principles around justice and dignity. To claim that these precepts are equivalent expressions of human rights in any operative or legal sense, however, is simply not historically accurate. Such a claim also fails to differentiate the subtle complexities as well as the specific historical and cultural meanings around the notions of freedom, rights, liberties, privileges, and power over time and in different cultures.[16]

The title of a much-cited article by Jan Herman Burgers, "The Road to San Francisco: The Revival of the Human Rights Idea in the Twentieth Century," reflects the second approach. Burgers speaks of a "revival" of the human rights idea in 1945. It is as if the mid-twentieth-century declarations of human rights principles were a logical and inevitable rebirth of natural rights philosophy. But this cyclical view of change works to flatten historical time. It leaves little need to examine concretely when and why human rights norms became part of a global discourse reshaping international diplomacy. Although Paul Gordon Lauren draws on an impressive array of historical evidence for the global spread of notions of freedom and liberty and, after the eighteenth century, rights claims, his study is a retrospective account of the evolution of human rights visions. Within a dynamic of repression and struggle, Lauren nonetheless makes the triumph of human rights ideas in 1945 an inevitable product of its own history. For the long time frame before the mid-twentieth century, he uses the two concepts—natural rights and human rights—as one.[17]

Natural rights philosophy was an essential ingredient in the establishment of liberal constitutional governments that created new legitimacy by protecting and safeguarding the so-called natural rights of man—to life, liberty, and property (or happiness), as they were originally conceived. These were the guiding principles of both the American and the French revolutions during the Age of Democratic Revolutions in the Atlantic world (1776–1825); they are enshrined in the two seminal documents of the age, the U.S. Declaration of Independence (1776) and the French Declaration of the Rights of Man and Citizen (1789). At the time, however, natural rights defended civic equality for all citizens before the law but limited political citizenship to those (white) male heads of households with property and wealth; they also allowed slavery as a form of property. A notion of rebirth, then, leaves out the whole post-Enlightenment history of political thought and action that critiqued the limitations of natural rights principles. For more than a century and a half, radical, socialist, feminist, nationalist, and anticolonial struggles emerged to defend alternative visions and strategies to achieve justice, dignity, freedom, and equality in society. Indeed, it was only through the interventions to enfranchise the disenfranchised in the wake of global nation-state building that political and civil equality became so clearly intertwined.[18]

Natural rights and human rights principles impose very different understandings of duties and obligations on the bearers. Natural rights contracts are, in effect, civic affairs among citizens, which are seen to constitute legitimate government; they require no further obligations to those outside the particular political society. These contracts activate territorial sovereignty. In contrast, by guaranteeing all human beings rights in international law, human rights precepts subject the actions of state and military officials (and, according to feminist interpretations, private individuals) within state borders to international scrutiny. They shift the location of accountability from domestic to international institutions, such as U.N. bodies and treaty committees and, recently, international criminal courts, and they mobilize public opinion. They work to loosen the absolute prerogatives of sovereignty. Human rights purviews are international; they draw on but are greater than natural rights traditions.

Reflecting the many controversial issues at the heart of global politics, this book brings a social historian's perspectives to a study of human rights advocacy over the sixty years of its operations. What drives these mobilizations are human beings caught in real-life crises. Human rights crises are never generic. They may be about grave breaches of community norms of life, liberty, personal security, or social justice, but they take place at precise moments in time and in distinct communities. Human rights tragedies are tangible events about people with faces, names, families, and histories. They must be placed in their specific historical contexts. Approaching human rights as a powerful language of resistance, this "new" social history assesses individual and group agency embedded in discursive and structural contexts. With its attention to social actors and the play of scale, it demonstrates how social structures are built up from transnational interactions.[19] These premises are the first contribution of social history to the discussions.

The second contribution, the transnational perspectives of rights advocacy, offers new ways to assess the ongoing institutional developments in U.N. oversight, the formation and work of permanent international NGOs, and the developments in international law. They feed into both constructivist and progressivist interpretations and, at the same time, permit a more precise account—known in the historians' guild as "historicization"—of structural advances and setbacks at the international level. Social history supports the work of those legal scholars who see international human rights law as a "living system" in mutual interaction with concrete manifestations of social unrest and injustice on the ground. According to this view, there is a "large gray zone separating emerging social values from the well-established legal rule."[20] It is in this "zone" that new community norms are forged through direct confrontations with abuses and inequities. Since 1945, human rights principles increasingly have operated in this zone to bridge the gaps between shifting social norms and existing obligations and commands of the law. Many of the social movements analyzed in this book have broadened human rights understanding and implementation and supported new legal instruments; others still are pushing for change. The interaction between events on the ground and changes in international law shows unmistakably how understandings of the law turn on insights beyond the topic of law itself.

The third contribution, the anchor in historically precise moments, permits a focus on the wider international contexts for the unfolding of events. It opens a global perspective, not in the sense of providing an all-inclusive global survey—a task beyond the competency of a single author—but as an accounting of the human interventions that have sustained the system and pushed it in new directions. As evolving struggles, these events have their own chronology, one that defies neat categorization or a straightforward linear development from decade to decade. They peak at certain moments and subside, only to leave the living with the agony of acknowledging the horrors of the past. This rhythm lends coherence to the organization of the book.

Matters of Organization and Themes

The book's organization reflects the concerns of a social historian. Thematically driven, it presents a distinct interweaving of human rights advocacy movements in a nonlinear chronology that opens new interpretations. Chapter 1 raises the historian's question of why the human rights system was founded only after World War II and not earlier. It sees the answer in two contradictory international developments resolved only in 1945: the emergence in the early twentieth century of increasingly transnational movements and organizations linking change in the domestic and international orders, on the one hand, and the evolution of international law, on the other. This tension rarely has been explored in historical research. It then examines the legal and institutional changes taking place between 1945 and 1949, which "made" the human rights revolution under the auspices of the fledgling United Nations. Finally, it dissects the contentious debates and compromises that went into formulating the Universal Declaration of Human Rights by the new U.N. Human Rights Commission between early 1947 and late 1948. Now considered international law, the declaration still serves as a reference point for human rights advocacy in the international and national arenas. The proclamation of universal human rights principles left open what it would mean for people at risk around the globe.

Pushing the meanings of international human rights norms and practice were resistance movements on the ground and the development of transnational and state advocacy networks. The many protest movements that break out around the globe, however, do not generate equal recognition. Not every victim can speak and not every tragedy feeds into collective memory and institutional mobilization. Only some images, it appears, effectively galvanize collective outrage. It is not enough to affirm our common membership in one Cosmopolis, as Mary Midgley does, where "their" business becomes "our" business as a matter of our own self-interest.[21] Public outrage is selective, constrained by the very inequalities and prejudices that divide human communities into many antagonistic and suspicious groups. There is no automatic collective moral response to human suffering and pain. So the questions still remain: Which victims' causes become part of international debate, at what point in time, and why? What produces identification with the plight of distant others?

Part I acknowledges this stark context. It centers on an emerging orthodoxy in the definition and implementation of human rights guarantees through a confluence of geopolitical forces that drew, uncharacteristically, three exemplars of people's struggle into the international arena. This set the stage for an international engagement with newly defined human rights violations. Chapter 2 juxtaposes the antiapartheid movement and its shifting allies abroad and the anti-Soviet dissidents with their transnational supporters; it follows their developments throughout the Cold War era, 1952–90. Chapter 3 examines the mothers' responses to the forced disappearance of their children and family members through the vicious state tactic of rooting out its so-called enemies. Part I shows how these formative movements and causes operated simultaneously in local and global contexts; the points of intersection strengthened domestic struggles as they established the first U.N. rules of intervention, gave rise to new international law, and inspired the founding of permanent human rights NGOs, such as Amnesty International. They revealed as well that mobilized public support responded to concrete and immediate human tragedies; there were multiple human rights publics overlapping in time. Furthermore, these struggles created new roles for victims and their NGO supporters who, in the first two decades of U.N. operations, had only limited access to commissioners monitoring violations. What seems today the self-evident role of NGOs in U.N. oversight was achieved only through hard struggle.

In different regions of the globe, the transnational mobilization around these causes helped establish the types of rights abuses demanding immediate international attention. These were the systematic abuse of *political* authority and the *state* repressions of individual freedoms and liberties and of democratic rights to political participation. Together, they shaped new types of international interventions pushing compliance. These violations, of course, were grave abuses of human rights, but they were only part of the interdependency of rights understood as necessary for human well-being by the original architects of the Universal Declaration. On the face of it, they seemed to correspond to Cold War dichotomies between political and civil rights (the so-called "negative" Western freedoms from an arbitrary state) and the economic and social rights (the so-called "positive" socialist and welfare principles of state obligations). The Cold War, however, was less cause than context for this priority, although it may have reinforced the wide receptivity to the dominant paradigm favoring political freedoms. For different reasons, the same priority was an inherent characteristic of the early human rights movements. Looking at the events below the surface showed at the same time that the people in struggle had a much more complex understanding of their own causes than the dominant international model of human rights defense admitted.

Part II argues that large-scale mobilizations by women's and labor activists for more inclusive priorities emerged around the mid-1970s, partly in response to the limitations of the orthodoxy. These groups, to be sure, had their own independent historical trajectories as transnational movements extending back into the late nineteenth century. They had helped establish the groundwork for societal receptivity to universal rights and many of their advocates pushed for inclusion of specific protections under the broader rubric in 1945. But the new context of the human rights era transformed the foundational assumptions and methods of mobilization of these earlier movements.

Chapter 4 traces the shift in thinking and organizing by women's groups as they confronted ongoing violence and violations in their work for economic development in the 1960s and early 1970s. From the principle of sex equality, which their activists had inserted into the U.N. Charter, they moved to gender analysis with its recognition of difference. Through their efforts, and sustained by transnational advocacy for gay rights as well, gender became a new category of protection in international law. The gender perspective, furthermore, challenged the orthodox location of violations in public spheres alone by demanding accountability for abuses taking place in the private arenas of domestic family life and customs. Not surprisingly, its advocacy elicited strong opposition from traditionalists regardless of their place in the global divides of culture, levels of wealth, and political systems. Chapter 5 explores understandings of economic rights and social justice, also reshaped in the human rights era. Despite the efforts of the leaders of the new postcolonial nations starting in the mid-1970s to defend a collective "right" to development, the industrial power elites have been unwilling to negotiate equitable solutions to the gross injustices of global and regional economic inequality. The widening gaps in levels of wealth, exacerbated by neoliberal globalization since the 1970s, essentially placed the heavy burdens of poverty and social deprivation on the transnational labor migrant. Affirming rights inherent in the human person irrespective of territorial place, many of these immigrants and their NGO defenders have created networks around a notion of rights no longer tied to its traditional anchor in political citizenship.

As part of grassroots movements addressing social, familial, and community relations, advocates of women's and migrants' rights also have taken their claims to court, turning to both domestic and regional judicial systems. By pressing a legal claim, they began a process of incorporating international law into domestic case law, using legal strategies to extend the human rights culture of humane treatment, equality, and nondiscrimination into social life and to rearrange power. They also have broadened the law to nonstate actors, holding multinational corporations responsible, for example, for abuses of labor and for environmental degradation. Many of the legal gains, however, have led to serious backlash at the level of society.

Part III argues that the "long" decade of the 1990s—from the formal end of the Cold War (1989–91) to 2005—represented its own era in human rights history. Maintaining the thematic focus, it pulls together patterns of continuities under changing circumstances as well as of new departures and challenges for human rights advocacy. Despite widespread expectations of peace at the end of the Cold War, many societies faced internal strife, civil war, and genocide. No longer constrained by Cold War stalemates, the Security Council developed new patterns of intervention that went beyond established precedents. It sent "humanitarian" missions into fragmented societies, combining armed force, relief services, and human rights oversight with a bold agenda of peacebuilding and social reconciliation. These missions contributed to heightened interest in modes of "transitional justice" and accountability, which emerged as key characteristics of the decade. They fed into ongoing efforts on the ground to handle the aftermath of trauma and tragedy, for mothers who still had not learned of the fate of their children and other family members and for members of other societies undergoing the difficult transition to more democratic rule. These pressures from many settings brought out the need to confront the wrongs of the past in order to move into a different future. From the challenges of the decade, Part III also suggests some of the strategies necessary for effective human rights advocacy in the future. Its end point in 2005 reflects the first effort of U.N. reform in its sixty-year history, prompted by the unsolved problems of the "long" 1990s.

Chapter 6 examines the ambiguous legacies of "humanitarian intervention" as a new strategy to safeguard people at risk, focusing on events in the breakup of Yugoslavia and the genocide in Rwanda. It examines the work of these missions on the ground in their role as intermediaries between beleaguered communities and U.N. decision-makers. Unable to prevent the tragedies, the Security Council, freed from the familiar stalemates of the Cold War, moved beyond the Nuremberg and Tokyo precedents and established ad hoc international criminal tribunals to try leaders of Yugoslavia and Rwanda for international crimes. It extended this model of international justice to other conflict situations and, in the late 1990s, created the permanent International Criminal Court, with its potential to universalize accountability for grave breaches of international criminal and human rights law.

Chapter 7 explores as a social microcosm the U.N. World Conference against Racism, the first world gathering in the new millennium. Called in part to address the explosion of ethnic violence, mounting societal anger at migrants, and minority vulnerabilities in the globalizing world, it gave marginalized groups a world stage for a while. It demonstrated the ongoing work to defend against the global economic forces and state structures that exacerbated inequalities on the basis of racial, ethnic, and minority status. Reflecting the 1990s' climate of accountability, grassroots pressure also brought to the fore historical grievances that had lasting consequences into the present—among others, the demands for reparations by Africans in Africa and the diaspora for the slave trade, slavery, and colonialism, as well as the clash of narratives between Israelis and Palestinians. In addition, the timing of this world conference—it ended three days before the September 11, 2001, attack on the United States—offers a unique lens through which to assess the immediate unfolding of the U.S.-led "war on terror." Many of the debates and preparatory efforts at the conference became even more relevant for the post-9/11 world. So, too, did the significance of international human rights laws for a more just international order. The outlines of this potential development also had become clear by 2005, the end point of this study. This book follows a chronology, but one that marches to its own beat.

At the point of writing this book, the balance sheet on the impact of human rights in the international affairs of peoples and governments is incomplete. It is, after all, inappropriate to use the vocabulary of victory and defeat in human rights contexts. The defense of rights principles requires constant vigilance partly because it coexists with the practices of political and military power. To place human rights achievements under the label of progress is to simplify the movements: their outcomes are never guaranteed. But their actual track record over the past sixty years narrates the hopes and bitter struggles that have altered the course of international and domestic relations.

Chapter 1
Raising the Bar, 1900–1949

> The Charter of the U.N. specifically mentions the promotion of Human Rights. Where these rights are flagrantly violated, it is the duty of the U.N. to step in for their protection. If a State accepts a policy of discrimination on the ground of race or colour that State must explain and justify its policy before the bar of the world.
> —Hansa Mehta, Indian representative on the Human Rights Commission, 1950

A near consensus among scholars and journalists charting the impact of human rights principles on state behavior sees 1945 as the pivotal moment in the emergence of a formal human rights system—of norms, laws, and permanent intergovernmental bodies committed to rights formulations and oversight. Political scientists substitute the word "regime" for "system," drawing attention to a binding set of norms and rules relating to specific thematic areas of international coordination. Through comparative inquiry regarding other international regimes, this literature assesses the human rights structure in terms of a spectrum of implementation possibilities, from setting standards to monitoring to binding enforcement on the states.[1] This work, too, is anchored implicitly in the new patterns of institutional coordination that emerged in 1945 as part of the global effort to rebuild international political life after World War II.

The focus on a historical moment—1945—is a shorthand tool that carries with it a much longer purview. For political scientists, the new post-war international regime was a logical outgrowth of developments in international relations extending back centuries. In the standard narrative, this history was dominated by the wars and tensions between sovereign states and empires and by the competing principles of collective security, the treaty law system, and the mechanisms of international concert designed to regulate the areas of mutual concern and interest among sovereign entities. Other scholars interested in the history of ideas also point to earlier moral and religious traditions and rights principles that seemed to make the international commitments to human rights self-evident in 1945.

These two perspectives converged in the way many contemporary activists understood their own work and times. René Cassin, one of the authors of the Universal Declaration of Human Rights, made the point in 1947 when he claimed that in the war the "great fundamental principles of mankind had been forgotten." For Cassin and others in the fledgling United Nations, older traditions of humanist aspirations could be refashioned into guiding principles to serve as the foundation of a new peaceful international order.[2] At the same time, Cassin's work in the U.N. Human Rights Commission seemed to promise an institutional breakthrough in bringing human rights issues to a new level of international coordination. It is not surprising, then, that 1945 can be considered both the culminating point of historical investigation into human rights genealogies and a new starting point of inquiry into international mechanisms defining and safeguarding rights. In the history of human rights, all roads seem to lead to, or radiate from, 1945.

This observation, however, begs an important question. Why was the human rights system created in 1945 and not earlier, say, in 1918 after World War I or even in 1899 at the Hague Congress, which established the first Permanent Court of Arbitration? The framing of this query reflects the historian's retrospective sensibilities and at the same time— even in the face of a known outcome—engagement with the past that has no automatic or predetermined path to the present. The past is as open as the present to human agency, even under the substantial weight of structural continuities and power imbalances. For a social history of human rights advocacy, the question turns attention to the ways contemporaries made sense of their location at the end of the nineteenth century, as they increasingly crossed territorial borders in their efforts to create more just and equitable social, national, and international systems.

My approach locates the origins of the human rights system in the clash of two competing international developments, starting at the end of the nineteenth century. The first was the increasingly transnational nature of the struggles against injustice and oppression that was becoming a permanent fixture of international society at the time. Its advocates drew on and made operative a wide range of values and visions, including notions of a just order, a common humanity, and a brotherhood of the races; some claims also were phrased in rights language and sought diplomatically sanctioned legal protections. These movements were launched from many so-called centers—from London; Washington, D.C.; Berlin; Tokyo; and Shanghai. The second was developments in positive international law negotiated by sovereign states to regulate their mutual interests. Territorial sovereignty was the cardinal principle of the international order regulated by law. By the later nineteenth century, states' interests began to embrace humanitarian issues, whether the fate of the enemy wounded soldier or the postulate of a high law ("of humanity") to govern the conduct of war. These humanitarian potentials, however, were constrained by the defense of state sovereignty in the international legal system.[3]

Both developments have been largely obscured in historical research, which is written primarily from the perspective of the nation-state. A product of some of the same forces shaping new national identities— such as rising literacy rates, media circulation, and market linkages —groups in national societies and colonial spaces developed identifications with like-minded individuals across borders who were seen to share experiences and a common history of oppression. As some historians have noted, these foundational identities were both fictional and operational. They were fictional because they were premised on a unitary consciousness of interests based on a set of shared experiences and histories that were seen to transcend differences in location, culture, levels of wealth, and even languages. This "fiction," of course, leaves subsequent historians the task of scrutinizing these movements for the internal contradictions that often limited their effectiveness.[4] By the early twentieth century, these transnational identities were material and operative, creating international movements and organizations across the globe premised on the idea of the international solidarity of the group. From both national and international settings, activists involved in transnational causes intervened in foreign policy and proposed alternative agendas to those set by state elites and the colonial powers. From different venues of oppression, these transnational linkages and coordinated actions set new bases for rethinking the global order and the place of human beings within it. Juxtaposed, these developments showed that the unmistakable trend in the "internationalization" of sentiments, identities, and organizations ran up against the centrality of sovereignty in international law and state practice, which upheld the order of states, empires, and colonial possessions. This clash between the defenders of the old state order and the mobilization pressures of transnational civil society was broken only in 1945, when human rights as visions moved from their limited and particular use in transnational mobilizations to enter the language of diplomacy and to challenge the geographical and thematic limitations in the coverage of international law. While resting on prepared and fertile ground, human rights principles enshrined in international law in 1945 represented not a culmination of developments but new understandings that made universal rights central to the collective security tasks of international society. Anchored in human well-being, they also changed spatial relations to blur the once sacrosanct lines that had cordoned off the sovereign territorial units in the international arena, except for the self-identified areas of mutual interests.

Transnational Struggles and International Visions

The pace of global interconnections quickened in the early twentieth century. It was then that growing numbers of activists involved in a host of national reform, revolutionary, and anticolonial causes became increasingly aware of their global position and interconnectedness. Whether through journals and newspapers; study and travel abroad; or the creation of international organizations with headquarters, visible leadership roles, and periodic congresses, the activists began to link their movements with others outside their territories. From different geographical sites and perspectives, these groups of activists developed transnational identities that pushed beyond national frontiers and opened new channels of communication. At the same time, governments began to create the first permanent intergovernmental agencies, which set for their member states around the globe uniform rates and standards for expanded postal and new telegraph services and also coordinated common health and sanitation measures to prevent the spread of communicable diseases.[5]

These new expressions of global interconnections took place against the international system of imperial conquest and rule that was binding the globe to the imperial centers in Europe as well as to the United States and Japan. In the early twentieth century, the world's political imbalances had reached an extreme. Formal European colonial empires stretched across most of Africa, large parts of South and East Asia, and many islands of the Pacific. The government of Meiji Japan established rule over Formosa in 1894 and annexed Korea in 1910. The United States, through its gains in Hawaii, the Philippines, Puerto Rico, and Cuba, extended its power and influence more purposefully in Asia, the Pacific, and Latin America. Roughly half a billion people fell under the formal control of foreign colonial administrators.[6]

These empires rearranged space in regions that were not under the internationally sanctioned protections of the state as a sovereign unit in the international arena. They also impacted labor markets at both the global and local levels. Imperialism, after all, involved serious competitive struggles over resources and labor. In tandem with shifting consumption patterns, new labor forces collected at crucial nodal points:

the Chinese laid railroad beds in the American West, Filipinos worked the sugar cane fields of Hawaii, South Asian indentured laborers and shop keepers were in southern and eastern Africa as well as the West Indies, and black West Indians moved along the seaboard docks of the United States to Panama and also to England. These patterns of labor migrations followed the massive movements of slave labor in earlier centuries that had created the African diaspora in the New World. These migrant communities became crucial incubators for radical rethinking of each group's place in the larger world community at a time when "the ends of the world are being brought so near together," as the authors of an Address to the Nations of the World by the Races Congress stated in London in 1900.[7] Throughout their often mobile labor careers, community members sustained contacts through diverse publications and institutional ties. Significantly, by the early twentieth century, their own immigrant settlements also affected politics and perceptions among intellectuals in their countries of origin.

Recently, historians have developed innovative cultural methodologies to explore the dynamics of empires, stressing the formation of new identities and public policies that were products of the reciprocal ties between the imperial center (the metropole) and the colony. The approach is an improvement over earlier research methods that traced the influences flowing from the center and left unexplored the impact of colonial rule back home. Some of the new research demonstrates how white female emigration projects of the British, Dutch, and imperial German colonial offices and societies in the early twentieth century used women to establish normative family life in the colonies and to draw sharp racial borders between coexisting communities. Other research points to an increasing use of colonial images for domestic projects of slum clearance and settlement and traces parallel developments in urban planning of new, modern, and airy colonial cities, such as the creation of New Delhi around 1900. Still other research notes how advertisements circulating in the press to sell goods popularized gender and racial differences, while private philanthropic bazaars offered Berlin shoppers, for example, "Cameroon Chocolates, New Guinea cigarettes and drawings from Mesopotamia," among other exotica.[8] In the metropole, imperialism had become part of the marketing and consumption of goods in everyday life. Ironically, the very transnational character of the European nineteenth century—the introduction into domestic life of new knowledge, products, and material objects from outside the territorial borders—served partly to reinforce a Western sense of superiority, whether constructed through the shifting fortunes of Ottoman and Prussian-Austrian military contacts or, as in late imperial Germany, by popular enthusiasm for the plains Indians of the American West, that "vanishing race" of peoples. This knowledge easily served to reinforce a wider Western belief in its civilizing mission, which ranked the peoples of the world along a hierarchy of criteria for entrance into the so-called modern world. Similarly, attributes of civilized nations also made their way into international law.[9]

The growing force of transnational identifications duplicated and, at the same time, transcended the imperial map. This was true of the two large movements for political change that were international in scope: socialism and feminism. In 1889, workers' parties and associations from countries in the heartland of the industrial West established the Second International, a permanent organization coordinating workers' international struggle for socialism from its headquarters in Amsterdam. Meeting in periodic congresses in major European cities in the years prior to World War I, they embraced the cause of colonial labor and offered searing commentary on the disastrous consequences of colonial exploitation and rule. In the majority view, the social costs of imperialism at home and abroad made a mockery of the claim to "civilized" status by the advanced capitalist nations. They acknowledged the ways capitalist markets pitted colonial labor against workers in industrial societies yet envisioned a "special role [for] workers of the civilized world" to bring all labor together "irrespective of nationality" in common action toward the goal of socialist revolution and "human brotherhood." Through the titles of their party newspapers, furthermore, they deployed such notions as "equality" and "justice" and, by helping found parties, trade unions, and associations outside the West, spread the cause of socialism around the globe. Delegates from colonial territories attended and addressed these gatherings, as in 1904, when a representative from British India, Dadabhai Naoroji, spoke before the international congress in Amsterdam.[10] The Third (communist) International continued this practice well into the 1920s and 1930s.

A similar set of international organizations increasingly coordinated organized women's movements across the globe, pressing a variety of domestic reform agendas. Formed out of the antislavery movement of the 1840s (one of the first transnational humanitarian causes) and tested in a series of campaigns across borders, which initially challenged state-sanctioned prostitution and then championed temperance, these commonalities led first to the founding of the International Women's Council (IWC) in 1888, with its emphasis on harmony and commitment to embrace the widest number of national women's groups possible. By 1904, the suffrage proponents broke away to form the International Women's Suffrage Association (IWSA), dedicated solely to the goal of women's full incorporation into political citizenship in the nations around the world. And, in 1915, in the middle of World War I, progressive and pacifist women laid the foundations for the Women's International League for Peace and Freedom (WILPF), opposed to the use of violence and force in all arenas of national and international life.[11] Both the IWC and the WILPF remained active organizations that helped shape the transition of organized feminism into the human rights era after 1945.

Early in the twentieth century, the constituent components of the women's internationals centered on the Atlantic world; members also shared a middle-class status and high levels of education, characteristics as well of the few women from the colonies who managed to attend the women's congresses. The leadership, however, sought regular contact with non-Western feminists. For example, in 1913, to promote dialogue, Carrie Chapman Catt, president of the IWSA, together with Aletta Jacobs, head of the Dutch branch of the international group, made a "tour around the world" to learn firsthand about the situation of women elsewhere. Their report described holding "public meetings in many of the towns and cities of four continents, four great islands and on ships of three oceans" and also corresponding regularly with representatives of "the most advanced . . . women's movements" in countries they did not visit on this particular journey, among them Egypt, Palestine, Japan, Philippines, Java, China, and the Ottoman Empire.[12] In 1907, the competing brand of feminism in the socialist movement founded the Socialist Women's International, with its prominent leadership based in Germany.

Perhaps not surprising, in the colonized and semicolonized spaces of the world, intellectuals, reformers, and activists also began to develop new understandings of the global situation. They could turn the notion of "civilization" on its head and appropriate it for alternative politics. Many, indeed, came to see the world not only in terms of center and periphery but also in relation to identities that linked colonized peoples together. For many Chinese intellectuals in the early twentieth century, for example, these understandings made the fate of Poland (removed from the European map through partition in the late eighteenth century), the Ottoman Empire as the "sick man" of Europe, colonial India, as well as the recent annexations of the Philippines and Hawaii directly relevant to China's global place, perceived also to be weak and vulnerable to imperial dismemberment. By rethinking history, nationalists in colonial and semicolonial settings drew new dynamic regional identities that saw neighboring peoples as racial "brothers" in a revitalized Asia connected intricately to the Pacific and Africa.

Extricating itself in the late 1890s from the unequal treaties imposed by the colonial powers, Japan emerged as a natural center for this new Pan-Asian identity—as a powerhouse and potential challenger to Western domination and also as a recent member of the "white" imperialist powers. Notions of Pan-Asianism were nurtured by politicians; spread through journals, poetry, and publications; transplanted abroad by student organizations; and debated at people's congresses, as those in Shanghai and Nagasaki in the mid-1920s. Anticolonial leaders had their own institutional and media circuits for the ongoing exchange of information and ideas in the idioms of the shared experiences of oppression and exploitation. Nationalist sentiments also reflected perceptions of affinities from the circulating flows of labor migrations, which had brought Chinese laborers to Java, Indonesia (under Dutch colonial rule), and to mine work in the Transvaal after the Boer War (1899–1902) in South Africa. Pan-Asianism, then, embraced neologisms, such as "new race," and reworked older Chinese ideas of "common civilization." These understandings produced a strong sense of commonality, rooted in race and kind, expressing an Asian solidarity not confined to territorial borders. From the other side of the globe, drawing on the shared experiences of oppression from the slave trade and slavery in the Atlantic world, "men and women of African blood" began a sustained struggle in 1900 that also defied geographical territory. It presumed a common necessity for "millions of black men in Africa, America, and the Islands of the Sea, not to speak of the brown and yellow myriad elsewhere" to secure the "right" to seek entry into the "opportunities and privileges of modern civilization."[13]

From different origins and with different goals, the near simultaneity of these struggles emerging in different regions of the globe reflected intersecting perceptions of historical injustice and commitments to the power of a people to bring about substantive change, whether at the level of domestic reform, new regional collectivities, or peaceful international societies. The movements, to be sure, coalesced around appreciably distinct rubrics that offered a common agenda to their diverse groups of constituents. The realities were more complex, however. Thus, advocates of socialist revolution and feminist change were among the many exiled nationalist revolutionaries congregating in Tokyo in the years after 1900. Similarly, the career trajectories of individual advocates, who were the lifeblood of any movement for social change, captured a fluidity of identities belied by fixed political rubrics. For example, nationalist M. N. Roy, who launched a "pen" revolution for Indian independence in Berlin in 1923 with his influential publication, *The Vanguard of Indian Independence*, earlier had sought to bring communist revolution to Mexico. Over his long activist career, Trinidad-born Marxist radical George Padmore ultimately renounced socialism and moved to Pan-Africanism, coordinating the correspondence between African and Caribbean nationalists and unionists. In addition, Mary Church Terrell tirelessly sought to bridge the gaps between white and black women's causes in the United States. Recognizing divisions within the rubric "women" over race and color, she nonetheless sought common political alliances and brought her perspective on the "colored question" to the 1904 Berlin International Women's Congress.[14]

The sense of an intertwined world found parallel expressions beyond transnational struggles. It also came from the many world's fairs and exhibition displays taking place in different regions, starting in the mid-nineteenth century. These exhibits reproduced power hierarchies—privileging, for example, the great imperial powers as well as the white "races of man" with pride of place in the exhibition halls; they also exoticized "the other" and differences. If in some small way they offered an entry point for new understandings of the complexities of cultures; the varieties of customs; and the wide range of local manufactories, goods, and products, they also provoked protests and riots at the perceived affronts to more egalitarian sensibilities of human achievements.[15] Similarly, the activities of museum collecting and running charitable foundations in many Western countries reflected the extent of information, personnel, and institutional forms circulating in the Atlantic world. Boards of directors in one locale drew capital, patrons, and inspiration from the wider Atlantic community. Although they were implicated in the imperialist project, the historian Akira Iriye calls these agents, as well as other scientists, artists, and academics, members of "epistemic communities," reflecting identities not tied to distinct territorial borders.[16]

The expansion of contacts over shared agendas also led to the proliferation of new, private nongovernmental associations cooperating across borders in matters of health, welfare legislation, sex trafficking, and even sport; they also increasingly linked people of like-minded persuasions, as in the creation in 1894 of the World Young Women's Christian Association. By 1910, international organizing for a variety of causes had proceeded sufficiently far across the "entire globe" that a Central Organ for International Organizations was established in Brussels, Belgium, to collect and distribute information on the structures and operations of these new societal-driven transnational organizations.[17] Early in the century, two major types of international bodies—intergovernmental organizations established by formal treaty agreement among states as well as transnational nongovernmental associations—coexisted and vied with states and empires as participants in the geopolitical arena.

However contradictory and complex, the emergence of transnational movements against injustice comprised an important ingredient in human rights history. Their precise role requires careful assessment. First, the dynamics of transnational identification with like-minded individuals led, seemingly logically, to a substantial rethinking of the basis of international relations and a redrawing of the international map. Each movement developed international institutions and mechanisms that connected its local efforts to similar ones abroad. These coordinated struggles—rooted at the time in distinct components of the human community—demonstrated the discursive link that emerged between identifications beyond the immediate territorial border and new critiques of the geopolitical status quo.

Shaped by the teleological drive of Marxist ideology, many workers saw in the success of socialist revolution a radically new international community based on equality, justice, and peace. My point is not the accuracy of the prediction but the step to the vision of an alternative world order. A similar path also informed many women participants in their international organizations. Embracing a wide spectrum of political views, most adopted a vision of the complementarity of the sexes as they grappled precisely with what it meant to be a woman in organized public life. Most probably also would have accepted the sentiments of May Wright Sewall, which she expressed at the IWC meeting in Berlin in 1904. "Each sex," she proclaimed confidently, "has its place, but in order that each sex shall occupy its place and fulfill its duties, to both sexes must be given the same freedom, the same independence."[18] At the time, most saw women's activism as infusing public life with distinctly feminine attributes. This was true also of socialist women who, in their daily politics, confronted the masculine biases of Marxist class theory and its organizational structures and strategies. From this essentialist understanding of difference came a new vision of the international order. Especially for the suffrage proponents, the granting of women's suffrage was the precondition for a fundamentally more peaceful international order. As women entered the decision-making apparatus of the state, or so the argument ran, they would bring a new maternal ethic of care to the diplomatic arena. Again, my point is not the veracity of the argument but the linkages between redrawing domestic place and rethinking the nature of the international order. Equally illustrative of this changing consciousness were the emerging Pan-African notions, which produced new drawings of the map literally, centering on Haiti, Abyssinia, and Liberia as interconnected nodal points for a new order that would embrace the needs of the "darker races of Mankind."[19] From distinct configurations of transnational society, advocates demonstrated the international implications of the local projects for social, sexual, and political liberation.

The second observation is less straightforward and comes from careful reading of language—of the concepts, images, and values activists used to express their visions of struggle and place in the world.[20] Strikingly absent in these early transnational mobilizations was a language of human rights, although the point is not surprising in the case of anticolonial struggles, which, at the time, tended to center on the new collectivities of "nation," "people," or "race" as solidarities for common action. More attuned to sociopolitical transformations than rights, anticolonial nationalist thinking expanded its purview beyond the state to mobilize similar kinds of peoples (or races) for the project of freedom and independence. In addition, much of Pan-Asian thinking turned on an alternative conception of "civilization" than that offered by the West, which, through the Pan-Asian lens, spelled mainly violence and conquest. Particularly after Japanese military successes in the Russo-Japanese war (1904–5), many intellectuals saw Japan as offering an alternative model for the future, blending the fruits of Western science and technology with the Asian values of harmony and community. This perspective divided the world essentially into distinct geopolitical blocs, with an ultimate logic of "Asia for the Asians."[21]

Other groups in transnational alliances drew their moral power from a conception of the bonds of common humanity. By the late nineteenth century, indeed, this language of humanity found resonance in may different settings: in reform agendas rooted in notions of human progress; in humanitarian appeals for aid for the victims of natural disasters, including floods and earthquakes in far-off lands; and in the powers of photojournalism, which, working through searing images of refugees, of victims of state oppression, or of women and children who "bore the brunt" of war, captured, and also shaped, what the reading public was coming to understand as humanitarian crises.[22] In the early twentieth century, this embrace of a common humanity, however, was circumscribed. Even the politics and strategies of the transnational movements for rights did not make operational the presumption of universal humanity. The appeal was for *their* full humanity and only limited efforts reached horizontally to the other members of the human family.

Yet, many historians have appropriated these early transnational movements—particularly the international socialists and feminists who deployed a language of rights—as equivalent human rights movements or, at a minimum, as examples that led logically to the inclusion of human rights vocabulary in the U.N. Charter in 1945.[23] But this assumption is questionable. Despite the universalist appeal to sisterhood as a "common union," linking women of the "North lands and South lands," for example, the call for women's vote in practice reinforced class and racial hierarchies, a point driven home unmistakably at the 1923 congress of the IWSA in Rome. Then white women delegates from South Africa, advocating women's suffrage, were part of the political elite slowly extending the discriminatory racial laws at the base of apartheid South Africa. Similarly limiting, the 1900 Pan-African appeals to transcend the racial binaries "between white and black men" rested on an acceptance of the progressive stages of development in the culture of a people. Shared levels of culture were to overcome the exclusion of people of color from the "great brotherhood of Mankind."[24]

A more careful examination of the political vocabularies of liberation struggles reveals that in these grassroots people's movements the use of "human rights" emerged in specific contexts. Thus, in Europe, proponents of adult (universal) suffrage in the first decades of the twentieth century made their case on the basis of universal principles such as human rights (in contrast to what they saw as the limitations of women's suffrage). Marxists, too, spoke of human rights (in the German, *Menschenrechte*), but framed the notion in stark opposition to the existing system of domestic constitutional rights (as products of the evolution of natural rights), which, as they put it, upheld capitalist power and privilege. Using this logic, the achievement of international human rights was possible only after the socialist revolution. At times, for pragmatic reasons, a case made on the basis of human rights deflected the critics' efforts to dismiss distinct arguments for rights as necessarily limited and partial. Thus, human rights language was used purposefully by advocates of the full civil equality of black people in early twentieth-century America. For the influential reformer and critic W. E. B. Du Bois, furthermore, human rights also captured his expansive vision that intricately linked U.S. civil rights causes and those in the West Indies to the future liberation struggles of oppressed peoples in colonial Africa.[25] If limited and contradictory at times, the language of a common human bond or shared claims and entitlements was fundamental to any subsequent effort at universalizing rights principles. In the early twentieth century, this potential still ran counter to the sovereign prerogatives and exclusionary practices enshrined in international law.

International Law and the Limits of Rights

In their studies of the components of early internationalism, historians largely have neglected the movements to codify the "laws of war," those binding conventions governing the way wars are fought (*jus in bello*), known today as international humanitarian law. On the intergovernmental level, the codification work at the cusp of the twentieth century was an important catalyst for building permanent international structures, in some ways serving as a precursor to the League of Nations created after World War I. On the transnational level, too, this work attracted considerable interest among a diverse group of activists drawn from many parts of the globe. Their numbers included, among others, international pacifists, members of women's international suffrage alliances, supporters of the International Red Cross and Crescent societies, and lawyers' professional associations.[26]

When connected to human rights history, the codification efforts offer new insights into the uneasy relationship between law and justice. At both the national and international levels, law is a complex institution. It upholds dominant power structures and, thus, contributes to systemic injustices; it also is a tool to bring about social change toward greater equality and fairness. In the early twentieth century, the principles of international law, which defended state sovereignty and empire-building, helped construct an international order that dragged against the evolution of supranational norms.

From its origins in the emerging system of states and empires, the work of international law served two major functions. First, it regulated the duties and responsibilities of states in matters of mutual concern: opposing piracy on international waters, securing diplomatic immunities and protections of their own subjects and property abroad, ensuring redress of injuries to aliens, and providing care for wounded enemy soldiers on the battlefield. The state in its necessary intercourse with other states in the international arena became the main object of the law; with remarkably few exceptions, individuals were not covered under international law. Second, international law rested on the principle of nonintervention, which defined and confirmed sovereign status. That is, international law set a state's domestic affairs outside its proper jurisdiction. In principle, then, states had no right to intervene in the internal affairs of other states. Even in the revolutionary movements for national independence spreading throughout the Atlantic world in the early nineteenth century, international law came into force only after a new state had been established by rebellion. In practice, powerful Western state leaders periodically used both religion and language as criteria to intervene and promote the causes of minority peoples in the territories of other (weaker) states, but the principle of the inviolability of domestic jurisdiction remained the cornerstone of the international order regulated by international law. Much of this law was formulated through bilateral agreements; starting in the mid-nineteenth century, however, multilateral treaties became the main expressions of international law.

International humanitarian law governing military conduct in warfare was codified through international treaty, beginning at the first Hague Congress in 1899. There, representatives of twenty-six sovereign states, drawn nearly exclusively from Europe but also from the United States and Mexico, attended the meeting. The number of states rose to forty-four at the second Hague Congress in 1907, including fourteen from Central and Latin America as well as Japan, China, and Thailand [Siam] in East and Southeast Asia. Treaty provisions allowed for state accession; according to the design, as more states signed on, the law became more nearly universal.[27]

This movement at The Hague capped a full half-century of previous efforts to "humanize" warfare through multilateral agreements initially among a Concert of Europe. Most significant had been passage of the Geneva Conventions in 1864, which established safeguards for sick and wounded soldiers on the battlefield and simultaneously created the International Red Cross and, after negotiations with the Ottoman Empire in 1877, Red Crescent societies, headquartered in Geneva. Organized in national branches, which extended down to local communities, these relief organizations promised impartial, humanitarian aid to wounded soldiers of any nationality under the new internationally sanctioned status of inviolability, symbolized by the red cross and crescent. Although originally tied closely to the state, these groups were among the first NGOs in transnational contact operating under international law.[28] Through the Geneva Conventions, states accepted new duties and obligations to soldiers and civilians alike and pledged to ensure uniform implementation by the commander of each belligerent army. Tested in continental and colonial warfare, by 1906 they also had begun to expand the status and rights of prisoners of war. While agreements among states, these "laws of war" singled out certain types of individuals for legal protection in wartime: wounded soldiers, noncombatants (civilians), and prisoners of war. The Geneva Conventions were incorporated into the 1899 Convention on the Customs and Practices of War on Land (Art. 21) and made part of the Final Acts of the Hague Congress.

An unlikely source had set this "wheel of progress" in motion, as one contemporary European author described the codification movement, placing it among the defining hallmarks of the age. In 1898, at the request of the autocratic czar, the Russian foreign minister Count Mouravieff called for a select conference of state officials from around the world to work together to reduce the mounting budgetary expenditures for armaments, which so negatively "affect[ed] public prosperity," and also to enhance the prospects for peace.[29] After a cool reception, a second circular expanded the topics to include arms control and proposals for international arbitration to prevent armed conflicts among nations. The Dutch government, neutral in the great game of geopolitics, agreed to host the meeting at its capital, The Hague; the first conference opened on May 18, 1899.

Declaring the "preservation of the peace" a worthy goal of international policy, the work of codification, in fact, sought to impose proper rules and regulations for the conduct of armed warfare between states. If the work was cast under the rubric of peace, codification was as much about accepting the inevitability of war as developing the collective means necessary to maintain the peace. The congress deployed the new language of humanitarianism to bind the fate of humanity together through a common set of rules for warfare.[30]

The work at The Hague codified nineteenth-century law around the customs and practices of war on land and sea and eventually included aerial bombardments. Written, as the architects put it, with the "interests of humanity and the ever-growing requirements of civilization in mind," the Final Acts of 1899 set limitations on state military practices in wartime. Despite its grammatically indirect construction, Article 22 clearly captured the authors' intent: "The right of belligerents to adopt means of injuring the enemy is not unlimited." Drawing on positive law, it declared that the only legitimate object of warfare was to "weaken the military forces of the enemy." It, thus, opened a humanitarian space where the "necessities of war" were expected to "yield to the requirements of humanity."[31] The Final Acts prohibited a whole host of military actions, including the use of certain types of modern technology (hollow-point bullets, explosive projectiles, and poison gases); they forbade "treacherously" killing or maiming the enemy as well as destroying enemy property, towns, villages, or buildings—acts that were seen to bring "excess" suffering to soldiers and civilians alike. Preventing excess suffering was the humanitarian imperative. Other articles also governed military authority over an occupied territory. The Final Acts, too, established a Convention for the Pacific Settlement of International Disputes. It strengthened the principle of international arbitration, made it compulsory in restricted cases (initially involving contract debts), and established a Permanent Court of Arbitration seated at The Hague and served by an International Bureau, which kept the court's records. This experiment in multilateral law established permanent institutions in international society that put a face on the new norms and values in the law.

Codification was an empirical project based on existing positive laws. It drew on the state manuals of military law, such as the Lieber Code issued to the Union Army of the United States in 1863, and on the common practices of states. However, a number of contentious issues remained unresolved, notably the status of civilian insurgency. The statesmen for the smaller states, particularly Holland and Belgium, wanted a right of resistance to military occupation; representatives of the larger states, particularly Imperial Germany, wanted to declare civilian armed resistance illegal under all circumstances. Furthermore, the architects of the code also recognized that much customary and moral law had not been included in its work yet continued to exist as unwritten customary principles. Here the authors appealed to the normative traditions of natural law doctrines.

To handle these issues and overcome the particular impasse on civilian insurgency, Fedor Fedorovitch Martens, the Russian delegate, proposed a compromise. Known as the Martens Clause, it was inserted into the Preamble of the 1899 Fourth Convention. As Martens put it in his speech, he did not want to leave decisions about military conduct solely to the "arbitrary judgment of the military commanders." Thus, he invoked a higher law, what he called the "laws of humanity," which had ongoing validity even after the adoption of a treaty norm. The clause suggested that behaviors not explicitly prohibited by a treaty may be prohibited because they contravened this higher law. Martens said, in part, "Until a perfectly complete code of the laws of war is issued, the Conference thinks it right to declare that in cases not included in the present arrangement, populations and belligerents remain under the protection and empire of the principles of international law, as they result from the usages established between civilized nations, from the laws of humanity, and the requirements of the public conscience." Nearly the exact words were in the Preamble. Because the code was not exhaustive, states remained bound by customary international law regulating state military conduct, regardless of whether they had signed a particular convention. Subsequently, the International Military Tribunal at Nuremberg in 1946 used this principle to establish subject jurisdiction over so-called crimes against humanity—as grave breaches of international customary law.[32]

Despite references to a higher law of humanity and the vigilance of the public conscience, the authors of the Hague Conventions could not escape the contradictions inherent in their own international project. Given that state officials negotiated the treaty, they limited the scope of international jurisdiction, deferring to the norms of sovereignty and military autonomy. In the language of the day, the Final Acts exempted the internal "political relations of states" and the "orders of things established by treaties" from the jurisdiction of the Final Acts. They also failed to include any enforcement mechanisms to prevent—or subsequently prosecute—the excesses committed beyond what was militarily necessary.

Significantly, the deliberations at both Hague congresses, in 1899 and 1907, took place against the backdrop of imperialist wars that were placed outside the reach of international law. Imperial rule was imposed through deadly cycles of conquest and resistance. However, the imperial powers declared these colonial wars over land and resources purely internal matters of empire and, thus, off limits to the international community. Inventing a legal fiction, they labeled the geography of colonial areas "dependent territories" and placed them squarely within the borders of empire as a matter of internal jurisdiction. In ideological terms, the very norms of humane warfare were seen to differentiate the "civilized" nations from the "savage" peoples. In circular fashion, the conventions on the laws of war were open only to the so-called civilized states, which affirmed this status by adhering to the laws of war. Colonial peoples, by definition, were deemed uncivilized and stateless, persons who anyway would not follow the canons of accepted military behavior.[33]

Furthermore, the "laws of war"—and the customary principles—applied only to wars understood as wars: armed conflict between sovereign nations and empires. The wars against colonized people at the dawn of the twentieth century became "total wars," unrestrained by law and custom. Imperial armies used "scorched earth policies" to defeat the enemy and at times "concentrated" the remaining population on the land into camps. The concentration camp was invented in colonial contexts and used by the Spanish against the Cuban rebellion in 1896, by the British against their Boer enemies in the Southern African War (1899–1902), and by the United States in its brutal pacification efforts in the Philippines in 1899. During the Nama and Herero uprising against German colonial administrators and settlers in 1904–7, furthermore, official German policy sought the near annihilation of the native populations. These wars were grim examples—and repeated in the century to come—of wars undertaken with no sense of any common human bond with the enemy. Hannah Arendt, the post-Holocaust ethical philosopher, understood the formative role of imperialist conquest and rule in the "origins of totalitarianism" in Europe. Behind the "stagnant quiet in [early twentieth century] Europe," she observed with searing clarity, the period of imperialism tested the patterns of rule and unrestrained warfare that resurfaced in the genocides of fascist totalitarianism. According to Arendt, the whole era of imperialism, with its bureaucratic formulas and racist authority, was a "preparatory stage for coming catastrophes."[34] It also had an immediate and a devastating impact on colonized societies. Given these harsh geopolitical realities, the total wars of the colonial era could not produce collective sentiments in favor of universalizing rights. The law itself had perpetuated a stark divide between "civilized" nations and "savage" peoples, who were left unprotected.

Despite the mobilizing slogan of a world made safe for democracy after the carnage of World War I, the League of Nations coexisted with the unequal system of imperial and state power at the center of international relations. Its covenant was a collective agreement among sovereign states to preserve international peace and stability. Following legal traditions, it exempted the "internal affairs" of the member-states and imperial powers from international interference. The League, however, experimented with distinct modes of sovereignty and minority protections under international law, broadening the scope of rights talk among defenders of the system as well as among its critics.

The victor powers initially also made some efforts to punish states and individuals for violations of the law during the war: thus, harsh reparation terms were imposed on the defeated German nation for its presumed responsibility for the outbreak of the war. In addition, the Entente leaders in 1915, drawing on the Martens Clause, charged the Ottoman government with "new crimes . . . against humanity and civilization" for its brutal deportation policies and massacres of its Armenian citizens. In the 1920 Treaty of Sèvres, which aimed at the partition of the defeated Ottoman Empire, several articles provided for war crimes trials against officials for the killing of their citizens. Similar trials were required of Germans also accused of war-time atrocities. The effort to bring the Ottoman government to justice floundered on the nationalist military successes in defending a new Turkish nation centered in Anatolia. And, although some accused war criminals were brought to trial in Leipzig, Germany, this effort floundered on the ambiguities of the law. Meeting resistance at the level of state and society, these innovations failed to establish guidelines for criminal proceedings in cases of atrocities against citizens or crimes in excess of military necessity.[35]

The League of Nations marked a decisive advance in intergovernmental organization. Headquartered in Geneva, it was a permanent international body, open to all sovereign states and governed by an assembly of these states as well as by a small Council of Great Powers. A Secretariat coordinated the League's business; the Permanent Court of International Justice (following on the heels of the Hague Court) handled disputes involving international law. Furthermore, the League was joined in Geneva by the International Labour Organization (ILO), one of the first of many formal affiliations among intergovernmental bodies around issues that were seen to require transnational cooperation. The ILO, too, had been part of the peace treaties, a step by the victorious powers to stave off labor unrest and socialist revolutions that had engulfed many parts of Europe at the end of the war. In a new departure in law, the ILO was able to set international work standards and living conditions for labor, which applied universally to all the contracting state parties.[36] In addition, the League also coordinated an increasing number of volunteers and agencies concerned with epidemic disease prevention as well as cross-border sex and drug trafficking, among other transnational issues.[37]

Members of many large, prewar transnational groups already involved in rethinking international relations expressed misgivings about the organization and purpose of the League. Meeting at nearly the same time as the Paris Peace Conference at the conclusion of the war, representatives of the Second International, for example, called for a league of peoples (and not of nations) and a true democratization of the principles of self-determination and international cooperation. Likewise, members of the Women's International League for Peace and Freedom at its Zurich Congress in May 1919 condemned the terms of the "peace" established by the League. Other women's groups, such as the IWC, pushed for the admittance of women to all League offices and committees. They had hoped to make the full legal and political equality of men and women a prerequisite for state entry into the League, but the proposal was not accepted. Added transnational pressure came from the first official Pan-African Congress in Paris in February 1919. The fifty-five delegates wanted to turn the colonies over to an international organization and establish collective responsibility for the "just treatment" of natives in Africa.[38] As in the women's proposal for equal participation in the League bureaucracy, some of this language on native peoples was inserted into the covenant.

In this fluid climate of anticipation, the League confronted two major issues with implications for rights principles. The one concerned the colonies seized in war from the defeated nations, notably Germany's African colonies and the Ottoman Arab provinces of Iraq, Syria, Lebanon, and Palestine. The other involved minority peoples in the states carved from the European territories of the former Russian, Austro-Hungarian, and Ottoman empires. Historians recently have reexamined these policies as part of a new interest in rights talk.[39]

In the postwar era, outright annexations of former colonies were ruled out, in deference to the strong opposition of powerful leaders such as Woodrow Wilson, ideological mentor of the League, as well as to transnational opinion openly hostile to such a step. The League, thus, created three types of mandates based on liberal imperialist assumptions about stages of development toward eventual self-rule. Not part of national sovereignty, these territories were administered "in trust" for "the peoples not yet able to stand by themselves under the strenuous conditions of the modern world" (Art. 22). In addition, the mandate powers faced oversight by a Permanent Mandate Commission.[40]

Some mandates, notably the one given to South Africa over the former German colony of South-West Africa, were "annexation in all but name" and furthered the dispossession of black Africans from their lands. In other cases, oversight mitigated some of the harsher colonial practices involving military service and labor, as the ruling powers calculated their interests in the glare of international scrutiny. If the new research shows that the mandate system did not accelerate the step to independence, it served, in Pedersen's judicious analysis, as a transitional system between formal empire and full independence. To the many sources of geopolitical change, including native anticolonial movements and the metropole populations' growing concerns with the ethics of empire, Pedersen added the intersecting role of international bodies, generating new norms and talk. Besides, indigenous nationalists in the Middle East, in particular, and in Africa and the Pacific learned different "transnational political practices," including effective deployment of international norms in the "halls of international organizations."[41]

Confronting colonial issues, the League legitimized at the same time the redrawing of the map of Europe according to the principle of national self-determination, which had served as the Entente power's vision of a new world at peace after the armistice. Carving new national borders to reflect linguistic and religious criteria, the victor powers nonetheless feared for minority rights, responding in part to the transnational pressures of prominent Jewish activists. Confronting systematic discrimination and oppression, vocal leaders of European Jewish minorities had been pushing the issue of minority protections at diplomatic and peace conferences starting in 1878. It became a vital question under League auspices which imposed Minorities Treaties on the governments of the newly created states.[42] Written as bilateral agreements, the treaties became part of the multilateral new order guaranteed by the League. They ensured all inhabitants of the newly formed nation-states in Europe the full protection of life, liberty, and law "without distinction of birth, nationality, language, race or religion." They also guaranteed minority peoples inside the sovereign nation a certain measure of cultural autonomy, establishing group protections. Compliance became a condition of the states' full membership in the League while, reciprocally, protection of the political and civil rights of the minority group was made an obligation of the international community through the mandated development of procedures for oversight and implementation (including taking petitions). Similarly, the victor powers also imposed minority protections on the new Turkish nation sanctioned by the Lausanne Treaty in 1923. Protections, however, were extended only to distinct religious minorities in the state and not to the ethnic groups (for example, Kurds) within the dominant Muslim community.

In a recent article, historian Mark Mazower analyzed the geopolitical context that, as he put it, "abandon[ed]" minority protections in favor of the post–World War II system of human rights. Yet he penned too stark a contrast between individual and group rights: minority treaties gave all *individual* nationals an equality of citizenship rights in addition to measures for *group* autonomy in, for example, explicitly guaranteeing Jews the right to their Sabbath (Saturday) in labor contracts and in conducting legal business. Rights claims often embrace contradictory principles, which are prioritized and balanced differently at distinct historical moments.[43] In the end, the League proved to be ineffectual and weak, unable to safeguard the peace or minority protections. Its failure opened the floodgates for the horrors of the Holocaust and the wholesale slaughter of other minority peoples during World War II. In the evolution of international law, however, its experiments with sovereignty set new boundaries between international authority and state power. In addition, the minority clauses broadened the debates beyond the stark dichotomy between the "civilized" nations and the "savage" peoples that was set by the Hague precedent.

Concentrating on mandates and minorities, this historical literature has missed the growing opposition to the limited scope of rights upheld by international law. Within the post–World War I treaty system, new patterns of societal pressure to expand League guarantees came from two directions. The first proposal sought to extend the minority protection principles of rights to the "internal affairs" of all member-states of the League (as Woodrow Wilson originally had proposed). The second questioned the long-held sovereignty norm that the status of women was a matter of domestic jurisdiction alone.

The first proposal, in effect, broadened the formulation of rights by calling for guarantees to ensure the "international rights of [all] individuals," affirming porous boundaries between individual rights and group rights in contemporary thinking. The proposal was put before the Assembly in 1933 and 1934 by a delegate from the Republic of Haiti, then under U.S. occupation—and both times unsuccessfully. The resolution nonetheless testified to new thinking about international law among Chilean and Parisian jurists as well as to Pan-American collaborative work and networking on issues of shared interest, such as security and arbitration, despite intense state rivalries in the Western hemisphere. In addition, it spoke to wider intellectual contacts across the Atlantic world around questions of democracy and social justice.[44]

The second proposal was pushed by Latin American women's organizations, which, too, had been increasingly involved in inter-American affairs. Led in the early twentieth century by feminists from Uruguay and Argentina, these activists became well practiced in the politics of lobbying the Inter-American Conferences of States on their own issues of mutual concern, such as family life, public health, child welfare, and women's suffrage. In the case of Latin American women, it appears that the wider hemispheric contacts were the impetus for parallel work on the national level; similar ties among women's groups also sustained Pan-Pacific identities distinct from those in Europe and America. Many of these local leaders also participated in women's international organizations and advocacy, redoubling the work of lobbying for women's causes in Geneva.

The heads of the women's advocacy networks were appalled at the absence of women in official administration and leadership posts at the League despite Article 7, which opened all bureaucratic posts to women and encouraged them to become members of the state delegations to the Assembly. After 1929, the leaders became increasingly alarmed at the consequences of the world economic depression for women's right to work, a principle defended by the ILO. In addition, the rise of fascism was seen as a serious threat to women's position in society. Ten Latin American delegations at the League, reflecting widespread concerns back home, took the lead in calling for a forceful response to the "encroachments upon the rights and liberties of women." The Liaison Committee of Women's International Organizations, established in 1931 to coordinate the international work of a wide range of women's reform societies, mobilized its affiliated organizations for a tandem public relations campaign. Bowing to considerable international pressure from 1935 on, the League agreed two years later to sponsor a "comprehensive and scientific inquiry" into the status of women worldwide, the first such broad investigation into the domestic life situation of women around the globe. Women's organizations had come together and turned a gender-specific issue into a matter of grave international urgency. As earlier, the interwar period faced contradictions in the uneven application of legal rights under growing transnational pressures. But these many efforts were not framed in the explicit language of *human* rights.

The 1940s: Reformulations and New Linkages

The distinctive contribution of human rights to international relations was the explicit linkage of human rights protections to an international order of peace and security. Human rights language expanded the safeguards that states put into place to promote international cooperation from their original sources in "respect for treaty obligations," for the "implementation of existing international law," and for the maintenance of "honorable relations between nations."[45] Collective security now was seen to require the defense of human rights norms and principles. This point explains my earlier focus on the ways members of many transnational movements moved from supporting particular causes in local contexts to rethinking the basis of the international order of states. Human rights also posited the fundamental equality of human beings. The embrace of a conception of a common humanity was a precondition for this radical shift. Only in the 1940s did these two components converge and reshape treaty law.

In the first three decades of the twentieth century, human rights language was not the common currency of formal diplomacy. After the Bolshevik Revolution, Western leaders increasingly centered their ideological claims on "freedom" and "democracy," which they deployed against the so-called twin evils of communism and fascism. Soviet leaders promoted anti-imperialist struggles globally as part of their push for socialist revolution, and Japanese officials sought to bind Asian nations more closely to them through anti-Western policies, implementing, however, a peculiar form of anti-imperial imperialism, which accelerated after 1937.

At the level of society, proponents of rights guarantees began to form separate groups, as in the creation through French and German efforts of the International Federation of the Rights of Man in 1922, a forerunner of the International Federation for Human Rights (FIDH). Prominent intellectuals such as the writer H. G. Wells also worked for the "rights of man." In the interwar years, for example, Wells linked the universality of his new codes of rights and duties to a comprehensive vision of an interdependent world community.[46]

As a specific lexicon, "human rights" entered the diplomatic arena through the spread of Allied wartime propaganda leveled against the Axis powers of Germany, Italy, and Japan during World War II. Human rights language worked to crystallize the purposes of the war and the meanings of its sacrifices: the creation of a new world community that would protect human rights and fundamental freedoms as the basis of international peace in the future. By late 1941, the Allies included the Soviet Union, after Hitler invaded Russia, and the United States, after the bombing of Pearl Harbor by the Japanese. In pragmatic terms, human rights represented a bridge language to cement, however uneasily, this coalition of politically diverse states joined against fascism. Arguably, the formulation of this term came with less baggage than either "democracy" or "freedom"; it also appealed to the socialist defense of economic rights and social welfare provisions. Indeed, the Soviet Constitution of 1936 was one important document that helped shape the discussions around the precise cataloging of human rights after 1945.[47]

Although not detracting from the moral appeal or the normative legal potentials of human rights, this argument explains the rather sudden and widespread appearance of human rights language in the battleground for world public opinion during World War II. In pamphlet form in multiple vernaculars, the idea literally was dropped from the sky; it was broadcast on radio; and it was used to mobilize the colonies for the war effort. A proclamation issued by twenty-six Allied countries in January 1942 was typical of the nature of the appeal. It read, "Complete victory over [our] enemies is essential to defend life, liberty, independence and religious freedom, and to preserve human rights and justice in [our] own lands as well as in other lands."[48]

Simultaneously, this idea of universal rights was picked up by a large and diverse number of people around the globe. "Human rights" became a new term to express many different values and goals behind existing struggles against injustices. Asking oppressed people to join the fight for freedom against fascism only made the struggle for their own freedom and rights more insistent. For example, fully recognizing that "in the war" South Africa was fighting "against oppression and for freedom," the African National Congress (ANC)—the major opposition party to white minority rule in the country—drew up a Bill of Rights and an Atlantic Charter for Africa. Tellingly, the African blueprint was modeled on the Atlantic Charter proclaimed by U.S. President Franklin Roosevelt and British Prime Minister Winston Churchill in 1941 to crystallize the "common principles" in the Allied fight for "a better future" for the world. Renouncing territorial aggrandizement, it defended self-determination, global economic prosperity, and a future of peace. Its principles upheld the right of a people to choose its own government; long part of anticolonial struggles, these values were penetrating even deeper into oppositional politics, inspiring, as in the African Charter, new maps of the continent free of colonial rule. By 1946, the ANC had incorporated the call for "fundamental human rights" into its platform.

René Brunet, a French official with the League of Nations, graphically captured this mounting support for human rights principles at the organizational level of transnational civil society as well. Writing in 1947, he reminisced about the flows of exchange as the war progressed: "Hundreds of political, scholarly and religious organizations have, by their publications, appeals, manifestations and interventions, spread and impressed the idea that the protection of human rights should be part of the war aims of the Allied Powers, and that the future peace would not be complete if it would not consecrate the principle of international protection of human rights in all States and if it would not guarantee this protection in an effective manner."[49] Brunet was on the mark. This compelling framework was embraced by Jewish groups pushing for a world charter, church organizations with international linkages, trade unionists as part of international alliances, peace movements, and all manner of women's groups.[50] It also fed into the liberation struggles against the Japanese occupation and, subsequently, into the nationalist movements opposing the return of the European colonial powers to Asia. Thus, Indonesian nationalists proclaimed a new constitution on August 18, 1945 (one day after the Japanese capitulation), which incorporated respect for human rights as well as fundamental freedoms for ethnic minorities. Two days later, the liberation leader Ho Chi Minh declared Vietnam's independence from France. Quoting from the 1776 American Declaration of Independence, he said, "All men are created equal." He went on to explain, "In a broader sense, this means: all the peoples on the earth are equal from birth, all the peoples have a right to live, to be happy and free." For the Indonesians and Vietnamese, however, there was "no easy walk to freedom," as Westad put it succinctly.[51]

Despite the widespread commitment to a new world order and a growing appeal to human rights, incorporation of the principles into the U.N. Charter—the foundational treaty document of the postwar order—was not automatic. The outcome required the timely intervention of transnational voices and regional blocs determined to see human rights become a permanent fixture of the peace after the war. Significantly, the Dumbarton Oaks proposal by the Allied greatpowers (the United States, Great Britain, the Soviet Union, and China) held in Washington, D.C., between August 21 and October 7, 1944, which set the blueprint for the future United Nations, downplayed concrete references to human rights principles, despite their high visibility in the propaganda campaigns of the war. British and Soviet leaders were opposed and the United States reacted negatively to the Chinese effort to mention explicitly the "equality of the races." Disagreement meant a weak draft proposal; its publication led to a storm of protest and action by government representatives and transnational groups.

Foremost among these actions were public protests in Latin and Central American countries, which had been spared as battlegrounds in war. In February and March 1945, the Chapultepec Conference (on the problems of war and peace) in Mexico City came out decisively for the international protection of fundamental rights to ensure the peace and called for an inter-American human rights convention. Reflecting pressures at home, some Latin American delegations, notably Panama, arrived at the San Francisco meeting in spring 1945, which established the United Nations, with full drafts on hand of an International Declaration on the Essential Rights of Man, which they hoped to insert into the charter. Other countries also responded to mounting public pressure. In an effort to prevent a repetition of isolationist sentiments that had kept the United States out of the League of Nations, the U.S government invited members of forty-two prominent NGOs to travel to San Francisco as official consultants to the state delegations. The American groups consisted of well-known representatives of labor, women's, and religious groups, as well as lawyers; they worked to overcome opposition to amending the Dumbarton Oaks plan, which had divided the U.S. delegation.

John P. Humphrey, the Canadian lawyer later responsible for the first U.N. draft statement on human rights, credited these NGOs and individuals with anchoring human rights principles into the charter. In no uncertain terms, he wrote that these groups, "aided by the delegations of the smaller countries, conducted a lobby in favor of human rights for which there is no parallel in the history of international relations." And even Kirsten Sellars, a cynic about the embrace of human rights principles by the leaders of the Western powers—she argues that U.S., British, and French leaders have used human rights merely to placate domestic opinion—nonetheless credited the public campaigns in San Francisco for putting significant pressure on the key political decision-makers.[52] Because of their efforts, human rights were mentioned seven times in the U.N. Charter.

Human Rights and Postwar Reconstruction

The human rights revolution inaugurated by the charter rested on new international legal foundations. In contrast to the historic precedents, the postwar reconstruction of intergovernmental cooperation in 1945 made human rights principles universally applicable as part of an international treaty law system binding on the participating states. The universal protection of human rights became a matter of international law.

A series of international treaties that were drafted, passed, and ratified between 1945 and 1949 rewrote the jurisdiction of the law. Human rights principles were codified before they were theorized. Chronologically, the first was the London Agreement of August 8, 1945, signed by the United States, the Soviet Union, Britain, and France, and adhered to, subsequently, by nineteen other states.[53] This charter established the first International Military Tribunal at Nuremberg to hold individual Nazi leaders responsible for clear breaches of international law: crimes against the peace, based on 1920s law; war crimes codified by the earlier Hague congresses; and crimes against humanity, using the Martens Clause precedent. A similar tribunal was created by the American occupation authority in Japan in late 1946 to prosecute war criminals in the Asian theater of war, but it was not established by international treaty. The courts narrowed the areas of personal immunity for high civilian and military officials who had violated international or customary law. They rejected a defense on the basis of "reason of state" or "due obedience," declaring that an accused could no longer appeal to the sovereign prerogatives of defending the state or claiming to follow orders.

A second, and cornerstone, treaty was the Charter of the United Nations, signed originally by fifty-four participating states; it entered into force on October 24, 1945. In stark contrast to the League covenant, it adopted the voice of the people of the states newly joined in a United Nations, making the "self-determination of peoples" and "respect for human rights and international cooperation in humanitar-

ian matters" declared purposes of the world body. It established permanent organs and committees to oversee these goals, vesting decision-
making and execution in a General Assembly of all state members and
in a smaller Security Council with veto powers given to its five permanent members—the United States, Britain, Russia, China, and France,
the major victor powers of World War II. It established, as well, an Economic and Social Council (ECOSOC), promoting international cooperation in economic, social, and humanitarian matters, and a Secretariat,
running the day-to-day business of the organization. U.S. statesman
George F. Kennan summarized its meaning later when he wrote that the
United Nations is "the only living . . . symbol of the community of fate
that links all the people of this planet."[54]

A third treaty was the Genocide Convention, passed unanimously by
the General Assembly on December 9, 1948. At the time, "genocide"
was a newly minted term in international criminal law, coined by a Polish
Jewish lawyer, Raphael Lemkin. From the early 1930s on, Lemkin had
been pursuing a personal campaign to broaden international law to
criminalize racial massacres; he defined these types of murders as the
killing of the *gens* (Latin for "clan" or "group"). Although Lemkin's
new formulation was not part of the Nuremberg Tribunal's formal jurisdiction, in the trials themselves prosecutors began to speak of Nazi genocide. In time, genocide has come to symbolize the ultimate evil of which
human beings are capable. In addition, the General Assembly also
adopted the Universal Declaration of Human Rights on December 10,
1948, a date celebrated in many parts of the world as human rights day.
Not passed originally as treaty law, it proclaimed a broad set of rights
and protections to serve as a universal standard for all human beings,
everywhere.

Prodded by the International Committee of the Red Cross, a diplomatic conference of sixty-four states adopted substantive revisions of the
Geneva Conventions on August 12, 1949. Part of the legal revolution in
the postwar era, the conference rewrote the "laws of war" to aid the victims of war, effectively replacing many of the provisions of the Hague
Conventions. In particular, the Fourth Convention expanded the safeguards on civilian life, liberty, and property during war; it was the first
time that civilians were singled out in a separate legal instrument.
Adopting a set of shared articles, the conventions, furthermore, affirmed the continued force of customary obligations on states in wartime (Common Article 3).[55]

The new formulations of rights were not made solely at the level of
law. Between 1945 and 1949, they were matched by an activist climate that
drew the fledgling United Nations into many pressing moral and political problems of the day. Its members were determined to overcome the

League's weaknesses. In early December 1946, for example, the General Assembly looked into a complaint lodged by India condemning the rampant discrimination against south Asians by the white population in South Africa. In an uncharacteristic diplomatic move, it cast an intrusive eye into the domestic affairs of a state. A few days later, it also recommended that member-states adopt measures consistent with the equality principle in the charter and give women the same political rights as men. As earlier, this proposal did not become a condition of U.N. membership.

The fate of Mandate German South-West Africa, administered by the Union of South Africa, also became an urgent political matter. Through the president of the ANC, "Africans in South Africa" sent a protest telegram to the United Nations forcing the new human rights values into global politics. The message cataloged South Africa's discriminatory racist policies "at home": Africans had "no share in government, [and thus] no part in negotiations . . . South Africa denies political and economic rights to her 8 million Africans . . . 83 percent of the land is reserved for 2 million Europeans." Such blatant discrimination precluded the incorporation of other African territories into the state. Subsequently, the General Assembly also went on record opposing the transfer.[56]

As part of the ongoing international discussions of the League mandate regime, Palestine also entered the international agenda. In early May 1947, the General Assembly set up a Special Committee on Palestine. This multinational group took evidence on conflicting claims from the Jewish Agency, the umbrella organization to oversee the establishment of a Jewish national home, as well as the Arab Higher Committee, and sent delegates to investigate "all questions and issues relevant to the problems of Palestine." The issue became compelling when the British government summarily announced that it was withdrawing from the empire—from Palestine to India to Burma. As a consequence, the U.N. Special Committee in 1947 recommended a partition of Palestine. The proposal acknowledged the legitimacy of the Zionist claims to a homeland in the face of the near destruction of European Jewry in the Holocaust. The Arab states rejected partition, demanding the integrity of Palestine. This decision set the stage for ongoing confrontations on the ground over the land of Palestine, initially in the 1947–49 war, which brought about the creation of the state of Israel but failed to provide an acceptable solution to the status of the Arab residents in former Mandate Palestine. The United Nations has remained involved in ongoing negotiations for a permanent solution.[57]

Expectations for new international commitments also remained high at the level of transnational advocacy. In 1947, W. E. B. Du Bois, the long-time Pan-African advocate, lodged "An Appeal to the World" through the United Nations, protesting the treatment of Negroes by the U.S. government. His justification showed how the creation of the United Nations seemingly opened new avenues for the hearing of grievances. Du Bois asked to whom his petition should be addressed and acknowledged that many people would see it as a "domestic question which is purely a matter of internal concern." Yet, he described how a state's discrimination against its own citizens challenged the rights of people everywhere and defied the "ideals and work" of the new United Nations. He then answered his own query. "This question . . . becomes inevitably an international question and will in the future become more and more international, as the nations draw together." In a similar fashion, the U.S. Civil Rights Congress in 1951 charged "genocide," connecting the U.S. government's adherence to the Charter of the United Nations mandating respect for rights with the legal prohibition of genocide codified in the 1948 convention (which the government had not ratified). If not a new demand—referencing the slave trade and slavery, the petition bemoaned the wait of "three-hundred years"—it drew its moral force from the requirement of prevention in the Genocide Convention. The moral-legal nexus of human rights instruments was changing the language and strategy of transnational advocacy. But the expectations of immediate redress—matched by other appeals around slavery, aboriginal peoples, and trade union issues that came to the attention of the General Assembly in its early years—remained unfulfilled by the intergovernmental body.[58]

The United Nations represented an older pattern of organization, bringing together for mutual benefit a collectivity of sovereign states. At the same time, responding to transnational pressure, it proclaimed universal human rights, admitting norms that had the potential to erode sovereign prerogatives. Its charter universalized the principles of nondiscrimination, protecting people on the basis of religion and language, here drawing on the original criteria that underpinned earlier diplomatic interventions. Reflecting growing anticolonial pressures (the charter was written at the cusp of the breakup of empires), the Chinese delegation pushed for the inclusion of "race" as an added category of protection; the horrific abuses of Nazi racial doctrines guaranteed its wide embrace. And, because of the substantial presence of organized women's groups in San Francisco, most notably from Latin and Central America, the charter specifically affirmed "the equal rights of men and women."[59]

As a product of great power, small state, and people's bargaining, the charter established the organizational structure and lines of authority for the international protection of rights. Figure 1 shows the original six

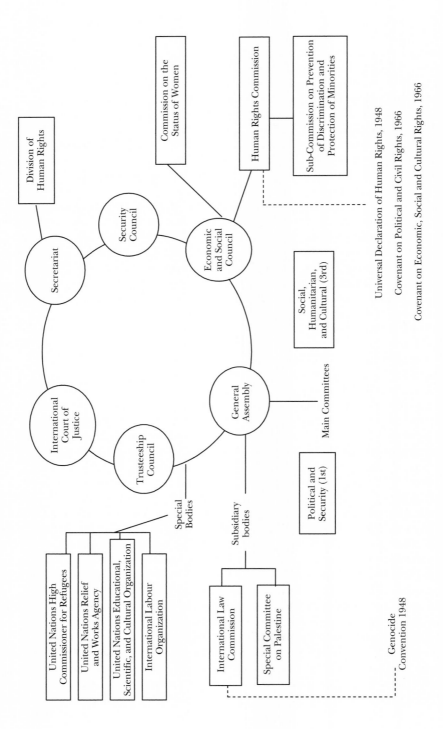

Figure 1. The early U.N. human rights system, 1945–51. This figure shows the human rights "revolution" as it was instituted in the early United Nations. Adapted from the official U.N. Web site, www.un.org.

principal organs of the United Nations, each with a distinctive place in the emerging human rights system. The General Assembly, Security Council, Economic and Social Council, and Secretariat remain the major international organs involved in human rights work. The figure also shows the Trusteeship Council, which supervised the territories put under U.N. administration with the dissolution of the mandate system.[60] The charter created the International Court of Justice as the principal judicial organ of the United Nations to adjudicate disputes between states, including vital issues that involve human rights principles.

The Charter of the United Nations also called on the Economic and Social Council to establish a commission "for the promotion of human rights" (Art. 68). At the passage of this article, U.S. Secretary of State Edward Stettinius cautiously predicted that "the unanimous acceptance of this proposal may well prove [to be] one of the most important and most significant achievements of the San Francisco Conference."[61] The only functional committee specifically mentioned in the charter, the Human Rights Commission (HRC) has been at the center of contentious debate and policy formulation, testing the lines between sovereign prerogatives and human rights. Although not explicitly mentioned in the charter, the Economic and Social Council in 1946 created a Commission on the Status of Women, drawing on League precedents. Figure 1 also shows subsidiary bodies to the General Assembly, specifically the International Law Commission (ILC) established in 1948. A product of the "codification movement," it has been at the forefront of the continuing developments of international law. The ILC, for example, drafted the Genocide Convention. The figure also notes a number of new international bodies for the care and protection of refugees established in response to war crises on the ground—the United Nations High Commissioner for Refugees and the United Nations Relief and Works Agency.

Emerging from the carnage of World War II, the charter set the preservation of the peace as one main purpose of the United Nations It called for "collective measures [to be taken] for the prevention and removal of threats to the peace, and for the suppression of acts of aggression or other breaches of the peace" (Art. 1.1). And it declared, although somewhat ambiguously, that "armed force shall not be used, save in the common interest" (Preamble). Seeking to put muscle behind this commitment—and going further than the precedents—the charter authorized the Security Council to take all necessary measures to preserve peace, including the threat or use of armed force against an offending state (Arts. 41, 43). By charter designs, only the Security Council can impose economic, military, or other sanctions on a state seen to be threatening international peace and security. In its original intent, the architects of the United Nations put the possibility of military force behind the council's mandate to preserve collective security. They exempted the articles authorizing force (Chapter VII: "action with respect to threats to the peace, breaches of the peace, and acts of aggression") from the domestic jurisdiction defense. That is, a state placed under Chapter VII sanctions cannot appeal to the domestic jurisdiction protections of Article 2.7, in the same charter. The efforts to ban acts of aggression and define the limits of armed self-defense have remained largely dormant since their formulation. Thus, the human rights system developed in a difficult climate, as part of an international system that has remained relatively powerless to overturn the fictions of so-called defensive wars.

The organizational blueprint of the United Nations inserted human rights principles into its committee structure; in and outside the world body, the state members continued to pursue their own calculated interests. In this uncertain terrain, one of the first practical decisions of the new Human Rights Commission limited its range of action. Early in 1947, HRC members ruled they had no authority to investigate complaints of human rights violations by the alleged victims. Petitions by individuals, groups, and organizations (or "communications" as they are known in official U.N. circles) were sent to the office of the Secretariat, where, in deference to sovereignty norms, they remained buried under stacks of paper. The many vocal transnational advocates of justice had very different understandings; as the U.S. Civil Rights Congress, they spoke about "our right of petition" and of a corresponding "duty of the General Assembly to hear our complaint." For years, however, the HRC would not act against, or publicly name, a state that was charged with violating the human rights of its people.[62]

The HRC turned to other tasks, notably the setting of norms and standards as well as initiating comprehensive studies. Between January 1947 and December 1948, its eighteen members opened a debate about the philosophical and practical underpinnings of the rubric "human rights." This debate proved truly consequential. Drafting the Universal Declaration of Human Rights, they cataloged a range of rights, and some corresponding duties, which set the norms for the ensuing struggles that tested their actual meanings in everyday life. The Universal Declaration has provided the overarching framework within which the human rights system unfolded—with its own priorities and biases and in confrontation with critics within the system, pushing for greater universality, and those outside, who rejected the notion of universal human rights.

Debating International Human Rights: Controversies and Compromises

Despite the expectations of many representatives in San Francisco, the charter did not contain an International Bill of Rights; rather, it proclaimed the absolute necessity of these rights for the future peace and it purposefully left the negotiations over their enumeration to the Human Rights Commission, organized in June 1946. With Eleanor Roosevelt, widow of the president and a liberal voice in U.S. politics, as chair, the commission worked nearly two full years on multiple drafts of the document. In retrospect, perhaps, the arduous debates in the commission itself and in its parent body, the General Assembly (followed by the reading public) were an advantage for meaningful intercultural and political exchanges. The many months of discussion allowed for the participation of diverse groups and voices with multiple agendas and interests. In time, through decisions of the International Court of Justice and the ratification of new international human rights treaties, the Universal Declaration became the authoritative interpretation in international law of the references to human rights in the charter.[63]

Because of their avowed universalist ends, these U.N.-led debates represented one of the earliest efforts to confront the many different political, cultural, and religious traditions that comprised the so-called global community, itself being fashioned by these types of agreements. In the heady days of postwar reconstruction, the framers' shared goals of international peace worked to bridge many divides, even among ideological adversaries. Roosevelt could have been speaking for others when she said, after a particularly difficult moment in the negotiations, that her government was willing "to surrender a certain amount of national sovereignty in an effort to join with the other nations of the world" in establishing a new normative foundation for international politics.[64] Although they did not prevail, these were remarkable sentiments, capturing the particular moment.

Drafting the declaration involved numerous phases of tough negotiation and artful compromise. It produced a document unique in its foundation, formulation, and coverage. The task of drafting originally was given to a four-person nuclear (preparatory) committee, representing the leadership of the HRC, with Roosevelt as chair, Peng-chun Chang, the Chinese nationalist representative who had been educated in the West, as vice chair, and the Lebanese Christian Charles Malik as the commission's executive secretary (rapporteur). Included in this small group was John Humphrey, director of the Secretariat's Division of Human Rights (created in 1946), who served as the liaison to the HRC. Challenged by the Soviet Union as too narrow, the drafting committee expanded to eight, adding representatives from Australia, Chile, France, the Soviet Union, and Great Britain. Each member came with formidable credentials and many later took other important leadership roles in the United Nations.

This committee worked at the discretion of the full eighteen-member Human Rights Commission, which constantly intruded into the drafting stages. Operating at the beginning of the decolonization movements, two of its most vocal participants, Dr. Hansa Mehta and General Carlos Romulo, came from the newly created nation-states of India and the Philippines, respectively. Malik was from Lebanon, evacuated by the British and French in 1946. Other active members were from Egypt, nominally tied into the British Empire, and Iran, formally independent. On the HRC also were representatives from Panama and Uruguay. At various phases of deliberation, the Human Rights Commission presented drafts to the full U.N. membership in the General Assembly, consisting of fifty-eight states by late 1948. Thus, delegations from Pakistan, Sweden, Mexico, Cuba, Ecuador, and South Africa, among others, weighed in, offering comments and substitute amendments. In terms of regional balance, however, people from Africa and Southeast and East Asia, still under colonial domination, were seriously underrepresented at the time.

Members of the drafting committee broadened their scope and conferred also with a host of international NGOs. Their instructions authorized them to "consult any document or person deemed . . . of relevance to their work." During the negotiations, commissioners heard from the Coordinating Board of Jewish Organizations, seeking to advance the interests of Jews in the post-Holocaust climate, and the International Committee of the Red Cross. They took testimony from many groups given formal consultative status in the United Nations, including the prominent International Council of Women, the left-leaning Women's International Democratic Federation, and the International Federation of Christian Trade Unions. Other newly created intergovernmental agencies, such as the United Nations Economic, Social and Cultural Organization (UNESCO), undertook broad global surveys on rights policies on behalf of the commission's work and the newly created Commission on the Status of Women also weighed in. In the main, the prewar, well-established international NGOs from the West dominated this consultative landscape. Despite the obvious biases of international power, representatives of many traditions engaged in the debates and discussions over rights formulations for the new era. The Syrian delegate Abdul Rahman Kayala, a prominent Sunni nationalist from the mandate period, may have reflected the prevailing optimism when he observed that the process was not the "work of a few representatives in the Assembly or in the Economic and Social Council." For him, the final document reflected "the achievement of generations of human beings who had worked towards that end."[65] Many different visions were being drawn together in a way that based rights on the presumption of the inherent equality of all human beings.

The task of drafting a universal agreement by such a diverse group of people in and around the Human Rights Commission was daunting, indeed. The authors faced big philosophical and political conundrums as well as nagging matters of detail. They had to negotiate on the principles that might ground (or authorize) human rights as well as on substantive matters such as the proper balance between rights and duties as well as freedoms and social responsibilities. They had to determine the types of rights that would be guaranteed and balance the two large traditions of rights that had a global currency: the so-called negative rights (the civil and political freedoms *from* state oppression in the natural rights tradition) and the positive obligations *on* the state to provide social, economic, and cultural entitlements (from the socialist, labor, and welfare capitalist traditions, among others). It remained a question whether the Universal Declaration be written as a "common standard of achievement for all peoples and all nations," as its proposition claimed.

The authors of the declaration immediately recognized the impossibility of formulating a philosophy of human nature or other shared ontological (originating) foundations that would be universally accepted. Their own historical perspectives, customs, traditions, and values were too ingrained, meaningful, and diverse for any such undertaking. Rather, they set their sights on negotiating a set of shared practices that they could agree were necessary to uphold human dignity and worth, which had been so egregiously violated in their recent past. The declaration, therefore, made no reference to God or to a single transcendent source of authority as the basis for human rights. Nor did it appeal to any universal theory of morality beyond the commitment to behave in a way that sustained human dignity. And it made no claim that human beings endowed with reason could arrive ultimately at one incontrovertible Truth. Rather, the declaration was an agreement on a code of behavior for members of the international community. It was silent about the metaphysical, moral, and religious reasons that might lie behind such a commitment, allowing each and every participant his and her own specific beliefs. In this respect, it differed from natural rights theory that underpinned the U.S. Declaration of Independence and the French Declaration of the Rights of Man and Citizen. As products of Western thought, these historical documents grounded their authority in a transcendent Christian God and in human nature purportedly established by God. A similar metaphysical appeal was not possible in a document seeking to address the globe's human communities. The declaration was an agreement to establish a culture of activism to build the legal, institutional, and normative preconditions for the unfolding of human dignity in international political society.

"All human beings are born free in dignity and rights," stated Article 1, proclaiming the inherent dignity and fundamental value of each human person placed at the center of the agreement. "They are endowed with reason and conscience and should act towards one another in a spirit of brotherhood," it concluded. The authors made an appeal to "reason" and "conscience," two of the shared attributes of human capacity, which permitted people to know they had rights. This knowledge, in turn, allowed them to form one human community based on actions that reflected and promoted a "spirit of brotherhood," a communal vision long in vogue in earlier transnational struggles for justice. The authors, then, did not legitimize rights by making them a "natural" expression of human nature. The ethical philosopher Bhikhu Parekh reworked the point in a different context. "Our concern," he said, "is not to discover values, for they have no objective basis, but to agree on them." Put another way, the broad agreement to protect human rights came not from nature but from "history"—from the knowledge of the evil that human beings can do to one another.[66]

As Article 1 proclaimed, the declaration enshrined dignity as the most cherished value of human beings. This widespread commitment to dignity across different political systems and cultures was rooted in part in common beliefs from diverse religious traditions and customs and in part in the activist traditions defending autonomy, self-actualization, and independence—both personal and collective. Although not part of classical European natural rights philosophy (in eighteenth-century Europe, for example, dignity applied to aristocratic independent status), it became a fundamental principle of both international feminist and labor critiques of natural rights, measured by the demand for women's full participation in the state (i.e., their independence from men) or by the proposition of the dignity of labor (i.e., personal affirmation through work). The same idea, expressing a common humanity, penetrated deep into anticolonial thinking. While multivalent, the concept of dignity captured the change in consciousness that had underpinned the widespread resonance of universal human rights by the end of World War II.[67]

Article 2 of the Universal Declaration extended its principles to the whole of humanity divided into multiple components. To the U.N. Charter's four categories protected from discrimination—language, religion, race, and sex—the General Assembly added color (because of the sensitivities of many colonial and former colonial peoples), political opinion, national or social origin, property, and birth. Shunning formal minority protection clauses, the declaration sought to safeguard all types of minority status from discrimination; as Figure 1 also shows, the HRC's working sub-commission conceded the importance of minority protections. Furthermore, the declaration authors prohibited discrimination by the accidents and histories of geographic place. Pushed by the Chinese and Egyptian delegations against the opposition of the colonial powers, Article 2 explicitly extended its guarantees to colonial peoples: "No distinction shall be made on the basis of the political, jurisdictional or international status of the country or territory to which a person belongs, whether it be independent, trust, non–self-governing or under any other limitation of sovereignty." This article marked a decisive step toward universality in principle in contrast to the geographically limited defense of rights in the League covenant. The declaration, however, left unresolved the contradictions between the universal promises of human rights and the political system of colonial rule and dependency functioning openly in the international arena. In subsequent years, the national liberation struggles of colonial people for their dignity and independence unfolded under the self-determination norms of the Charter of the United Nations.

Significantly, the framers of the declaration used other words than "individual." They protected the human person and referenced "everyone" and "no one." "Everyone has the right to life, liberty and security of person" (Art. 3). "No one shall be held in slavery or servitude" (Art. 4). "Everyone has the right to recognition everywhere as a person before the law" (Art. 6). Mehta, who, in the epigraph, so eloquently crystallized a rising threshold for state behavior as a result of human rights thinking, convinced Eleanor Roosevelt to adopt gender-neutral language as well. At women's urgings, the Universal Declaration of Human Rights moved away from the "rights of *man*."[68]

This decision reflected other negotiations and compromises. During the debates, a serious controversy developed around two fundamentally antagonistic understandings of the underpinnings of rights, sharply formulated on the one hand by Roosevelt's insistence on liberal natural rights theory and, on the other, by Alexandre Bogomolov, the Soviet delegate's defense of the socialist theory of rights. For Roosevelt, rooted in the West, individuals possess rights in the state of nature; they come together to form political society in order to safeguard their inalienable rights, understood to be those of life, liberty, and property. Legitimate state authority exists to protect man's fundamental natural rights, which comprise a sphere of freedom independent of state interference. Roosevelt's position stressed rights over duties and conceived of the individual existing prior to the state.

Bogomolov countered with an equally complex political philosophy. Historically, socialists emerged as vocal critics of the state authority constituted by liberal natural rights theory. In their conception, this type of state rests on private property and defends class wealth. (Property indeed was declared sacred in the 1789 French document.) The "rights of man," constituting political society and citizenship, in socialist analysis, are nothing but masks for "egotistic man," the "individual withdrawn into himself, into the confines of his private interests and private caprice, and separated from the community," as Marx put it in 1843.[69] The socialist position stresses the collective good of society premised on social equality. Without social security, it argues, there is no liberty. If, ultimately, the state apparatus was expected to wither away, state membership nonetheless ensures the collective well-being of all inhabitants, who pool resources, labor, and talents together for the common good and receive their just rewards according to needs. Bogomolov's position conceived of collective interests above individual ones.

Most participants in the debates, however, were uncomfortable with the logic of *both* positions. They carved out a middle ground, backing Charles Malik's compromise solution, which substituted the word "person" for "individual". While seemingly splitting hairs, Malik made an important distinction that found wide support. In his view, a person was more than an individual; a person was someone in constant interaction with his or her social world, both shaped by and shaping it. Persons were social beings. Ultimately, this substitute term was accepted by the advocates of the Anglo-American liberal position and by the Soviets and their state allies. It also appealed to many representatives of other cultures and traditions, whose fundamental values also stressed social relationships and communal ties.

In deference to these cultures' concerns with duties as well as with rights, the declaration also included Article 29. Slipping into use of the male gender, it said, "Everyone has duties to the community in which alone the free and full development of his personality is possible." The historian Johannes Morsink, who examined the phases of the negotiations in detail, argued that the word "alone" had great importance.[70] Through the inclusion of this word, the architects affirmed their understanding of human beings as social actors, intricately intertwined with families, communities, social groups, and all sorts of associations and organizations. The majority view did not conceive of individuals existing prior to or apart from social and political society. Rather, it envisioned human beings as having responsibilities to the social collective. However, the proper relationship between rights and duties as well as freedoms and responsibilities, seemingly reconciled in Article 29, remained divisive in theory and in practice.

Until the moment of drafting, human rights as a concept had been vague and unspecified, partly accounting for its appeal to many people during and immediately after the war. Groups ranging from religious organizations to labor to those fighting against colonial rule could insert their own understandings and values into the malleable rubric. The declaration concluded this fluid moment by enumerating the rights to be defended by collective action. In this sense, it marked a baseline of protections, a universal "standard of achievement" for all peoples, everywhere. Later struggles under its banner, however, have deepened protections and expanded the list. The declaration, as it turned out, was only a beginning.

Human rights activists and theorists today speak of the two generations of rights that were upheld in this historic document. By order of seniority, the first generation was the so-called political and civic rights founded in natural rights theory, even though, historically, they were in tension. Classical natural rights principles enshrined civic equality but not political equality; only through subsequent historical struggles did the two principles become intertwined. In 1948, the framers subsumed these redefined notions of natural rights under human rights principles as the first generation. The declaration proclaimed legal and civic equality (Arts. 7–11), and it called for freedom of thought, conscience, opinion, association, and religion, as well as guarantees for equal access to political participation (Arts. 18–21). Many of these principles had found wide currency outside the West. The second-generation category affirmed economic, social, and cultural rights; these too spread across the globe as part of international labor protections fought for in industrial and colonial settings, social democratic traditions (which were strong in Latin America in the 1940s), and the movements for socialist revolutions. The declaration upheld these rights, including social security, health protections, free choice of employment, and wide access to cultural opportunities (Arts. 22–27). It defended property but referenced both its liberal and collective forms. In addition, Article 16 guaranteed men and women of full age the right to marry and found a family. Despite the Nazi persecutions of homosexuals, including women accused of asocial sexual behavior, there was no active discussion at the time about preventing discrimination on the basis of sexual identity and preference.

In 1948, the majority of the framers understood this enumerated list of rights as mutually reinforcing. In the terms of the day, human dignity required both political and civic freedoms as well as economic security and cultural opportunities. Much of the literature on human rights, however, glosses over these foundational debates in 1947 and 1948, reading developments backward through the prism of Cold War dichotomies and implying that political and civil rights had been at the core of the human rights revolution.[71] The framers saw their formulation as a total package essential to human dignity. Only through subsequent developments did the two generations of rights become dissociated in law, rhetoric, and much practice.

To be sure, Cold War rhetoric as part of the superpowers' battles for influence already was heating up in the many stages of negotiation. As a matter of principle, the U.S. delegation, for example, voted against every work-related article in the declaration (each passed anyway). Furthermore, partly because of the opposition of the two superpowers, the document remained a declaration and not a treaty, as had been the original intent of those drafting it. By 1948, neither the United States nor the Soviet Union wanted to be bound by the treaty form, showing that Cold War tensions rested on many areas of mutual agreement. The General Assembly nonetheless had expected to transform the declaration into a single binding treaty; given the ideological tensions over power spreading around the globe, the effort floundered by 1954. Subsequently, the Human Rights Commission worked on two separate conventions, drafting the International Covenant on Civil and Political Rights and the International Covenant on Economic, Social and Cultural Rights. Completed by 1966, both conventions came into force in 1976. At the level of international diplomacy and U.N. norm-setting, the emerging constellations of states had enlisted human rights in the great game of geopolitics.

When it came to a vote in the General Assembly in early December 1948, no delegation opposed the declaration. Eight countries abstained and their reasoning foreshadowed many of the subsequent tensions that constrained the implementation of human rights protections in the international system of politics. Six representatives of the emerging bloc of Soviet countries abstained in good measure because the declaration did not go far enough to promote the role of the state as the guarantor of rights. Saudi Arabia refused to vote on cultural grounds. Its representative noted that Article 16 (proclaiming equal marriage rights for men and women) and Article 18 (ensuring freedom of religion) contravened the country's religion. In the face of universalist assertions, this Islamic country defended the integrity of its customs and traditions. From its inception as a state, Saudi Arabia embraced a conservative religious code as the common law of the land. In the emerging nation-states in the Middle East, the autonomy of personal-status law also marked the civic order; there, national elites made compromises with religious authorities for power.

The last holdout was South Africa, which took a position opposite that of the Soviet bloc. For South Africans already under scrutiny by the General Assembly for their racist domestic policies, the declaration went too far. Although the declaration was not a treaty, the white South African delegates feared it eventually would impose obligations on the state. They predicted, correctly as it turned out, that it would become the authoritative statement on human rights, binding under charter membership. "If such an interpretation were accepted," they said to the full Assembly, "those member states which voted for the Declaration would be bound in the same manner as if they had signed a convention embodying those principles."[72] Confrontation with the abuses of their own regime brought to a head the first major clash between the prerogatives of state sovereignty and the new norms of human equality and dignity for all. Mehta understood well that the human rights revolution had raised the bar for membership in regional and global society.

*   *   *

The creation of the universal system of human rights between 1945 and 1949 draws the historian's attention to the international level. This early history establishes a seemingly logical pattern for the continuing effort to set international norms and standards. In the 1950s, developments followed rapidly at both the international and regional levels. New human rights laws were written by the Commission on the Status of Women as well as by the ILO. Regional human rights systems also emerged. In Europe, the European Convention (for the Protection of Human Rights and Fundamental Freedoms, 1953) proclaimed rights as the "common heritage" of the governments of Western Europe (in contrast to the situation in Eastern-bloc countries). Similarly, the Organization of American States (OAS) created an Inter-American Commission on Human Rights (1959) to consult with the states in promoting and protecting rights in the Western hemisphere.[73]

These steps left vital questions unanswered. What would this system mean for people at risk? How would these guarantees be mobilized? Who would be protected? How far would states and people go in demanding change in the domestic practices of other states? In the context of geopolitical power, to what extent could human rights principles erode the fundamental norm of state sovereignty at the basis of the international order? Hardly predetermined, the answers to these questions were tested at the level of daily struggle in the continuing intersection between transnational movements for rights on the ground and an international institutional structure newly charged with human rights oversight. This shifts the focus to the major dynamic pushing the *evolution* of human rights advocacy, oversight, and laws: the points of contact between the local and global arenas. From this perspective, Part I traces the emergence of a human rights orthodoxy, which became the face of human rights talk and mobilization until the later 1970s.

Part I
An Emerging Human Rights Orthodoxy: The First Round

After 1945, proponents of the new international system of human rights protections faced all the uncertainties of the evolving postwar world. Although institutionalized in U.N. committee structures and defined through declarations and law, the proclamation of human rights had not been matched by adequate enforcement powers. Thus, the meaning of the rights agenda at the level of society remained very much open and in dispute.

In matters of international law concerning the relations among sovereign states, the place of universal human rights protections was ambiguous from the start. The Charter of the United Nations defended the time-honored norm of domestic jurisdiction, which made the state the "master" in its own house and set limits on the influence of international law in a state's internal domestic affairs. Following this norm, as noted earlier, the U.N. Human Rights Commission—the showcase international organ responsible for all matters of human rights deliberations and decisions put before the interested public—refused to investigate the numerous written allegations submitted to it by individuals and groups who claimed to have been victimized by state actions. For twenty years, the HRC "closed the door" on the victims.[1]

Yet, the legal situation was not this simple. Not only had the proclamation of universal human rights implied a common international agenda of protection that stood at the state's doorsteps, the language of the same article in the charter suspended domestic jurisdiction once the Security Council invoked its powers under Chapter VII to sanction state behavior. It implied that domestic jurisdiction had to be understood in the context of the overall purposes of the United Nations, which linked peace and security to the protection of human rights and fundamental freedoms. This modification of law already had been anticipated in a 1923 decision by the Permanent Court of International Justice to settle a colonial dispute between Great Britain and France under the League of Nations. Concluding its case, the court wrote presciently, "The question whether a certain matter is or is not solely within the jurisdiction of a state is an essentially relative question; it depends upon the development of international relations."[2] The jurists, in fact, had anticipated the major stakes for the implementation of human rights in the post–World War II era. Because the human rights system was tied to the geopolitical world of international relations, the question centered directly on whether converging alliances of states and people promoting rights protections across borders would erode the domestic jurisdiction clause. This was the first major challenge to the nascent human rights system as its advocates grappled, too, with the big issues confronting the people of the world in the aftermath of World War II.

As in the breakthrough period 1945–49 in human rights history, which combined older aspirations and new departures, so postwar peoples and communities faced ongoing as well as new challenges. Many had been set in motion well before the war, as in the demand for self-determination and independence by colonial people but grew more insistent as the war progressed. In the territorial theaters of war, the focus turned on the fate of refugees and displaced persons and also on issues of economic recovery and the rebuilding of bombed-out infrastructure and physical plants. Still others were newly emerging challenges, as in the growing geopolitical competition for power and influence between the United States and the Soviet Union, the two acknowledged postwar superpowers and antagonists. Although this tension, too, went back to the 1920s, its complicated postwar history is subsumed under the label "Cold War."[3]

From different origins and contexts, the many challenges converged in the immediate postwar era. Not surprisingly, then, the diplomatic negotiations and the ensuing relations among empires, new superpowers, and aspiring states—on one level, the key international players determining the territorial and domestic maps of postwar reconstruction—centered on problems of profound implications for society. Pushed partly by social ferment from below in many parts of the globe, the substance of international politics became suffused with tensions surrounding the actual meaning of terms such as "sovereignty," "self-determination," and "citizenship," as well as "economic development" and "human welfare." These complicated and fluid notions became the highly charged watchwords of postwar reconstruction. They also set the larger framework within which the first efforts to define and defend human rights protections took place.

It is difficult to convey the real sense of openness and possibility that also characterized the way people understood the immediate postwar era. The ending of the war had unleashed many different and, to be sure, often conflicting aspirations and expectations. Indeed, the very terms used by historians to capture the political and social developments of the age for purposes of analysis and comparison—"decolonization," "Cold War," and "state-building," among others—contain limiting assumptions, as if the outcome were predetermined. But these implicit limitations miss the sense of the possible in the postwar era, even for the imperial authorities, who expected to return to their colonial possessions in Africa as well as in Southeast Asia after the war and did so in Indonesia and Indochina. They also draw attention from the prewar visions of Pan-Africanism as well as transnational labor alliances, which for a time after the war seemed viable and inspiring options to many leaders and activists still involved in anticolonial struggles. They neglect, too, the ongoing nature of political debates about the groups in society to be included in political decision-making. These themes also had a long history in the struggles of labor, women's organizations, and religious communities, which had emerged as alternative voices, challenging the elite-based nationalist campaigns against colonial rule in the 1920s and 1930s.[4]

It also is true that the first decades after the war saw a closing of many of the options. Viewed in retrospect, the postwar world was being shaped mainly by the realist orientation of the political elites in the most important states of the globe. Their strategies and priorities reflected three driving motivations: stability, territorial integrity, and security. The expanding international system of states, which continuously was mirrored in the organs of the United Nations, rested principally on the shared values of geopolitical realism.

In Europe, these calculations meant a de facto division of the continent into two increasingly armed and hostile camps: the countries of Western Europe (including Great Britain) tied financially and militarily to the United States and those Soviet-bloc states of Eastern Europe, where single-party communist regimes were forced to mirror the Soviet system (see Map 4). The war, however, did not end in a peace treaty; the borders reflected the total defeat of Nazi Germany by the victorious Allies converging from east and west. The territorial expression of this new political reality was a divided Germany and a divided Berlin, the country's historic capital city, with each side eventually incorporated into its respective military alliances of North Atlantic Treaty Organization (NATO) nations and Warsaw Pact countries. In this way, for the first time in history, the United States became a European power, and the Soviet Union, absent since 1917 because its leaders were preoccupied by internal revolutionary transformations and global designs, returned to help dictate European events. For the sake of stability, the cessation of wartime fighting also was met by formal population exchanges, with the expectation that political stability best could be achieved through a process of ethnic homogenization, a policy already set in motion by the Nazi genocide and the forced removal of people in its occupied East.[5] The exceptions of multiethnic Soviet Union and Yugoslavia make the general point. Despite the wartime Declaration on Liberated Europe promising free political choices to Europeans, with their eventual deliverance from Nazi oppression, no sustained effort was made to ensure that its principles would be met in the establishment of new authorities in Eastern Europe. With many states near bankruptcy and the population fully exhausted after the war, there was no political will for a continuing hot war.

Ultimately, too, the disruptive challenges of decolonization were channeled into more orderly patterns of nation-state independence that followed the colonial maps. The process itself, however, was messy and costly in human terms, at times involving communal bloodletting, as when the Europeans pulled out of their colonies without taking responsibility for the ensuing chaos during the difficult period of transition. This happened in 1947, after the British left South Asia, in the bloody war of independence that created modern-day India and Pakistan. It is estimated that about a million people died and twelve million were displaced; in addition, the political fate of such border territories as Kashmir remained in dispute, created occasions for future wars, and, in the need to maintain rule, developed increasingly arbitrary and violent state policies. Over time, the human traumas and the memories of the wholesale destruction of families, villages, and communities during these independence struggles slowly fed into alternative narratives of war, ethnicity, and nation-building that both reflected and promoted an expansion of human rights activism globally. At the time—and tragically repeated in case after case—the impact of realist assumptions in statebuilding did not factor the morality of human suffering into the calculations of state interests.[6]

Decolonization, then, became a formal process codified in law and U.N. practice. Whether through peaceful negotiations with former colonial masters or, ultimately, through armed struggle for liberation, the very processes behind the emergence of new nations (and their recognition by the United Nations) set limits on the international principle of self-determination, long used by people in their struggles to claim self-government and appropriate forms of democratic rule. Under the constraints of the postwar consensus on geopolitical stability set by powerful states, the claim of self-determination was limited to colonial peoples alone and not to minorities within the colonial state or to any other state or, for that matter, to indigenous peoples around the globe. Here, too, the watchword was on territorial integrity as the basis of a stable international system of states.

The new United Nations, therefore, did not act on alternative claims to self-determination outside the colonial context. Separatist movements, which sought their own state-building schemes in the immediate postwar years, were brutally suppressed, with little international outrage or attention. Cold War historian Odd Arne Westad made the following point: "The fiction [that] an inclusive nation existed within the mostly haphazardly drawn borders created by the colonial powers led to untold misery for those who did not recognize themselves as part of that entity."[7] The point applied to many "nations," of course, not just to former colonial territories. It was true for Azari and Kurdish separatists brutally suppressed by the Shah of Iran, with Stalin's approval, in 1946; it was true for Tibetans incorporated into China by 1956; and it was true for West Irians in the former Dutch New Guinea opposed to their incorporation into Indonesia in 1963. This list—admittedly incomplete—demonstrates the normative nature of much postwar state-building promoting national integration.[8] Self-determination had been narrowed to colonial independence and dissociated from rights imperatives.

The careful research of decolonization scholars shows how nation-building, too, increasingly closed down many political options that had seemed open after the war in light of the long decades of struggle by groups in society for freedom and independence. Africanist Frederick Cooper speaks of "gatekeeper" states, a term that could be applied equally to political developments outside the African context. It draws attention to the administrative and political continuities between the colonial and the independent state in its duplication of increasingly centralized political rule and deep suspicion of independent political groups and organizations.[9] Beneath the postcolonial maps graphically cataloging the remarkable rise in the number of new independent nations after 1945 was social tension over who would be included in state decision-making and increasing frustration over the continued gaps between the industrial and the developing world.

In the first postwar decades, decolonization also became a new terrain of Cold War tensions as the different "camps" of antagonists sought political advantages in the transfer of formal power from colonial administrators to local and national officials. Offering competing models of modernity to an increasingly global audience, both U.S. and Soviet agents had few qualms about intruding into the domestic affairs of states. This could take the more indirect form of offering foreign aid to new allies or the more insidious form of arming competing factions within the states. On the ground, each superpower flaunted—or defended—the normative principle of state sovereignty when it suited its economic and strategic interests. In the big picture of postwar developments, then, it seems easy to lose the focus on human rights—except to catalog an ongoing set of human wrongs, which, for the most part, were left unexamined at the time. In the relations among peoples and states, the system continued with business as usual.

Reading human rights histories as an intersection of concrete social struggle and international response, Part I demonstrates that it was in the interstices of this realist system of states that a defense of human rights principles was first launched successfully. This campaign began to erode the very assumptions of realism from which it emerged. The pattern was not fully anticipated by international developments that had been put into place between 1945 and 1949. Given the constraints of the international system of states, it was unclear how people at risk might use new human rights principles and guarantees to press for intervention. It was also unclear what "intervention" meant in a human rights context dependent on state action.

The answers are in the historical record. They show that three distinct manifestations of grave injustices in the societies of states set the initial agendas for large-scale human rights mobilizations across borders; each was shaped by a set of geopolitical contingencies that ensured sustained international attention and coordinated action. Cumulatively, they established important guidelines for subsequent human rights advocacy and network-building as well as creating permanent human rights NGOs. The movements also established the major precedents for formal NGO participation in U.N. monitoring efforts. Together, they helped fashion the first human rights publics. One was the antiapartheid struggle in South (and southern) Africa and its state and transnational allies committed to racial equality in the new postwar world that had declared the universality of human rights. A second was wide receptivity to the many claims of Soviet dissidents, who pushed for autonomy and freedom in a challenging vision of civil society. The third was the principle of bodily integrity and freedom from torture in the terrible human tragedy of disappearance, a tactic of terror used by dictatorial regimes to cow their civilian populations. The very nature of these causes spoke to wider audiences, confronting many of the same issues at home.

Examining the historical record offers a distinctive interpretation of the human rights system and its chronological unfolding. As a confluence of rigorous, transnational mobilizations, the early human rights causes created an orthodoxy in the understanding of what constituted human rights violations and, thus, what types of abuses would or would not mobilize an international response. My use of "orthodoxy" is designed to capture a limitation in the purview: the orthodoxy at the time drew societal attention to the injustices done to individuals and families as well as to racial and minority groups by an arbitrary and abusive state. Until the mid- to late 1970s, the heart of international debate and action centered on opposing the state's arbitrary use of power in repressing individual liberties, whether by legal segregation, the denial of political rights and freedoms, or the infringement on the right to bodily life and liberty. This emerging consensus even generated its own influential symbol of injustice—"the prisoner of conscience," coined by Amnesty International when it was founded in 1961. Pushed most successfully by state and transnational alliances in the three formative cases discussed in Part I, the collective response by U.N. organs (and other regional security arrangements) challenged the once sacrosanct norm of domestic jurisdiction, slowly eroding its authority, at least in cases of the systematic abuse of political authority by state actors. By the end of the 1970s, international responses in these three cases had set important precedents for human rights "interventions"—testing the whole gamut from resolutions and proclamations to economic boycott and sanctions. Through the cumulative work of these early mobilizations, human rights discourse helped legitimize resistance to an oppressive state.

By carefully historicizing the three distinct human rights movements over roughly four decades, Part I writes its own chronology, demonstrating many advantages of interlinking the three disparate movements for interpretive purposes. In this way, it overcomes other limitations of the existing literature, which typically provides a truncated chronology of human rights history: a burgeoning set of activities between 1945 and 1949, then a period of quiet and inaction, followed by a revival in the 1970s. In contrast, my approach keeps in focus the formative influences of the struggles on the ground in southern Africa and, to a lesser extent, Eastern Europe in the 1950s and 1960s; international actions from above often followed precisely the trials and tribulations of domestic crises and struggles on the ground. By 1967, the pressure from below opened a new period of monitoring in the United Nations and, subsequently, in regional security arrangements, such as the Helsinki Accords, which wrote a final peace treaty for Europe in 1975. It also gradually allowed more opportunities for transnational NGO advocacy groups to intrude directly into the international negotiations among states. By the 1970s, the stage had been set from many directions for a new burst of human rights actions and activities.

As Part I also shows, the chronology is not simple; the 1970s did not mark a clean transition from one type of advocacy to another. The antiapartheid struggle was an exceedingly long one, concluded only in 1994, with the nation's first multiracial election on the fundamental basis of "one person, one vote"; Soviet dissident struggles were crucial elements in the dissolution of the socialist political systems in the Soviet Union and its Eastern-bloc allies between 1989 and 1991; and, tragically, the tactic of disappearing state enemies continues to this day. In each case, furthermore, the difficult transitions to new systems of rule brought about partly by the human rights movements' pressure for change were shaped by the constitutional and institutional assumptions of the earlier struggles. In short, implementing much of the orthodoxy often set a new context for expanded human rights work even after a formal conclusion of the struggle.

Chapter 2
Cold War Politics and Human Rights Publics: The International Antiapartheid and Soviet Dissident Movements, 1952–90

> Gross internal violations of human rights cause aggressive behavior in international relations and thus endanger other nations. Such . . . reasoning helped overcome the objections of domestic jurisdiction and played an important role, for example, in the imposition of sanctions against South Africa for its policy of apartheid. In the Helsinki Final Acts, it is [also] reflected.
>
> —Vojin Dimitrijevic, professor of international law, Belgrade University, 1981

By 1949, with their address to "the people," the agreements negotiated in the new U.N. bodies and commissions had proclaimed the international moral linkage of all humanity. Human beings had rights regardless of status, birth, geography, or nationality. They had protections and guarantees through the operative international principles of nondiscrimination and the self-determination of peoples. It was a bold agenda but one that remained at the level of abstraction.

In international politics, the growing intersection of two transnational movements gave the first concrete expression of this affirmation of shared identity. Rather than remain in local or national contexts away from the spotlight, these movements forced human rights agendas into the heart of international diplomacy. One was the domestic struggle against the system of apartheid in South Africa, with its shifting alliances of states and peoples abroad. The movement was fighting the legal system of racial oppression, which tightened in South Africa with the victory of the National Party in 1948, at the moment of passage of the

Universal Declaration of Human Rights. Its ultimate global reach means that the human abuses implied by the term "apartheid" are understood worldwide without translation. The case was brought before the General Assembly at its first session in 1946 as a *political* problem between South Africa and India. Originally a matter of bilateral diplomacy, it gradually forced concerns with grave human rights violations in a state's domestic life into diplomatic negotiations.

The second involved the coalitions supporting Soviet and Eastern European dissidents after 1975 when a security conference of states established the final peace in Europe (the Helsinki Final Act). Feeding off cycles of domestic discontent in the Eastern-bloc countries and the Soviet Union, a traditional instrument of interstate diplomacy facilitated a dramatic surge of human rights NGO mobilizations.

Both movements originated in struggles that essentially predated the human rights currency, so they are critical test cases to examine how and why oppressed people came to embrace human rights visions as a way of galvanizing their own struggles for dignity. Deploying historically different meanings of self-determination—as national independence and peoples' rights to democratic governance—they reconciled the two in a new vision of this powerful geopolitical concept. The South African movement in the 1950s and early 1960s, furthermore, shows that the geography of human rights mobilizations was hardly limited to the West.

To juxtapose the antiapartheid and Soviet-dissident movements in one chapter is not usual and requires some comment. There exist two excellent and distinct historiographies on the topics; however, the movements intertwined in ways that largely have been overlooked by both groups of historians. The transnational perspective encourages a reshuffling of national narratives. The decision to interrelate these movements explains as well the long time frame for this chapter, extending through the traditional dating of the Cold War, 1946–89. It permits a careful assessment of Cold War politics in the unfolding of these struggles. Above all, the operative word is "juxtapose," not "compare." I am not equating the two struggles; they overlapped in time but were unmistakably different in goals, in demographics, and in the structures of rule and oppression they faced. And they mobilized different constituencies of supporters across territorial borders, revealing the distinct identities of emerging human rights publics. Just as many different strands of transnational opposition had converged in the 1940s to help proclaim a common human rights standard for all, so subsequently the work under this unifying rubric devolved into more distinct channels of advocacy.

Early on, both movements confronted the clash between adherence to universal human rights principles and the time-honored defense of state sovereignty, which the architects of the human rights system had left unsettled. Both sought to bring the states' domestic policies into compliance with the new set of human rights legal norms. From the perspective of the evolution of international law, these transnational advocacy projects set key precedents that challenged the inviolability of domestic jurisdiction in cases of state political repression.[1] Because of their pressure at the national, regional, and intergovernmental levels, U.N. bodies and regional agencies as well as the affiliated law commissions have limited the scope allowed for the defense of domestic jurisdiction.

To focus on matters of law and international diplomacy, however, misses part of the point. Popular identification with advocacy networks is never really about abstract principles of law; it is about concrete and immediate human tragedies, which are reflected in the work of the specific advocacy networks. Drawing on graphic depictions of a population under siege and firsthand accounts of the plight of victims, the people involved in these historic movements became new and vocal players in global politics, disseminating from the bottom up different types of information about what was happening in local contexts than that found in the standard accounts of the state-dominated media. The movements launched global campaigns, organized letter-writing actions, established defense and aid funds, sent emissaries to oversee trials, sought ties with U.N. committees and commissions, and developed new monitoring mechanisms. In short, their highly conscious activists invented new styles of international advocacy, which then were picked up by other groups also embroiled in human rights conflicts. From these empirical cases, human rights scholars analyze the politics of transnational advocacy.[2]

Global Diplomacy and Local Politics

According to Clyde Ferguson, law professor and activist who served as the U.S. representative to the U.N. Commission on Racial Discrimination, "No more persistent and intractable issue" emerged to challenge the new universalist commitments to human rights than the South African apartheid regime.[3] Its brutal system of laws and authorities upheld white supremacy, although whites comprised little more than a sixth of the total population in 1990. This policy of discrimination was incompatible with the newly formulated principles enshrined in the Universal Declaration.[4] Put another way, the antiapartheid struggle developed in the context of the broad movement for decolonization that was gathering momentum after World War II. Indeed, the increase in the numbers of new nations from former colonies ensured its centrality in the U.N. agenda. Between 1956 and 1963, for example, twenty-eight new African states entered the General Assembly; three years later, African and Asian nations (64 states combined) comprised more than half of the total membership of the United Nations (117 states). A similar shift in membership took place on the Human Rights Commission. The final ending of empire in Africa, wrote Frederick Cooper, reflected "cross-border connections within Africa and engagement of Africans with international organizations."[5] The same process kept international attention on the situation in South Africa for decades.

Scholars of international relations often place the movements for national liberation squarely within the human rights agenda of the world body.[6] The reference appreciably is to the self-determination and nondiscrimination principles enshrined in the Charter of the United Nations and the Universal Declaration: self-determination became the legal foundation for the establishment of the sovereign state from the colonial territory. In 1960, a coalition of newly independent states in Africa and Asia in the General Assembly ensured passage of a resolution on the Granting of Independence to Colonial Countries and Peoples. It said that placing "peoples [in] alien subjugation, domination and exploitation constitutes a denial of fundamental human rights, is contrary to the Charter of the United Nations and is an impediment to the promotion of world peace and co-operation." It made colonial rule incompatible with the human rights principles of the U.N. Charter. It also took a direct stand against the liberal basis of much older international law that had underpinned the mandate and trustee systems for the people "not yet ready" to enter the modern world. The resolution stated clearly: "Inadequacy of political, economic, social or educational preparedness should never serve as a pretext for delaying independence." It put "now" in place of the great power principle of "not yet." Its positions marked a fundamental shift in law, affirming decades of anticolonial struggles worldwide.[7] But other aspects of the newly proclaimed human rights agenda, including viable democratic practices or the right of association, found little acceptance by many new leaders in Africa and Asia facing the daunting problems of state-building and economic development. These principles of internal political and economic organization were not on the list of topics driving diplomatic negotiations or international debate in the first years after World War II.

South Africa was the critical exception. The struggles against apartheid created and sustained the first real links, making a state's internal policies relevant to U.N. diplomatic negotiations and committee work. South Africa, however, was not a typical colonial setting. White South Africans (the Dutch and later French Huguenots, known subsequently as Boers or Afrikaans) had been living on the Cape land since the mid-seventeenth century; British settlers arrived early in the nineteenth century. Whites were citizens in their own country, controlling the state apparatus that dominated the majority African and also South Asian and "colored" populations. In this sense, it was the abiding anger at racial injustice, carried over from earlier anticolonial movements and so palpable at the U.N. founding conference, that drew the state's domestic policies into international scrutiny.[8]

The connections were not made at the international level alone. They were sealed by the centrality of human rights language in the political agenda of the African National Congress, the main black opposition group determined to overthrow the whole system of apartheid and create a nonracial, democratic state for all the people. The ANC drew on a much longer struggle for racial equality in South Africa. Even before World War I, there had been mass protests and riots against racial discriminatory policies and laws, such as the Asiatic Registration Bill (1907), limiting South Asian immigration and domicile, and the Natives Land Act (1913), which segregated residence by race. In the early 1940s, the ANC explicitly embraced human rights as a fundamental goal of its struggle for racial justice. The ANC's Youth League Manifesto (1944)—a challenge to the old leaderships' failures to act according to the "demands of the times"—demonstrated how the new vision rewrote priorities and strategies. Its authors were a group of determined young leaders who subsequently led the ANC's struggle, among them Nelson Mandela, Walter Sisulu, Oliver Tambo, Ashby Mda, and Anton Lembede. Rejecting the race doctrines at the basis of white oppression of black people, which left Africans "without security," the manifesto promised to transcend race through new political doctrines that defended "full and free citizenship" and a "free and unhampered life" for all. The authors pledged to turn the ANC into a powerful national movement, promoting new political thinking (what they labeled "specialized political attitudes") among the still "amorphous mass" of the people. According to the blueprint, this transformation in attitudes required clear goals of political action against the "inhuman" apartheid system.

These goals were spelled out in subsequent years. A 1948 Basic Policy statement, for example, stressed fundamental human rights guarantees for "all nationalities and minorities" secured by a democratic constitution; it also called for land and property rights, better health services, full literacy, and democratic control over the workplace (known as "industrial democracy"). The ANC leaders maintained transnational contacts with émigré groups abroad and saw their own work at home as part of wider global liberation movements and, closer in, of a shared African nationalism embodied in the "struggle for freedom."[9] These efforts to reshape national goals culminated in the Freedom Charter (1955), which guided the South African liberation movement through its subsequent turbulent history. The charter's values stressed multiracial cooperation and harmony. "South Africa," it began simply, "belongs to all who live in it, black and white, and . . . no government can justly claim authority unless it is based on the will of the people." In addition, it affirmed economic justice and land redistribution.[10]

Equally important, this national program became localized through the parallel "grassroots," or local, protest movements continuing in rural areas and homelands for access to arable land or education as well as efforts at tax relief and the removal of corrupt chiefs and leaders.[11] Moments of widespread anger and violence expanded local purviews; through heightened attention, they brought the ANC's political goals to local communities. In March 1960, for example, a major rural uprising erupted in Pondoland in the Transkei, part of four large-scale peasant protests during that year. There, tensions had been mounting for years over the government's effort to impose Bantu authorities on a people with a long tradition of tribal self-government and jurisdiction over the distribution of land. This official effort to shift power in newly created "homelands," or Bantustans, provoked widespread opposition, including the refusal to pay taxes and boycotts against traders seen as sympathetic to the government. The government responded with violent repression; the police killed eleven protesters and, by their own accounts over the course of the conflict, arrested 4,769 men and women. The government also banished the leader, Anderson Khumani Ganyile. Sentiments quickly turned against the chiefs and the movement took on "new features," according to one author. At large public gatherings, people adopted the "full program of the ANC and its allies as embodied in the Freedom Charter."[12] This conflict moment extended the national agenda by making it part of local idiom; it also forged important links between rural and urban communities in struggle. These new channels of communication were helping transfer "rights consciousness" into community struggles. Although those on the ground never lost sight of "local wrongs," the shared agenda subsumed many local causes into the wider political struggle for self-determination. The intersection of international, national, and local politics in the antiapartheid movement represented the opening salvo in the development of institutional mechanisms and transnational links making universal human rights standards relevant for pressing national and local struggles.

Despite the best efforts of the white government to use its domestic jurisdiction prerogatives to halt debate, South Africa remained on the U.N. agenda as a bilateral problem over "minority" rights and as a challenge to international law, once the government illegally annexed its mandate territory, German South-West Africa (Namibia). In 1952, the fundamental premises justifying international scrutiny shifted to what was called the "race conflict." Thirteen Arab and Asian member-states

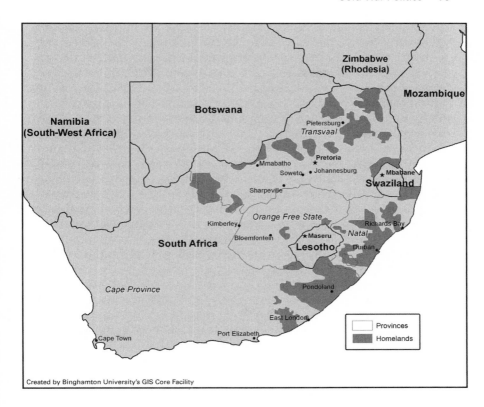

Map 3. Apartheid South Africa.

demanded international action because of the government's systematic violation of the human rights provisions in the U.N. Charter and the Universal Declaration. This violation, they argued, constituted a "grave threat" to international peace and security. They also raised the possibility of the Security Council authorizing punitive measures to force compliance. Subsequent resolutions became increasingly insistent on the need for effective multilateral action, including sanction options against the racist regime. The position rejected the whole system of apartheid because it denied opportunities for human development and dignity. Within the decade, the separate issues had merged under a common rubric, "The Policies of Apartheid."[13] Not only were peace and security at risk but also the fundamental values proclaimed for the postwar world.

The timing of this shift was important because it underscored the rhythm of heightened international concern, inseparably linked in this conflict to moments of domestic crises. In 1952, through cross-race collaboration, the ANC leaders launched a mass movement of civil disobedience across the country, a campaign of defiance against many of the recent laws hardening white political and economic control. The unrest, repression, arrests, and subsequent "treason trials" accounted for the new sense of urgency among U.N. member-states in the early 1950s. A similar peaking of international concern took place in 1960, as a response to the Sharpeville massacre of sixty-nine unarmed protesters who were burning the passes (the identification cards) needed for travel in the country. Under a state of emergency, the government banned the ANC and its rival, the Pan-Africanist Congress (PAC), a more militant group that had broken from the ANC a year earlier, and passed draconian legislation, including the Sabotage Act. The Sharpeville tragedy is well known because it galvanized international outrage, but the violence of repression was a daily fare for the masses, as events in Pondoland that year attested. In response, the General Assembly took a series of innovative steps, notably creating the Special Committee Against Apartheid in 1963 as a liaison body with direct access to the General Assembly and the Security Council (see Fig. 2a). That year, too, the Security Council adopted (nonmandatory) policies to limit arms sales to South Africa. In a similar cycle, sustained international pressure to force change followed the 1976 crisis in Soweto, in which the armed forces killed schoolchildren demonstrating against the inferior quality of education in the Bantustan. In popular memory, June 1976 became known as "the power days."[14]

At the outset, international pressure on South Africa came most prominently from the representatives of independent African states. As decolonization gained momentum, the independent nation became the norm of international politics. South Africa, the most industrialized and powerful country on the continent, was a holdover from a colonial past that was seen to have no real future. By 1960, it had become a pariah state in international affairs. It is no wonder that the people's liberation was of vital concern to new African leaders. Their revolutions stood for the hope and dignity promised in self-determination. Listen to the words of Julius K. Nyerère, spoken when he was chief minister of Tanganyika in British East Africa. At a March 1961 meeting to rework the basis of the British Commonwealth, given the new political reality of independence, Nyerère captured the collective sentiments that animated the opposition. He put it eloquently: "In our struggle for self-government and independence we have spoken of brotherhood and the equality of man. . . . The *apartheid* policies now being practised in the Union of South Africa are a daily affront to this belief in individual human dignity. They are also a constantly reiterated insult to our own dignity as Africans, about which we cannot be expected to remain indifferent." African leaders were hardly indifferent: a strong commitment to principles drove their policies, at times even overriding the more traditional economic and strategic calculations at the basis of state actions.[15]

Innovations in law and U.N. human rights monitoring also followed the particularly charged link between apartheid and decolonization. Together with Asian colleagues in the United Nations, African leaders spearheaded passage of the International Convention on the Elimination of All Forms of Racial Discrimination, the hallmark legislation of the decolonization era, unanimously adopted by the General Assembly in 1965 (see Fig. 2b). As binding treaty law, it stood against racial segregation and apartheid. Reflecting the seriousness of the abuses, the law established an eighteen-person committee to ensure compliance, a "historic procedure," according to Arthur Goldberg, the U.S. Ambassador to the United Nations at the time. It mandated that signatory states submit follow-up reports to the committee, which also was able to receive independent evidence directly from individuals and groups.[16]

This provision marked a significant shift in U.N. organizational practice, which, with a few exceptions—as in the work of the Trusteeship Council—skirted direct contact with the alleged victims. The overall climate in the United Nations however, was becoming more open to the voices of the aggrieved, in part because of the graphic pictures of the suffering coming from South Africa. Thus, an optional protocol to the international Political Covenant in 1966 allowed its committee to hear complaints from individuals. Notably, the same provision was not included in the parallel Economic Covenant. The notion that individuals could petition for equitable resources and state provisioning of education or welfare was not accepted. Hidden behind the drama of liberation struggles, an orthodoxy in human rights thinking was emerging in the international arena, which pushed for differentiation between "human rights" and "human needs," to borrow one "classic" formulation of the divide used by contemporaries in testimonies to the U.S. Congress or before the Human Rights Commission.[17] It meant that economic deprivation and poverty would not be sufficient grounds to activate the international machinery. But the societal crisis of apartheid was, and the response also reshaped the monitoring agenda of the Human Rights Commission and its sub-commission.

In deference to state sovereignty, the HRC and its sub-commission had refused to act on local complaints about states' violations of human rights. In addition, they also had kept secret the name of any accused state. Prodded by the same state coalitions that were proposing new laws, the Economic and Social Council in June 1967 authorized the first breakthrough in monitoring procedures. The change was unthinkable without the sustained pressure on the U.N. organs to act against the apartheid state. Resolution 1235 gave the HRC and its sub-commission authority to review the individual complaints about violations coming to the United Nations, which had been shunted aside for twenty years. The sub-commission was directed to bring to the attention of the HRC any situation that revealed a "consistent pattern of violations," primarily as "exemplified by the policy of apartheid . . . in the Republic . . . and in the Territory of South West Africa . . . and racial discrimination as practised notably by Southern Rhodesia." Making the systemic violations of apartheid the benchmark, the same resolution also empowered the two rights oversight bodies to undertake "thorough study" of other patterns of large-scale violations. Passage of this resolution gave the HRC new powers to study violations. It opened new channels for the vertical flow of information.

Debate under the new resolution centered nearly exclusively on the situation in southern Africa and, as a result of the Israeli occupation of Palestinian territories after the 1967 war, on Israel. For nearly a decade, however, most complaints still followed the standard practices: the states, intergovernmental agencies, U.N. organs and committees, and the Special Committee Against Apartheid brought most of the complaints to the HRC. Nongovernmental organizations with consultative status were allowed to present evidence, but they could speak only for a limited time at the end of the debate. Broadening direct access to victims and local NGOs with no official U.N. status came only at the end of the 1970s, as Chapter 3 shows.[18]

In the 1950s and 1960s, a coalition of states had pushed for international action against the apartheid system, in a rhythm partly dictated by events on the ground. Pressure was most effective on the intergovernmental bodies run by majority vote: the General Assembly as well as other affiliate organizations, such as UNESCO, the ILO, and the World Health Organization (WHO). In these agencies, African representatives simply "brought all business to a standstill" until South Africa was forced to withdraw. In 1974, the country lost its General Assembly credentials. A decade later, the Universal Postal Union, one of the earliest intergovernmental agencies, expelled the country from its ranks.[19] A broad international consensus rejected official dealings with the white-run government.

But South Africa also had powerful defenders. The conflict became embroiled in Cold War politics, as both the United States and the Soviet Union sought political advantages with the retreat of the European empires. The developing Third World became one of the central terrains of the Cold War and South Africa emerged as an increasingly vital sphere of influence for both ideological camps. Rich in mineral wealth and markets, the country became a strategic ally of powerful Western nations in common cause against the threat of communism. Through the simple bipolar lens, the U.S. leaders, for example, saw white South Africa as a Christian bulwark against communist expansion on the African continent. For its side, the Soviet Union had been sympathetic to anticolonial struggles since the Bolshevik Revolution of 1917. In the 1950s and 1960s, it supported the liberation movements in Africa, seeking its own alliances. After the death of Stalin in 1952, Politburo leaders accepted alliances with countries where the possibilities for socialist revolution still lay in the future. The Soviet Union and the German Democratic Republic (East Germany, the GDR) became the major supplier of aid and, eventually, of arms to the ANC through much of its years of struggle. Within South Africa itself, Communist party members supported early ANC campaigns; after the party was banned in 1950, many joined the ANC and helped write the Freedom Charter. The charter at the time was branded by the Western media as a dangerous communist document.

South African authorities also played up the dangers of communism. The white population overwhelmingly supported the Nationalist government throughout its reign. Speeches of politicians and the Afrikaaner press showed that most whites believed majority rule spelled "chaos," the spread of "disorder on the continent," and the eventual "triumph of communist conspiracy." In this analysis, "subversion, communism and external pressures" on the country went hand in glove with the same result, the overthrow of the government.[20] In fact, the U.N. structure shielded the regime from most demands for mandatory boycotts and embargos, which only the Security Council, under Chapter 7, could impose. The council still operates today by the threat of veto from any of the five permanent members. It became deadlocked on South Africa and never passed mandatory economic sanctions, although it imposed an arms embargo on the regime in 1977. Representatives of the United States, Great Britain, and France—South Africa's largest trading partners until the demise of the Nationalist government—repeatedly vetoed stringent economic sanctions. Historian George Frederickson quoted a young ANC activist fed up with the position of the United States in the United Nations. After one such veto in 1952, he wrote, "[Its] stand is rotten and the Eastern nations have beaten the West on the colour issue. . . . I think America has lost African friendship. As far as I am concerned, I will henceforth look East where race discrimination is so taboo that it is made a crime by the state."[21] The statement was naïve on many accounts, but for those demanding the right of self-determination, official U.S. policy stood on the wrong side of the liberation struggles.

Border Crossings and Societal Bridges

For many South African activists on the ground during the first twenty years or so of resistance to apartheid after 1945, the Soviet Union and its Eastern-bloc allies (aided by many Third World countries) provided much-needed material, psychological, and political support for the hard and dangerous work of liberation. The life story of one activist, Gladys Tsolo, offers a compelling account of the personal meanings of what otherwise are abstract statements about the avenues of support. These channels were tangible, life changing, and sobering. Interviewed in 1978 at a Dutch institute, Tsolo's recollections were unique and revealing on many levels.

A little-known figure, Tsolo is testimony to the many strands of antiapartheid struggles that made up the whole—narratives indeed that are lost in a study that centers on the iconic (male) leaders of the movement. At home, the antiapartheid struggle was complex and multifaceted, reflecting many different identities and transnational connections that included women's issues, labor struggles, and different ideological perspectives, ranging from communism to Pan-Africanism. These diverse and complementary ties abroad helped explain the relatively peaceful transition to democratic rule ("one person, one vote") after 1990.[22] Tsolo's recollection shed light on the situation for black men and women under apartheid and explained her path to armed resistance. She left South Africa and lived in East Germany from 1965 to 1973. At the level of personal history, then, Tsolo linked the early South African liberation movement to Soviet and East German support; she also opened a window into the system of political control in the GDR. She made no mention of societal discontent with the East German system, although from living there she was much less positive about life in the East than activists in South Africa had imagined it to be.[23]

Tsolo's path is but one example of the connections that drew South Africans to socialist countries. Parallel changes in consciousness—particularly after the brutal repression of the Hungarian uprising by invading Soviet troops in 1956—also were preparing the ground for new progressive politics in Western societies. Not yet tangible in terms of concrete networks, these shifts brought a new level of societal support to the antiapartheid movement, creating different modes of transnational advocacy in the 1960s. These societal changes also began to forge links across the ideological divides of Europe. Given the timing of the interview in 1978, Tsolo unwittingly reflected these historical changes. In many ways, her interview was a microcosm of the border crossings—of people, ideas, and causes—that were creating new societal bridges for human rights advocacy.[24]

Tsolo grew up in the 1950s in a coal-mining district in northern Natal where, she said, many people were "in struggle but not aware of the political situation." They experienced the full effect of poverty, hardship, and injustice but had not yet grasped the importance of organized resistance or what the Youth Manifesto had called "political attitudes." After 1955, gatherings of five or more people were officially banned, so community restlessness coalesced at Sunday church services and school committee meetings. She remembered singing "Come Back, Africa" during church sermons; her family was Methodist. In later years, with growing grassroots support, people took this same inspiration into the streets, adding song, dance, and trotting to the repertoire of opposition movements.

At its core, apartheid was a racialized form of labor extraction, which tore at the very heart of family life, turning many women as well as men into social activists. It relied on migrant male contract labor for work in the mines and urban factories, coupled with legislation such as the Removal Act of 1964 that forced people from areas declared white where they had farmed and lived all their lives. They were removed to the ethnically structured "townships," which were mired in poverty and offered limited work and educational opportunities. Between 1960 and 1980, over two million African blacks were transferred to these so-called Bantustans through evictions and the destruction of black urban neighborhoods.

Tsolo's father worked in Johannesburg until the Removal Act. She described the impact on the family. "Most of the men were usually away from the home. . . . The men only came home once every three months, or once every two months if they were better off. So the women were carrying the social and economic burdens of the community." As she put it, women were "running the homes, raising children, planting the fields." From these gendered sites and roles, women were drawn inexorably into resistance; they were always "on the scene" defending their families and children, even in the face of danger. They were part of all local actions from the burning of passes to demanding better education for their children to protesting the bulldozing of squatter camps (on so-called white land located near available jobs). Because apartheid's vicious system of control and humiliation permeated all aspects of life, struggle became a part of daily existence.[25] Opposition followed a wide continuum of methods, from naming a child "Freedom" for the Freedom Charter to petitioning the government to forming organizations such as the Human Rights Welfare Committee for the Banished. Its leaders were banned in the 1960 crackdown.[26]

Tsolo's political awakening came after going abroad to study. She wanted to train as a nurse, but "because of the system . . . there were no vacancies for nursing or for training for Black women. I waited for two years for training, from 1960 to 1961, without any success." In contrast to European colonial practice, the apartheid government made little effort to maintain even the pretense of preparing African men and women for the challenges of "modernity." The system was premised on keeping black South Africa separate, allowing only some men and women limited opportunities to prepare for a career in teaching or nursing through the Bantu system of education.

In 1962, Tsolo went to neighboring Botswana hoping to pursue her medical studies; there she met political refugees and exiles from South Africa who had fled the country after the massive suppression of the opposition in 1960. In response to the crackdown, the ANC had given up its strict position on nonviolence and sanctioned selective reprisals. In 1961, it set up an armed movement known as *Umkonto we Sizwe* trained partly abroad. Its aims remained carefully delimited, however, with no indiscriminate "targeting" of white people. Despite massive state violence and reprisals, it is clear—in retrospect—that armed resistance against apartheid sought to avoid levels that would preclude future cooperation between the races. The ANC, nonetheless, was condemned in the West as a violent terrorist movement bent on a communist takeover.

Tsolo joined the ANC and its armed wing in Botswana. The ANC sent her first to Dar-es-Salaam, Tanzania, and then through Cairo to Russia, ostensibly for further studies but really for military training. Of Russia she wrote, "We were not given the same military training as men but were trained to be military nurses." She still wanted a "proper" medical training and, after much pressure on her part, was sent to East Germany. It was in the GDR that she met and married Mike Tsolo, a political refugee who had been a grassroots leader of the Sharpeville protest movement. Mike was a member of PAC; Gladys joined the faction as well.

Gladys Tsolo received the medical training she wanted in the GDR and became a midwife but only after "much difficulty," as she put it cryptically. Her reminiscences were silent on the question of daily interaction with East German citizens. It is clear that both Tsolos were the beneficiaries of the education and work opportunities that the socialist country gave refugees and students from colonial countries. The GDR prided itself on bringing the fruits of its progressive health-care system to Third World countries through traveling hygienic exhibitions and lectures. The importance of public health to the dignity of labor became the German socialist state's own self-promotion in Cold War propaganda battles for the hearts and minds of the people in the Third World.[27] Through this route, the regime sought to counter West German policies that penalized states for establishing diplomatic relations with its East German rival.

Tsolo did not describe what it was like to be a black woman in GDR society. Rather, she wrote in some detail for so short a recollection about the stultifying political situation that she found in the GDR. Of her time in East Germany, she said "We Azanians there were completely cut off from the struggle and the outside world, unless someone was lucky enough to have a powerful radio. . . . In 1966 there was a very strong campaign of indoctrination in the GDR. There was no chance to think and develop political consciousness."[28] What bothered her the most was not being able to have independent politics. The regime took a hard line against PAC, so no debate over strategies and goals of liberation was possible. There was no chance, she said, to exchange information or to travel. "All travel to the West was forbidden." In short, she found the political atmosphere "very oppressive." Forced to be silent, she could not accept the GDR because, as she said, "I was not persuaded democratically." From 1968 "I tried to get out. However, marriage and pregnancy prevented me from leaving until 1973." Whatever propaganda value the East German regime received in the developing countries with its public health and medical services was offset partly by the negative memories that activists like Tsolo carried with them about political life in the East.

By November 1978, the date of the interview, Tsolo had carefully positioned herself squarely *between* East and West.[29] The intervening years had brought considerable change in the political landscape for grassroots antiapartheid activists: opportunities had opened up for travel and support in Western societies and not just in Soviet-bloc states. Tsolo's interview took place while she attended a symposium at the Institute of Social Studies in The Hague. This institute was part of a network of organizations funded by UNESCO, one of the leading intergovernmental agencies that early on had rejected South African membership. In the 1970s, its General Conference began aiding the southern African liberation movements by funding refugees and political activists. It sponsored training and legal programs for South Africans and Namibians in Tanzania and Zambia as well as at the institute.[30]

In The Hague, Tsolo participated in a conference called to discuss women's liberation and national liberation. At the time, the topic was at the center of heated debates in the emerging global women's human rights movement. This new global movement in many ways is inconceivable without the specific sensibilities to women's lives that had been developing in the course of decolonization, nation-building, and national liberation, as shown in Part II of this book. By the late 1970s, Tsolo was part of this new social milieu, which could draw on career activists' passions as well as long experiences confronting the traumas and tragedies of women's lives under apartheid.

What mattered most for Tsolo in the interview was the chance to tell the stories of the many courageous local women involved in South Africa's liberation. She did not want their histories to be overlooked in the future as they had been in many of the accounts that were generating international outrage. Tsolo spoke of prominent women such as Lilian Ngoyi, leader of the Women's Federation, founded in 1954, who had helped galvanize women's protests against the pass laws and also brought the language of human rights to the petitions and local protests. The Fed provided organizational coherence for sustained political actions. She mentioned Dorothy Nyembe, also active in women's mass protests and who was still languishing in prison at the time of the interview, and Ellen Molapo, leader of the Garment Workers. Tsolo praised the dedicated nurses who, during the bus boycotts, walked miles to and from the hospitals and clinics and were there to help the victims shot by the police during the riots, and also the many women at the Crossroads squatters' camps and elsewhere. Responding to the degradation of rural family life, the women had moved to the camps to be near male workers, desperate to put down roots, although the authorities came repeatedly to demolish their flimsy shacks. And there also were the poor "widows of the liberation struggle," whose husbands—often the subjects of considerable international discussion and concern—were in prison on Robben Island, or elsewhere. Yet, these "widows" were keeping their families together. Tsolo's identity as a woman in struggle had opened her to the necessity of women's liberation. If, ultimately, she subsumed women's issues under the cause of national liberation, she also condemned the international silence around "the conditions of ordinary women in Azania." Tsolo was part of a wave of activists bringing new testimony to light about racial and gender injustices in the struggles for national liberation. She was an indispensable part of making the women's human rights movement truly *global*, by forcing a different perspective than the Western feminists' into the global debate. And, with her graphic details of the inhumanity of South Africa's system of apartheid, she also brought to the transnational level the compelling case for racial oppression as a fundamental affront to human rights' roots in human dignity.

Although indirectly, Tsolo's personal history called attention to profound changes in society that had broadened the base of support for the many sides of the South African liberation movement. These same societal mobilizations eventually meant widespread transnational support for dissident struggles in Eastern Europe and the Soviet Union. In the 1950s, few transnational groups in the West had defended the liberation movements in Africa. The broad-based Defiance Campaign of 1952 led by the ANC, for example, received little attention in the Western media. To be sure, it opened some channels across the Atlantic between U.S. civil rights and South African antiapartheid leaders, as seen in the correspondence between Secretary General of the ANC Walter M. Sisulu and George Hauser, founder of the U.S. Congress of Racial Equality (CORE), who established a small American support group to aid the defiance actions.[31] But these cross-national contacts were exceptions. Despite a long tradition of Pan-African politics that tied black activists in the United States with those in Africa, Cold War hostilities estranged the former allies. Many civil rights leaders, staunchly anticommunist, were unwilling to challenge official U.S. government policies toward Africa or its support of the South African white minority regime. In turn, the speeches by American civil rights leaders simply found little resonance among South African liberation leaders.[32]

Similarly, the dissidents in socialist countries remained relatively isolated from one another and from support abroad in the 1950s and early 1960s. Self-described *samizdat* groups (literally, the "self-published" at home in contrast to exile writings abroad, the *tamizdat*), circulated makeshift flyers, newspapers, broadsheets, manifestos, letters, and petitions offering a self-generated humanist critique of the arbitrary exercise of power under state socialism. They faced harassment, dismissals, arrests, "show" trials, internal exile, and imprisonment in labor camps (the gulags) or in mental hospitals.

In 1968, a group of anonymous founders and editors in Moscow came together to bring out the clandestine *Chronicle of Current Events*, which became a major source of independent information about the plight of dissidents working for change.[33] The authors defended this step by calling on universal principles, notably Article 19 of the Universal Declaration guaranteeing "freedom of opinion and expression." Simultaneously, with their actions, the group implemented its right "to receive and impart information and ideas through any media and regardless of frontiers." It was a bold act in the context of the state's monopoly of the communication media and control over debate. Publication complemented the work of the first official human rights group in the Soviet Union, the Initiative Group for the Defense of Human Rights. Within a year, Valery Chalidze and Andrei Sakharov began coordinating the paper's distribution; the publication was copied by hand and spread throughout the country and abroad. Individuals such as Nina Antonivna Strokata-Karavanska were responsible for its translation and circulation in the Ukraine and elsewhere. In time, Sakharov, a nuclear scientist turned human rights activist, became a powerful symbol of the Soviet dissident movement.[34] As in South Africa, these alternative sources of information and public mobilizations began to describe the political situation from the point of view of activists on the ground.

They also found new audiences abroad. By the late 1960s, the international climate had changed dramatically, bringing new groups into domestic politics and thereby changing the face of international relations. Against the backdrop of war in Southeast Asia, tensions seemed to peak in 1968: from the unrest in Mexico City to the upheavals of the Cultural Revolution in China to the crushing of the Prague Spring, which had sought to democratize socialist Czechoslovakia, to the student barricades erected in Paris and the student protests erupting in Belgrade, the capital of the Serbian socialist republic of Yugoslavia. In many parts of the globe, student radicals, new feminist groups raising consciousness about women's oppression, movements fighting for civil rights, and antiwar organizations questioned the old institutions of politics—the traditional political parties and labor unions—and, as important, their political categories of class and nation. Old definitions gave way to new rubrics and causes: gender, the environment, ethnic diversity, nuclear freeze, and human rights. Promoting these causes seemed to require new transnational organizations working cooperatively. It is perhaps not surprising that those launching the *Chronicle* in 1968 defined their cause in human rights terms.

In many respects, the change in political attitudes for Europeans had been prepared by the Hungarian uprising in 1956. For the populations of Eastern Europe and the Soviet Union, its brutal suppression by Soviet arms had meant beginning disillusionment but also a newfound commitment to work with the ruling communist parties for change. The year 1956 also shattered illusions for many left-leaning democratic and socialist groups in Western Europe. Many indeed had been enamored of the Soviet Union after 1945—its bold social experiment, its language of peace, and its undisputed antifascist credentials. In light of the state's commitment to human equality and economic welfare, they also had been willing to overlook the political stranglehold on debate, mobility, and associational life. But in the 1960s, some progressive groups began to draw new connections between the "great anti-imperialist struggles in the Third World" and the dissident strivings for greater democracy in Eastern Europe and the Soviet Union. They were opening a new basis for increased contact between the people separated by the walls of the Cold War. In intellectual discourses and activists' agendas, there was a remarkable convergence of political visions across the divides of North (the industrialized world) and South (the developing world) as well.

The South African antiapartheid struggle became a compelling source of inspiration for this new vision of global politics, which was inspired by Third World struggles.[35] It laid the groundwork for a societal turn to human rights politics.

These intersections had been the catalyst for the founding of Amnesty International, one of the earliest and still most effective permanent international human rights monitoring organizations. Galvanized in the mid-1950s by the "treason trials" of antiapartheid activists in South Africa as well as by the harsh sentences imposed on Hungarian dissidents after their unsuccessful uprising against the communist system in 1956, British lawyer Peter Benenson launched Amnesty International in 1961 to defend political prisoners throughout the world. It took a stand against state repression of opposition groups anywhere, transcending the Cold War practice of hurling charges of human rights abuse only against one's enemies. The organization's tactics combined a global perspective with a very specific approach: it worked through ever-expanding circles of like-minded individuals (tied together by work, church, or neighborhood), who "adopted" specific prisoners (known as "prisoners of conscience") considered to have been wrongfully convicted. Seeking a neutral space in the Cold War—an "armistice" in Benenson's terminology—each circle took up the case of three prisoners: one from an anticolonial struggle, another from a communist context, and a third from a Western country, notably at the time the then-dictatorial regimes of Portugal, Spain, or Greece. Through letter-writing campaigns and petitions, the groups pressured the governments for the prisoners' release and tried to ensure that their fate remained in the media spotlight. Not as neutral in the geopolitical game as it claimed early on, Amnesty International's campaign of action resonated at home and abroad. To its growing numbers of supporters, it seemed so "distinct from traditional politics."[36] By 1977, about 20,000 members participated in each monthly campaign. Soon after publication of the *Chronicle*, Amnesty International published an English and a Russian version in New York City. This organization was focused on bringing new information to the international scene. Not acknowledged at the time, its politics worked to narrow the symbols of human rights abuses to the cause of the lone (male) *political* prisoner.

New Patterns of Transnational Pressure: Antiapartheid Mobilizations

The public dialogues opening in the 1960s were matched by new transnational coalitions of NGOs increasingly allied to intergovernmental and regional committees that directed the international campaigns against apartheid. They added societal dimensions to the existing state alliances. Subsequently, in an innovative step, a treaty accord in 1975 established formal roles for NGOs in monitoring state abuses, creating a plethora of people's organizations sharing the name Helsinki Watch. Most of these groups were new to the postwar scene; none had been part of the consultative processes that helped write the Universal Declaration. They had been called up by the specificity of the human rights crisis. Their place in the U.N. human rights machinery was evolving simultaneously.

The antiapartheid mobilizations drew on a wide number of support groups. They tested new patterns of advocacy designed to coordinate transnational action by individuals and groups in society. Through print and new television media, activists appealed to ordinary people in different countries to take action to stop a human tragedy in a distant land. Prominent was the Boycott Movement, founded in England in 1959, following a call for international boycott by ANC members a year earlier at an All-African People's Conference in Ghana. The ANC had said at the time, "When our local purchasing power is combined with that of sympathetic organizations overseas we wield a devastating weapon." ANC leaders were determined to take their case beyond Africa and reach people in Western European societies.

The massacre at Sharpeville turned this British group into the more ambitious Anti-Apartheid Movement (AAM), calling for sanctions; it established independent branches throughout Western Europe during the 1960s. For years it was headed by Ambrose Reeves, a bishop who had been deported from South Africa in the crackdown in 1960 because of his egalitarian views. Other groups emerging to oppose apartheid included the International Defense and Aid Fund for Southern Africa, a coalition of organizations that extended from Denmark to Switzerland. The fund offered legal defense and other assistance to prisoners and their families accused of crimes against the state. In a complementary undertaking, it also supported the growing numbers of refugees fleeing state repression in the southern regions of Africa. Part of its money came from a trust fund set up by the United Nations, with contributions from member-states, designed to help those most in need in the struggle. This is only a short list, but it indicates the new types of organizations that promoted a "heavy volume of publicity" on a daily basis against the regime.[37]

These organizations had a unique ally in U.N. institutional circles. Remember, in 1963 the General Assembly had created a Special Committee Against Apartheid. It was the first U.N. committee shunned by Western representatives, who refused to serve on it. Without Cold War blockages, it became an activist group, establishing close working ties (a "partnership," in the words of E. S. Reddy, its first principal secretary) with many NGOs emerging in the 1960s as well as with concerned governments, particularly those in the Organization of African Unity. Reminiscing in 1994, Reddy conceded that "no United Nations committee had ever developed such intimate relations with non-governmental organizations." In his words, these societal groups offered him "useful advice" and proposed many "new initiatives for international action"; the committee even sent representatives abroad to meet with NGO heads in their home countries.

These ties were partly strategic. The strength of international anger at the racist regime allowed Reddy to do an end run on the Human Rights Commission. In U.N. circles, the climate for NGOs had become less hospitable than at the time of the drafting of the Universal Declaration; a rule change in 1952, for example, had limited the ability of NGOs to circulate statements. Reddy simply bypassed HRC jurisdiction and established new channels of communication. In 1964, he also authorized an independent group of experts in law and administration to study prison conditions in South Africa and report back on torture and—in typical U.N. formulation—other "gross violations of human rights" faced by prisoners and detainees. In the course of its investigation, the group heard the testimony of twenty-five eyewitnesses and received twenty-three written statements. Through direct ties to victims and their legal aid groups, it documented the state's repressive system of law, which enforced social order and defended the racial hierarchy. It also revealed widespread use of torture and other inhumane practices, such as indefinite detentions and solitary confinement. From this early innovation, similar firsthand investigations by working groups became more common in U.N. human rights circles. Prodded by the committee, for example, the HRC established a working group of jurists in 1967. The collaboration across borders not only deepened professional ties but also helped set the criteria for continued developments in international law. In addition, through its strategic alliances to states and targeted NGOs, the committee also called for an embargo on arms, ammunition, and oil and pushed for a U.N. blockade to cripple the state's economy.[38] Fig. 2a shows the place of this Special Committee Against Apartheid in the institutional innovations that were changing the face of U.N. oversight.

In building international pressure, the antiapartheid alliances targeted core constituencies and expanded to reach a widening circle of the public. The original members of the British AAM, for example, consisted of South African exiles and students living in Great Britain, former colonials from Anglophone Africa, and members of the small African disaporic communities in England. Its component parts were a near duplicate of the types of members who had responded to the call for Pan-African mobilizations earlier in the century. Increasingly, they were joined by other citizens' groups already involved in a range of public activities, including petitioning and demonstrating for peace, nuclear disarmament, and welfare and labor reforms. Chief among these supporters were trade unionists, aided by the International Trade Union Conference (ICFTU), church groups, and peace activists. Citizens' organizations in Great Britain and Western Europe, which later established contacts with groups in the socialist East, developed from this social milieu. In the early 1960s, the AAM, working with its branches abroad and coordinating activities (when possible) with the ANC leadership, implemented the call for boycott. It first targeted South African wines, fruits, potatoes, and cigarettes.

The antiapartheid mobilization was a trans-Atlantic phenomenon, reaching U.S. shores in the 1960s. Throughout the Cold War years, U.S. officials consistently maintained their primary geopolitical goal of limiting Soviet influence in Africa and they continued to shield South Africa in the Security Council. But in its bilateral ties with the country, the U.S. government was forced to respond to pressures of the international antiapartheid movement, increasingly defended by growing numbers of opponents of apartheid at home.

Change came in the 1960s. The Vietnam War (1962–75) was a powerful catalyst for the new politics, part of the growing social ferment of the decade, which electrified anti-imperialist sentiments and heightened attention around the globe to the racial character of the wars of liberation. Mounting opposition to the war domestically meant that civil rights leaders were more willing to take a stand against the U.S. government's Cold War policies toward popular liberation movements. They began to link their own goals of racial justice and democracy to the black liberation movements in South Africa. If the transition was gradual, it nonetheless became a hallmark of the struggle against the Jim Crow laws segregating the races in the South.

Already at the time of the Montgomery, Alabama, boycott (1955), Martin Luther King Jr., the eloquent leader of the American nonviolent civil rights movement, linked his domestic actions to wider liberation struggles. "The oppressed peoples of the world are rising up," he cautioned. "They are revolting against colonialism, imperialism and other systems of oppression," a veiled reference to Jim Crow. In a speech in London on his way to receive the 1964 Nobel Peace Prize in Oslo, Norway, King was much more explicit about the bonds that tied the U.S. civil rights movement to the liberation movement in South Africa. He said, "In our struggle for freedom and justice in the U.S., which has also been so long and arduous, we feel a powerful sense of identification with those in the far more deadly struggle for freedom in South Africa."[39] Acutely aware of the different contexts, from his own domestic base King nonetheless was seeking to forge new transnational politics in the name of democracy and racial justice.

The antiapartheid cause became part of the social protest movements that were driving Americans and others into new politics and the streets in the mid-1960s: civil rights, women's rights, antiwar protests, and student protests. These movements both mirrored and supported the complex and interlocking strands of the antiapartheid movement in South Africa itself. Although sustained in the United States in good measure by the struggles for civil rights and black consciousness, the South African issue had emotional and immediate appeal to many groups: those opposing the Vietnam War, second-wave feminists discovering a lost history of women's involvement in public life and confronting the different paths to liberation, and many students demanding reform of the academic curriculum to include Third World authors and perspectives. Because of the central relevance of South Africa to the many debates about democracy, freedom, racial justice, and women's equality, the cumulative effect of protests began to ripple more broadly through American society.

Public opinion in the United States was responding partly to widening media coverage of the "free Mandela" campaign, one of the first and most successful global campaigns to use the life story of one individual to make tangible the terrible costs of rights oppression and to capture the broader struggle against apartheid. Nelson Mandela had been one of the leaders of the ANC charged with treason under the Sabotage Act in the Rivonia Trials of 1963. Along with six others, he was sentenced the next year to life imprisonment on Robben Island. The government had hoped these leaders would fade from view, but the opposite happened. Mandela was revered in popular memory at home, even among individuals who had not been especially political. He remained "the symbol of leadership and struggle." Norah Dlamini, interviewed in the mid-1980s, reminisced about the period of mass unrest in the late 1950s: "I remember we had the . . . bus boycott in Alexandra and the stayaways. We used to go to the offices in the bottom of town to see Nelson Mandela—you know how it is with a famous person. You just want to know what he looks like. I never met him—I just saw him when we went past. In the 1980 petition [circulating in the country] all the people were saying he must be released." Tshidi Phutela summed up popular sentiments of Mandela with a simple statement: "That was a good leader."[40]

The world campaign to "free Mandela" (and political prisoners more broadly) drew sustenance from and in turn supported the domestic struggle. Launched by the AAM and the Special Committee at the time of the Rivonia trials, it crisscrossed the globe, finding defenders from luminaries to government officials to town councilors to common people. In part, Mandela himself helped guide it. His letters and manifestos were smuggled out of prison, translated, and published widely. The first international call to action reflected many of the values that sustained the campaign. Those on trial, it said, would not be facing trial at all "in any rational society." They were "leaders of a popular struggle for the defeat of racist rule, for the recognition of rights regarded as natural wherever a common humanity is acknowledged. . . . [Their] trial is the struggle of all men for freedom; their trial is the trial of all men who want to be free." Campaign tactics included hunger strikes; signing petitions demanding Mandela's release; coordinated celebrations worldwide at the time of his birthday, July 18; and strategic pressure at key international meetings, as during summits of the superpowers, as well as conferences of Commonwealth nations and European parliaments. In 1984, both houses of the U.S. Congress adopted a "Mandela freedom resolution." One report estimated that organizations comprising "no less than 250 million people" signed petitions on Mandela's behalf over the course of the campaign.[41]

In the growing clamor accelerating in the 1970s, Americans became increasingly active, launching a successful divestment campaign. Individuals and members of churches and synagogues lobbied city councils and state legislatures to divest their funds from South Africa and pressured investors and stockholders to force changes in portfolio management. Students and some alumni demanded universities follow suit and so did individuals involved with public institutions such as the Smithsonian. Consumers also waged coordinated boycotts against companies such as the Polaroid Corporation, implicated in the pass laws system because of its use of photographs for identification. In 1985, responding to student and community pressure as well as protest actions, ninety-five colleges and universities partly or fully withdrew their investments from South Africa. Other universities used their formidable economic clout to pressure businesses to curtail work in South Africa or to adopt just and fair labor practices (the Sullivan principles).[42] By 1990, twenty-seven state governments, ninety cities, and twenty-four counties had pulled their holdings from South Africa.

At the federal level, congressional action by black caucus members in 1986, supported by Democrats and moderate Republicans, overrode a presidential veto by Ronald Reagan and passed the U.S. Comprehensive Anti-Apartheid Act (CAAA). Reagan was engaged at the time in what he called "constructive dialogue" with the South African regime, an effort to encourage change by quietly pressuring in the background. Congress demanded action. The CAAA redirected American foreign policy, establishing an elaborate sanctions structure, and, perhaps most important, detailing what it would take to lift the sanctions. Ending the sanctions required releasing political prisoners, discontinuing the state of emergency, and legalizing all political activity. It also meant opening a meaningful dialogue with the majority population over democratic rule, according to the "one person, one vote" principle, the long-standing goal of the original antiapartheid coalition of states. When the law passed, more than 200 U.S. corporations doing business in South Africa sold their operations and the remaining industries began to adhere to the new business and labor guidelines more favorable to workers. Even with these changes, the United States still remained the second-largest trading partner in South Africa during the years of sanctions, doing $1.6 billion a year in business.

The economic bite from government and corporate sanctions and boycotts in the United States—and duplicated elsewhere—exerted a sizeable toll on the racist regime, as did continuing domestic protests and actions. In 1986, the ANC inaugurated "people's power," a mass grassroots movement to replace official government authorities with people's courts, street committees, defense units, and new union organizing. The government's policies of repression also were draining; toward the end of the 1980s, half of its armed forces were deployed in the black townships to keep public order.[43] Ultimately, the wide publicity of the "free Mandela campaign" helped secure Mandela's release from prison on February 11, 1990, marking the moment of irrevocable change for the South African regime. Significantly, the political transition from apartheid to democratic rule took place according to the CAAA requirements for ending sanctions. By 1990, the question no longer was "if" but "when" the formal transition would take place.

The historical patterns set by the confluence of local and international actions in the antiapartheid movement had a contradictory impact on human rights developments more broadly. On the one hand, these transnational pursuits were the first test and foundational model for many future human rights mobilizations. Decrying the inhumanity of apartheid, they brought the human rights principles of freedom and justice into the concrete day-to-day operations of U.N. committees and commissions, setting precedents for oversight and sanctions in the future. On the other hand, their concentrated message fed into a wider climate that restricted the types of human rights abuses demanding international attention and action. In a different way, the Helsinki Final Accords also contributed to this limitation.

Helsinki Human Rights Organizations

A second major source directing human rights advocacy, the Helsinki Final Act of 1975 established patterns of regional monitoring outside the U.N. structure. It gave rise to a host of citizens' initiatives and NGO watchdog groups, which essentially operated parallel to the continuing work of the international antiapartheid networks. The Final Act was a product of a regional Security and Defense Conference in Finland, meeting between 1973 and 1975, part of a "thaw" in superpower tensions known in the standard Cold War narrative as "the era of détente."

Initiated by Soviet leaders determined to legitimize the European map established after World War II, the conference brought together representatives of thirty-three European countries, the United States, and Canada. The Final Act formally recognized the reality of Soviet power in Eastern and Central Europe and affirmed the sovereign integrity of the territorial borders of the socialist states that had been created after the war. The signatory states agreed to "respect each other's right to freely choose and develop its political, social, economic and cultural systems as well as its right to determine its laws and regulations." The agreement confirmed the inviolability of the existing frontiers of Europe.[44] With sovereignty so centrally entrenched in the accord, Soviet Politburo Chairman Leonid Brezhnev believed he could make a concession to Western representatives, who also pushed for the inclusion of respect for human rights and fundamental freedoms.

A forerunner conference in 1970 issued a Friendly Relations Declaration also placing national self-determination—territorial sovereignty —at the basis of the international order of states ensuring friendly relations among peoples. This document, however, had not mentioned human rights. In the interim years, transnational pressure had been building, reflecting the growing contacts between citizens' groups in Western and Eastern Europe over peace and nuclear freeze as well as environmental concerns. Socialist state planning from above had paid little attention to environmental costs, with increasingly clear consequences. The deteriorating landscape was raising vital questions in societies with no space for independent advocacy about who to hold accountable—and how to do it. In this shared climate, mounting concerns arose with the human costs of Cold War barriers, particularly how sealed borders separated families and impeded travel, scientific and student exchanges, and the flow of information.

The Helsinki Final Act defended human rights in two ways. It committed the signatory states to respect human rights and fundamental freedoms (Article VII) and, while mentioning political, civil, and economic rights, drew specific attention to "freedom of thought, conscience, religion or belief" as well as to the rights of minorities to "equality before the law." Adhering to the broad scope of rights in the Universal Declaration, it singled out the defense of political rights, including freedoms of speech, press, belief, movement, and association. These priorities shaped the actual processes of monitoring. Reflecting the popular issues of family reunification and travel, it also had a section on "Co-operation in Humanitarian" fields (known as Basket III) for its list of specific proposals to enhance people-to-people contact across the East-West divide in Europe. Here, the signatory states pledged to address family issues, travel, and youth exchanges, as well as to improve the circulation and flow of information across borders.

In a remarkable step, the Helsinki Final Act also set up a schedule of intergovernmental conferences to oversee compliance, beginning in Belgrade, Yugoslavia, in 1977 and projected to Madrid, Spain, in 1980 and Ottawa, Canada, in 1985. That is, government representatives agreed to a mechanism of *official* oversight to monitor compliance. These Helsinki negotiators, whether from Western or socialist countries, knew the precedents already set by U.N. organs and committees in the ongoing fight against South Africa, as the epigraph shows. For Vojin Dimitrijevic, the Helsinki procedures for compliance reflected the same legal principles first tested in South Africa: in matters of human rights (for peace and security), domestic jurisdiction arguments no longer could be used to bar states from "intervening."[45] These interventions had followed the gamut from special investigations and working groups to resolutions to various forms of pressure—all short of armed intervention. The Helsinki accord precluded armed intervention by affirming the right of the state to sovereign independence. But it also confirmed that human rights principles were matters of legitimate concern to the community of states. To be sure, the continuing antiapartheid mobilizations on the ground were not strictly about U.N. oversight or matters of international law. Yet, they showed that breakthroughs in the law and international procedures were inconceivable without a people's mobilizations at home and, increasingly, in transnational alliances abroad.

A similar configuration of people's movements within a multilateral framework for action confounded Soviet expectations after 1975. As it turned out, the Final Act was only the first word in a set of changes quickly enveloping the socialist world in Europe. The principle of an individual's right to know had "a most extraordinary and probably unforeseen development."[46] It meant that the Helsinki Accords were translated quickly into every language in the Soviet Union and Eastern Europe; they spread quickly across the region.In a process that caught socialist authorities off guard, the grassroots response was immediate, turning isolated dissidents into coordinated human rights defenders.

The *samizdat* groups had created fertile ground for this shift; already claiming a public civic role, they had established crucial networks and contacts for new developments.

The Helsinki groups were a more serious challenge to the authorities through the breadth of their organizations and programmatic coherence. The prototype for Helsinki watchdog groups appeared first in Moscow in spring 1976. Called the Moscow Helsinki Watch Group, its founders proclaimed a common task for the post-Helsinki era: to gather "written complaints" from Soviet citizens about violations of their rights and forward them to the participating governments. The next year, similar Helsinki initiatives spread further east into Siberia and also into the Transcaucasian regions as well as the Ukraine, Georgia, Armenia, and Lithuania. Their leaders expanded contacts and shared information and sent petitions documenting their cause to the United Nations. But Soviet authorities, aided by their well-placed Eastern European allies in the world body, effectively squashed U.N. action. Only in 1985 did the Human Rights Commission, for example, establish a working group on Defenders' Rights to investigate the increasingly widespread repression of dissidents monitoring their countries' adherence to the Helsinki principles. According to a U.S. report, by 1978 the new human rights organizations had become "catalysts, drawing together the disparate struggles of soviet dissent." These ranged from matters of press censorship to conditions of political prisoners in labor camps and psychiatric hospitals to the denial of independent unions and collective bargaining to specific problems of religious and ethnic minorities and to the right of emigration, particularly for Jews who had suffered renewed outbreaks of anti-Semitism after the June 1967 war and Israeli occupation of Arab territories. The official Soviet hostility to the Zionist state was the excuse in many quarters for domestic persecution of Jewish citizens.[47] The shared organizational rubric—Helsinki Watch—embraced many different causes.

For these opposition movements, the human rights framework opened a novel strategy. Using the language of the accords, the citizens' groups demanded that Soviet authorities comply with their new obligations under international law. They also increasingly referenced the rights and liberties that were guaranteed by their own constitution. That is, they called on Soviet leaders to fulfill their obligations enshrined in their own constitution and in the many U.N. conventions the country had ratified beyond Helsinki, such as the two international covenants. Throwing "rights talk" into the limelight, the obligations of the law became central to the dissidents' case. So, too, did their organizations, which were not only the vehicle for change but, in embryonic form, embodied their vision of a free society—a place of autonomy separate

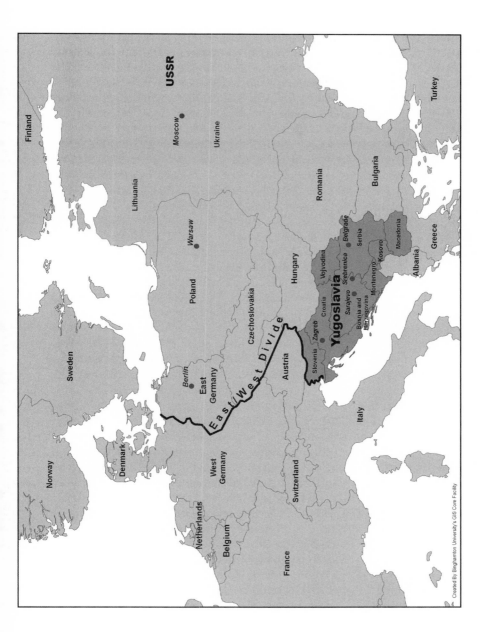

Map 4. Cold War Europe, 1945–89.

from the state to ensure independent civic action. Soviet leaders moved harshly against these new private associations—closing them down, outlawing their activities, and arresting their members. By 1978, officials had imprisoned or banished most of the early founders of Moscow Helsinki: among them, Yuri Orlov and Vladimir Slepak, on charges of anti-Soviet propaganda, and Anatoly Shcharansky for treason. Petro Grygorenko was stripped of his citizenship while traveling abroad.

Similar organizations appeared in the other socialist countries of the Soviet bloc. Historian Padraic Kenney called this type of associational opposition "civil society" dissent.[48] He drew attention to the conceptual framing of these movements by contemporaries—dissident intellectuals in Eastern Europe in the mid-1970s—and subsequently by political and social theorists. The contemporary Hungarian intellectual Miklós Haraszti, for example, saw the reconstruction of "civil [i.e., "bourgeois"] society" as a "necessary corrective to Communism's defects." Similar ideas were found in the writings of the Polish strategist Adam Michnik as well as the Czechoslovak writer Václav Havel, whose slogan "live in truth" became a watchword for many intellectuals who were the backbone of civil society dissent. They were bent on carving out new protected spaces for associational life and for the open exchange of ideas and views. Collectively, they opposed the states' monopolies on information and decision-making and sought to engage in substantive dialogue with the authorities over the nature of freedom, liberty, and collective responsibility.[49]

These ideas also encouraged organizational experiments. Foremost among them was Charter 77, a self-defined "free and informal and open association of peoples of various convictions, religions and professions" determined to legitimize "non-party" voices in the running of the state. It originated with a group of 240 individuals in Czechoslovakia, who signed a petition, which named three spokesmen for the group: Havel, the philosopher Jan Patocka, and a former government official, Jiri Hajek. Its principles underscored the importance of civic activism—of reconstructing society to defend fundamental rights, which were "daily and systematically violated by the government." The causes for these violations lay in the monopoly of "power and ideology" by the Communist party, which subordinated all institutions and organizations in society to its authority. Reaching the crux of the matter, the authors acknowledged that responsibility for preserving rights rested with the state: "But not on it alone. Every individual bears a share of responsibility for the general conditions in the country, and therefore also for compliance with the enacted pacts, which are as binding for the people as for the government. The feeling of this coresponsibility, the belief in the value of civic engagement and the readiness to be engaged, together with the need to seek a new and more effective expression, gave us the idea of creating Charter 77."[50] The charter listed a range of rights that the government had pledged to respect by its adherence to the Final Act but which it still had not implemented. It stressed freedom of expression, freedom from fear (of political reprisals for speaking out), the need for education for all irrespective of political views, and freedom of religious confession. The name "77" came from new diplomatic opportunities: the group presented this document to the intergovernmental compliance conference meeting in Belgrade in 1977. The association became a formidable organization in Czech society, with close ties to Polish, Hungarian, and Romanian opposition clusters.

Unique in its ability to bridge the intellectual-manual divide and win wide support among workers in society was the Polish Workers' Defense Committee (KOR). The group had emerged to champion workers' rights and became linked to the powerful trade union movement, Solidarity, formed in 1980 and headed by Lech Wałęsa; at its height, one of every two Polish adults was a member of the union, which had become a serious alternative to the state. The imposition of martial law in late 1981 curbed the union's activities. Among other important organizations were the Democratic Opposition in Hungary, the Peace Movement Working Group in Slovenia, one of the six socialist republics in Yugoslavia, and the Initiative for Peace and Human Rights in East Germany. Increasingly, these organizations made contact with like-minded groups in the West. There, they found receptive audiences. Amnesty International, for example, adopted many "dissenters"—a label Amnesty International preferred because many on trial dissented from their governments' claim not to violate human rights principles—who landed in prison.[51]

Other Helsinki Watch groups were established in Western Europe as well as in the United States, most notably Human Rights Watch (originally Helsinki Watch). Founded in 1978, it has evolved into one of the most influential permanent international NGOs in the human rights community today. Its early phases of work, however, conformed to the multilateral agenda established by the Final Act—including its priorities on state abuses of individual political freedoms. For these purposes, the U.S. Helsinki Watch issued detailed, thorough, and documented reports on compliance, drawing on information from its growing contacts with dissidents in socialist countries. Its focus remained overwhelmingly on the political situation for organized dissent—on the absence of civil society, in the language of the day. Given the socialist welfare net, its efforts concerning worker protections (or economic rights) turned exclusively on the need for independent trade unions as well as the right to strike and bargain in the public arena. But even these issues, typically, were given only one-tenth of the space in the reports.[52] In its early operations, the U.S. group duplicated the political biases in human rights monitoring. By 1982, Helsinki committees in thirty-seven countries formed an International Helsinki Federation based in Vienna, Austria, to coordinate and defend the work of Human Rights Watch members more broadly.

The Helsinki Act, of course, applied to *all* state members that had signed it. The accord, thus, offered an opportunity to shift international attention to the record of Western countries, including the United States, beyond the precedents set by Amnesty International, which had been directed against Western authoritarian regimes. Arthur J. Goldberg, former U.S. Supreme Court justice and head of the U.S. delegation to Helsinki, was justifiably skeptical about the possibility. After participating in the Belgrade compliance meeting, he wrote wryly, "The United States and other countries of the West had their performance questioned at the Belgrade meeting, and some of the questioning was constructive, for our own record of performance is by no means perfect. Questions should aid our respective countries to improve their records. I wish others were of equal mind." Goldberg was prescient, indeed. The dominant view in the United States—among officials and the wider public—has tended to regard human rights violations as problems "out there" but of little direct implication for reform at home. Nonetheless, despite its decisive focus on the violations by socialist countries, the Helsinki initiative supported a number of new domestic NGO monitoring efforts in the United States. For example, in the late 1970s a Citizen's Committee in New York City developed close ties with civil rights organizations that also were pressuring for racial justice in South Africa. Another in Washington, D.C., turned attention to the situation of not only blacks at home but also migrant workers, prisoners, and native Americans.[53] By somewhat circuitous routes, distinct advocacy networks of human rights constituents began to reinforce one another.

Civil Society on Trial: The Case of the Belgrade Six

A trial against a group known as the Belgrade Six, which opened in Yugoslavia in late 1984, graphically captured a number of characteristics of the new civil society dissent. The arena of law became a central battleground between the dissidents and government authorities. At stake in this new legalist context, with its talk of rights, were the ties between state and society.

To be sure, Yugoslavia was somewhat of an anomaly in the socialist bloc. Its first communist leader, Marshall Josip Broz Tito, had broken with Stalin in 1949. The country embarked on an independent foreign policy that often allied with Third World countries; it was not a member of the Warsaw Pact, the socialist Cold War military alliance. The government saw itself as representing internationalist values and more open politics. Authority, however, remained centralized in Communist party rule. Times were hard in Yugoslavia in the mid-1980s (as elsewhere in the East)—as reflected in economic stagnation, rampant inflation, mounting international debt, and stirrings of ethnic strife over economic development and investment strategies.

The trial showed how the Yugoslav government's adherence to the Helsinki Final Act transformed internal debate over the terms of governance. The six defendants were determined to unmask the state trial for what it was, a "political trial." They received considerable publicity at home and abroad and their cause mobilized a network of transnational groups committed to the principles of judicial due process. As was typical of the many dissident movements, transnational support came from professional groups, notably from writers, scientists, and lawyers. Srdja Popović, a Belgrade attorney specializing in human rights cases and the leading defense lawyer for one of the accused, noted before the trial date, "The case [against the Belgrade Six] is unique in many respects. So [far] more than five hundred people have signed a petition demanding that the Six not be prosecuted. In my whole career, I have never before seen it that defendants in a political trial are supported by compatriots—in most cases nobody wanted to be connected with them. Many protests have also come from abroad, although the defendants were relatively unknown."[54]

During a police raid of an apartment in Belgrade in April 1984, twenty-eight people were arrested and six eventually were charged with "hostile propaganda" and "using the gathering to conspire to overthrow the government." They faced a five- to fifteen-year prison term. All were intellectuals standing outside the establishment career ladder: Milan Nikolić and Vladimir Mijanović were sociologists (the latter unemployed at the time); Milan Miodrag was a scriptwriter and filmmaker; Pavuľško Imširović, a radio station publicist; Gordan Jovanović, a twenty-three-year-old philosophy and art history student; and Dragomir Olujić, a freelance translator. According to Helsinki Watch, which immediately took up their cause, all had been active earlier in some form of opposition politics; they had served time in prison. The first three had been involved in the 1968 student protest movements and four had demonstrated in front of the Polish Embassy in Belgrade, denouncing the harsh measures taken against the Polish trade union movement (Solidarity) in late 1981.[55]

At the time of the arrest, the defendants were participating in what they called a "free university"—an independent gathering of people in a private apartment outside the stultifying censorship of official university life. In this "free" space, people came together to discuss all manner of contemporary issues and problems as well as historical and theoretical perspectives. Known to the authorities, these types of gatherings had been taking place in the capital for seven years.

As a makeshift institution comprising a rudimentary civil society, this university was a place for an exchange of ideas that was not allowed in government-controlled institutions and media outlets. The discussion in April had centered on "the nationality problem," a particularly sensitive topic for government leaders seeking to maintain their power base over an increasingly restive population that was beginning to bring ethnic identities into political life. Tito's 1974 constitution had paved the way, creating six republics that matched, although imperfectly, the ethnic and religious differences in these former Balkan lands. As Map 4 shows, the Yugoslav Socialist Republic consisted of Serbia, the largest republic, as well as Croatia, Slovenia, Montenegro, Macedonia, and Bosnia-Herzegovina, and also two autonomous provinces carved out of Serbia, Kosovo (90 percent ethnic Albanian) and Vojvodina (with sizable numbers of Hungarians). Tito's death in 1980 opened up a constitutional struggle over power and resources that increasingly was being played out in ethnic terms. In 1981, for example, ethnic Albanians in Kosovo, led by students, took to the streets demanding higher wages, greater freedom of expression, the release of political prisoners, and a new status as a republic in the country. Decrying "Albanian separatism," the Serb government began to curb the province's autonomy; leaders in Croatia and Slovenia also became increasingly alarmed about their own lines of authority.[56] The trial played out against a backdrop of mounting ethnic antagonisms that were being mobilized as part of a struggle for power.

At the time of the crackdown in Belgrade, the ruling communist elite was divided into hardliners and reformers; similar divisions were also appearing in the other socialist countries in the face of compounding problems in state and economy. The leadership also was split on how to deal with dissidents. It appears that the hardliners were behind the arrests, fearful that reformist communists might be allying with dissident intellectuals in society. The arrests, then, were designed to intimidate and silence the reform movements in society.

The defendants were self-proclaimed independent intellectuals who defied easy labeling. They positioned themselves between two dangers, as Milan Nikolić put it in his "final words" to the court: between the "restoration of Stalinism" (bureaucratic rigidity and authoritarian rule) and the "restoration of capitalism" (state and corporate capitalism and the domination of managers over workers). In this sense, they offered a complicated picture of the politics of socialist dissidents; they did not identify with Western definitions of freedoms, which were tied so closely to market economics. They also showed that broad-based transnational support turned on specific issues—the shared commitments to the rule of law and civic freedoms, which were the points of common concern. The international realm of publicity and mobilization often was a simplified distillation of highly complex local settings. In the case of the Belgrade Six, it missed the ideological nuances that made up the daily politics of these dissidents' strivings.

As Nikolić expressed it, the Six wanted to bring democracy, self-government, and economic self-management to socialism. They advocated a return to the democratic traditions of socialism to ensure the "possibility of a majority of the people [taking] their destiny into their own hands."[57] They applied self-determination to political life within the state as the best guarantor of more democratic and humane politics. In retrospect, it was perhaps naïve to assume that civil society politics automatically would be tolerant and inclusive and would serve as a brake on arbitrary power. But those were the assumptions of the 1980s. The trial also had its dramatic side: it included accusations of beatings and torture of those arrested, a forty-two-day hunger strike (which won the defendants release from prison for the duration of the trial), and a mysterious death of one of the original twenty-eight arrested suspects, Radomir Radović.[58]

The post-Helsinki world shaped the lines of defense. Arguments centered on the provisions in the Yugoslav Constitution (for example, its declaration of freedom of thought and belief and guarantees of scientific and artistic creation) to expose the government's abuse of power. The defendants held state authorities accountable for their failure to implement the corpus of international law they had agreed to. Any violation of human rights "whoever performs it" was "unconstitutional and subject to sanction." As they saw it, the state had to acquire a new legitimacy by subjecting all of its political bodies to the provisions of the constitution. In short, they called for the state to become legal again. They were determined to use the trial, again in Nikolić's words, "to expose the people who indict us."

Given the nature of politics, the strategy was not about approaching those in power. As Vladimir Mijanović stated in a direct "Appeal to the Public," the defendants addressed their case not to the court, which under the circumstances could be neither "independent" nor "impartial," but to the public: to the Yugoslav public actively following the trial as well as to an international public already deeply concerned about the legal abuses of such patently political trials. Of those abroad, Mijanović specifically mentioned the different "defense committees" formed in several other socialist countries as well as "international NGOs" devoted to the protection of human rights. "I am not appealing to the court," he said pointedly, which, in his view, could issue only a "legal sanction for an arbitrary political decision" already made. "My appeal to the public is not to protect myself [however] but . . . to provide an indirect protection to all those who may find themselves in the same situation by arbitrary decisions of some individual from the top layers of authority." He called on the mass media to produce "professionally correct and relatively full reports of the trial in spite of the restraints and political risks [its writers] will endure."[59] In late 1984, Mijanović was on the cusp of an emerging global network of instantaneous communications, which he tried to enlist for his own cause.

The appeal was not without effect. Within Yugoslavia itself, open letters circulated widely, defending freedom of thought and expression, and many newspapers throughout the republics reported in detail on the trial. So did others, abroad. In the new climate of monitoring, the case became an international cause. Amnesty International and Helsinki Watch organized urgent writing campaigns to defend the accused. The American Bar Association sent observers to the court as did Amnesty International, although the Yugoslav government refused to allow members of the Helsinki Commission to observe the proceedings, a ruling that was met with much dismay because it was "not in accord with the spirit" of the Final Act. The U.S. embassy in Belgrade sent observers to the trial every day and a three-member delegation from the United States sat in on the proceedings: Adrian W. DeWind, for the American Bar Association; Aryeh Neier, for the U.S. Helsinki Watch; and George Ginsburg, for the International League of Human Rights. From these perspectives, the legality of the trial, judged according to a growing consensus on international canons of law, was itself on trial. As in the case of South African trials and prison politics, the abuses of legal standards elicited professional outrage. For example, the American Bar Association protested vigorously when one of the defense lawyers was arrested and sent to prison in the middle of the trial, depriving the accused of counsel. There also was a general outcry when the prosecution arbitrarily added a new charge to the indictment as the trial was proceeding. The charge was inflammatory, indeed: the accused had sympathized with Albanian separatists in the province of Kosovo.

Support abroad was extensive. The European Parliament passed motions condemning the "taking of legal action against persons who have simply expressed their opinions" and called on the Yugoslav government to discontinue the proceedings. European governments passed similar resolutions, as did party factions within parliaments. Organized by the European networks for peace and human rights (*Friedens-und Menschenrechtsbewegung*), public demonstrations during the trial took place in front of the Yugoslav embassy in Bonn and in many other European capitals. Furthermore, the archive contains alphabetical listings as of February 1985 (and a note indicates it is only a partial list) of ten prominent international NGOs that lent their support to the defense.

Other materials listed by country the individuals and groups who were speaking out for the defense. Weighted toward Europe, this list shows a geographic breadth from Australia, Canada, India, Mexico, Argentina, and the United States. The Argentine Adolfo Pérez Esquivel, for example, was on the list. As Chapter 3 shows, Esquivel was one of the most prominent activists in Argentina who fought the brutal military dictatorship that was disappearing its citizens between 1976 and 1983. Esquivel had received the Nobel Peace Prize in 1980 for his courageous stand. His example shows a transnational activism that transcended distinct causes and geographies. For the United States, furthermore, forty-four members of the House of Representatives and two senators, Paul Tsongas, then on the Committee on Foreign Relations, and Edward Kennedy, lent their names to the widening protest movements. A separate Committee Against Intellectual Repression in Yugoslavia also had been established, comprised nearly exclusively of university faculty members. In tune with the typical pattern, professionals, among them many university professors and lawyers, provided the active core of the concerned and mobilized Americans defending the Belgrade Six.[60]

The intense international scrutiny of the trial helped influence the outcome. Through diverse avenues of support, the defendants had become well-known international figures. As a result of both internal and external pressure, and also reflecting growing misgivings among many members of the party elite who feared that the trial hurt Yugoslavia's international standing as a tolerant and nonaligned state, the court gave lighter prison sentences than anticipated. Nikolić, Miodrag, and Olujić, whose cases were separated from the others, received between one- and two-year prison terms; the case against Imširović was dropped altogether; Jovanović and Mijanović were sentenced to twenty months in prison; Mijanović was able to leave Yugoslavia in 1987 and move to the United States. But the prognosis for the future remained uncertain. Reflecting wider European sentiments among progressive circles, the German Green Party member Petra Kelly complained that the prison sentences "still [were] an injustice." A Western diplomat also was cautious: "The authorities have retreated some but that does not mean that the cause of human rights has been advanced."[61] His words turned out to be quite telling but not in the way he had anticipated.

Repression of dissidents did not have the desired effect. Generally in Eastern Europe and the Soviet Union it bred more discontent and international scrutiny. Furthermore, it did nothing to address the pressing problem of economic stagnation. Within the Communist parties, reformist leaders—as had emerged in Yugoslavia—began initiating programmatic changes. In the Soviet Union in 1985, for example, the Communist party elected Mikhail Gorbachev as secretary general. He initiated two reform principles, which became paradigmatic for many proposals for change from above beginning to affect all European socialist societies: *perestroika*, which meant "reconstruction," and *glasnost*, which implied a new openness to public debate. Although the events in each socialist country took their own course, the civil society groups played a formative role in an accelerating momentum of change. In Poland, for example, the "counter-society theorized by Michnik and others . . . was emerging as a *de facto* source of authority and initiative." In Czechoslovakia, by 1989, Charter 77 members (the group had been renamed Civic Forum) entered the cabinet as working partners with government officials. The end goals of this change remained complex, however. For many socialist reformers and activists, the watchword was Europe "as imagined from the East," with its prospect of "affluence *and* security, liberty *and* [social] protection."[62] There also were nationalist undercurrents, as glimpsed in the trial of the Belgrade Six, an alternative appeal to ethnic nationalism for social identity and political cohesion.

* * *

The international antiapartheid movement and the socialist dissidents with their transnational allies are vital to the narratives of both the human rights activists reading their own history and the general scholarly literature. As historical cases of decades-long struggle, both seem to hold instructive examples for how transnational networks bring norms and values to the international arena. As the political scientists Keck and Sikkink put it, the antiapartheid coalition launched "one of the most successful transnational campaigns in the human rights era." Historian Audie Klotz noted similarly that by securing universal suffrage in South Africa in 1994, "the domestic and international pressure to end apartheid [had] succeeded."[63] The postapartheid era reflected the dramatic impact that coordinated pressure by an international coalition of states and peoples could exert on a repressive regime.

In the prominent narrative, human rights advocacy stood at the heart of several of the most important transitions in global politics and power in the late twentieth century. Its activists received many international accolades, including the Nobel Peace Prize. Among the recipients in the formative phases of human rights developments were Andrei Sakharov (1975), Nelson Mandela (in 1993) together with F. W. de Klerk of the

African Nationalist Party for negotiating the relatively peaceful transition to democracy in South Africa, Amnesty International (1977) for its work in Argentina, Adolfo Pérez Esquivel (1980), and Lech Wałęsa (1983). A prestigious international prize of long pedigree, it honors the values of peace, nonviolence, regional crisis management, and international cooperation in global politics. With its embrace of human rights activism, the prize highlights the values that are seeking to make the security of human beings more central to the calculations of international diplomacy and state power.[64]

Examined as historical entities, the two formative human rights movements were not simple success stories. Only detailed examination of the specifics of advocacy work can assess the limitations of their politics. The transnational campaign of states and NGOs indeed swept aside the legal impediments to racial equality in South Africa. The movement had been less able to secure social and economic rights for the majority population mired in poverty. In the South African example, the system of *legal* racial segregation became the growing target of international public outrage; it has proven more difficult to mobilize effective international campaigns against the multiple abuses of racial segregation when and where they are not legally imposed. And, although much of the human rights literature sees Helsinki as a pivotal moment in the "internationalization" of human rights discourses, the assessment is not historically accurate.[65] Whatever the intent of many of the dissidents—in their original efforts to "humanize" socialism, many remained committed to the principles of collective welfare and social equality and found the transition to liberal market economies after 1989 bitter and difficult— Helsinki internationalized the discourses on civic rights and freedoms. There was no similar broad-based embrace of the principles of economic justice, which would have meant a full internationalization of the values inherent in the Universal Declaration. Through a broad consensus of states, the HRC and U.N. organs rejected efforts to include international monitoring of states' economic policies in the legitimate criteria to restrict state sovereignty.[66] Rather, they set crucial international precedents for defining human rights violations in political terms. If the outcome seemed to reinforce the Cold War ideological divisions over rights, the causes were more complex, inherent partly in the constraints of the domestic struggles at the time.

The next chapter continues the same line of analysis. Its theme forms part of an ongoing set of domestic and international events, which created the political orthodoxy in human rights advocacy. The chapter explores the crisis of forced disappearance, which peaked as a transnational cause between 1973 and 1983. It examines this unfolding crisis through the eyes of the mothers of the disappeared, whose courageous acts drew increasing international attention to the terrible problems at home. These self-styled mothers-turned-human-rights-activists pushed U.N. monitoring practices in new directions, opening U.N. organs to NGO influence, a critical step in the broadening of NGO advocacy in international relations. In addition, these movements from the southern regions of the globe also contributed to an expansion of international criminal law. The mothers' movements defy easy generalization and, in some ways, served as a bridge for the new advocacy networks addressed in Part II of this book.

Chapter 3
Mothers' Courage and U.N. Monitoring of Disappearance, 1973–83

> A society that does not fight for its rights becomes a sick society, a
> society that lives in fear and horror that it can happen again. That
> is what happened here in Argentina and this is what makes us, the
> human rights organizations, survive. We can't sit peacefully at
> home.
> —María Adela Gard de Antokoletz, a Mother of the Plaza de Mayo

Starting in the early 1970s, evidence of cases of "disappearance" compiled by exiles, refugees, local organizations, and individual survivors
began to trickle out of many countries in Central and South America. It
was not the first time that the word had appeared in public, however.
Several journalists used "disappeared" to describe the chaos of state
repression after the Guatemalan coup in 1954 and again in 1964 during
a military takeover in Brazil. But the situation received immediate and,
as it turned out, sustained international attention after September 1973,
when Chilean General Augusto Pinochet, with backing from the U.S.
Central Intelligence Agency (CIA), overthrew the democratically
elected socialist leader, Salvador Allende Gossens. At the time, Chile was
one of the leaders among the nonaligned member-states of the United
Nations, with close ties to Western Europe as well. The country had one
of the most vibrant democracies in Latin America, and its representative
sat on the Human Rights Commission. A Chilean delegate had served
on the HRC for twenty-three of the first twenty-nine years of the HRC's
operations.[1] Chilean voices, thus, had been part of the international
machinery addressing human rights issues from the start. At the interna-

tional level, then, a particular geopolitical constellation of interests meant that these reports would be taken very seriously.

The international climate, too, seemed quite auspicious for U.N. attention, not the least because of the emerging era of détente. Although outside the jurisdiction of the world body, the negotiations opening at the time at Helsinki promised a "thaw" in Cold War tensions. The Final Act incorporated human rights standards into a multilateral diplomatic treaty and, importantly, sanctioned the right of private citizens to monitor their state's compliance with the new standards. The numbers of NGOs proliferated in the countries tied to the Helsinki agreement, developing networks and coordinated strategies across borders.

At the same time, a similar pattern of new human rights organizing was occurring in Latin America. There, the Chilean coup, which had sent shock waves throughout the continent, was the "watershed" event in the creation of human rights organizations and networks. As political scientists Margaret Keck and Kathryn Sekkink pointed out, the "Chilean organizations that were formed to confront government repression . . . became models for human rights groups throughout Latin America and sources of inspiration for human rights activists in the United States and Europe." It is no surprise, then, that in 1975 it already seemed to an international expert in nonstate actors as if an entirely new global phenomenon were emerging, what Johan Galtung called the "invisible continent of nonterritorial actors." Unable to escape the metaphor of geography, he nonetheless captured the interconnections of communications and organizations beginning to reshape global politics. The number of international NGOs—not only those involved in human rights issues—increased fivefold from 1972 to 1984, from 2,795 to 12,686. A list of human rights organizations compiled in 1981 in the developing world recorded the largest number in Latin America (220), followed by Asia (145) and then Africa and the Middle East together (123).[2]

Interpretations are always matters of perspective, however. The Cold War thaw, with its openings for human rights politics, eased tensions for a while at the center. The election of Jimmy Carter in 1976 as president of the United States reinforced the change; he made the defense of human rights a central element of his administration's foreign policy. But the situation was different on the periphery, where Cold War interventions accelerated, at times with deadly consequences. The mounting instability and civil strife in southern Africa after the demise of the Portuguese Empire in 1974, for example, reflected the direct involvement of white South Africa, supported by the United States. Among other interventions, these two countries armed, trained, and funded the rebel groups trying to bring down the new governments in Angola and Mozambique, which also were providing refuge to the ANC militias. Cold War tensions also reconfigured alliances in the Middle East, particularly after the Israeli victory in the 1967 war. Just as South Africa became a key player for U.S. interests in southern Africa so, too, did Israel and somewhat later Iran and Saudi Arabia in the Middle East. The Soviet Union increasingly was arming and supporting Egypt, Syria, and Iraq. This geopolitical balance relegated most human rights calculations to the sidelines.

Central and South America, too, were key battlegrounds in the Cold War struggles for influence. The United States was determined to prevent Soviet "footholds" in the area, a strategy made doubly imperative by the Cuban revolution of 1958, or so it seemed to all subsequent U.S. governments. The revolution increasingly became communist, willing to export its own brand of revolutionary politics. To meet the challenges, the U.S. government made covert operations a central part of its policy calculations in the 1950s. After the CIA-inspired military coup in Guatemala in 1954, for example, American operatives started to fund, train, and support right-wing military leaders and paramilitary bands in counterinsurgency techniques throughout the region. They actively aided military dictatorships in their efforts to defeat leftist insurgencies and shared a deep skepticism about all progressive movements for change, from land reforms to workers' rights to cooperative buying to movements for expanded democratic practices. The Cold War easily framed these complex and multidimensional struggles as simple divisions between democracy and communism, good and evil. These CIA operations were top secret and often hidden from congressional oversight.

In its origins and by design, the state policy of enforced disappearance also was clandestine and shrouded in mystery; it left little evidence of the crime and no body. Initially, even those most affected, the families and friends of the people who were disappeared, remained in a state of confusion. Only subsequently—and at first through the courageous efforts of family members and the new domestic human rights NGOs formed to deal with the crisis—did the full extent of the state tactic of terror become clarified and documented. But this process of clarification was neither straightforward nor assured; at every turn in the international arena, in bilateral diplomacy, and for domestic consumption, state military officials simply denied knowledge of the fate of the disappeared—and continued to do so long after the crisis abated. The military leaders continuously justified their radical repression as necessary to defeat a ruthless communist enemy determined to destroy the state.[3]

The major breakthrough in bringing the crisis to light occurred in the years between 1973 and 1983. The dating is an approximation, of course, because disappearance has a long and complicated history that extends before these dates and continues long after. But during these years a particular clustering of evidence revealed a "new face of terror" that was erupting in many regions of the globe, although with particular intensity in Central and South America.[4] In these same years, the accumulated weight of evidence pushed U.N. monitoring practices beyond the precedents set by the antiapartheid movements. The forging of new ties between families, NGOs, and key U.N. officials broadened the role that victims and groups would be able to play in official U.N. oversight procedures. It also moved international attention away from its overwhelming preoccupation with specific countries to a new thematic approach, which highlighted for the first time the transnational nature of human rights violations. The official government use of disappearance as a tactic to intimidate and silence its population, furthermore, fit in with and, in turn, fed into the emerging dominant understandings of human rights violations, requiring forceful international attention. In its human implications, disappearance violated an individual's right to life, liberty, and personal security. It was, indeed, about vicious state abuse of power. No one group was more instrumental in drawing public attention to this secret policy of terror than the Argentine mothers, who became known as the Mothers of the Plaza de Mayo. From the southern regions of the globe, under an unfolding tragedy, a group of local mothers emerged to play a decisive role in reshaping the international debate on rights and expanding international human rights law.

Mothers' Losses and Public Outrage

In early May 1977, fourteen middle-aged, mostly working-class women walked purposefully into the Plaza de Mayo, the main government square in Buenos Aires, the capital city of Argentina. A seemingly unremarkable event, it was in fact a courageous act of public defiance. The previous year, on March 24, a brutal military coup had installed a new government of National Reorganization, destroying all semblance of constitutional rule. The reigning junta immediately declared a state of siege and prohibited public gatherings of more than two people. It promised to rid the country of what it called the communist subversives and terrorist enemies of the Argentine state. Following the coup, the foreign minister, Vice Admiral César Guzetti, spoke openly about "a sickness," which had "contaminated" the body politic. Pledged to combat this avowed public disease, the junta expanded a clandestine policy of kidnapping and disappearing people who were targeted as state enemies and subversives. It opened what now is known as the "dirty war," a secret war and campaign of terror against its own citizens (and some unfortunate foreign nationals caught in its net) that ran from 1976 to 1983. In the leaders' calculations, the population had to be terrorized so that it would not support the left-wing guerrilla movements: hence, secrecy and silence surrounded the disappeared person, but the kidnappings occurred in broad daylight, and electricity was shut down in neighborhood raids in order to maximize public terror and ensure silence. In patterns that rippled across borders, disappearance also increasingly was adopted as a weapon against the civilian populations in other countries. During the dirty war, the use of disappearance as a governmental strategy of social control was so extensive that it turned the word *disappear* into a transitive verb in human rights vocabulary.[5]

Each woman entering the Plaza that day in May had suffered a terrible personal tragedy: her son, daughter, son-in-law, or daughter-in-law had been taken away, often right before her eyes, and disappeared with no trace. Eduardo Rabossi's painful experiences show that the strategy had a multiplying impact, affecting friends, colleagues, neighbors, and parishioners in addition to the mothers (and fathers). As he remembers it, a group of people entered the house of three of his friends and "well, they were taken away. And they said that they had been taken to such and such a division, that they were going to some police station, and I went there and there wasn't anyone there. This produces a psychological effect—that's what the strategy [of disappearance] is trying to do, because you don't know what to do. The strategy is this, that the relatives, the families, the colleagues don't know what to do."[6] As occurred in every case, the relatives spent desperate days, weeks, and even months shunted from ministry to police headquarters to city morgues and back again, as they pressed for information about the fate of their loved ones. Repeatedly, they were met with official silence or outright denial that the person had disappeared; they were even met with a countercharge, that the person in question had fled the country as a terrorist.

Yet the mothers knew differently. Listen to a confrontation on the Plaza between María del Rosario de Cerruti and a police officer who was taking her statement before arresting her. He first accused her of being a communist, to which she recollected replying, "I am coming to the Plaza to look for my son." He then accused her son of being a communist. "My son is not a communist," she answered defiantly. "He is a young person who thinks and acts politically. I don't care what party he belongs to because I am not defending a political party. I am looking for my son who has the right to think."

A similar conviction sustained Hebe de Bonafini, who later became one of the most influential and outspoken leaders of the group of women known as the Mothers. In the course of the deadly seizures by state officials, she suffered extraordinary loss—the eventual disappearance of both her sons and a daughter-in-law. After her first son, Jorge, had been dragged away by the authorities (as she later learned from an owner of a small grocery shop in the neighborhood), she remembered trying to reassure her frightened second son, Raúl, who wanted to hide at a friend's house. "Why in the world should you hide if you have done nothing?" she asked him. The mothers' strength came precisely from the knowledge and understanding they had of their children's lives, potentials, and futures. María del Carmen de Berrocal, another Mother, captured their shocked sense of injustice at the arbitrary destruction of lives. She said of her son, "Everything was important about him, his studies, his work, his political ideas. Every part of his life was important, his marriage, the birth of his children, his work. He had so much, his dreams, his ideas, all cut off."[7] In these mothers' conceptual universe, their children had the right to pursue the gift of life that they, as mothers, had given them.

Initially isolated through fear and silence, in time the women began to recognize one another in their endless vigils around the corridors of state offices. Taking the initiative, one mother, Azucena de Villaflor de De Vicente, invited a group to her house to discuss the bewildering situation. She subsequently was disappeared never to reappear. At the outset, however, Azucena coordinated the women's activities, helping them write letters, draft petitions, and search for information in the daily press. These joint undertakings proved momentous. The Mothers later would put it simply: "Our lives were divided into before and after," a reference both to the extraordinary sense of solidarity and strength they received from associating with one another and also to the ways their own families and private lives had been pulled apart by the crisis. The search for missing children took the women out of their homes and often meant leaving their other children alone or with family and friends. Some husbands (and other relatives) were fearful and resentful of the mothers' increasingly vocal opposition; a number of marriages broke up. Even supportive husbands had to adjust to new domestic gender arrangements. The few fathers who originally joined the group soon left it when the cohesion around motherhood proved politically effective. The necessity to continue to work to support the family anyway reinforced a gender division of labor in this emerging sphere of human rights politics. When the mothers decided that day in May to go public with their demand that the president of Argentina tell them about the fate of their children, none of the women had had any experience in the formal world of politics. They were not without political savvy, however. In advance of their demonstration, they contacted the press (only members of the foreign press showed up) and chose a time (Thursday at 3:30 P.M.) when the banks closed for the day and the Plaza likely would be filled with people should the police attack them. With this decision, wrote journalist Iain Guest, "One of history's most remarkable human rights movements had been born."[8]

This statement, of course, became clarified only in time. Initially, in entering the Plaza, the mothers had no other purpose than to draw public attention to their plight. Yet even this goal proved difficult. Throughout the dirty war, a majority of the Argentine population carried on as if untouched by the terror; for many, life indeed maintained its familiar routines. As the Mothers remember it, at first they were met with considerable skepticism by the onlookers at the Plaza. The certainty of their position, however, gave them a dogged perseverance. They had gone public to demonstrate an alternative reality: their homes had been violated, their trust in the state shattered, and their ability to care for and protect their families destroyed.

The junta had consolidated power partly by proclaiming the sanctity of the traditional Christian family with its bedrock gender role divisions as the basis of a revitalized Argentine state. The Mothers revealed the extent to which the regime continuously brutalized the home, eroding the so-called boundaries between public and private life. In their public defiance, the Mothers turned the regime's maternal ideology on its head, mobilizing it for oppositional politics. Their search for the truth, furthermore, meant an unrelenting quest for information. Seeking advice from local human rights organizations and lawyer relatives, the Mothers learned the legal tools to obtain it: they wrote writs of *habeas corpus* and other formal petitions. They also tirelessly interviewed those few individuals who had returned from the prisons, learning the gruesome details about torture, maiming, brutality, and murder that were going on behind closed gates. More and more, the Mothers became aware of the extent of the authorities' crimes. All were at risk: men, women, children, and even the unborn. A parallel group known as the Grandmothers of the Plaza de Mayo emerged almost simultaneously with the Mothers. As the Grandmothers also would learn, the regime confiscated the infants born to pregnant detainees, many of whom had been raped, and adopted them out, the girls to low-level policemen's families and the boys to the homes of military officers. Over the years, the founder of this organization, María Isabel Chorobik de Mariani, kept wondering whether any of the young girls she saw on the streets of an appropriate age might be her own granddaughter, Clara.[9]

In time, too, the Mothers developed a set of ritual practices that decisively marked their politics and drew transnational public attention to their cause. Theirs was body politics in its most corporeal meaning. The junta caused people to disappear, leaving no trace. In time, the Mothers learned the painful truth about the suffering of their children and the children of other families: disappearance was accompanied by the torture of the victim, a brutalizing and maiming of the body designed in part to prevent later identification. The Mothers put their own bodies on the line, with their vigils every Thursday afternoon at the Plaza, demanding information. With absolute predictability, they returned to the Plaza to reenact their histories. At one point, prodded off the benches by the police, they began to walk counterclockwise around the Plaza, signaling defiance; this march, too, became their trademark. Denied entry into the formal institutions of power, whether of the state or church, they claimed an alternative sanctuary in the open Plaza and the streets. To identify one another in the crowded settings of demonstrations and processions, they began to wear a white headscarf (a *pañuelo*, reminiscent of a baby's diaper), symbolizing life, not mourning. At the outset of their campaign, the scarf typically was embroidered with the date of their child's disappearance. The Mothers made no concession to any loosening of the authenticity of facts.

A combination of highly personal as well as political contexts drew the Mothers into the human rights orbit. They brought to their politics two seemingly distinct principles. The one was a maternal ethic of care that placed the greatest stress on family and community well being and on the values of nonviolence and peace. The second was an unrelenting belief in truth, which sustained them in their tense confrontations with a brutal and repressive regime. What they learned about the state's inhumane practices also convinced them of the need for full democracy, an open and a transparent government that was responsive to its own citizens. During those early months of confusion, they had turned to local human rights organizations for help, drawing on their expertise. There were, for example, the Ecumenical Movement for Human Rights, the Argentine League for Human Rights, the Center for Legal and Social Studies, headed by Emilio Fermín Mignone and also Adolfo Pérez Escuival's Service for Peace and Justice, founded in 1973 to provide legal and other aid to Chilean refugees who had fled Pinochet's military dictatorship. Mignone's daughter had been taken May 14, 1976, shortly after the Argentine coup. He soon was giving advice to others in similar situations: "So I said, send a letter to Amnesty International, to the Red Cross, go to the curia, go to see the bishop, write a letter to the Organization of American States, write to the United Nations, and organize people, to form groups. My wife was one of the first to become a member of the Mothers of the Plaza de Mayo."[10] The Mothers followed his advice, sending detailed evidence of their own cases to Amnesty International. They tapped into the new channel of communication that had emerged locally in the early 1970s and, in turn, revitalized it with their passion and principles.

Other possible options for protest had been closed off. Despite increasing international concern with the situation of disappeared Argentine labor leaders by agencies such as the International Labour Organization, leftist politics had all but shut down under the dictatorship. The Argentine Catholic Church hierarchy proved no ally, either. Although many Mothers originally had been devout churchgoers, they became disillusioned with the subsequent complicity of the Church leadership in the regime's crimes, experiencing firsthand how cathedral doors were shut tight, providing them no sanctuary from police beatings in the public squares. Through a highly compressed political baptism, they fully embraced the human rights community. Its values of life and the right to personal security spoke directly to their own experiences. Its framework, too, transformed their visceral demand to learn what had happened into a more sustained campaign not only for the right to know but also for accountability. They made justice their own personal cause—justice in the sense of obtaining the truth about what had happened to their loved ones and, increasingly, as a demand for individual accountability for the grave injustices of the brutal dictatorship. When several of the Mothers in late 1978 traveled to Washington, D.C., and on to New York City to address the United Nations, they presented a distinctive calling card. It announced simply, "We are the Mothers of the *disappeared* from Buenos Aires, Argentina, and we are coming to discuss human rights."[11] As a concept, human rights seemed particularly able to combine a profound sense of family tragedy with an understanding of human wrongs that violated international values.

The Mothers became well-known figures of global stature. Beginning in late 1978, they started to travel extensively abroad and often were given full honors accorded otherwise only to heads of state. They first went to cities in France and Italy, subsequently to Canada and Australia and, eventually, to Soviet-bloc countries and North Korea, transcending Cold War divisions and making disappearance a matter of international urgency. In early 1979, they traveled to Geneva, Switzerland, and met with Theo van Boven, who had been appointed director of the U.N. Division of Human Rights two years earlier (see Fig. 2a). Van Boven was an activist director, determined to make human rights more central to all U.N. operations. He developed close ties with the Mothers—and other relatives' groups of the disappeared.[12] The Human Rights Commission, too, met in Geneva. Why the Mothers found such an extraordinary international following tells a lot about the human rights system at this moment in time—in the later years of the 1970s. It returns attention again to new possibilities opening in U.N. and international monitoring practices.

The Culture of Responsibility

Under the pressures of the early antiapartheid mobilizations of states, the Human Rights Commission, and its sub-commission in 1967 developed new rules to take into account the many communications about human rights violations coming from individuals and groups on the ground. Through direct access to these specific reports, the U.N. bodies were asked to find patterns of grave violations and make a "thorough study" of the situation, consulting accredited international NGOs as part of the inquiry. These procedures were made matters of public debate among the state representatives on the HRC. No longer were such grave abuses shielded by the domestic jurisdiction protections of international law nor were they kept confidential. In deference to sovereignty, the HRC had not publicly named any state in violation of international norms except for South Africa, which it did so repeatedly from 1952 on. South Africa was the proverbial exception that proved the rule.

The original scope of inquiry in 1967 limited investigations to the abuses of apartheid, which became the standard for a possible study of other "gross violations." An opportunity soon opened in the aftermath of the 1967 war in the Middle East. With its victory in June, the state of Israel unilaterally annexed East Jerusalem and occupied the remaining Palestinian territories. Its actions contravened established international law from the start, which in the eyes of many state delegations made the situation a matter of great concern to U.N. organs. Soon after victory, for example, the Israeli government began financially to aid Jewish settlers in the West Bank, Gaza, and the Golan Heights even as some of its citizens, starting in the summer, founded new settlements on occupied land. But the Fourth Geneva Convention, protecting civilians, prohibited a victor power from moving its population into occupied territory. Building settlements, furthermore, came at the expense of Arab-Palestinian homes, which were demolished. Concerns also were raised about the treatment of Palestinian prisoners and detainees and the expulsions of so-called Palestinian "agitators."[13] By December 1967, the General Assembly created a Special Committee on Israeli Practices to monitor the situation on the ground (see Fig. 2a). The Human Rights Commission never established its own working group but coordinated its monitoring techniques with the Special Committee. Many of the same states pushing to censor Israeli policies were in the coalition that simultaneously demanded rigorous international sanctions against South Africa. Israel rejected any intervention by the United Nations as an encroachment on its sovereign right to administer the Arab territories won in war. Even more successfully than in South Africa, U.S. power and its veto in the Security Council shielded the state from coercive U.N. actions. This geopolitical reality has left the problems of human suffering festering on the ground. Furthermore, the limited use of public exposure to the near exclusive condemnation of South Africa and Israel alone opened the HRC to the countercharge of politically motivated actions.

Confidentiality still remained the norm in U.N. human rights over-sight. The principle was strengthened by a subsequent Security Council resolution, no. 1503, which passed in 1970, establishing new procedures for reviewing communications. This resolution broke with precedent by allowing the HRC for the first time to take action on the local petitions by individuals and private organizations. If a working group of the sub-commission established persuasive evidence of gross violations, HRC members could undertake broad-based fact-finding missions and appoint a secretary (or rapporteur) or an investigation committee to report on the situation. They could initiate direct contact with the accused government to secure the needed information. However, to promote a dialogue with the targeted authorities, the Security Council made these proceedings confidential; it returned, in effect, to the older rules of silence.[14] In implementing these resolutions, the director of the Secretariat's Human Rights Division played a pivotal role. He made the original decisions to send the confidential communications to the rele-vant U.N. commissions and affiliated agencies and his office provided necessary resources, background materials, and personnel to coordinate the investigation. Furthermore, he could open his office to the expertise of NGO officials.

But the climate for NGO participation in U.N. oversight remained fluid and uncertain. There had been disruptive charges of political bias in the mid-1960s: of the 206 international NGOs accredited by the Eco-nomic and Social Council in 1966, all but sixty were based in the United States. Caught in Cold War political maneuvers, the NGOs underwent new credentialing two years later. This system of classification, which still is in force, divided the NGOs into three categories, setting rules for par-ticipation in U.N. deliberations: category 1 allowed the NGOs to set agenda items and prepare written and oral statements; category 2 allowed oral interventions and limited written submissions; and category 3, comprising the roster NGOs, permitted only written arguments. Each NGO, furthermore, had to be financially independent, democratically organized, and willing to refrain from "unsubstantiated or politically motivated acts" against any of the member-states.[15]

It is no wonder that these international NGOs, seeking legitimacy out-side the institutional divisions of Cold War politics, quickly embraced the Mothers. These women embodied a personal commitment to activ-ism, without which the human rights movement cannot exist. Their ethic of personal responsibility precluded staying quietly at home, as my epigraph to this chapter poignantly notes.[16] They were going to mobilize and shame others into doing likewise in order to shake up the public stunned and silenced by terror. Their public courage was even more remarkable given the psychological strain disappearance placed on the relatives. A missing person is the "living dead," according to Dr. Esther Saavedra, a Buenos Aires psychologist who worked with the relatives. For the remaining family and friends, uncertainty suspended the normal process of grieving and ritual mourning for the dead. In this situation, Saavedra said, "Grief can't be normal." In addition, many family members were fearful that public protest might cause serious harm to their loved ones.[17]

Emerging after mid-decade, the Mothers embodied the human rights culture of responsibility, catapulting its moral outrage and demands for justice and truth into the international arena. In 1979, when they came to Geneva and met van Boven, they spoke for all the relatives who could not be there. During the height of the conflict, the journalist Guest saw the Mothers unmistakably as the prototype for relatives' organizations elsewhere. He wrote that the "Argentine Mothers had inspired relatives in other countries where disappearances had become a feature of the political landscape and, as in Argentina, the search for the 'desaparecidos' was being conducted by the mothers of the families."[18] By going public, they were willing to use the values of human life and dignity as operative criteria to condemn a dictatorial regime. Father Luis Angel Farinello, a local Buenos Aires priest involved in social justice causes who was imprisoned by the junta, captured the importance of this activism in the local setting. As he experienced it, Argentine society had lost its dignity under the dictatorship. Reflecting back, he said that only the Mothers had the dignity to stand up to the regime and cry out "never forget." In Farinello's view, then, these acts of public defiance were the first steps for the Argentine people to regain their dignity and self-respect.[19]

By wielding the maternal imagery so effectively, the Mothers also garnered considerable emotional and ethical support abroad. Their public persona helped loosen the rules of silence in the U.N. human rights monitoring system. Indeed, their ethic of personal responsibility was a direct challenge to the many silences that still shrouded human rights conflicts in international diplomacy. It overcame the paralysis of indifference. As a report by an independent commission investigating forced disappearance put it in 1986, whether born of fear or apathy "indifference is the worst enemy of human rights." These sentiments dovetailed with the convictions of van Boven. For him, silence was "the biggest threat to human rights." He described his first operating principle unequivocally: "I have always felt that our primary duty is toward the peoples in whose name the United Nations Charter was written and I have maintained that whenever necessary, we must speak out on matters of principles, regardless of whom we please or displease within or outside the Organization." Believing the Secretariat had to be held accountable to the people, van Boven developed unusually close contacts with the victims of repression and extended consistent institutional support to the work of international and domestic NGOs. As he put it, the NGOs were "important two-way means of communication" between U.N. organs and private citizens, offering "indispensable" support to carry out the U.N. missions.[20]

For their part, the NGO networks functioned to promote and protect this activist culture on the ground. They provided resources, money, legal aid, and, literally, international protection—at least for specific individuals who came to the attention of the network. To the Argentine human rights advocate Adolfo Pérez Esquivel, these vertical ties were a matter of life or death. On April 4, 1977, he was imprisoned and brought to a torture center in Buenos Aires. A well-known lawyer involved in aiding Chilean refugees, Esquivel headed an international NGO, the Service for Peace and Justice, providing legal aid to many other victims of military oppression. His own disappearance caused an international uproar. Partly to ease tensions during the world soccer championship match between Argentina and Holland, the junta released him after thirty-two gruesome days in prison. He wrote, "I believe that in my case, well, my life was saved thanks to international solidarity. If it hadn't been for that, they would have killed me right away. And not because I was a guerrilla, not anything like that, but because I worked for peace, for human rights, not with violence. . . . And I always think about these people who didn't have anyone's help, who were really alone. I never felt alone, because eighty thousand things could happen to me, but I knew that people were helping me. But thousands of prisoners had no one."[21]

Standing together with the activists is one main purpose of human rights NGOs. Human Rights Watch has described its work precisely in these terms. On the dedication page of one of its investigative reports is the following statement: "We stand with victims and activists to prevent discrimination, to uphold political freedom, to protect people from inhumane conduct in wartime and to bring offenders to justice."[22] The principled and courageous defiance of the Mothers embodied this activist ethic and propelled the Mothers to international prominence. They became the human link between the local tragedy and the international institutions and human rights machinery mobilizing on its behalf. In time, they were aided by and helped sustain new human rights networks building up around the abuse of disappearance, which was not confined to Argentina.

Of course, the Mothers never had the world stage to themselves. However emblematic they were of the human rights culture of responsibility, their struggle also revealed the many impediments that work against rights advocacy in the system of states. The extent of international condemnation and scrutiny of Chile had not gone unnoticed by powerful military circles in Latin America in general and in Argentina in particular. The Argentine military leadership was determined not to repeat the "mistakes" of Pinochet, who openly had targeted and murdered his enemies. The Argentine officers were very much aware of the new climate favorable to human rights principles in international diplomacy, whether in the Carter administration, in criteria for military aid recently imposed by Western European countries, or even in the U.N. support of Helsinki monitoring. As Guest demonstrated, they spoke dourly of the menace of the HRC, calling it "the anteroom to the tribunal of international public opinion." The Argentine junta mounted its own version of the truth, even employing a U.S. public relations firm to improve its international image.[23]

Junta leaders had a different explanation for the phenomenon of disappearance, which they propagandized throughout Argentine society and took abroad to the HRC and other monitoring bodies in Geneva. Not unlike the South African apartheid government, the Argentine officers saw themselves as a Christian bulwark against a powerful communist menace. They also found shifting levels of support by influential states in the international arena. Argentina was a member of the HRC throughout the dirty war and its representative skillfully used the principle of confidentiality to keep the country off any public list of states accused of human rights violations. During controversy, the play of state interests prevented the HRC from acting forcefully to defend the cause of victims. This limitation continued to plague the HRC throughout its history.

Breaking the Silence

When van Boven took over as director of the Human Rights Division, he found considerable dissatisfaction in many corners with the HRC's monitoring procedures. Despite the constraints on NGO participation, their representatives had become increasingly "bold" in mentioning offenders, and innovations had followed the Chilean coup. The United Nations had not acted in prior cases of military coups, believing they posed no threat to international security. But soon after the Pinochet coup, the nonaligned community at the United Nations began to push for an effective response to growing evidence of wholesale terror unleashed by Pinochet's military dictatorship. These nonaligned groups found unexpected support from the Soviet Union and the socialist-bloc countries concerned about the plight of trade unionists and other leftist groups in Chilean society. The Soviet Union—aware of its home-grown dissenters and soon to face its own human rights movements—usually opposed the efforts to give U.N. monitoring bodies more teeth. Through a newly consolidated consensus, an individual—President Allende's widow, Hortensia—was permitted to address the Human Rights Commission in 1974 as a representative of the Women's International Democratic Federation. This was the first time a spokesperson for an NGO openly criticized a government to the HRC in person. The meeting set new possibilities for dealing directly with the surviving victims and the relatives. In 1975, the HRC established the Working Group on Chile, ensuring continuous monitoring of the situation on the ground (see Fig. 2a). By limiting attention to Chile alone, the HRC still followed the model of South Africa and Israel, concentrating on a single state. However, its directive expanded "gross violations" to include detentions, torture, and disappearance, offering new ways to configure human rights abuses outside the national construct.[24] The sub-commission put the issue of detention and torture on its regular agenda and invited international NGOs such as Amnesty International to submit reports and information on the topics.

Prior to becoming director, van Boven had served on the HRC as part of the Dutch delegation. He had been instrumental in establishing the Working Group on Chile and joined its direct fact-finding mission to the country. Well versed in the HRC's operating style, van Boven was determined to erode the hold of confidentiality on the HRC, which, as he put it, "extended protection to governments who pretend to cooperate while shutting out both the international community and the oppressed people." He raised a set of difficult questions that still lie at the heart of transforming proclamations of universal protections into meaningful and effective strategies. He conceded the need to cooperate with the offending state but bitterly resented the passage of time this required, during which the victims continued to suffer. He asked, how can we deal with governments that do not act in good faith or that abuse the procedures of the commission by pretending to cooperate while in fact allowing violations to continue? He was not alone in having these concerns, and he found allies in new hires at the Secretariat and among a number of states, including Senegal, Ghana, Egypt, Panama, and Jordan, which were willing to make innovations. The addition of ten new members to the HRC in 1980 also aided his quest.[25]

Ultimately, van Boven did not break the rule of confidentiality, but he used the cause of enforced disappearance, which, for him, was a particularly heinous crime and barbaric practice, to initiate permanent changes in U.N. oversight. Together with his international allies, he expanded the powers of investigation in the United Nations, establishing lasting precedents for appointing rapporteurs, special representatives, and theme-oriented working groups. He also developed procedures for working groups to take "immediate action" in crisis situations to help people at grave risk.

At the time, the tragedies of enforced disappearance fit with the orthodox model of rights monitoring, sanctioning international interventions when a state abused the freedoms and liberties of its citizens. In this sense, van Boven helped define what I have called the "orthodox position" in the official implementation of human rights guarantees at the international level. But he also initiated a much wider agenda, helping broaden the types of situations that were brought before the United Nations. By 1981, he already was offering a critique of this orthodoxy, which he labeled the "tendency . . . to see human rights in too narrow terms."[26] Thus, he set precedents for a more direct confrontation with the structural and economic inequalities of the global world. The changes that he helped initiate in the later 1970s were significant for the emergence of the new advocacy networks examined in Chapter 5. In all cases, van Boven's passions reflected the links, which he deepened and broadened, between his office and the victims on the ground.

In the United Nations, institutional change came rather quickly, as Fig. 2a shows. Under increasing pressure from anguished relatives, in 1978 the General Assembly called on governments to undertake speedy investigations of alleged disappearances. The next year, the Economic and Social Council urged the HRC to make disappearance a top priority and asked commissioners to develop effective mechanisms to act quickly—evidence showed that the first few days were the critical moments to intervene to help the disappeared reappear. In this setting, the HRC began to move from a scrutiny of the policies of a particular state to a thematic focus. This step was innovative both for the breadth and nature of inquiry, and it set precedents for future thematic working groups on mass exodus, summary arrests, and torture. Over Argentina's objections (which were supported by the representatives from Uruguay and Brazil), in February 1980, the HRC created the U.N. Working Group on Enforced or Involuntary Disappearances.[27] Five HRC members—serving as individual experts and not as representatives of their countries—comprised the group. Its operations reflected a new principle of "immediate intervention" to stop the abuses through direct contact with victims and relatives. Departing from earlier procedures, the group took firsthand testimony from the survivors and families and also sought to open a timely dialogue with the accused governments, thus working as an intermediary between governments and victims. The group's published reports named the states under credible suspicion of forcibly "disappearing" their own citizens. In its first year, the group investigated fifteen countries from various parts of the world.

By 1985, the working group had contacted thirty-eight governments, although the Argentine representative of the junta refused to forward the requests for information to his government. The working group proclaimed an international *habeas corpus* rule, but it lacked enforcement powers and in its first six years acted on only 6 percent of the 10,000 cases that came to its attention.[28] Its work nonetheless reflected a new international standard for state behavior—disappearance had not been mentioned explicitly in the Universal Declaration or in the list of crimes under the jurisdiction of the Nuremberg Tribunal. With the advantage of hindsight, it is clear that the question of full accountability is handled best at the national level through what now is called processes of "transitional justice." In a reinforcing fashion, the different levels of investigations also worked in tandem.

Mapping a Violation: The Transnational Perspective

The shift to a thematic focus by the working group reflected the nature of the evidence coming to the U.N. decision-making bodies. Appearing in many regions of the globe, enforced disappearance shared characteristics that set it off as a distinct typology within the category of rights violations by an abusive state, although it typically also involved other violations, such as illegal arrests, torture, and murder. For government officials disappearing their opponents, the strategy preserved a façade of legality, internally for the citizens and externally for international consumption. State officials claimed ignorance and blamed their opponents for the chaos. The Argentine generals' response to the Mothers' insistent inquiries was the same refrain they instructed their ambassadors to give to all questions about disappeared foreign nationals: denial of any knowledge of wrongdoing and refusal to deal with the fate of the disappeared person.

A study in 1986 mapped out the political geography of disappearance, offering a number of suggestive points. The report was prepared by the Working Group on Disappeared People established by the Independent Commission on International Humanitarian Issues, which had been created in 1982 with General Assembly support but which worked independently of the United Nations. The authors showed, for example, that cases of disappearance were relatively low in apartheid South Africa (although, importantly, the South African government was condemned by the U.N. working group in December 1980 for disappearing detainees). As the independent group put it, South Africa "has a sufficient arsenal of laws and regulations at its disposal" to ensure the imprisonment and execution of any "real or imagined" opponents of the regime. During states of emergency, this working group added, the state has the power to acknowledge openly the use of "disappearances" as a security measure. In its modes of repression, then, the South African police state selectively used disappearances in times of declared emergencies and did so openly and in defiance of world public opinion. The working group also noted that Soviet-bloc countries rarely disappeared opponents. At the height of their human rights crises, soviet dissidents were exiled, banished to remote regions of the country, expelled, and, as in the case of the Belgrade Six, accused and tried publicly in court. These dissidents, then, could use all the political strategies developed by prisoners to draw media attention to their cause, ranging from hunger strikes to orations and closing arguments during the trial to smuggling out letters from prison. For someone disappeared, it was left to the relatives to use these same tactics, and many indeed went on hunger strikes to dramatize the unknown fate of the family member.[29]

Generalizing from the data, the authors also noted that the tactic was used typically by the leaders of what they called "insecure" dictatorships and "semi-democracies." Both types of regimes relied heavily on outsiders for foreign aid and military support. Observing the landscape, they wrote that disappearances "occur in countries with traditions of democratic government, as in Argentina, or in those burdened with a dictatorial heritage which can paralyse the process of reform, as in Guatemala and El Salvador."[30] They also could have mentioned Chile, which had been unique in the region for its electoral democratic stability. Given preexisting democratic traditions and institutions, military dictators had trouble relying on the courts to do their bidding, however much they sought to pack them. They simply avoided the publicity of trials and disappeared their targeted enemies. In other cases, the authoritarian governments counted on the fears and panic surrounding disappearance to reinforce other military and paramilitary tactics of violence that also were being used to control their populations.

Offering other insights, the working group related the need for secrecy to the strength of a state's legal and military traditions as well as to its reliance on outside military and economic aid. These ties of dependency gave the donor states potential leverage on the country, particularly if its abusive human rights record became a matter of public record and aroused considerable transnational outrage. From the perspective of the dependent state, this situation put a high premium on secrecy—on disappearing alleged enemies of the state.

The independent working group nearly perfectly described the situation of many Latin American countries at the time. Many were client states of the United States. However, the events in Chile had led, among other things, to the founding of the Washington Office on Latin America (WOLA), headed from 1974 to 1986 by Joe Eldridge; the organization, an effective lobbying group for Latin American human rights causes in the U.S. Congress, still is in operation today. Its heyday coincided with a reassertion of human rights principles in U.S. foreign-policy decision-making, which followed the contentious debates over the Vietnam War and the Watergate scandal of the Nixon presidency, both weakening the American executive branch for a time. Between 1974 and 1977, for example, the U.S. Congress passed a series of amendments to the Foreign Assistance Act, prohibiting military and economic aid to any country that "engages in a consistent pattern of gross violations of internationally recognized human rights." Its language reproduced the exact wording of U.N. resolutions. The legislation also instructed U.S. representatives on development banks and lending agencies to deny loans to countries that were seen to practice flagrant human rights abuses.[31]

For a while, the many allegations surrounding disappearances in Argentina restricted the flow of U.S. financial and military aid to the country even as U.S. covert operatives used Latin American military leaders for clandestine work. Hard-line Argentine General Leopoldo Galtieri, who took over leadership of the junta in 1981, helped train for a while the "contra" exile army fighting the leftist Sandinista government in Nicaragua after 1979. Subsequently, to get around the strict prohibitions set by Congress against assistance for military activities in Nicaragua, the Reagan administration secretly diverted funds from the sale of arms in Iran to this contra army. Knowledge of these illegal activities have come to light only sporadically as, for example, during the hearings by the independent counsel probing the Iran-Contra scandal starting in 1986 and also through the gradual opening of classified national archival collections.[32]

New evidence from Latin America also shows that many of the right-wing military regimes began cooperating in the wars against left-wing insurgencies. In 2000, the opening of key military files in Brazil revealed a coordinated agreement starting in the 1970s among many Latin American dictatorships to kidnap and kill each other's opponents. Secretly named Operation Condor, it linked the regimes of Brazil, Argentina, Chile, Bolivia, Paraguay, and Uruguay in a bloody plot to disappear one another's nationals. According to human rights reports, in Argentina alone 118 exiled Uruguayans, 51 Paraguayans, 49 Chileans, and 9 Brazilians were "disappeared" during the dirty war.[33]

In this context, it is not surprising that Latin American countries figured prominently in the official U.N. monitoring reports condemning disappearance. Indeed, when the five-member U.N. working group indicted fifteen states in late 1980 and set the precedent for publishing statistics on disappearances each year thereafter, ten of the fifteen states on the list were located in the Americas. A similar report in 1985 indicted sixteen states and nine of those were Central and South American countries. However, countries outside the hemisphere also were accused of sanctioning disappearances, including, in 1980, Cyprus, Ethiopia, the Philippines, Indonesia, and South Africa. Five years later, the list also named Iran, Iraq, and Lebanon in the Middle East, and Sri Lanka in South Asia. Most of these latter cases appreciably involved opponents of the state apparatus or its dominant ruling groups; some reflected abuses of internal civil strife caused by emerging armed succession movements. Disappearance, undeniably, had become a global phenomenon. But the fact that the official reports centered on countries from one region of the globe opened U.N. monitoring bodies to the charge of "politicization"—of selectively condemning the bureaucratic "authoritarian" regimes in Latin America for their human rights records and neglecting the "totalitarian" violations, particularly those kept in the limelight by the work of the Soviet dissident networks. The Argentine representative made this particular case repeatedly to the HRC.

Differentiating among human rights abuses was crucial for the development of international law; enforced disappearance has become an international crime against humanity, a vehicle to hold individuals legally responsible for the terrible inhumane act. General Assembly resolutions in 1978 and 1992 condemned the tactic as an "affront" to human dignity and a "grave and flagrant" violation of the collective values of life, liberty, and security. The documents demanded that states cease and desist using the tactic and urged them to hold their security forces responsible for all actions that might lead to such crimes. In the mid-1990s, disappearance was included in the list of crimes prosecuted by the international criminal tribunals dealing with the aftermath of ethnic cleansing and genocide in Yugoslavia and Rwanda, a subject for a later chapter. It became part of international criminal law before it was codified in its own convention. As Fig. 2b shows, only in December 2006 did the General Assembly pass the Convention for the Protection of All Persons from Enforced Disappearance; it is not yet in force. Significantly, this treaty reflected many of the same innovations pioneered in the late 1970s: it affirmed a nonderogable right to habeas corpus and adopted "urgent actions" plans—humanitarian field inquiries—to protect victims as soon as possible.[34] Distinctions in the types of violations are not only important for law, they also form the grid of human rights history, focusing historical investigations onto one precise area of danger and terror.

The Relatives' Transnational Networks

Latin American relatives' organizations estimated that between 1973 and 1983, about 90,000 people were disappeared from 13 countries on the continent. In Argentina alone, 30,000 people were disappeared in the dirty war or, at least, this is the generally accepted figure for something as shadowy as disappearance. The strategy, however, had its own tragic rhythm of intensity. Disappearing enemies abated in Chile by 1978 and in Argentina by 1980. By then, both dictatorships essentially had crushed their leftist armed opponents—a nascent civilian leftist opposition in Chile and armed guerrilla groups in Argentina. In the process, however, they dragged many other people into their net—lawyers, social activists, radical priests, doctors caring for the poor, social workers, and students. The evidence gathered since the crisis also showed clearly that disappearance was not randomly applied. Most of the disappeared had been active in a wide variety of social justice causes, but, also, most had virtually no connection with the armed left-wing guerrilla movements, as the Mothers continually pointed out.[35] For the relatives, ending the policy of disappearance still left the fate of the disappeared unexplained.

The advocacy networks mobilizing around disappearance in the years after 1973 were instrumental in bringing the whole hidden problem to light in the first place. Inspired partly by the untiring work and high publicity of the Mothers, similar mothers', grandmothers', and relatives' organizations emerged in countries facing the same crisis. In Chile, a group of women had already formed the Association of the Detained-Disappeared in 1975; four years later, the Mutual Aid Group was established in Guatemala, a group of about thirty women, who carried out public protests, including night vigils. Mothers' organizations also emerged in Sri Lanka to demand accountability for the violent confrontations between ethnic Tamils and Sinhalese leaders in the country's disastrous civil war. In 1981, furthermore, the Latin American groups succeeded in forming a Federation of Families of Disappeared Persons and Political Prisoners (FEDEFAM). The coalition pooled resources, coordinated information, and, most important, helped relatives contact the relevant U.N. organizations in Geneva. A group of relatives in El Salvador, known subsequently as the Marianella Garcia Villas NGO for its leader who was murdered under suspicious circumstances in March 1981, developed a particularly effective strategy to publicize the unfolding human rights crisis in that country. They used photographic documentation for human rights purposes. The members took pictures of the gruesome evidence of the bodies of disappeared people, many of whom had washed up from mass graves where they had been dumped; they then gathered the testimonies of relatives able to identify the dead. The group brought these graphic pictures and testimonies to Geneva, where they found strong allies in Theo van Boven and his colleagues, who were deeply shaken by the weight of evidence pouring in. Speaking specifically of the mothers' and relatives' groups, van Boven admitted, "It was thanks to them, in fact, that we could carry on our work, because I've always claimed that 85 percent of our information came from NGOs. We did not have the resources or staff to collect information ourselves, so we were dependent. They did a lot of work which we should do at the U.N."[36]

A wide amalgam of identifiable groups coalesced around advocacy for the disappeared. In their heyday between 1973 and 1983, these included intergovernmental agencies such as the ILO, which published lists of disappeared labor leaders in Argentina and elsewhere, and the Inter-American Commission on Human Rights, which organized two highly publicized investigations into the situation in Chile (in 1974) and Argentina (in 1980).[37] Mounting public pressure all but forced the Argentine junta to allow Amnesty International into the country to investigate human rights' conditions there in 1977. Simultaneously, government officials engaged in a serious propaganda campaign, seeking to keep their policies on the ground hidden from view. Amnesty International countered with a forthright report. For its overall efforts that year, Amnesty International shared the Nobel Peace Prize, an international vindication of its views in the public battle over truth with the junta. To the prize committee, its actions showed that "ordinary man and woman is capable of making a meaningful contribution to peace." And it added, "This is remarkable in an age when we live with the desperate pressure of the conviction that only the military powers equipped with nuclear arms are in a position to decide, for one and for all of us, the question of war and peace."[38] It hailed the international NGO for saying no to violence, torture, and terrorism and for saying yes to human rights and human dignity. That same year, the Dutch branch of Amnesty International sent several women to establish contact with the Argentine Mothers and help spread their message to Europe and beyond.

Demand for information also came from states concerned about the fate of their disappeared citizens. Over the course of the crisis in Argentina alone, fifty governments, including the Swedish and French, made urgent inquiries to the junta about their citizens who had disappeared. The disappearance of two French nuns, Sisters Alicia Duman and Léonie Duquet, for example, kept the issue alive before the French public for years. A Swedish case had important long-term consequences for international criminal law. Through evidence that only subsequently came to light, an Argentine captain, Alfredo Astiz, in early 1977 arbitrarily shot and wounded a young Swedish woman, Dagmar Hagelin, on a street in Buenos Aires in broad daylight in front of witnesses; she then was dragged away and disappeared. Despite numerous inquiries at the time, the Swedish government ran up against the stone wall of silence. A Swedish court later convicted Astiz *in absentia* of killing the young girl.

This case spurred Hans Danelius, a member of Sweden's Foreign Ministry, to press for a torture convention with universal jurisdiction; he wrote the first draft in 1977 and submitted it to the Human Rights Commission. Although it took seven years before the General Assembly finally adopted it, this Convention against Torture and Other Cruel, Inhuman or Degrading Treatment or Punishment (1984) was the most important piece of international criminal law to be generated by the horrifying details about the abuses of forced disappearance (see Fig. 2b). Its origins combined a personal mission to redeem a senseless death and the strong evidence of the systematic use of torture as part of the government's campaign of disappearance. Besides, the HRC and the international community of lawyers long had made arbitrary detention and torture a matter of urgent study and action. Amnesty International, too, had been directing an international campaign against the practice, which was used extensively at the time, as it documented in 1984. For the Amnesty International authors of the report, torture was integral to a government's security goals and had it own rationale: "Isolation, [sexual and other forms of] humiliation, psychological pressure, and physical pain are means to obtain information, to break down the prisoner, and to intimidate those close to him or her." The torturers themselves were trained specialists and, even if they knew their actions were criminal, operated under the full protection of their superiors. Whatever the rationale—protecting the greater good, for example—Amnesty International judged it an unacceptable evil under all circumstances. Ethically, it was an affront to human dignity and the international customary norms of the right to humane treatment. It also was counterproductive because the victims gave any (false) testimony just to stop the pain.[39]

Demonstrating the continued importance of the antiapartheid movements to innovations in human rights laws and practice, the authors of the Torture Convention purposefully adopted the criminal law approach of the Apartheid Convention of 1973 (in force in 1976). In its specifics, the Torture Convention prohibited the intentional infliction of "severe pain or suffering" for the purposes of obtaining information or a confession. It allowed no exceptions to the rule whatsoever, not for a "state of war or a threat of war, internal political stability or any other public emergency." As with the Apartheid Convention, the law's juris-diction was universal. Torture was an extraditable offense, meaning that the state had to either prosecute a person accused of torture or extradite the person to a country willing to turn the case over to the competent authorities (Art. 7), but it also had to refuse extradition of a person who would be in danger of facing torture back home.[40]

The cause of disappearance radiated far beyond the law. Exiled Argentineans and refugees abroad brought added attention to the trag-edy. Demonstrations at the Plaza de Mayo in the political center of Bue-nos Aires found echoes in protest marches before the Palace of Nations in Geneva, where the Human Rights Commission held its meetings. The exiles had been mounting demonstrations in Geneva since 1976, float-ing banners asking about the fate of a son or daughter. Their questions hit a receptive chord in Swiss society, for five Swiss citizens also had dis-appeared. Solidarity committees sprung up around the country; for a time every Thursday, concerned Swiss citizens marched in front of offices of the Argentine airlines to demand a full accountability. With this heightened publicity, augmented by the powerful pull of national identification, citizens groups in local communities abroad began to form in solidarity with the beleaguered relatives and helped raise money for their cause.

In this context, the Mothers of the Plaza de Mayo as mothers living a terrible human tragedy—the theft of their own children by the state—remained a potent symbol of defiance and truth. Their case attracted other mothers in solidarity outside the crisis sphere, encouraging the establishment of support committees in Mexico City and Paris and school funding drives in cities such as Berlin, among other examples.[41] Although they received considerable financial backing, the Mothers maintained their own independent agendas; with the funds, they incor-porated formally in 1979, setting long-term democratic goals for the country. In 1980, when Esquivel received the Nobel Peace Prize for his legal advocacy work on behalf of Latin America's disappeared, some felt the Mothers deserved the prize and the choice reflected a gender bias toward individual male activism. However, several of the Mothers accom-panied Esquivel to Oslo and shared the stage with him. In a powerful gesture of gratitude, he gave a third of the prize money to the Mothers' organization. Through these gendered controversies over international recognition, the prominence of a mothers' group was aiding efforts to redefine the fundamental work and tactics of the women's international organizations.

The mothers' and other relatives' groups in crisis-wracked societies developed a two-pronged strategy to exert influence on powerful states. With different emphases and sites, these tactics were not unlike the ones first developed and used by the international networks defending black South Africans and, nearly simultaneously, Soviet dissidents. Advocates for the disappeared established effective mechanisms to bring their own histories to the United Nations in Geneva and they exerted considerable bilateral pressure on great power states as well. Given the Cold War constellation of state power, like their contemporaries active in the anti-apartheid movement, they turned primary attention to Western states and, in particular, to the United States as the ally of many dictatorial regimes in Latin America. These human rights groups learned quickly that they could influence government decision-making by working with its foreign embassy staff in their own country. The sympathetic foreign officers would channel the information to the appropriate institutional committees back home. During the Carter administration, for example, the Mothers developed a good working relationship with the U.S. ambassador's secretary in Buenos Aires, Ted Harris; he often attended their weekly vigils. They maintained close personal ties with U.S. Assistant Secretary of State for Human Rights Patricia Derian. Along with many others, they testified before the U.S. Congress and in relevant subcommittee hearings on foreign aid and human rights. They also influenced the content of the reports put out by the State Department annually assessing the human rights records of countries abroad. These patterns were duplicated in other national settings. Partly because of such pressure, the U.S. government halted all military aid to Argentina in 1978. U.S. Ambassador Harry Schlaudeman candidly acknowledged the effectiveness of this pressure on the Argentine junta. Writing specifically about the Mothers, he noted in 1980 that "clearly, [their] persistence in calling for an accounting has [had] a substantial effect on the military. . . . The governments' maneuvers in the OAS General Assembly strike me as signs of considerable strain and even fear within the armed forces."[42]

The dual strategy of pressure directed internationally and nationally became less effective by the early 1980s, when the Cold War began to heat up again at the center. In the United States, the Reagan administration came to power in January 1981 determined to reassert Cold War priorities globally. The new administration officials opposed the attention given to human rights principles by the Carter presidency, which they saw as dangerous to U.S. national security interests. They pointed to the recent political upheavals in Nicaragua and Iran in 1979—the victory of the left-wing Sandinista government in Nicaragua and of the radical Islamic revolution of Ayatollah Ruholla Khomeini in Iran. In their analysis, they found that pressure on the previous governments to comply with human rights principles had left these regimes dangerously weak. The point, they said, was not to weaken allies but to defeat Soviet power. They found support among a growing number of nonaligned nations concerned with the Soviet Union's invasion of Afghanistan in December 1979. As it would become clear later, 1979 was a pivotal moment in the shifting patterns of regional alliances. In the short run, these sentiments affected the monitoring climate in the United Nations.

Prodded by Argentine authorities who all along had fought to keep the principle of confidentiality alive in the Human Rights Commission, van Boven was maneuvered from his powerful office in 1982. The Secretariat's human rights division then was moved from Geneva to New York City. Many international NGO activists bemoaned the demotion. Representing the views of forty NGOs with millions of people from "all regions, religions and ideologies," they had nothing but praise for van Boven's work and role in securing a robust life for the advocacy groups in U.N. operations. In a letter of support to the Secretary General, they wrote, "As nongovernmental organizations working in the field of human rights we can testify to the immense contribution he has made in assisting the Commission on Human Rights and other human rights organs to strengthen the international system of protection. . . . He has also focused attention upon the most urgent issues and upon the plight of especially vulnerable groups, of victims of violations and of those engaged in the struggle on their behalf. In consequence hopes have been awakened among those whose rights are repressed or denied."[43]

But the shift had consequences. Between 1983 and 1986, the U.N. working group no longer received relatives' firsthand testimonies and began to deal more closely with the accused governments. In 1983, the HRC dropped Argentina from its (confidential) list of suspect countries. By then, the junta had lost power. Hoping to solidify its authority after years of dictatorship, the Argentine junta had invaded the Falkland (Malvinas) Islands in 1982, a disputed territory that the British had controlled since 1833. Argentine military defeat by the British on the battlefield brought immediate changes in the direction of democracy: a lifting of the ban on political parties and planning for democratic elections. The end of the dictatorship in Argentina had less to do with the ability of the advocacy networks to undermine junta military *power* than with its humiliating defeat in a real—and not a dirty—war. But undeniably, the cumulative effect of publicity and pressure had weakened the regime's resolve. Ironically, this democratization process removed much of the U.N. pressure for accountability and left alone local groups like the Mothers, who again became emblematic in the human rights community for demanding accountability and truth even from the struggling new democratic states.

Mothers and Transitional Justice

As did all the human rights NGOs in Argentina, the Mothers greeted the election of President Raúl Alfonsín in October 1983 with great anticipation. They expected justice and a full accounting of the tragic events of the recent past. Without a full reckoning and accountability, the new democratic government would be burdened with a terrible legacy that would hamper its future. During its heyday, the U.N. working group also had come to similar conclusions. The preconditions for a successful transition to a viable democracy required bringing to trial those responsible for the massive human rights abuses. Otherwise there could be no healing of the personal and collective traumas.

But matters of truth are also issues of power. After 1983, the balance of democratic power in Argentina was precarious. The military apparatus remained strong and unrepentant. Many in the population simply wanted to forget and move on and let time heal the wounds rather than force a systematic search for truth. Furthermore, widespread acceptance of a "dual evil" theory also worked to promote passivity. This view in effect explained the junta's tactics as evil, to be sure, but necessary in the face of the equally evil threats of armed left-wing terrorism.

In this shifting climate, the Mothers of the Plaza de Mayo remained steadfast in their opposition to any compromises with the truth for any reason. In 1984, they changed the inscription on their headscarves to read, "Bring Them Back Alive." A scathing indictment of the Alfonsín government's wavering course (supported by large segments of the population), it said in effect that my child was alive when he or she was taken. It put the focus on what happened and not on exhuming and identifying the bodies of the dead. If the child has died, who is the killer, they continued to ask.

Such principles led to a split among the Mothers; some were willing to accept compensation from the government and exhumation of the body, even if it allowed the crimes to go unpunished. The majority of the Mothers took a different stand. They brought the same passion for truth and justice to the vacillating democratic government as they had to the brutal dictatorship. The Mothers' position, however, has not always been popular with the public fearful of such challenges to military power. In the late 1980s and the 1990s, they suffered verbal abuse, public attacks, and even beatings. Nonetheless, they have remained a consistent witness to the horrors and have fed the understanding of how important memory is to the human rights culture of justice and truth. Keeping memory alive is necessary not only for individual and collective healing; it also is a political act and guardian against the return to the old politics, which had allowed such horrible atrocities in the first place.[44]

In April 1985, the Alfonsín government opened one of the first trials in Latin American history against nine of the high junta leaders for human rights abuses under their watch. It indicted, tried, and found guilty, among others, General Jorge Rafael Videla, Admiral Emilio Massera, Brigadier Ramón Agosti, General Roberto Viola, and three members of the third junta. Luis Moreno Ocampo served as assistant prosecutor, initiating 711 cases of illegal abductions.[45] Because of this bold step, many of the hidden details about the junta's secret weapon of terror came to light, helping to set the record straight. The Alfonsín government also began criminal proceedings against lower-level officers, many of whom still were on active duty. Despite a law passed in December 1986 that halted any new prosecutions (the Full Stop legislation) and a Due Obedience law the next year that prevented prosecution of officers who were just "obeying orders," fearful military leaders repeatedly threatened the democratic government; several revolts challenged its authority.

Three months after his election in May 1989, President Carlos Saúl Menem gave blanket pardons to all those who had participated in the dirty war. He also pardoned those accused of abuses during the Falklands War as well as the participants in the three military coups against the government. From his weak position, Menem bowed to military power, giving full amnesty to the perpetrators of the human rights abuses and of the unconstitutional challenges to the elected government. The democratic Argentine state could not defend the principle of full accountability. Whatever its role in promoting social stability, amnesty offers neither truth (and the possibility of a full accounting of the events) nor justice (because the perpetrators are not punished). It is incompatible with the core universal human rights principle of individual accountability for crimes. For a society that has been brutalized by its authorities, it cannot bring about social reconciliation and peace. It is no surprise, then, that the Mothers maintained their vigil every Thursday well into the new millennium.

The Mothers' lived principles offered one answer to the challenges of political transitions—and of how to move on. The power relationships in Argentina in the 1980s provided two contradictory solutions: one of criminal liability, the other of amnesty. The big political transitions that are at the center of Part I of this book—the end of apartheid and a post-communist European world—also made the question of accountability for past crimes compelling. South Africa became emblematic for an alternative solution between the two poles experienced in Argentina. In 1995, the post-apartheid government in South Africa set up a Truth and

Reconciliation Commission, drawing on recent experiments with this mode of reconciliation. As the name implies, it offered amnesty to those who gave a full public accounting of their role in the vicious apartheid system for the sake of social peace; in that sense, it put truth before justice. The United Nations has brought this model to other traumatized societies through its peacekeeping missions, for example, in El Salvador in 1992, Guatemala in 1994, Sierra Leone in 1999, and East Timor in 2001.[46] In the postsocialist countries of Eastern Europe, furthermore, many people also have grappled with various ways to handle past atrocities committed by officials of the former regimes. Because of the widespread societal confrontations with the past in rebuilding shattered identities in many regions of the world, the question of accountability became vital in human rights circles in the 1990s, as noted in Figure 4.

*   *   *

The Mothers of the Plaza de Mayo helped ignite international outrage at a tragedy unfolding in their own society. Their courage and conviction worked to galvanize new human rights networks, bringing to light the dark hidden secrets of state terror. They became figures of enormous respect, receiving many accolades, prizes, and invitations to travel and speak around the world. Among the requests was an invitation from the organizers of the World Conference on Women, meeting in Copenhagen in 1980. Reports from representatives of local women's organizations at U.N.-sponsored conferences testified to the Mothers' importance in the emergence of a global women's human rights movement, which began to form after the mid 1970s.[47] They served as inspiration for new feminist international organizing around human rights.

Yet, the Mothers felt awkward and surprised at attending this large, energetic international women's conference. At the base of their politics was concern for family, children, and community, as well as collective values of social welfare and democratic governance. Outside the context of state terror, their direct descendents, arguably, were organizations such as the Mothers of East Los Angeles, a community group concerned with the impact of toxic-waste dumping on poor neighborhoods in North America. East Los Angeles mothers brought the same collective values of community well being into the public arena. The Argentine model also directly spawned groups such as the MADRE, founded in 1983, a U.S.-based transnational network of organizations today providing social welfare and health services to beleaguered communities. These mothers emerged to help strengthen women's roles and, thus, family and community ties, in conflict-ridden societies, operating first in Nicaragua and El Salvador and, in 1992, establishing a kindergarten in

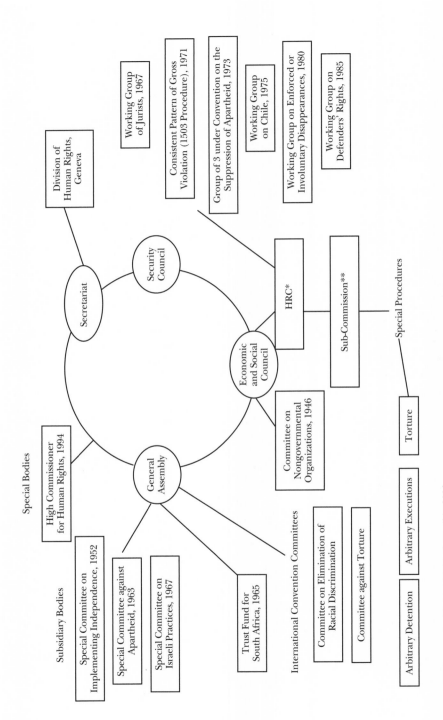

Special Bodies

Subsidiary Bodies

Special Committee on Implementing Independence, 1952

Special Committee against Apartheid, 1963

Special Committee on Israeli Practices, 1967

Trust Fund for South Africa, 1965

International Convention Committees

Committee on Elimination of Racial Discrimination

Committee against Torture

High Commissioner for Human Rights, 1994

General Assembly

Secretariat

Security Council

Economic and Social Council

Division of Human Rights, Geneva

Working Group of Jurists, 1967

Consistent Pattern of Gross Violation (1503 Procedure), 1971

Group of 3 under Convention on the Suppression of Apartheid, 1973

Working Group on Chile, 1975

Working Group on Enforced or Involuntary Disappearances, 1980

Working Group on Defenders' Rights, 1985

Committee on Nongovernmental Organizations, 1946

HRC*

Sub-Commission**

Special Procedures

Arbitrary Detention

Arbitrary Executions

Torture

*It became the Human Rights Council in 2006.
**The name changed to the Sub-Commission on the Promotion and Protection of Human Rights in 1999.

(a)

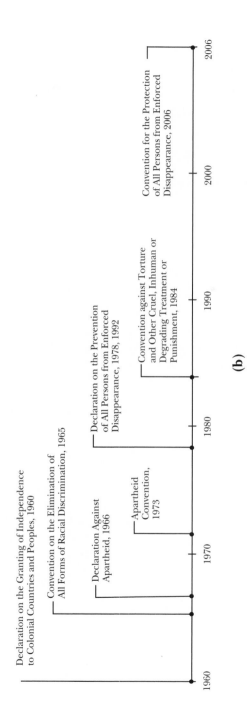

Figure 2. The growth of major U.N. mechanisms to prevent abuses of political rights and freedoms: (a) The chief U.N. oversight bodies responding to popular pressure against state excesses. Adapted from the official U.N. Web site, www.un.org. (b) Chronology of major international resolutions and laws concerning political rights and freedoms. Adapted from the official U.N. Web site, www.un.org.

Nablus in Palestine's West Bank. The group also was active in the historic boycott against South Africa.[48]

In 1980, however, the Argentine Mothers were at the center of an international women's gathering seeking to hammer out a variety of positions on distinctly feminist agendas. Among the critics of the Mothers' form of politics have been feminists, including many from Latin America. From the feminist perspective, activists and scholars point out shortcomings in the Mothers' analyses, particularly their failure to subject family life to searing critique for its gender inequalities and differential access to resources and power. As these critics noted, the Mothers have recognized the strains on family life under the dictatorship but failed to examine the gendered nature of power within the family or the family's role in limiting women's opportunities in political, social, and economic life. Nonetheless, international feminists at the time were able to see in the Mothers oppressed and culturally subordinate women from a poor country who courageously stood up to official brutalities. In their everyday politics, the Mothers lived the most important feminist contribution to political thought and action: bridging the gap between the so-called public and private spheres of life.

At the time of the Mothers' first acts of defiance, a global women's movement was beginning to coalesce around recognition of the gender-specific vulnerabilities of women and, particularly, of violence directed at women in many different cultural and political contexts. Establishing transnational links partly in the context of U.N.-sponsored efforts to promote economic growth, these groups intersected with others concerned with the structural problems of global inequalities as impediments to human rights values. These activists shared dissatisfaction with the limitations of the definitions, implementation, and symbolic politics of orthodox understandings of human rights violations. By the later 1970s, their visions fed two distinct, although at times overlapping, advocacy struggles: one for gender justice and the other for economic justice, for citizens and noncitizens alike. Part II turns to these new challenges developing within the human rights community.

Part II
The Debate Continues: Critics and New Mechanisms

The 1970s brought together a new set of historical conjunctures that challenged the principles and practices of human rights advocacy around the globe. They added different voices and arguments to the existing debates about how best to protect and enhance human dignity in society. In part, these trends reflected much longer histories—of feminist internationalism, union and labor mobilizations across borders, reformers in both industrialized and colonial settings committed to economic development and social welfare, and ethno-religious community linkages. These networks had started to redraw societal relationships along transnational lines early in the twentieth century. They represented continuities in historical developments, capturing the presence of highly mobilized social groups with defined reform agendas.

Yet, many of these groups found their voices marginalized in the processes of consolidating state power and sovereignty after World War II. Under the immediate pressures of postwar financial and political reconstruction as well as the struggles for national liberation, their own platforms for reform had been effectively postponed. If increasingly closed out of political and public life, their advocates nonetheless sustained their day-to-day patterns of mobilizations at the local, regional, and national levels. And, at the macro level, many international NGOs, representing the wider cross-border coalitions for change that continued into the postwar era, established close working ties with the new U.N. organs involved in human rights oversight, from the General Assembly to the Economic and Social Council to the Human Rights Commission to the Commission on the Status of Women. Reflecting grassroots perspectives, they sought to move debates beyond the dominant discourses, which had framed violations principally in terms of the state's abuse of individual rights.

That alternative notions about the preconditions for genuine human dignity coexisted with an emerging orthodoxy should come as no surprise. As Part I showed, many complex strands of struggle came together in the three iconic human rights movements that ultimately helped underpin the reigning perspectives. In South Africa, the overarching goal of the demise of apartheid and the victory of the ANC "led to the subordination of local struggles in the name of unity against the common enemy."[1] These initiatives had given way temporarily to the vocal national priority of democratic inclusion. Similarly, the views of Gladys Tsolo in the late 1970s reflected a tension—and one duplicated in many anticolonial struggles—over the place of women's rights in the shared goals of national liberation and racial justice. Yet women's voices, so essential in the long decades of anticolonial movements, became marginalized in the power hierarchies of the newly emerging nation-states of the globe. With searing commentary, Elizabeth Thompson wrote of a "national [gender] pact" between the nationalist elites and religious authorities that took women's challenges to the patriarchal family order and its personal status laws off the official agenda of nation-building after independence.[2] The construction of the political order reinforced the masculine character of postcolonial regimes.

Discontent continued to seethe in post–World War II societies. By the 1970s, these alternative sources of mobilization in virtually all regions of the globe were beginning to coalesce into new, broad-based human rights coalitions pursuing their own agendas. Working within the existing human rights framework, they advanced ideas about women's human rights and defended, in another line of argument, fundamental rights to economic and social development, including broad access to education, health care, decent housing, food, and social security. These alternative perspectives launched a serious critique of the human rights system's claim to universality.

For the women's organizations among them, it meant a gradual shift from the vision of sex equality enshrined in human rights instruments to new understandings of gender vulnerability—vulnerability that indeed differentiated the experiences of women from men. This turned attention to family life, a hitherto hidden arena of violations. For the advocates of development, it meant confronting the grave human costs of the inequalities of the world economic order, which remained deeply entrenched in the postwar world. Seeing economic development as a collective international responsibility, proponents supported a new generation of "solidarity" rights, which linked state economic and human social development together. It shifted focus from the liberties of the individual within the state to collective responsibilities as the basis of social cohesion and solidarity.

These contributions did not remain at the level of substantive debates alone. The new advocates also formed transnational coalitions. The transnational emphasis differed from the state-oriented and geographic focus of the highly publicized rights struggles against state abuses unfolding in global politics at the time. The first major human rights networks drew international attention to specific states and regions; they mobilized support across borders against state injustices, attracting pockets of backers from members of many different societies throughout the world, but these supporters had little practical interaction with one another. Therefore, the patterns of advocacy examined in Part I did not include confronting directly the cultural or political differences that might strain the alliances. In contrast, the newer coalitions tackled problems on a worldwide scale. Initially working on a global level through the U.N. organs, they came face to face with the many sources of cultural tension and social division within the movements themselves. In addition, they faced serious and vocal opposition not only at the state level, with its institutional power and authority, but also at the societal level. Thus, they confronted challenges from many sides, critiquing dominant paradigms within the human rights community, on the one hand, and seeking to deflect serious societal opposition to their principles, values, and priorities at home, on the other. In addition, the leaders of the dominant state players in international relations saw neither of these clusters of violations by themselves as necessarily threatening to international peace and security. These cases of human suffering were not brought to the U.N. Security Council; they did not activate embargoes, sanctions, the freezing of assets, or other forms of collective pressure that can be placed on states or individuals to force compliance (as first tested against apartheid South Africa). Rather, to promote change, the women and men making the new gender arguments and demanding social justice have turned to other mechanisms, most notably, to a combination of social mobilization and court challenges. In this way, they reveal the state to be a complex institution in human rights struggles. The legal system can be used to force domestic legislative and administrative changes and bring new human rights principles directly into the fabric of daily life in societies.

Through somewhat circuitous routes, the immediate impetus for the *new* formulations of rights principles came from the same source: the U.N.-sponsored work on development which, in surveys, inquiries, and technical assistance programs, extended deep into local communities. The challenge of economic development had been high on the international agenda, making it one of the key mobilizing sentiments of the early postwar era. Its promises readily captured the expectations of former colonial peoples and their new leaders, who envisioned an international order of states that would ensure growth, education, and welfare for a world still divided by huge imbalances of political and economic power. Here, they drew direct precedents from colonial administrators who, in the 1930s, had promoted "progress and development" in their efforts to stave off the movements for national independence. However limited and piecemeal, these authorities had introduced export crops, expanded education and health provisions, promoted women's occupations, and invested in large public projects such as the building of dams.[3] Many features of the colonial states were carried over into the successor regimes, particularly the belief in a state-directed mobilization of resources for development and its allocation to support a clientage network. A similar belief in state planning also characterized sentiments among Europeans turning to the challenges of postwar reconstruction; there, too, a strong state seemed a prerequisite for providing social services and security.

As part of overall postwar planning, the victor powers had agreed to tackle the shortcomings in the international financial and trade system, responding in part to the dislocations of the world depression in the 1930s. Forty-four allied nations met at Bretton Woods, New Hampshire, in 1944 to establish new institutions, rules, and regulations for an international monetary system to manage commerce and trade. The agreement created the International Bank for Reconstruction and Development (a forerunner of the World Bank) and the International Monetary Fund (IMF), ensuring the availability of long-term capital for investment projects, monies to finance short-term imbalances in international payments, and provisions to stabilize currency rates pegged to a gold standard. It also called for a General Agreement on Tariffs and Trade (GATT, the forerunner of the World Trade Organization) to open national markets to international trade.

The redesigned international trade and financial system favored the economic interests of industrial countries. It set low prices for raw materials, putting primary producers at a decided competitive disadvantage, and charged high prices for manufactured imports and technology. Early on, it also intervened to defend the old power hierarchies; among the first loans were those given to France and Portugal to fight the wars of liberation sweeping through colonial territories. Already in 1946, the Soviet Union refused to support the plan and, together with its satellite countries, stood apart from the emerging institutions of a world economy established under "free" market conditions. Divided Europe, indeed, came to reflect competing paths to development and growth.

It is striking that in the first two decades after World War II, the societal mobilizations around development priorities domestically and internationally were pursued with little attention to the unfolding human rights debates. It is as if the postwar era had given rise to a number of separate international regimes: human rights norms and emerging law, agreements governing international lending institutions and trade, the policies of the World Health Organization and its agencies, and the international labor codes of the International Labour Organization, all distinct parts of the seemingly interconnected global machinery. In the early years, there was little overlap in agendas, either conceptually or institutionally; they seemed to be operating according to separate rules. For example, between 1955 and 1966 the Human Rights Commission held no advisory seminars on the topic of economic development. Its informational promotion lay with political rights and liberties and, to a lesser extent, with women's and minority rights. Furthermore, reflecting the closing of democratic options, many Third World leaders, too, put development strategies before rights and freedoms and placed national priorities squarely on resource mobilization for economic purposes. This strategy was known as "The Full-belly Thesis" and set the principle of "one man one bread" over "one man one vote"; it found widespread acceptance throughout the Third World, according to the influential Ghanaian scholar Adu Boahen, who, in 1992, was seeking to bridge the gap and bring human rights principles and economic development together as necessary complements.[4] Similar conceptual tensions also characterized official IMF and World Bank policies, which from the start paid little attention to the needs of labor as a fundamental social resource or to human rights concerns. Indeed, World Bank officials did not even reference human rights language until the 1990s. By then, however, its definitions and understandings were contested by independent human rights NGOs involved in the day-to-day work of seeing to people's social, generational, and economic needs.

Reflecting Third World interests nonetheless, the United Nations emerged as a highly receptive forum to coordinate international goals for national development. The addition of so many new nations from former colonies made the shift inevitable just as it had ensured international attention to self-determination and racial justice principles. In proposing measures to promote sustained economic growth, the General Assembly took the lead and, in 1961, launched the first U.N. Development Decade. For its efforts, the General Assembly relied on other U.N. organs, notably the Economic and Social Council and, increasingly, the Commission on the Status of Women. It also coordinated its work with affiliated agencies, among them the ILO, UNESCO, and the U.N. Food and Agricultural Organization, and dealt with such lending agencies as the Inter-American Development Bank, established in 1959. It also created the U.N. Development Programme to coordinate delivery of international development assistance at the local level.[5]

To conclude the U.N. Development Decade, the General Assembly initiated a systematic statistical inquiry into the concrete impact of the efforts to promote economic growth in local communities. The Commission on the Status of Women emerged as a linchpin organization in this extensive information-gathering process, reviewing for the General Assembly for a while the many reports and responses to questionnaires prepared by grassroots organizations increasingly drawn into the global effort to assess the effectiveness of policies on the ground. Reflecting conditions in rural and urban communities, these reports offered vivid descriptions of the life situations for men and women living in poverty around the world, noting the presence or absence of health services and prenatal care, educational and work opportunities, including the extent of food supplies, housing, and social infrastructure. These firsthand accounts and statistical studies prompted a reevaluation of development priorities, shifting U.N. attention from its previous emphasis on national growth (gross national product, GNP) statistics to the human impact of development policies. By the mid-1970s, these new calculations purposefully linked human rights with development priorities in the United Nations. By 1977, members of the Human Rights Commission, at the time creatively seeking new thematic rubrics to hold states responsible for gross violations of human rights, also began to incorporate the goals of economic and social rights into their working agenda. They began to put forth a fundamental right to development, for peoples and states, in an effort to reorient the work of the international human rights system.[6]

The timing of the shift, however, was not propitious for a new world order premised on human social needs and justice. The opening salvo in what has emerged as an ongoing effort to rewrite the rules of trade and finance in ways more favorable to developing countries took place at a moment of global economic crisis and the restructuring of the international financial regime along more liberal economic lines. With the oil embargo by the Organization of Petroleum Exporting Countries (OPEC), led by Saudi Arabia in 1973, and the onset of global recession, leaders of the industrialized West jettisoned Bretton Woods and put in place new economic freedoms for international currency exchanges, trade, and investment. To pay for the rising cost of fuel and continued development assistance, Third World states took on more and more debt (and this was true even for some countries that had adopted state socialism, such as, for example, Tanzania). Rewriting the rules for borrowing, the international lending institutions imposed new requirements, notably structural adjustment policies (SAPs) that demanded debtor states agree to large cuts in government institutions, education, social and welfare services, and infrastructure investment. Everywhere, SAPs called for the dismantling of the public sector of the state. In many instances, debtor states, which were given little chance to negotiate the financial terms, have been forced to reservice the debt even if it means diverting money from existing educational or health services.[7] With the premium on privatization (and no longer government responsibility for collective well-being), Third World standards of living began to deteriorate significantly.

After the mid-1970s, these policies accelerated economic globalization—as a particular neoliberal creation of free market economics. Globalization, a large, complicated, and politically charged subject in its own right, has become a way to characterize many of the disparate forces that are directly impacting people's lives, whether they live in industrial, semideveloped, or underdeveloped societies. For our purposes, after the mid-1970s, human rights debates and advocacy became deeply entangled with many contentious debates about the character and impact of globalization.

Undeniably, the continuous processes of global integration provided a new and challenging context to human rights advocacy, particularly for the new networks emerging in the 1970s that were seeking to reorient the work of human rights advocacy globally. The debates showed clearly that the term "human rights" was fluid and malleable and deployed for many different purposes and interests. Under the emerging conditions of free market globalization, two alternative uses of human rights language in economic discourse have collided. On the one hand, a powerful strand of argument, particularly for the influential neoliberal advocates who increasingly dominated the world's financial and trade regimes, linked development under "free" market conditions to the promotion of democracy and human rights. Still operating "free" of influence by the major U.N. organs responsible for human rights formulations and oversight, neoliberals nonetheless have adopted some of the same language, enlisting it to justify their lending policies as compatible with—indeed, even necessary for—the realization of human rights potentials. In their conception, economic freedom (which means the dismantling of state regulations and provisions) promotes human rights by expanding market forces. Although the argument was anchored in the language of free market reforms, it returned to the dominant focus on political freedoms and individual liberties. In other words, it was the older orthodoxy dressed in a harsher and more taxing garb.

On the other hand, the critics took as their starting point the values of social cohesion, collective responsibility, and mutual interdependency. The organizations in their advocacy networks embodied the very principles of mutual support that lay at the heart of their vision of society. These advocates added to the values of democracy and transparency the satisfaction, through *collective* effort, of people's fundamental social needs for education, culture, affordable health care, food, housing, and access to clean water, among other public goods. In essence, they have returned to the more holistic view of human rights as understood by the original authors of the Universal Declaration of Human Rights.[8] As such, they also were seeking to push the work of permanent, mainstream human rights NGOs in new directions.

The chapters in Part II take as their starting point the challenges of globalization as they emerged from the high hopes and expectations as well as frustrations around development policies after World War II. Although different in theme and cause, each chapter examines the historical intersections of newly emerging human rights advocacy networks with the often piecemeal and ad hoc responses to the shifting characteristics of globalization. Both global coalitions have had to confront the corrosive impact of neoliberal globalization and the mounting geopolitical and social tensions that its policies have generated. At the same time, they have built extensive transnational networks, tapping the new communication technologies of the global age that broadened personal contacts and expanded the transnational flow of ideas and information.

Chapter 4
The Gender Factor since the 1970s: Universality and the Private Sphere

> Sometimes people ask me if women are tortured worse than men. And I say, "It's not even ethical to ask that question. Torture is torture is torture is torture." But the military does tailor torture to women.
> —Alicia Partnoy, an Argentine disappeared who was returned

With an economy of words, human rights activist Alicia Partnoy pinpointed a crucial dilemma that has accompanied women's efforts to negotiate their role and place in movements for change and liberation. Full integration into the movement can lead to the submergence of women's specific interests and needs while a separate mobilization safeguarding these issues easily is marginalized. The struggles over human rights causes are no exception.

In their scope of coverage, human rights norms and laws are gender neutral, embracing humanity as species; in principle, they extend their protections to men and women equally. Thus, the international Convention against Torture applied to all men and women who found themselves imprisoned and the potential victims of torture. For added insurance, the Charter of the United Nations and Universal Declaration of Human Rights explicitly prohibited discrimination on the basis of sex, using the standard scientific category of the day seemingly confirmed by human biology. These foundational documents proclaimed the fundamental equality of men and women.

Partnoy's remarkable insight complicated the presumption of equality. On the one hand, that it might make a difference if the tortured body were male or female was morally repugnant to her. Torture is torture is torture, she said in no uncertain terms. On the other hand, as an

Argentine "disappeared" who later was returned as a political prisoner, she had been dragged into political life, terrorized, and had experienced firsthand the traumas of physical and psychological abuse by the government. Reflecting her own life experience, the key word in her statement is "but"—torture is torture, to be sure, but the military systematically applied different tactics to women. As she describes it, women were raped, their breasts were electrocuted, and they were sexually humiliated. Above all, the Argentine perpetrators understood that women were the most vulnerable as mothers and family members. Therefore, they threatened the women's children and other loved ones and stole the infants born in prisons and in the secret concentration camps and adopted them out to military and police families. Partnoy knew well that torture took on a gendered form.[1]

Without using the word, then, Partnoy acknowledged the importance of gender-specific experiences in the unfolding of human rights tragedies. Although the point remains morally sensitive, men and women do not necessarily experience human rights traumas in the same way. This is true even when the many other social variables that describe the human condition are taken into account, including class, religious, ethnic, or cultural differences. In addition, some rights violations essentially are specific to women's life experiences alone, and these easily are missed if men's lives are assumed to be the normative measurement for the goal of human equality. Among the more pressing rights violations is the systematic violence against women *as women*, whether taking place in the private sanctity of the family, in a public act of honor killing, or in the specific use of rape and torture of women and girls as a part of armed conflict and civil strife.

Recognizing people as gendered beings has meant a profound paradigm shift in human rights advocacy and law. It has called attention to forms of abuse and violation previously unrecognized by human rights monitoring bodies. It has broadened definitions of international crimes, written new human rights instruments, and has led to new case law. Gender has brought other tensions to the forefront of rights discourses, with the necessity to balance women's new claims against long-standing legal safeguards to religious freedom, for example.[2] In addition, the gender perspective also has altered the agendas of prominent international human rights NGOs such as Amnesty International and Human Rights Watch, which in their origins limited their actions to exposing state abuses of political freedoms. But even in these cases, they had failed to defend women imprisoned for pushing feminist causes. So pervasive is the language of gender today in public and private speech—and the same is true of human rights—that it is difficult to imagine a time when this was not the case.

Yet, gender as a legally protected category appeared nowhere in the foundational documents establishing the human rights system—not in the U.N. Charter, the Universal Declaration, or the two international bills of rights. Its introduction to human rights advocacy came through the organizational framework of the United Nations and its Commission on the Status of Women. These bodies offered institutional coordination and support for the efforts taking place throughout the globe to improve women's lives, whether in ongoing national liberation struggles, in the subsequent movements to rethink a new social and civic order and the terms of citizenship for postcolonial peoples, or in the sustained efforts starting in the 1960s to bring technological and developmental assistance programs to the urban and rural poor. The "second wave" feminist movements in the West, coalescing around the mid-1960s, also added vitality to women's international organizations.

As a central clearinghouse, the United Nations brought diverse women's groups together, beginning in the U.N.-proclaimed International Women's Year, 1975, inaugurating the Decade for Women, 1976–85. As a result of organizing and networking around three world conferences held during the decade, the diverse women's movements in the many regions of the world evolved into a women's *human rights* movement. Hammered out in tense confrontations at the conferences, gender—with its focus on the specificities of difference—in turn sustained the strategies to create a women's *global* movement. Forging cross-cultural dialogues, it recast the site of violations from the state and the public arena alone into the private family and the state's domestic family laws (the personal status codes). Activists who entered this realm of family life confronted clashing definitions of culture, which impacted the day-to-day negotiations over the meanings of human rights claims and the extent of coverage at the local level.

As an analytical construct, then, gender has transformed debates and strategies in the human rights community. Originating in women's histories, it encouraged new international organizing by lesbians allied in transnational networks and also movements for gay rights, which derived partially from an old tradition of rights causes extending back to the later nineteenth century.[3] The gender lens also gave rise to parallel movements to protect male children from sexual exploitation through pornographic media and human trafficking. By enriching social analysis, furthermore, its perspective reframes many of the transnational crises addressed by human rights advocates, revealing their gendered patterns, as in cases of transnational migrations or discrimination based on race or ethnicity. It is no wonder, then, that gender advocates—and the voices of many women among them—are at the intersections of a host of human rights advocacy networks also promoting social justice causes and the work of meeting human beings' basic needs.

The Commission on the Status of Women: Equality, Development, and Peace

The international human rights system that emerged after 1945 affirmed the equality of the sexes. This norm took two distinct forms, which had developed from earlier international feminist and socialist movements. Both forms measured "female" lives by comparing them to and against putative "male" opportunities and experiences. One mode, pushed most forcefully by the international labor movement and socialist women's organizations starting in the early twentieth century, sought equality in work opportunities partly through women's "protective" labor legislation, which accommodated—or so the argument went—women's dual roles as mothers and workers. Special labor protections for women workers, such as maternity pay or the prohibitions against night work, were designed to level the playing field with men in the workplace. Article 25 of the Universal Declaration of Human Rights captures this position when it ensured "special care and assistance" for motherhood and childhood.

The second mode was elaborated as formal nondiscrimination on the basis of sex, the goal of equality feminists. It mandated the equal treatment of men and women in all walks of life in the national and international arenas. In this equation, men's public lives were the (unspoken) norms and standards against which women's lives were measured. Its imperative required that women's life situation be brought up to the equivalent male standard. However, formal equality did not address the class, racial, or other hierarchies inherent in the prevailing system of economic and social power. It left basically untouched the inequalities of wealth and power that also fracture social life. The Universal Declaration nonetheless explicitly proclaimed that "all are equal before the law" (Art. 7) and upheld the principle of equal pay for equal work (Art. 23). Formal legal equality, too, was designed to give women the same opportunities as men.

Drawing on these norms, the Commission on the Status of Women was instrumental in promoting equality in the early human rights instruments and in the broader U.N. agendas (see Fig. 3a). At its first session in 1946, the fifteen all-woman organization—unique in the United Nations for having only women representatives of governments—defined its goals: "to raise the status of women, irrespective of nationality, race, language or religion, to equality with men in all fields of human enterprise, and to eliminate all discrimination against women in the provisions of statutory law, in legal maxims or rules, or in interpretation of customary law." Originally a sub-commission of the Human Rights Commission, its first chairperson, Bodil Begtrup from Denmark, asked that it be raised to full commission status. She faced the typical quandary, admitting that "plans for development towards full equality certainly is work for essential human rights"; she admitted, too, that many believed "women's problems should not be separate from those of men." However, she labeled such views as "academic" and "unrealistic" for the real world of action. The essential work for women, which "covers, in fact, the condition of half the population in the world," should not be "dependent" on the pace of another U.N. organ, she insisted. Begtrup and her colleagues opted for a separate organization in the U.N. structure to keep women's voices, perspectives, and needs squarely on the international agenda; their view prevailed. Ever since, the Commission on the Status of Women has struggled to maintain a viable place between the poles of ghettoization and submergence. From the start, unlike the HRC, it developed close working ties to the international NGOs, with consultative status; in the 1950s, an average of thirty to fifty organizations attended women's commission meetings.[4]

In the first decades of the Commission on the Status of Women, its members advocated for legal equality in all U.N. settings. They worked closely with the Human Rights Commission and other U.N. agencies, such as the ILO, UNESCO, and United Nations Children's Fund (UNICEF), to bring those agencies updated information on women's political and economic status around the globe. The chair attended all HRC sessions that drafted the two international bills of rights and made the issue of women's rights part of HRC seminar training programs. In addition, its members helped write a number of specific conventions pertaining to women's political rights (1952), to the nationality of the married women (1957), and to consent and the minimum age of marriage (1962).

Just as the members of the Human Rights Commission so, too, the original appointees to the Commission on the Status of Women had expected a robust mission that would take them into fact-finding and investigating cases of violations against the international norms of equality. But the same geopolitical pressures safeguarding state sovereignty restricted their actions primarily to standard-setting. The members, however, also were asked to read the many reports sent to the United Nations as part of its broad social and economic agendas to identify larger trends affecting the status of women worldwide (but not targeting specific violations). The commission, in fact, was placed in an anomalous position in the U.N. human rights framework, which shaped its subsequent orientation. It was called on to assess the long-term economic and social contexts as well as customary social norms impinging on women's life opportunities, but these contexts were not seen to be the responsibility of governments. Thus, the commission broke with the narrow political framework that simultaneously characterized the Human Rights Commission's efforts to develop viable modes of U.N. investigations and interventions. From the start, the commission's focus was on the social and economic impediments to women's advancement; it looked at wider societal contexts on the ground. Yet, its new members from the developing world were unwilling to turn international attention to the arena of traditions and customs on the agendas of many women's rights organizations since the late colonial era. Similar to the changes in the United Nations and the HRC, membership on the women's commission more than doubled in the first twenty years of operation and the numbers of members from new nations rose from nine in 1960 to nineteen in 1969.[5] The members struck a compromise position, which increasingly drew the Commission on the Status of Women into the U.N. debates and policy implementations around the international efforts to promote the economic development of new nations.

The first U.N. Decade of Development followed a statistical model of industrialization that measured growth by the rise in a country's overall GNP. Through coordination with the technologically advanced donor countries in tandem with regional and world banks and other lending institutions, the premium was on technology transfers to targeted areas in poor countries. These mainstream technical assistance programs paid little attention to women's place in society, the economy, or the household, as the reminiscences of John Mathiason testified. A thirty-year veteran staff member of the United Nations who retired in 1996, Mathiason began his career as U.N. staff expert statistician evaluating the effects of an agrarian reform program in Venezuela, one of the most ambitious community-building projects in Latin America at the time. Mathiason later worked in the U.N. Division for the Advancement of Women, which helped him bring a different perspective to his earlier work. He now sees the gap between the empirical facts and data deemed significant. As he explains it, "In several of the case studies I noticed that in a context in which most government change agents were rather ineffective, the most effective government officials dealing with the reform were women: local primary school teachers, mostly of peasant origins, and promoters of the community development program. . . . I did not report this in my findings since my colleagues and I did not think that it was significant." Mathiason also prepared a detailed assessment of a sample survey of 5,000 peasant households. It revealed a sexual division of labor in agriculture: "Women were predominant in certain operations like weeding and harvesting, men in others. Women were predominant in raising food for home consumption." When he assigned a value to that labor, "it was evident that the economic contribution of the woman in the household was generally larger than that of the man." He noted the fact mentally but adds, "When I completed my contract at the end of 1967, I did not include those findings in my report, nor did the report of the evaluation note them."[6]

Mathiason's empirical data, which he left unexamined, dovetailed with the contemporary findings from reports directed by the Commission on the Status of Women. These studies focused directly on women's roles in economic and community life. The commission was instrumental in gathering and analyzing these data and pushing the United Nations to integrate women into the overall plans for development. Its work showed conclusively that sustained growth was unrealizable if development plans failed to address women's economic, social, and reproductive needs. In gathering the data, furthermore, the commission relied on its affiliated international NGOs; their members, in turn, encouraged women's organizations around the globe to cooperate with the projects. One firsthand account noted that "women's participation in U.N. deliberations reflected their long and rich experiences in their own countries, dating back decades."[7] Keretse Adagala offered similar testimony from the grassroots perspective in Kenya. "The first Kenya development plan was about industrialization," she reminisced. "Somehow women were supposed to benefit from 'trickle-down' effects. But it didn't trickle down. . . . Women sat and said: 'Wait a minute! How are we going to benefit from *uhuru* [independence]? By about 1965 there was a spontaneous movement all over the country. Women built houses, grew crops to sell." Mabel Mulimo, an activist from Zambia, made a similar point: "The women's movement has been growing gradually from the time of the struggle for independence, though in those days it was just known as nationalism; gender was not an issue. But gradually the women's movement started agitating for an improvement in the situation of women. By 1971–72 we began to make our voices heard and government responded."[8] Nearly the same observations were found in reports from the Philippines to India. With the heightened attention to feminism in the West, key activists in women's organizations also began to pressure their own countries to make the advancement in the situation of women a key component in the state's foreign-aid policy.

The Commission on the Status of Women had brought many women from developing and industrialized countries together in common cause. Through its U.N. work for development, it sustained the focus on the needs of women *as a group* with shared claims and rights. Its role as coordinator also was vital to grassroots networking, increasing the circular flow of information from local communities to the international meeting halls and back again. Its reports, furthermore, revealed both distinct patterns of discrimination against women as women as well as their vital roles in sustaining the household economy and community cohesion. In 1975, a reorganization plan in the United Nations moved the commission from the Secretariat's Division of Human Rights to the Centre for Social Development and Humanitarian Affairs. To be sure, the women's commission continued to be a key liaison body and an important link for the ongoing evolution of women's human rights networks. It also remained central to the interconnections between work at the local and the international levels. The shift, nonetheless, was indicative of dominant understandings of human rights violations. With its work squarely in the efforts to aid the life situation of a majority of women living in urban and rural poverty, the commission no longer was an official part of the human rights machinery at the top. Simultaneously, the assumptions behind the change added urgency to new mobilizations that made economic deprivation and poverty vital human rights causes, as Chapter 5 shows.

The U.N. Decade for Women: Negotiating Place, Confronting Difference

By the early 1970s, U.N. attention had turned to the multiple problems of discrimination against women that dragged on economic growth. Pushed by the larger international NGOs at its twenty-fourth session, the Commission on the Status of Women prodded the General Assembly to proclaim 1975 as International Women's Year (IWY) and to convene a conference of U.N. member-states, intergovernmental agencies, and NGOs to address the global scope of ongoing discrimination against women. The proposal came from the older Liaison Committee of Women's International Organizations, the International Women's Council, and such groups as the Pan-Pacific and South East Asia Women's Association, the African Women's Conference, and the World Association of Rural Women.

The World Conference on the International Women's Year was held in Mexico City in 1975, and, later that year, the General Assembly proclaimed the Decade for Women, affirming the necessary connection between equality, development, and peace. The organizing framework linked the two contrasting goals of women's organizing, seeking to bridge the divide between Western feminists' focused push for legal equality and Third World women's urgent interest in economic development. It placed the need to raise women's status squarely at the heart of economic development schemes and declared both to be critical preconditions for peace.

The decade marked an expansion in the patterns of regional and global networking and organizing that crisscrossed territorial borders. It also led to inventions of alternative communication tools. Miriam Cooke, the scholar of Arab women's literature, remained keenly aware of the role of the United Nations in these developments. She wrote, "In 1975 the United Nations launched its Decade for Women. . . . Responding to women's local and international networking activities, it drew new attention to women and to their changing roles, responsibilities, and status in the world. The decade focused concern on the many forms of injustice that women endure, but it also celebrated the fact that women have become increasingly powerful and visible as they intervene in global politics."[9] The decade also added new mechanisms for increasing the international visibility of local activists and NGOs. In tandem with the simultaneous push to bring the work of the Human Rights Commission into closer contact with victims and their organizations on the ground, institutional changes around the mid-1970s ensured the NGOs a more formal place in international advocacy.

World congresses are U.N.-led multistate conferences of government officials to develop common policies on transnational problems not amenable to individual state solutions. Prior to the Decade for Women, world gatherings had addressed, for example, the global dangers of environmental pollution and unrestrained population growth. With an eye to offering coherent planning up to the new millennium, the United Nations organized four world conferences dealing with the specifics of women's lives and status within the human rights framework, the first in Mexico City during the IWY, followed by the second in Copenhagen in 1980, the third in Nairobi in 1985, and the fourth in Beijing a decade later.[10]

The U.N. initiatives brought increasing numbers of representatives from local women's groups face to face at the world congresses. These personal contacts and exchanges of information continued long after the meetings had concluded. A new set of communication networks grappling with language barriers and translation problems nonetheless made available to a growing readership many visual and printed texts produced in local settings. Known as "counterinformation" because it was neglected by the mainstream media, this collection of materials included "newsletters, bulletins, films, video-tapes, songs, poetry, books, photographs, magazines, art work, [and] human resources," as cataloged by the ISIS *International Bulletin* in 1976, one of the earliest and most extensive global feminist communications networks. The publication reported on all the different types of work and organizing around women's issues that was happening in local communities. Several years after the announcement, the *Bulletin* had a readership in India, the Philippines, Peru, Namibia, and parts of Latin America, in addition to

Europe and North America.[11] Furthermore, these modes of communication fostered closer ties between the women commissioners and other female officials in the United Nations and women's groups in diverse parts of the world. Attention to the developmental needs of rural areas started to bring human rights legal aid training as well as models of institution-building to illiterate rural women. Because of the accumulated local knowledge, program officials could reach low-income women where they actually came together in their communities: in mutual aid and informal self-help groups coalescing around the need to handle personal, family, and community problems.[12]

The proliferation of local initiatives with transnational and U.N. links can be seen in the rise in the numbers of female delegates and grassroots NGOs attending the world conferences on women. The constituencies brought their own understandings of their struggles to the international debates. In 1975, 125 of 133 member-states in the United States sent delegates, and over 70 percent were female. But the innovation lay elsewhere.

In Mexico City, the delegates experimented with a new type of conference that subsequently has become a permanent fixture on the international scene, instrumental in drawing wider audiences into the heart of human rights debates. The organizers set up a people's tribunal, which met at approximately the same time as the World Congress of government officials. Rather than calling on groups of experts and professionals, this "open forum" tapped NGOs and other interest groups, local leaders, and individual activists; it gave voice and visibility to those who generally were marginal to governmental authority and power.

Decentralized and more democratic than its official U.N. counterpart, the NGO forum contained a mix of workshops, seminars, audiovisual presentations, and entertainment as well as speeches by prominent international women to draw the attention of the global media to its many causes. For example, the NGO forum on women in Beijing in 1995 opened its plenary session with a videotaped message from Aung San Suu Kyi, the captive human rights activist and Nobel peace laureate from Myanmar. In addition, the international gatherings of states and NGOs typically were preceded by regional preparatory conferences, helping to facilitate wide participation and input as well as publicity. Regional meetings in Tokyo, Japan; Arusha, Tanzania; Vienna, Austria; Havana, Cuba; and Baghdad, Iraq; in 1984 paved the way for the Nairobi world conference, which met July 15–26, 1985, to "review and appraise" the achievements of the U.N. Decade for Women. With changes in technology, delegates increasingly have established links through preparatory satellite meetings.

The numbers of women and men attending these international NGO open fora on women's rights issues have risen dramatically, from 6,000 in Mexico City to 8,000 in Copenhagen to 13,504 in Nairobi (when 60 percent came from the developing world) to 30,000 in Beijing.[13] True to its origins, the forum setting both complemented and critiqued the work of government officials. Through it, the state no longer had the monopoly on speaking for its people in the international arena. With considerable publicity and fanfare, these gatherings were designed to appeal to as well as mobilize public interest in women's human rights causes, which state officials might rather leave alone. It is no wonder that such a movement toward inclusion also brought serious ideological and cultural tensions to the forefront.

Disagreements surfaced dramatically already in Mexico City, particularly at the NGO open forum, which replicated, in feminist idioms, much of the anger, frustration, and competition surrounding world integration. At the time, the divisions mirrored Cold War tensions as well as the gaps between industrialized and developing countries and regions. Above all, they reflected divergent understandings of women's needs, experiences, and rights, exploding any claim to a universal feminist discourse based on a single hierarchy of feminist reforms and strategies. In 1975, participants fought furiously over end goals as well as over the preconditions for change. The Western groups, energized at the time by the women's liberation movement, stressed women's oppression and, thus, the need for legal equality. Other perspectives, such as that of South African activist Gladys Tsolo, mirrored the heat of liberation struggles and still others, energized by the heady successes of national liberation movements, turned to the place of women and children in economic development, critiquing development strategies that neglected women. From their work on the ground, social and economic changes (not political and legal rights) were the necessary first steps in the struggle for equality. In the tense debates, which participants themselves experienced as "chaotic," the groups learned about each other's organizations, their differences, and their commonalities. Ten years later in Nairobi there was no consensus either, but none was expected; by then, the global women's rights movement had been forced to accept diversity and, most important, had "agreed to disagree." Symbol of this position of tolerance was a "peace tent," a safe haven set up to facilitate contact and dialogue away from the glare of the global media.[14] These U.N. people's forums provided an important venue for serious and sustained cross-cultural dialogues over principles and strategies.

In the legal arena, passage of the Convention on the Elimination of All Forms of Discrimination against Women, popularly known as the Women's Convention, established a common benchmark for global organizing around women's issues. During the Decade for Women, the

Commission on the Status of Women drafted the Women's Convention, the most important single piece of international law proclaiming women's rights in the second half of the twentieth century. It was endorsed by the IWY conference in Mexico City in 1975, adopted by the U.N. General Assembly in 1979, and made the centerpiece of a signing ceremony at the World Conference on Women in Copenhagen in l980. The process of pushing for state ratification of the convention also aided the efforts to define shared goals. In many cases, national women's groups joined across borders to advocate for ratification. The first sixteen articles of the convention defined the conditions that were hampering women's full achievement of their potential in all walks of life. The remaining provisions established a Committee on the Elimination of Discrimination against Women (CEDAW), a monitoring group to oversee compliance by the states ratifying the Women's Convention (see fig. 3a). As of November 2006, 185 states had ratified the convention, which mandates changing domestic laws and policies to conform to its principles.[15]

The preamble to the convention made clear that the members of the Women's Commission who drafted it were deeply concerned with the continuing patterns of discrimination against women around the world, despite the many human rights instruments guaranteeing sex equality. They were beginning to grapple with the insufficiencies of equality to guide actual implementation of human rights policies and protections. The preamble acknowledged that "extensive discrimination against women continues to exist," yet such discrimination "violates the principles of equality of rights and respect for human dignity" embodied in the existing human rights instruments. For the purposes of ensuring compliance, the convention advanced a clear definition of discrimination, interpreted as any "distinction, exclusion or restriction" that impaired the ability of women to enjoy human rights and fundamental freedoms in "political, economic, social, cultural, civil or any other field" of life (Art.1).

Foreshadowing new thinking, the remedies deviated from the sex neutrality norms that require the equal treatment of men and women. From the text and the work that went into preparing the convention, the drafters of the law recognized women's specific vulnerabilities to discrimination, which the formal equality principle did not address adequately. The convention's authors, thus, legitimized "temporary special measures" (affirmative action policies) to accelerate de facto equality between men and women (Art. 4). They also set up the monitoring body CEDAW, comprised of twenty-three experts on women's issues around the world: within a year of ratification and every four years thereafter, each state government must submit a country report detailing the progress it has made in meeting the objectives of the convention in the legislative, judicial, and administrative fields (Arts. 17 and 18). According to Rebecca Cook, a feminist legal scholar, the convention recognized that "the distinctive characteristics of women and their vulnerabilities to discrimination merit a specific legal response." For clarity, Cook added, "Where a law . . . make[s] a distinction that has the effect or purpose of impairing women's rights in any way, then it constitutes discrimination . . . and must accordingly be remedied by the state party."[16] Figures 3a and 3b locate the convention among the other major legal changes pushed by women's activists in the new global networks.

The concerns expressed by the authors of the Women's Convention about women's special vulnerabilities to discriminations in the late 1970s were being reinforced by the volumes of statistics pouring in from grassroots groups as part of the increased monitoring and reporting on women's life situations mandated during the Decade for Women. Many different groups and agencies were gathering data from all regions of the globe. The CEDAW documents of the reporting governments were supplemented—and often challenged—by alternative perspectives from their local NGOs determined to oversee compliance with the Women's Convention. Intergovernmental agencies promoting technological cooperation among developing countries issued reports mandated by the various action plans of U.N. world conferences as well. The accumulation of evidence showed disturbing conditions of poverty, violence, and systematic discrimination that affected women disproportionately. Formerly submerged and taboo subjects in U.N. quarters, such as the practice of female genital mutilation, made their way into the open forum agendas.[17]

Gendering Transnational Advocacy Strategies

Local activists, who increasingly linked their struggles with those of others abroad, confronted the limits of existing law. Their day-to-day work in communities made it glaringly apparent that human rights instruments and implementation practices did not provide adequate protections for the many forms of discrimination affecting women as females alone. This recognition became the impetus for sustained critiques of the substantial gap between the alleged universality of human rights protections and whole categories of human experiences left unexamined and unprotected.

From the perspective of women's grassroots activists in the late 1970s, the human rights culture had developed its own stamp of orthodoxy, which defined human rights abuses in certain ways and raised money and allocated resources for these, but not other, causes. Implementation remained partial, even as societal mobilizations for human rights causes had become a more prominent feature of international life, as in the work around the prisoners of conscience, with the disappeared, and in the antiapartheid and post-Helsinki mobilizations. In addition, many leaders of international women's NGOs were furious that the mainstream human rights organizations, such as Amnesty International and the newly created Human Rights Watch, were indifferent to the Women's Convention and unwilling to push for its ratification. These mainstream groups, so it appeared to women's activists, saw women's rights as secondary issues, a byproduct of long-standing social policies and customs but not central to human rights advocacy. Through a circulating chain of causality, organized women's groups began to think about gender-specific vulnerabilities and experiences to push international human rights law and monitoring in new directions.[18]

Since the mid-1980s, the reformulations of rights claims encouraged by the gender perspective raised women's rights to new prominence in the human rights community. Nahid Toubia, the first woman surgeon in the Sudan, captured a sense of new beginning when she noted, "The language of women's rights as human rights moved very quickly into the national and regional levels at a pace that far exceeded that of any previous movement on behalf of women internationally."[19] It entered the thematic seminars and studies of the Human Rights Commission, and between 1983 and 1986 the sub-commission initiated an investigation of the practices of "female circumcision" by the Moroccan expert Halima Warzazi.[20] In 1991, the ECOSOC and Commission on the Status of Women added gender-based violence as a new reporting rubric for states under the Women's Convention and, in 1994, the sub-commission established a separate secretary to monitor violence against women worldwide (see Fig. 3a). Through its own process of translation, women's gender claims were being integrated into the U.N. human rights monitoring bodies.

The human rights rubric, tested at world conferences and brought back to the local level, also welded together—however loosely and fraught with tension—a vast network of advocacy groups stretching across the globe. The complexity and diversity of its operations defy easy generalization. The transnational flows of information, contacts, and funding helped ensure that local initiatives—often transferred from other communities—became part of wider institutional networks. These ties can be mapped a number of ways, although the pictures remain illustrative at best.

In 1999, Sri Lankan lawyer Radhika Coomaraswamy described the lobbying efforts on behalf of the new gender network against violence. At the time, she was serving as the special rapporteur on violence against women for the Human Rights Commission. The lobby, she recognized, had become "an important factor in international politics," part of societal mobilizations impacting programs and mechanisms in the U.N. system.[21] Under her magnification, it was comprised of distinct networks, collectively demonstrating the extent of violence faced by women in all parts of the globe. It included a "humanitarian women's" lobby dealing with violence against women in armed conflicts and coalitions of African and South Asian women's groups pursuing women's and girls' health issues, including those NGOs confronting violence in such community practices as widow immolation and female genital mutilation. Representatives from North American, Latin American, and European women's groups highlighted domestic rape and abuse cases as well as sexual harassment at the workplace. Active, too, were Southeast and East Asian women's groups, supported by many Europeans, who demanded attention to the exploitation of sex trafficking and forced prostitution. Facing a global phenomenon, these advocacy organizations tackled the regional trafficking networks that defined this international trade in sex.

Coomaraswamy also mentioned Women Living under Muslim Laws, a Paris-based group founded in 1984 that "has made a strong case for including the violation of women's rights resulting from religious extremism as a major area of concern." The group was part of a growing movement concerned with the dangers for rights principles of *all* forms of religious extremism, a topic that became a central theme of the Beijing Women's World Congress. At the same time, these Muslim women were entering a wider intracultural debate about women's rights and matters of faith. According to Miriam Cooke, the Iranian Revolution of 1979 had put the question of "women, politics, and religion on the international agenda." As the first successful revolutionary theocracy in modern times, it challenged moderate Muslin regimes as well as Western nations with interests in the Middle East. Increasingly, for the mainstream Western media, Islam itself seemed threatening, draining all the rich diversity from Muslims who live under vastly different political and cultural systems. It made Islam into the sole marker of identity, as if it alone captured the reality of people's lives and worlds. Particularly for the many immigrants from the Muslim world in the West, these assumptions became so pervasive that by the 1990s they were labeled "Islamophobia," a new form of social prejudice. Coomaraswamy used these women's NGO to illustrate her point, but the group straddled different agendas in human rights advocacy. Participating in many dialogues, its members testified to the dynamic and evolving quality of cultures, responding to the shifting aspirations of women and men and to circulating debates about equality and justice.[22]

From the vantage point of the United Nations, Coomaraswamy

offered a rich description of the main strands of one women's global network. Others drew different maps of these operations. Anthropologist Sally Merry, focusing as well on organizations combating violence against women, examined their procedures through what she called the "localization" of human rights values. This localizing, however, was a product of a wider circulation of ideas and people. Through a process of continuous contact and negotiation at the top—as in the drafting of the Women's Convention—international advocates participated in broad-based consensus-building around international laws, standards, and general principles of relevance to women's lives. These agendas were translated for individuals in local communities by NGO activists, who brought various implementation programs to local communities. As grassroots undertakings, the specifics of the programs varied—even if the shelters, hotline connections, counseling services, and empowerment training programs shared similarities as transplanted models of intervention. To be effective, each had to fit in with the dominant cultural and historical traditions of the locality.

As Merry describes it, shelters in China explained the problem of abusive male behavior as vestiges of older "feudal" thinking, using Marxist idiom; in India, "domestic violence advocates [told] stories about powerful Hindu deities to promote self-assertiveness among Hindu women." The strategies for protection also varied according to available infrastructural and political options. In Hong Kong, for example, shelters worked to place the at-risk woman higher up on the list for public housing. India lacked public housing, so the strategy centered on legal changes to allow the battered woman to remain in the matrimonial home. China had limited shelters and activists relied on the "quasi-governmental mass organization for women—the All-China Women's Federation (ACWF)—to deal with gender violence." In every case, human rights concepts became a crucial "resource" in local struggles, with a power to "change the way people think and act," and, thus, impact longstanding cultural notions, such as a husband's prerogative to "discipline his wife through beating."[23]

Equally illustrative for assessing the dense array of women's networks is a focus on program coordination by a central international NGO, which provides resources, training, and technical assistance to community-based women's organizations. This is the approach of MADRE, which over the years developed an internationally recognized model of human rights implementation in crisis-torn societies; it received U.N. consultative status in 1996. The organization brings four components to each project, which centers on supporting small, locally based groups best able to identify immediate community needs and establishing partnerships with independent indigenous organizations doing parallel work. Its model trains and empowers local women (these also are the "partners for change") to take prominent roles in their communities; by raising money, it sends critical supplies of medicines, food, and educational materials to communities made destitute by war and civil strife (its humanitarian component); it educates in human rights laws both through its specific community training programs and by reaching lawmakers and judges in the countries in which it operates (its human rights advocacy approach); and, as a U.S.-based group, it seeks to educate the American public (its pubic education agenda) about human rights laws and alternatives to war. Under its human rights component, furthermore, MADRE also pays for individuals from its local projects to attend the relevant U.N. world congresses, facilitating the transnational circulation of ideas and helping ensure vibrancy in the interconnections between local and international initiatives. With its foothold in Nablus, for example, the group became increasingly active in developing mental health programs and medical training in occupied Palestinian territories. Here, it drew on its work in El Salvador, where it pioneered, in 1988, the use of mobile health clinics for families fleeing the bombing and violence of that country's civil conflict.[24]

The vitality of women's networks—as distinct mobilizations addressing women's needs and in tandem with other causes—encouraged some prominent spokeswomen to talk about a fourth generation of universal rights, to be added to the political and civil rights; to the economic, social, and cultural rights; and to the solidarity rights to economic and human development.[25] Among others, Coomaraswamy made the case for this new category in 1999. "It may be argued," she wrote cautiously at the time, "that women's rights are the fourth generation, radically challenging the private-public distinction in international human rights laws and pushing for the rights of sexual autonomy."[26] This category embraced human sexual identity and such protections as reproductive choice and health care, the integrity of the body, freedom from discrimination on the basis of sexual preference, and gender self-determination (the right to determine one's own gender identity). It defended against sexual violence of all forms.

The formulation, however, was not a "new beginning," as Toubia had said, but a reworking of women's claims in the international arena coupled with innovative strategies. Its recourse to international law set it apart from the mobilizations for women's rights that emerged at the turn of the twentieth century. It anchored these claims in an internationally accepted set of rules and regulations that challenged once-tolerated gender norms. It also welded together an extensive cross-cultural coalition around these continuously negotiated international norms. As an important corollary, this appeal to human rights laws—as well as the sustained pressure to change them—also helped moderate the views of the heads of mainstream international human rights NGOs, at first highly skeptical of women's arguments.

The strategy sought to expand the coverage of existing human rights laws to incorporate gender-specific violations and it insisted on implementing protections where none existed. In a common argument, activists and feminist legal scholars drew an analogy between domestic violence and torture, approaching domestic abuse by using the human rights definition of the crime to make their case. For example, the scholar Rhonda Copelon argued that domestic abuse was systematic and structural in nature, inflicting "severe physical and mental pain and suffering." It met the test of intentionality established by the U.N. Torture Convention, whether used in defense of family honor, as vengeance, or as battering pure and simple; and it was coercion. The artificial divide between public and private life cannot mask the common characteristics of torture in both spheres of life, she concluded.[27]

This argument has been persuasive. Listen to the words of Kenneth Roth, executive director of Human Rights Watch in New York, who acknowledged the earlier limitations in mainstream human rights monitoring. Writing in 1994, Roth admitted that the Covenant on Political and Civil Rights, which came into effect in 1976, contained "powerful, expansive phrases" with obvious potential relevance for the fight against domestic violence. The Political Convention stated that "everyone has an inherent right to life"; "no one shall be subject to torture or to inhuman or degrading treatment"; "every one has a right to security of person." Roth described how early human rights NGOs implemented these protections: "Despite the broad potential reach of the Covenant's guarantees, international human rights organizations, particularly in their early days, treated these provisions as if they applied only to the victims of politically motivated abuse (and then only if the abuse was at the hands of a government agent). It was as if the sweeping language of these provisions—'Every human being,' 'Everyone'—were replaced by the far narrower phrase, 'every dissident.'" As Roth explained, mainstream NGOs activated the protections only for dissidents and government opponents caught in a political crisis. Persuaded differently, Roth came to believe that the lack of an established political motive for domestic violence no longer precluded its consideration by international human rights organizations. Drawing on feminist analysis, he acknowledged that domestic violence had a political context. It served, arguably, as a form of social control by reinforcing the subjugation of women as a distinct gender category. Admitting that human rights organizations no longer asked the political views of a victim of execution or torture, why should it matter that domestic violence had little if anything

to do with the political views of its victims. "A woman killed by her husband for a supposed offense to his 'honor' is deprived of her life in . . .
an 'arbitrary' . . . fashion," he wrote, referring to Article 6 (1) of the
Political Convention.[28] Although Roth feared the possible dilution of
human rights causes into common crime matters, he agreed that international human rights monitoring had to protect women from the dangers and degradations of domestic and family abuses. Human Rights
Watch and Amnesty International have come to adopt gender violations
as essential to their mission. As part of a women's rights project, for
example, in 1995 Human Rights Watch published an extensive global
report on the range of assaults on women's human rights. Significantly,
it organized the report according to the different breaches of existing
international legal protections.[29]

Armed with this perspective, women activists seized on the planned
1993 U.N. World Congress on Human Rights in Vienna, only the second
world congress on the topic (the first was held in Tehran, Iran, in 1968),
to launch a global campaign to bring to wider public attention the gender vulnerabilities women faced across geographical, cultural, and socioeconomic divides. They also pushed to include gender-specific language
in the conference's final document. As they saw it, even with the new
attention to women's activism, the original agenda for Vienna had failed
to cover women's issues.

Coordinated by the U.S. Center for Women's Global Leadership,
organizers were determined to write a more comprehensive Final Declaration. They launched a multipronged, synchronized campaign, which
relied on the support of a host of women's NGOs, too numerous to list
in full. They ranged from the by-now familiar old groups such as the
IWC and the WILPF from the earlier twentieth century to the MADRE
to ISIS to Women Against Fundamentalism to a Latin American Committee for Women's Rights and to the Asia Pacific Forum on Women,
Law, and Development, which had emerged from the Nairobi International Women's Congress in 1985. They made extensive use of alternative media to publicize the campaign—through periodicals and feminist
radio stations and, in Vienna, offered open access so that women could
tell their own stories in their own words; these stories were further
broadcast by shortwave radio. The organizers also set up a press room to
communicate with the mainstream media. In addition, they circulated
petitions, including one calling for the incorporation of more women
into the conference planning process. Translated into twenty-three languages, it was signed by half a million people from 123 countries. Other
strategies included lobbying efforts at the regional preparatory meetings
held in Tunisia, Costa Rica, and Thailand, as well as the commissioning
of policy papers from professionals in such groups as Women in Law

and Development in Africa. The recommendations were forwarded to Geneva, Switzerland, where the international committee was meeting to prepare the final conference agenda.[30]

The centerpiece of the campaign enacted the proceedings of an international tribunal, which heard eyewitness testimony of gender-specific abuses set against the backdrop of human rights laws prohibiting such abuse. In Vienna, women's groups put on stage their key strategic arsenal. This mock trial done in earnest highlighted both the relevance of existing human rights protections for gender-specific violations and the failure of implementation on the ground. Thirty-three victims gave firsthand accounts before a panel of four judges, who were internationally renowned lawyers and officials. The testimony centered on the arenas of family life, the political sphere, the situation at work and during war, and the issues of bodily integrity. One judge, Elizabeth Odio Benito, minister of justice in Costa Rica, subsequently served on the International War Crimes Tribunal established later that same year to prosecute war criminals in the territories of the former Yugoslavia; she also became vice president of the International Criminal Court.

Evidence under the rubric "family violence" came, for example, from witnesses from Austria, Brazil, Costa Rica, Pakistan, Uganda, and the United States. Such a diverse geography spoke volumes about the global movement's strategic ability to bring together under one common rubric women who confronted local and specific violations, which ranged from "traumatic cases of domestic violence, both physical and psychological, to rape of women, defilement of children, and child marriages . . . and also the question of polygamy within the context of the prevailing AIDS scourge." Overall, the testimony was poignant and compelling, as in the case of María Olea, a Chilean, who fled to the United States to escape domestic violence. The United States, however, offered asylum only for a justifiable fear of *political* (and religious) persecution, so she became an "illegal" immigrant. She told her story:

I escaped my country, Chile, in 1988 to save the lives of myself and my two children. I escaped a dictatorial political system that offered me absolutely no support as a battered woman; rather, the system supports men who . . . abuse their women. Because of this, I was forced to leave Chile, believing that the United States . . . would give me the protection I needed by granting me refugee status.

But, when I arrived in the country, I merely became another undocumented woman, because the legal system doesn't consider domestic violence against women as grounds for refugee protection. So in this way, my family and I became people without a country, because we could not return to our home without facing a risk to our lives, and in the United States, as "illegals," we were invisible.[31]

The evidence presented before the Vienna tribunal documented the systematic patterns of gender abuse and the many biases in national laws that adversely affected women's life chances. It also reported on the patterns of ethnic cleansing unfolding at the same time in war-torn Yugoslavia; the meticulous presentation of the eyewitness testimony helped turn international attention to the Serbian army's and militias' use of rape, sexual slavery, and forced pregnancy as official policy in the conflict. This evidence reverberated well beyond the Vienna tribunal, as Chapter 6 shows. The tribunal, which met June 15, 1993, received good media coverage and its proceedings are available on video.[32]

The cumulative effects of the global campaign shaped the final Vienna Declaration, which was adopted by all 171 participating states. For the first time in human rights history, an influential human rights instrument asserted gender-specific language to establish more comprehensive protections against rights violations (see Fig. 3b). Article 1 (18) states, "Gender based violence and all forms of sexual harassment and exploitation, including those resulting from cultural prejudices and international trafficking, are incompatible with the dignity and worth of the human person, and must be eliminated." The article explicitly protects people from sexual harassment and gender-based violence. It confronts directly the use of cultural and religious traditions to exempt specific customs and practices from international debate as well as from the full force of international law. The authors confronted what they called "cultural prejudice," those traditions that harmed women specifically and restricted their options in life. Under the prodding of women's mobilizations, the declaration stepped into the sphere of family codes and religious traditions and laws that govern many aspects of women's lives around the world. It declares these spheres in principle no longer off limits to the universal applicability of human rights laws. The step in many ways culminated the conceptual and strategic breakthroughs that had been developing from the first efforts of the Commission on the Status of Women to promote women's rights in the U.N. agenda. It also has proven controversial.

Gender and Culture

By opening the possibility of declaring some cultural traditions as prejudicial to the international agreement on universal standards, the Vienna Declaration moved toward more comprehensive human rights coverage. On the level of principle, it met a number of the critiques pushed most vocally by international activists in the global women's movement. Internationally, it strengthened their resolve to debate the validity of a range of cultural practices directly impinging on women's life chances in multiple geographic settings. But it also meant confronting the challenge that cultural relativists pose for a universal rights system.

Cultural relativism is not bound to any one geographical place; it is a philosophical position that argues for the absolute moral authority of each separate culture. Its adherents see culture as the "sole source of the validity of a moral right or rule" and maintain that no one from the outside can judge the legitimacy of cultural practices. They reject any notion of universalism, as in a common standard of rights guarantees for all.[33] Rarely are the positions so abstractly stated, however: they are powerful mobilizing sentiments at the root of a defense of a particular collective identity. Other arguments against universal claims, notably the appeal to domestic jurisdiction and state sovereignty, were used as well by officials in South Africa and Argentina during the conflicts over apartheid and the fate of the disappeared, respectively. In their concrete impact, the struggles around rights, including the women's mobilizations, have meant continuing expansion of the norms and rules safeguarding fundamental human rights.

Yet, this intrusion into the sovereignty of the state through lawmaking powers has been met by vocal opposition, often on cultural grounds. In many postcolonial states, it has mobilized powerful memories of colonial domination, when foreign administrators used the powers of the law (and its language of rights) to abolish cultural practices they deemed "uncivilized" and "savage" (e.g., female circumcision). In the age of great power imperialism, colonial officials had stood behind the inherent justice of law. South Asian jurist and human rights critic Ashis Nandy reflects the sentiments among many scholars, officials, and publicists in former colonial territories, who are suspicious of legal traditions. The problem lay, in Nandy's view, in the disjuncture between the customs and values in indigenous cultures and the colonial inheritances of the modern nation-states. "The law is the central instrument in the colonial process that aims at erasing traditions and plurality and restructuring civil society along modern lines," he noted.[34] With legal homogenization, reinforced by international law, Nandy feared for the survival of distinct local cultures. Furthermore, historically, notions of culture often provided an effective source of local authority and strength. For example, during the protracted struggles for national liberation against colonial rule in the 1950s and 1960s, a defense of culture mobilized resistance and underpinned "new" political identities. In this setting, reconstructing so-called authentic cultural traditions helped to define the very groups fighting against colonial domination. In both examples, appeals to "culture" have served as a valid source of political and national identity.

Neither "culture" nor the presumed impartiality of the law have been unambiguous for women's position in social and political life, however. Feminist scholarship has shown, for example, that British colonial inher-

itance laws in South Asia deprived rural ethnic Tamil women of customary rights to land and resources and the process was duplicated
elsewhere. Similarly, nationalist movements against colonialism in the
name of culture—notably in the cases of India and Korea—turned
against indigenous middle-class women's movements as "inauthentic"
and "diversionary." In these liberation contexts, the struggles for wom-
en's rights often were dismissed derisively as Western imperialist impor-
tations. This discursive position did not incorporate women's own
experiences or bring their voices into the search for a new identity. In
Korea, ironically, nationalist movements (against Japanese colonial
domination) and imperial Japanese administrators even colluded in
opposing middle-class and literary women's efforts at female emancipa-
tion.[35]

The cultural arguments against universalism have become more insistent since the 1970s. Their intensity arguably is tied to the continuing
challenges of economic and technological globalization and to the
growing power of the global media to suggest consumption as a powerful source of value. Although cultural relativists have burst onto the
human rights scene dramatically on occasion—witness the vitriolic and
highly publicized debates over so-called Asian values that erupted at
international meetings and U.N. world conferences between 1991 and
1995—the most sustained and systematic use of culture to defend
against common human rights standards and values has emerged in the
debates about, and in the daily organizing around, issues of women's
lives and gender equity.[36] The tensions between universal human rights
norms and distinctive cultural practices become magnified when antagonists see the traditional and customary roles of women as integral to
their own sense of national, religious, or ethnic identity. In these contexts, then, efforts to change women's status are seen to threaten the
foundations of such national or group culture. It is not surprising, then,
that women's NGOs—and also gay and lesbian activists—working for
gender equity in local settings have confronted this cultural critique
most directly.

Emerging from a period of confrontation initiated at world conferences during the Decade for Women, women's networks established
ongoing patterns of cross-cultural collaboration. Coomaraswamy
showed how effective these groups were internationally, lobbying on
behalf of shared causes. These ongoing exchanges helped mitigate the
danger of an uncompromising universalism or the promotion of a single
emancipatory path reflecting the values of one tradition alone. Powerful
women such as Gladys Tsolo and other Third World activists ensured
dialogue with Western feminists and the increasing acceptance of multiple paths. The first effort to raise the issue of customary practices at early

U.N. women's conferences had led to mutual suspicion and recrimination. Gradually, it opened a new front in women's mobilizing, an *intra-cultural* push for change, similar to that taking place in the discussions around women and faith in Islam. In this context, the prime catalysts for change become the community activists and NGOs as well as converted elders, health practitioners, legislators, and leaders in local, national, and regional contexts.

This avenue for change complicates the presumption of an unbridgeable divide between universal values and cultural traditions. In their day-to-day activities on the ground, women activists have defined and refined strategies that, in practice, bring universal norms to bear on specific abuses yet simultaneously affirm the importance of positive cultural markers. The guidelines of one prominent NGO, RAINB♀, working to eliminate the practice of female genital mutilation (FGM) in many African and African-immigrant communities, reflect this slow, consensual approach to societal transformation. As its leaders put it, the group "calls upon all peoples of all nations to come together in empathy, solidarity and compassion, to create an environment where people feel safe to change their old ways without threat to their dignity, independence and cultural integrity."[37] Through broad-based institutional support, this organization encourages changes without undermining the positive bases of people's own identities. The process of change, however, is difficult to map; for every new gain, there is, appreciably, continued, renewed, or even new abuse.

Among the many gender advocacy networks, the coalitions working to combat the practice of FGM offer a particularly compelling test case to assess the intra-cultural efforts to promote gender change—as well as the many impediments to it. FGM was one of the customary practices deemed "harmful" at the Vienna World Congress on Human Rights.[38] African women's organizations working in global concert have taken the lead in eradicating the practice of FGM, including by sponsoring comprehensive programs among African immigrant communities in Europe, Great Britain, Australia, Canada, and the United States. The practice, furthermore, challenges the intellectual arsenal typically used by women's gender networks to counter the cultural relativists' arguments. Of the so-called customs and traditions said to require exemption from universal standards, the activists ask: What creates the "cultural authenticity" to which human rights values should be relative? Who is authorized to speak for a particular culture? Are the voices of the victims heard in the debate? In the case of FGM, women are not simply "victims" (of male violence, as in a situation of domestic abuse). One western Sudanese woman, Hawa, confessed, "I would like my daughter to escape circumcision but I can't change this old practice. Even if I refused, my mother would never allow her to stay uncut."[39] The answers to these questions are complicated because FGM is embedded in women's traditional identities as healers, mothers, and daughters. With women's active participation, it denotes the contested boundaries of societal control over the female body.

FGM is a rite of passage that marks female initiation into womanhood through various degrees of cutting of the female genitals. It is a rite preparing a young girl for marriage. In poor communities with limited opportunities for education or work, marriage is vital to a woman's survival; it also is central to community life. With wide variations in timing, in most cases the girl is between 10 and 16 years old when the ritual is performed; typically it is done in secret away from the village by a female practitioner and without anesthesia. Historically, the practice was found nearly exclusively along a large swath of territory throughout the middle of Africa. With labor migrations and refugee movements, it has been brought to other regions of the globe as well. In 1994, Nahid Toubia estimated that there were about 130 million women alive who had undergone the procedure.[40]

The subject remained off limits to human rights discussions for decades, partly because it was a gender-specific issue and fell outside the equality perspective and partly because older hostilities from the era of European colonial rule also made the topic taboo. Customs such as FGM—and also widow-burning (*suttee*) and seclusion (*purdah*)—were used to justify in the name of "civilization" the imposition of European colonial rule in Africa and also in south and southeast Asia during the second half of the nineteenth century. Despite the efforts of colonial rulers and missionaries to outlaw female genital operations, the rite continued because it remained essential to gendered understandings of marriage, family, sexuality, and femininity. Although its origins predated the birth of Islam, many imams drew on passages of the Koran and Islamic law to sanctify the custom. Similarly, some African Christian churches declared their independence from Catholic and Protestant missionaries partly by defending the practice as symbolic of authentic indigenous culture. Its survival, then, became synonymous with the survival of the oppressed people.[41]

Since the mid-1980s, in opposing the rite as a human rights violation, African women's groups have initiated a number of interrelated strategies. Part of a campaign of longer duration, they increasingly draw on transnational and international resources strongly opposing the practice. The groups have established continent-wide coordination through the Inter-African Committee on Traditional Practices Affecting the Health of Women and Children (IAC). Armed with the international laws and resolutions on the right to life, bodily integrity and health, and the rights of the child, as well as freedom from violence and discrimination, its national branches engage in human rights and health lobbying at the level of parliament, the judiciary, and the police. These national activists, through translated forms, make available for wide dissemination the pamphlets, brochures, and other documentary evidence of the international consensus against the practice. Partly as a result of this pressure, fourteen countries in Africa criminalized the practice of FGM by 2004. State bans indeed are part of the organized women's strategies.[42] But laws alone, as the colonial era showed unmistakably, are not able to negotiate changes at the level of family life and sexual identity.

Most strategies are community based, bringing change slowly through face-to-face conversion. They reflect the interlinking of local initiatives with international organizations that provide coordination, funding, and training as well as programs, policies, and strategies tested and refined in different settings. This approach characterizes the work of WOMANKIND Worldwide, an international British-based charitable organization founded in 1989 developing community programs to address the many needs of women in poorer societies. Duplicating the MADRE model, its Kenya branch has had some success in changing attitudes among female cutters, even though, as one confessed, people in the community "denounced" her and some imams "smear[ed] her name in some mosques." In turn, supported by Equality Now, a New York–based global advocacy NGO, WOMANKIND organized an international conference for reformed cutters in Nairobi in 2004. Designed to reinforce the work of reform, the gathering offered psychological and material support and options about training for other ways to make a living.[43] Many local activists see these expansive ties as strategic to their own causes. Amna Hassan, working with WOMANKIND to end FGM in Sudan, explained, "A major stumbling block in Sudan is the attitude of religious leaders. We went to the head of the Sudan's religious advisory division, asking for a decree against all forms of FGM, but they refused. We faced severe aggression and insults from some of them. We are trying hard to change their minds, and being part of WOMANKIND's programme is helping to bring other countries' experience into our arguments."[44]

In Ethiopia, WOMANKIND relies on the work of the Kembata Women's Self-Help Center (the Kembatti Mentti Gezzima-Tope, or KMG), located in Durame, the main town in the southern Kembata zone of Ethiopia. Kembata is both a geographical unit and a linguistic group, a recognized "nation" in the ethnic federal structure that has organized the Ethiopian state since 1991. Populated by people of the Islamic and Christian religions, Kembata has the highest population density in Ethiopia, with 277 people per square kilometer (while the average density in the country is 63 people per square kilometer). In 2000, Kembata's population was about 466,000 people of the 1.2 million in the larger zone. Population growth and landholding fragmentation have degraded the soil, safe water is scarce, grazing forestlands are vanishing, and severe poverty is endemic. The people's traditional solution—the seasonal migration of male labor to jobs elsewhere in Ethiopia—has ceased because of the federal government's recent policies of restricting inter-regional migration to the "home" area alone. Increasing numbers of young men are crossing national borders for work. Despite its green landscape—the major staple crop is *enset* (a banana-like food)—Kembata faces a "green famine."[45]

Ethnographic evidence generally from around Africa shows that the key predictor of the custom of female cutting is ethnicity or cultural group affiliation. The Kembata people historically practiced the rite, affecting 90 percent of the female population. It corresponded to the centrality of community life for adult development or "becoming." The rite made a young girl a part of the mature community and is seen to offer further protection from threats to community cohesion. Bridging individual and community values, Kembata society nonetheless is hierarchical and unequal, resting on gender, occupational, and wealth divisions. Other survey evidence, particularly from women's perspectives among the ethnic "nations" of Eastern Ethiopia, revealed the pervasive belief that "if men openly stated a preference to marry women who were uncircumcised, FGM would probably cease."[46] The practice is open to change.

The work of the KMG opens a number of critical lenses into the processes of gender change; it also shows that gender-specific advocacy, for maximum effect, dovetails with grave community needs—in this case for resource management and infrastructural support for sustained development. The center was founded in 1997 by Bogaletch Gebre, a native to the area. Simultaneously an international and local figure, Gebre has received wide acclaim in the women's human rights community; she is a sought-after lecturer and recipient of many awards. Her center, too, plays a key role as a vibrant link to the diasporic community (many of whose Web sites are shut down in Ethiopia). It also participates in the ongoing national dialogue over land reform, providing valuable baseline and household survey information in a country notoriously negligent in census-taking and record-keeping. In this way, it keeps the focus on women's rights to access valuable social resources.[47]

Gebre was one of the first girls in her village to be educated beyond the fourth grade, at a missionary school nearby; she eventually studied epidemiology in Israel and the United States. At a young age, Gebre had undergone the mutilation ritual. Involved later in medical and educa-

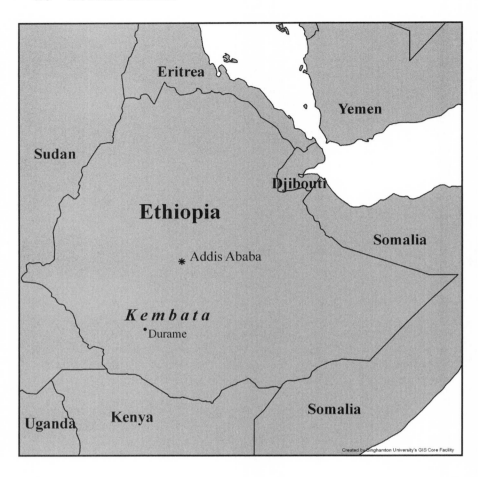

Map 5. The Kembata region of Ethiopia.

tional advocacy, she was determined to found an NGO to combat FGM, which, as she put it, was "physically and psychologically numbing. . . . I realized that what they really wanted to excise was my brain. It didn't work," she added.[48] While most local people do not see the FGM ritual as a human rights issue, Gebre is bringing rights talk to the community.

Building on her local reputation, Gebre launched her appeal at her childhood church, asking, "Do we think we know better than God what our bodies should look like? Where in the Bible is it written that we should do this?" Fundamentally geared to improving women's lot, whose fate still was to "carry water long distances, gather firewood, and prepare food," the organization sets the problem of women's lives and status in the wider needs of the community. It adopts a gendered approach, working with women and men to develop and test viable solutions. If improving women's life opportunities is the linchpin, the KMG implements three interrelated programs that tackle health and reproductive education, work opportunities in and outside agriculture, and the environment, under increasing threat from soil erosion and deforestation. It takes its educational campaign for women's health into the schools, churches, mosques, and community centers and shows videos hooked up to car generators of genital cutting to men living in remote communities. "Because FGM is typically carried out secretively and the girls are gagged to muffle their screams, many men have no idea of its severity." The group also has begun to help train former cutters to work as health practitioners in the AIDS crisis.

Although affecting all in the community, the degradation of the environment from the destruction of the forests and the threats to the water supplies was particularly hard on women, responsible for growing and processing food on small plots of land. It also threatened community existence. As Gebre put it, "Our people, especially the elders, feel these losses. . . . They feel especially the deforestation of Hamboricho Mountain, which was forested even when I was young. Now, it is growing bald from the bottom of the hill up." Drawing on former customs, she built a traditional roundhouse. Once, it had organized community life "according to gender with two sides: one for women and children and milking cows, the other for men and guests and animals they valued most, such as oxen and horses." In 2002, Gebre invited 300 men and women elders and, appealing to folk knowledge of the local flora, began a successful project to replant the landscape. This roundhouse subsequently became the center for community conversations, addressing the many other threats to community survival, including the scourge of AIDS. As a community organization, furthermore, KMG has worked to preserve local languages, several of which existed mainly in oral form.[49]

In the most dramatic gesture of change, the KMG in 2002 put on a marriage ceremony of two young staff members. The bride, Genot Girme (along with 4,000 girls in the area) earlier had taken a pledge to marry uncut; her groom, Adissie Abossie "strongly opposed" the ritual. The couple asked 317 girls to be bridesmaids, all uncut girls in the village, and the husband, along with his bridegrooms, affirmed to marry only women who had not undergone the ritual. Two thousand people showed up to celebrate. The national media covered the wedding ceremony in all major Ethiopian languages, bringing the subject into national debate—and attracting international attention. Uncensored by the government, this ceremony appreciably corresponded to official policy (FGM was banned by the government in 1994), which simultaneously was cracking down on local political opposition movements in the zone. Subsequently, Tafessa Jaara also reported interviewing couples from outside the region "who told me that they got married uncut, following the example of Kembatta women." An official report by WOMANKIND in 2003 offered a highly positive although cautious assessment of the anti-FGM work of the KMG; it was having an "extraordinary effect," helping to eradicate the practice in the southern zone, although the authors also admitted that resistance to change still "is strong."[50] Other sources have cataloged changing attitudes among practitioners but also recognize the continuing barriers to economic and educational gains for the women of Kembata: ongoing discrimination in employment and land acquisition and official neglect to translate human rights guarantees into statutory law. Equally to the point, Gebre acknowledged the community-specific nature of change: what works in one group may not be effective in another. As she put it simply, "Change must come from within" the community.

The social evidence from this one region of Ethiopia offers an unusual insight into the many layers of human rights advocacy. As evidenced by her speeches, many tours, and publications, Gebre is an active member of the women's human rights movement, sustained by and, in turn, essential to its work. But the people whom she reached did not necessarily embrace human rights, or at least its modernist core, with its commitment to law and state responsibility for eradicating abuse. Human rights values of empowerment and equality worked in tandem with other objectives and concerns. Examining the abuse of battering, Sally Merry came to a similar conclusion. As she showed, human rights were "crucial resources" in local contexts but not the only ones: victim understandings were complex and they continued to bring, for example, a belief in kinship obligations to their sense of injustice and wrong. Assessing another case of struggle over indigenous women's inheritance rights in Hong Kong in 1994, Merry showed that "it was not necessary for the rural women to have a deep commitment to human rights, since other parts of the movement translated global human rights approaches into the vernacular."[51] In expanding her organization's reach, Gebre enlisted the values and knowledge of local oral customs and gendered traditions. Yet her challenging marriage ceremony showed that gender change also broke with traditional ideas about hierarchy and inequality. Thus, she brought a new, if precarious, balance between universalist principles and the values of a local culture.

Gender and the Courts

As in the work for land reform in Ethiopia, local activists enlist the potentials of human rights laws in their cause; many groups use legal arguments as part of their educational and lobbying work. As a vehicle for change, the court increasingly has become an important site of challenge. Constituting and consolidating shifting social norms, the law can help bridge the gaps between new principles and existing practices.

Gender has established new fault lines of legal struggle. In part, these reflect the growing societal interconnections of the global age—for example, the patterns of transnational migrations that strain asylum, refugee, and immigration laws. At the Vienna tribunal, remember, María Olea described the consequences of the failure of U.S. laws to recognize gender-specific abuses as a basis for asylum. Partly, too, judges in national contexts have been willing to reference legal decisions from other national and regional courts and incorporate international human rights laws into their decisions.

In 1996, in a precedent-setting case in the United States, *Matter of Kasinga*, the Board of Immigration Appeals provided asylum to Fauziya Kassindja, who had fled Togo to escape genital mutilation. Her lawyers successfully argued that Kassindja met the existing criteria for asylum as a member of a "particular social group" (a gender) in danger of persecution should she be forced to return to her country. It was the first time a U.S. court ruled that a woman who faced fundamental violations of her bodily integrity could be recognized as a refugee. It led to a number of other test cases, notably of Rodi Alvarado, a Guatemalan who fled violent domestic abuse by her husband when the local police, refusing to investigate, claimed it was simply a "domestic matter," and also of Reina Izabel Garcia-Martinez, raped in 1993 by Guatemalan soldiers as part of their campaign of civilian intimidation. Despite concerted efforts of plaintiffs and NGOs to secure the right to asylum for women "fleeing countries that condone domestic abuse, genital mutilation, and other forms of acute violence," the Department of Justice and the Homeland Security Department have yet to establish the rule. The separate fight in court for each woman's case continues.[52]

Human rights regional bodies, as Chapter 5 shows in more detail, have been innovative in expanding human rights case law, including new rulings on gender issues. The shift is particularly noteworthy for the European Human Rights Court, established in 1959 under the European Convention for the Protection of Human Rights and Fundamental Freedoms. Its work has been pathfinding globally in applying these laws to curtail state violations. Reflecting broadening societal support for human rights values, an additional twelve protocols to the European Convention expanded the court's jurisdiction from its original focus on political and civic rights. New protocols abolished the death penalty (Protocol 6) and further safeguarded the rights of aliens and foreign nationals (Protocol 7).

Testifying to its growing role in the regional community, the court increased its workload and, in November 1998, was reorganized as a permanent body with judges sitting full time. From 1992 to 2002, the number of admissible cases rose from 189 to 577, reaching a high of 1,086 in the year 2000. The actual judgments delivered in the same period increased steadily over tenfold, from 81 in 1992 to 844 in 2002. In the latter year, for example, the court adjudicated a number of cases involving gender issues. It abolished Great Britain's ban on homosexuality in the military; defended the right of a father (living as a homosexual man) to visit his child of a former heterosexual relationship; and judged as impermissible differential treatment of married women under the Dutch pension law. Not all of its decisions have supported gender equity; in the same year, the court ruled against the right of a French gay national to adopt a child (*Frette v. France*, February 26, 2002). In the following year, in a pioneering transgendered case, the court favored a plaintiff's efforts to obtain financial reimbursement for the medical costs of a sex-change operation. Affirming "respect for . . . sexual self-determination" and "noting that gender identity [is] one of the most intimate aspects of a person's life," the judges overturned earlier court decisions, which, they said, had not reached a "fair balance" between the interests of the insurance company and those of the individual.[53] Furthermore, in a significant development in U.S. constitutional law, the Supreme Court's 2003 decision on the banning of state sodomy laws drew on legal precedents set by the European Human Rights Court. Writing for the majority in defense of constitutional liberty for gay men, Justice Anthony Kennedy cited a 1981 gay rights opinion by the European Court (*Dudgeon v. United Kingdom*), "the first time a decision of that court had been invoked by a majority of the Supreme Court."[54]

*   *   *

The judiciary has become a vital site of human rights struggles, demonstrating the existence of many complex layers of mobilization for human rights causes. Powerless to transform the structural basis of global economic and social inequality, national and regional courts since the 1970s nonetheless have been pushed to redress some of its glaring injustices. Court challenges have become integral to the strategies of new advocacy networks, defending, through social mobilization, the economic and social principles enshrined in the Universal Declaration of Human Rights. Just as the gender perspective developed partly in the context of the original human rights formulation of sex equality, so, too, the Universal Declaration helped formulate new visions. Responding to the global patterns of transnational migrations, activists used the declaration's language of "person" to challenge the historical links between citizenship and rights. Transnational migrants and their NGO defenders have claimed human rights divorced from any territorial foundation, which they seek to activate in the courts of their adopted countries, in regional courts, and through the complaint procedures of the Human Rights Commission, the theme of the next chapter. If these efforts testify to a "quiet revolution" in the legal landscape, they also have been met by loud opposition at the level of society.

Chapter 5
Citizenship, Socioeconomic Rights, and the Courts in the Age of Transnational Migrations

> The [Inter-American] Commission acknowledges that each State's immigration policy is its own sovereign decision; however, such policy has limits. . . . [It] should recognize legal foreign nationals' right not to be deported, except based on law, and should prohibit collective expulsion of foreign nationals, with or without legal status. Implementation . . . cannot result in cruel, inhumane and degrading treatment, nor in discriminations by reason of race, color, religion or sex.
>
> —Series E, Provisional Measures, *Case of Haitians and Haitian-Origin Dominicans in the Republic* (Dominican Republic), Order of the President of the Inter-American Court of Human Rights of September 14, 2000

In the mid-1970s, human rights visions became intricately linked to economic planning goals for members of the U.N. organs and commissions responsible for formulating and monitoring international rights. The shift was part of a set of wider changes in U.N. procedures, which, simultaneously, was expanding the role of local NGOs, victims, and their families in publicizing state abuse and also institutionalizing people's tribunals at U.N. world congresses. A coalition of new nations vitally concerned with development needs, and allied to socialist-bloc countries, stood at the forefront of the new agenda. Its members were armed with the statistics and detailed reports on societal conditions of life gathered worldwide during the first U.N. Development Decade. These reports offered vivid pictures of the human costs of continuing poverty and underdevelopment, reinforcing the dissatisfaction on the ground among aid-agency staff, development specialists, and women's groups with the prevailing industrial model of gross national product. It was increasingly clear to activists that the benefits of growth simply had failed to "trickle down" to most people in society.

A World Bank report in 1979 offered an equally bleak picture: for that year, its data counted over "800 million people in developing countries living in abject poverty." Translated into human terms, it meant that "forty percent of the people in the South are only barely surviving in conditions which are . . . 'below any national definition of human decency.'" The evidence convinced U.N. officials such as Jean Ripert, the Undersecretary-General for International Economic and Social Affairs, to call for change in the methods of analysis. "Economic growth," he said to the General Assembly in 1978, "while a necessary condition for development, is not itself a sufficient condition. Steps must be taken to ensure that opportunities and benefits associated with growth are widely and equitably distributed." His new criteria for investment centered on the dignity, security, and welfare of the human person. This shift turned economic development into an urgent human rights issue, placed before the Human Rights Commission.[1]

As with the families of the disappeared, the advocates of the new agenda in the 1970s found strong institutional support in Theo van Boven, strategically placed to disburse the relevant communiqués and help set the agenda for U.N. debate. The breakthrough resolution 1503, furthermore, had opened confidential communications to *all* violations; if the bulk still were on political and civil abuses (because individuals relied on NGOs to help prepare the complaints and most NGOs understood human rights as infringements on political freedoms), correspondence concerning abridgment of economic rights was sent to the International Labour Organization. But the changes in the mid-1970s were starting to blur the lines, as the HRC and its sub-commission, supported by the General Assembly, began to advocate for economic rights.

A flurry of proposals for rethinking development and rights coincided with van Boven's tenure as director of the Human Rights Division, pushed forcefully as well by the leaders of new nations, among them Kéba M'Baye of Senegal. Prompted by the General Assembly's call for a new international economic order (1974), the HRC and its sub-commission began to study the international dimensions of development; by 1981, they established a Working Group on Development, making it a "priority" item, as urged by the General Assembly (see Fig. 3a). It was the first working group able to meet between regular sessions since the HRC had drafted the Universal Declaration of Human Rights in 1947–48. The HRC also directed van Boven's division to prepare a comprehensive study of development challenges. Within the United Nations, information flowed in many directions.[2]

Under these auspices, the new view saw development as a global problem rooted in the injustices and inequalities of the international economic and social order and not simply a domestic issue for the states alone. Its solution required full international cooperation between and among rich and poor nations. The international economic, legal, and political structures, van Boven stated bluntly in an address in Santiago, Chile, in 1978, "function to the advantage of the privileged and to the detriment of the numerous peoples who live at the margins." He also recognized a lack of coordination among the international bodies pursuing economic development, from the world financial institutions to the U.N. aid and development agencies, and asked what role the U.N. human rights organs could play. The answer lay in the shift from the mathematics of growth to the calculations of human welfare, which elevated human rights criteria in the objectives of economic development. It made the "human person" the subject and not the mere object of development planning and returned to the original intent of the authors of the Universal Declaration, who had declared political *and* economic rights interdependent and indivisible. Taken together, these new debates in U.N. circles amounted to an effort to "reorient" the U.N. human rights program.[3] But the move was resisted strongly by the representatives of the powerful Western industrial states, who acknowledged neither the claims to certain material goods nor the obligations of states to recognize economic rights. They also opposed the effort to address the wider structural impediments to development. The preoccupation with economic issues, they said at the time, had turned the HRC's attention away from state abuses, such as those unfolding under the dictatorship in Uganda, in the "killing fields" of Cambodia, and with the violence in Burundi.

As van Boven understood, the U.N. human rights machinery was only one of a number of the international regimes addressing pressing economic issues. The debates in the mid-1970s took place against the backdrop of continuing economic and technological globalization, in which the human rights perspective, in practice, had only limited impact on international policies. Under the conditions of neoliberalism emerging in the early 1970s, globalization proceeded apace, with devastating consequences for standards of living in developing and, subsequently, industrialized countries as well. The authors' observations in the World Bank study in 1979 had captured trends that continued into later decades.

In the wake of the oil price shock, which reduced imports to industrial countries and led to structural adjustment programs for loans set by the World Bank and the International Monetary Fund, more money in 1980 flowed South to North to pay off debts and interest than North to South as development assistance to poorer countries. As one of the originators of the U.N. Women's Development Fund put it, the 1980s was the "lost decade" for development. According to another retrospective view, "In the period between 1970 and 1990, there was more inequality in the world than at any time before" and even after 1990 inequality did not decline significantly. The percentage of people living in extreme poverty fell (from 29 to 23 percent of the world's population between 1990 and 1999) because of its drop in East Asia and the Pacific; at the same time, in sub-Saharan Africa, the number of poor people rose, from 242 million to 300 million. The effect was "structural poverty," with "no room for millions of people either in the 'traditional' or 'modern' sector" of the economy. As Judith Blau and Alberto Moncada put it succinctly in a study in 2005, the decline that began in the early 1970s with economic globalization "never reversed course."[4]

The impact was not solely on extreme levels of poverty. The requirements for loan repayments forced the dismantling of the public sector and the health and welfare infrastructure of debtor nations, which from colonial times had been modeled partly on the welfare provisions of the Western powers. By the 1980s, these provisions, once regarded as the best guarantee of social stability and order after the devastation of World War II, came under assault by neoliberal politics in many Western countries as well. Everywhere, these policies challenged the role of government in providing social welfare and other collective needs, including access to clean water and electricity. Furthermore, for the developing countries, IMF and World Bank officials were the arbiters of the loans, allowing little opportunity for real negotiations over the terms. Thus, the liberalization in Senegal ended up eliminating one-third of the manufacturing jobs; when Brazil was forced to restructure its economy, the changes displaced small farmers in rice production, "creating food shortages in the country." In addition, the Vienna tribunal in 1993 heard graphic testimony of the impact of these programs on women's lives. Elaine Hewitt, for example, described the situation in the Caribbean, where many women, she said, have "sole responsibility for the economic well being of their children. Over 40 percent of all households are female-headed," yet there is no maternity leave or pay. The SAPs have deepened women's economic vulnerability. Hewitt could have been describing the situation of others when she said,

In countries like Trinidad and Tobago, Jamaica, Guyana, and Barbados, resources are used to service the external debt at the expense of the social sector. Cutting government expenditure . . . has meant reduced access to health care, education, housing and social security for women. The majority of those who have lost their jobs under these policies are also female, since women predominate in the social sector. In sum, this means greater poverty for women.

The sector of the population which benefited the least from the international loans (women and children) is now being made to bear the greatest burden.[5]

These conditions also helped account for the continuing rise in the numbers of migrant workers in the global economy. Their presence has become so pervasive that human rights activists and analysts captured the human dimensions of the phenomenon under the label "the new transnationals."[6] The term applies to all people who move across borders, not just to those looking for work. Migrants, after all, flee wars, civil strife, famines, and environmental degradation. But their movement is tightly correlated to economic development. Individuals would have been less willing to migrate if the postwar promises of sustained economic development had been met more fully. The social costs of underdevelopment—urban overcrowding, high unemployment, land depletion, and agricultural decline—contribute to the migratory patterns worldwide. In 1980, the General Assembly set up a Working Group on Migrant Labor, chaired by the Mexican delegate, and the sub-commission asked Halima Warzazi, who later also issued the comprehensive report on "female circumcision," to investigate the exploitation of labor through illegal and clandestine trafficking. These topics had come to the United Nations partly because of the growing concerns among representatives of Third World countries at Western Europe's heavy use of migrant labor to fuel its continued growth.

The cumulative pictures of the world economy from the ground became grist for new human rights causes. Responding to the human side of globalization, starting in the mid-1970s a new set of transnational advocacy networks emerged to address the many human rights challenges of the international and national economic order and of the flows of migrants crisscrossing territorial borders. Using rights language, they reactivated the economic and social principles behind the call for global justice, seeking to shift international debate from individual freedom onto collective responsibility for social well being. Human dignity and freedom, they argued, required clean water and food, health care, jobs, and labor protections as well as adequate housing. Just as the gender advocates, the groups pushing economic justice also served as critics of orthodox human rights thinking and advocacy; as with the women's groups, too, democratic participation and transparent government remained fundamental goals—although not the end point of, but the necessary precondition for, human rights struggles.

These views marked an alternative to the orthodoxy. Their challenge for mainstream international NGOs can be seen in the current Human Rights Watch Web statement of its official policies. Human Rights Watch explained its cautious conversion: "Since its formation in 1978, Human

Rights Watch has focused mainly on upholding civil and political rights, but in recent years we have increasingly addressed economic, social and cultural rights as well. We focus particularly on situations in which our methodology of investigating and reporting is most effective, such as when arbitrary or discriminatory government conduct lies behind economic, social and cultural rights violations." Its focus still remains on government violations, not on the nature or level of social provisioning. Complementing the point from a different perspective, MADRE faced skepticism at its founding. It noted that with its focus on *families* in addition to women, it did not fit with mainstream feminist organizing; nor did mainstream human rights groups originally accept its early attention to the economic rights it knew were central to women's lives, such as the rights to food, housing, and health care.[7]

In time, the many networks of overlapping advocacy for economic justice have become important—although consistently marginal—players in the human rights system. As human rights projects, these NGOs were shaped fundamentally by the framework of universal rights proclaimed in the U.N. Charter, the Universal Declaration and, in particular, the International Covenant on Economic Rights. In time, too, the courts have emerged to play a vital—if underexamined—role in the exercise of state power. The judicial realm had been a key arena in human rights struggles from the start. Confronting the flagrant abuses of the law was central to the Human Rights Commission's efforts to challenge the system of apartheid and uphold defenders' rights. Judicial decisions also brought social gains in gender equity. Starting in the late 1970s, in a process not fully anticipated in the human rights community, transnational migrants increasingly turned to international customary and human rights laws in their efforts to claim rights and expand the obligations and duties of states. These norms and laws have become a new source of vitality in immigration cases. Not surprisingly, as noncitizens, transnational migrants, whose status often is ambiguous in existing public law, have most vigorously pushed this process. Through litigation, individual migrants supported by a host of advocacy groups including their ethnic and religious organizations and communities, legal aid societies, and NGO coalitions defending noncitizens' rights, have used elements of international law (notably, the prohibitions on cruel and unusual punishment and nondiscriminatory principles) to limit the state's authority to set domestic agendas on immigrant residence, detention, and entitlements. They have forced changes in government policies and investments in social provisioning, at times confounding the ability of state authorities to regulate domestic policies and police their borders. The epigraph to this chapter captures well the challenges to exclusive state authority over foreigners and immigrants posed by the direct application of human rights norms in matters of immigration law.[8]

Pushed by the migrant plaintiffs, the judicial realm has become one of a number of transnational sites in the global age slowly reshaping the international system based on sovereign states. Of course, the very processes of globalization, with their premium on open markets and the free flow of capital and information, also have eroded key elements of national sovereignty, including the governments' ability to safeguard jobs. For the many people around the globe who feel threatened by the dislocations of globalization, these two interrelated challenges can be conflated easily. In national contexts, societal anger at immigration has led to xenophobic politics and even violence against migrants. This position seemingly pits the defenders of *human* rights, as an alternative to the politics of "othering," against those affirming national sovereignty and the exclusivity of citizenship. For migrants in their daily lives, these charged debates have hampered the implementation of judicial gains.[9]

The shift to addressing the injustices of the world economy and the plight of the economically and politically vulnerable within it raised difficult problems for human rights advocates. Theo van Boven seemed to have captured what is at stake for the system of universal guarantees and protections. The challenge was of "utmost importance," he noted, "for unless we can effectively bridge the gap between the realms of human rights and economics we risk the pursuit, on the one hand, of an international economic order which neglects the fundamental human development objectives of all our endeavors, and, on the other, of a shallow approach to human rights which neglects the deeper, structural causes of injustice."[10] He made the point at a U.N. seminar in 1980; it remains as valid today as it was at the time.

Globalization's Contradictions and the Universal Declaration

Globalization is a complicated topic beyond its intersection with human rights debates. Through trade, tariff, and market policies, it has transformed the basis of economic exchange and at the same time created new forms of inequality, both within the highly developed economies of industrial nations as well as in and with the developing world. The globalizing economy operates within a set of stark contradictions that underlie many of the challenges facing human rights advocates. Since the neoliberal reforms of the 1970s—and accelerating with the demise of the socialist bloc in Europe and the shift from planned to market economies in the 1990s elsewhere—global economic production and exchange have taken place under political conditions that value deregulation and freedom of movement for capital, finance, information, and technology. Under the rubric of free trade and exchange, components of the new economy seem to move effortlessly across borders. For some analysts, the transnational character of capital and technology spells the demise of national sovereignty, but the global economy continues to rely on nation-state laws to enforce the intellectual property and copyright laws as well as contract agreements needed for orderly capitalist reproduction. The operations of the human rights system mirror this complicated symbiosis between the global and national levels because many human rights conventions require corresponding changes in domestic legislation and administrative policies. Globalization, thus, transforms the state even as it continues to rely on state authority for its legal safeguards.[11]

Given the predominance of free trade and market ideology in the processes of economic globalization, it is all the more striking that the same freedoms do not apply to the movement of people across borders. Unlike capital and information, freedom of movement does not extend to labor, even if some bilateral agreements as, for example, the North America Free Trade Agreement enacted in 1993, eased the cross-border movement of personnel central to the information economy, among them bankers, international lawyers, and accountants. Similar freedoms do not exist for a majority of labor migrants in lower skilled jobs, although their work in domestic service, agriculture, construction, and the health care industry is vital to the health of the global economy. International law leaves the regulation of cross-border movements of people to the states; states defend the sanctity of territorial borders. The authors of the Universal Declaration of Human Rights had intended to proclaim new principles. However, confronted with the traditions of law and hardened by the Middle East refugee crisis in 1947–48, they left the states' authority over immigration intact. As it turned out, the Universal Declaration opened up different options for judicial interventions. This argument returns again to the debates that had surrounded the drafting of the Universal Declaration.

The architects of the Universal Declaration regarded freedom of movement within and across state borders, asylum, and nationality as matters of basic human rights, requiring international cooperation and agreement among states. They drafted and debated three articles, 13 through 15, on these principles. At the time, the lessons of World War II were raw. Under fascist authorities, Jews and Gypsies had been deprived of their nationality and rendered stateless. Without asylum from persecution, statelessness had left its victims naked and unprotected by law. To the members of the HRC writing the document, asylum seemed an inherent corollary to the principles of life and dignity, as basic as the guarantees of free thought and expression. So, too, did the right to a nationality. At the Second Session of the Drafting Committee, René Cassins put the principle simply: "Every human being should be a member of a national group."[12] By this understanding, a person's legal status in the world is tied to nationality. Moreover, the Universal Declaration affirmed freedom of movement and residence within states and the right of every person to leave any country and also to exit and reenter his or her own state.

In operational terms, the three articles were drawn narrowly, hammered out against the international problems of refugee status and settlement left over after World War II. The waves of Palestinian Arab refugees from the Arab-Israeli war of 1948 added fuel to the debates. From December 1947 to September 1948, around 600,000 to 700,000 Palestinian Arabs became refugees, most expecting to return after the hostilities ended. But wartime patterns hardened into permanent conditions. In June 1948, the government of Israel rejected a right of return; Arab states demanded repatriation and refused to absorb the refugees. Caught in political limbo, Palestinian Arab refugees came under the protection of U.N. relief agencies, most notably the U.N. Relief and Works Agency for Palestine Refugees (UNRWA), organized in late 1949. Assumed to be an ad hoc solution, the UNRWA has provided basic educational and health services for subsequent generations of Palestinian refugees in Gaza, the West Bank, Jordan, Lebanon, and Syria ever since. For more than sixty years, Palestinians living and born in the refugee camps in and outside Israel-Palestine have existed under the harsh and irregular conditions as stateless people.[13]

To the U.N. state representatives, this immediate humanitarian challenge showed the need for a permanent international body to handle the transnational dimensions of refugees and asylum-seekers. In December 1950, the General Assembly established the position of High Commissioner for Refugees (UNHCR), whose office coordinates the survival needs of people displaced across borders by wars and famines; it defrays much of the financial burden on the receiving states. In addition, it provides aid and shelter to asylum-seekers, thus partially meeting the objectives of those who had drafted the articles on the cross-border movement of people (see fig. 1).

The articles, however, were written to avoid addressing the related question of immigration and emigration. Bowing to existing international law, the authors left the setting of entry and exit policy to the sovereign authorities of each state. Thus, the right to leave any country (guaranteed by Article 13) was not matched by a corresponding right to enter another state (absent from the article); the guarantee, in effect, was empty. After much contentious discussion, aggravated by the deepening refugee crisis in the Middle East, an effort to proclaim an explicit right of asylum in another state was defeated. In its final form, Article 14 only ensured persons the right "to seek and to enjoy" asylum in other countries, but no state was required to grant it. Should asylum be given, the migrant had the right to enjoy it. Similarly, if all persons had a right to a nationality established by Article 15, no one had the right to become a citizen of a particular state. In the affairs of states, matters of entry and the residence of foreigners remained discretionary acts of public authorities, governed by positive state law.

With deference to sovereignty and under competing political pressures over state obligations to refugees in the immediate postwar era, the 1948 Universal Declaration circumscribed the right of mobility across territorial borders. For governments and regional blocs, immigration and emigration decisions have remained vital in the exercise of authority. At its core, immigration is about community identity and its fundamental values. In the international system of states, immigration policies help set the particular social composition of states and the communities within them. Seemingly at stake is the changing face of "the people" in a bounded territory. Thus, it is no surprise that the topic is at the center of so many contentious debates over membership, responsibility, and entitlements.

If the Universal Declaration perpetuated older international law, nowhere in the document were rights directly linked to citizenship. The language of citizenship also was absent in the subsequent development of international human rights laws. In this sense, the human rights "legal revolution" of 1945–49 broke with historical precedents that had tied rights exclusively to membership as "the people," that is, the citizens in a state. By attaching rights to human persons irrespective of territorial place, they have broadened the bases of legal claims. The shift to what historian David Jacobson subsequently called a "quiet revolution" in human rights history began to unfold only in the 1970s, with the stresses and strains of globalization in daily life on the ground.[14] It was the dramatic growth in the flow of transnational migrations that promoted new claims as did the legacies of colonialism, which continued to shape much of the migratory paths. At the same time, economic globalization has placed serious impediments to the effort to safeguard rights—even older, traditional labor rights—in regional and national settings.

Global Migration Patterns

The scale of transnational migrations is one of the most striking features of the global age—making it a problem of global concern. Since the

1970s, more people were on the move than ever before in history, rivaling the so-called "free" migrations of people in the nineteenth century, mostly from Europe to settlements in the Americas but also from China, Korea, and Japan to the Indian Ocean rim, California, and parts of South America. Their numbers reached around 50 million. These earlier patterns of migration were almost one dimensional in form—movements back and forth along a line, also establishing diasporic communities in their wake as, for example, with the settlement of the Chinese and the Hawdramauti (from southeastern Yemen) in the Indian Ocean world and Indonesia. In contrast, the contemporary patterns are more complicated, crisscrossing the globe from south to south—as in the case of Colombian workers in the Venezuelan oil fields or those from Togo, Benin and, Ghana, who worked in the Nigerian oil industry until 1983—as well as from south to the more developed north. In 2005, one-third of the transnational migrants resided in developing countries.

Although aggregate statistics fluctuate according to global political and economic conditions and say nothing about the personal meanings of the sojourns nor the living and working conditions, they demonstrate the breadth of the patterns. For 2005, the U.N. Department of Economic and Social Affairs put the number of international migrants worldwide at around 191 million, including refugees, who accounted for about 21 million. The figure represented a significant rise, from 75 million in 1965 and 120 million in 1990. Nearly half of the world's migrants in 2005 were women. These totals, however, do not include people moving within countries, such as the estimated hundred million internal migrants from rural areas to factory settings who have fueled the Chinese economic boom with its shift to market policies in the mid-1990s. They also neglect the internally displaced persons (IDPs), who are forced to move because of drought or war, which in 2006 was estimated at 12.8 million people.[15] And, of course, the statistics do not count the undocumented workers, whose circuitous routes and desperate plights began to attract so much attention in the media—and also among human rights defenders—in the latter third of the twentieth century.

Conforming to sovereign norms, much of the cross-border labor migrations continue to be regulated officially through work permits and other formal arrangements between sending and receiving countries, such as the historic "guest worker" programs. Guest worker exchanges were arranged in the United States, notably the Bracero program of Mexican farm labor, which lasted from 1942 to 1964. Under special programs (H-2), U.S. companies continue to import foreign low-wage labor to meet the needs of agriculture and other seasonal industries, as in the cyclical employment of Jamaican farm workers to cut sugarcane and harvest other crops. But these guest workers also "make chocolate in Louisiana, staff hotel desks in Florida and mow lawns in Missouri. They toil in some of the country's most difficult and dangerous industries, from shipbuilding to asbestos removal to forestry." A study in 2007 put their numbers at 150,000. Their vulnerability has spawned new NGOs, such as the Alliance of Guest Workers for Dignity, seeking to protect the workers' rights along the U.S. Gulf Coast.[16]

Beginning in the 1960s, many Western European countries also imported temporary workers from Turkey, North Africa, Yugoslavia, and Greece, who helped fuel the region's postwar economic boom. Their situation first brought the plight of migrant workers to the attention of the HRC. The European guest worker program ended officially in 1974, but many of the "guest" workers, defying the original intent of the program, became permanent residents of the host countries in the late 1970s. They pushed for "family reunification" policies and established enclaves of new immigrant communities. A similar labor program started up in the oil-rich Gulf states after 1973, using workers from Egypt, Yemen, and South and Southeast Asia.

As a societal problem, the presence of "illegal" migrants is one of the most contentious issues produced by the world economy. Even framing this issue (in English) through the term "illegal" reveals the deep levels of tension. If the migratory patterns of immigrants seem idiosyncratic and random, as structural phenomena they were set in motion by two historic forces. The timing of the one, ironically, reflected the official termination of guest worker and other programs as well as the onset of new legal migratory paths. First, as a consequence of the official ties to labor-exporting regions, people in local communities acquired information about work opportunities, migratory routes, family resettlement policies, and immigrant communities in the country importing the labor. Such information circulated widely and, when the temporary programs ended and the workers were forced to return home, these long-standing social ties emboldened people to move without documents. Second, global investment patterns produced a structural link; here, too, the choice of sites was not random. Typically, it reflected the zone of influence of the firm's base country as well as the continuing traces of colonialism in the postcolonial world economy.

This point is made convincingly by Saskia Sassen, who examined global migration streams, particularly those from lesser developed regions to Europe, the United States, and Japan. In her analysis, such migrations were a function of the exporting of jobs abroad (known as "outshoring" in the contentious globalization debates) and the impact of foreign aid and trade policies, which disrupted life in poor, rural communities. In a typical pattern, women migrated to the new jobs opening up in global factories of their own countries; 90 percent of the labor force of these global factories worldwide at the turn of the twenty-first century was female. The gender imbalances in rural communities in turn engendered migrations of male workers abroad but also of the women workers who, through their work in the factories, had gained firsthand knowledge about life and work opportunities in the more prosperous country sponsoring the factory, setting the stage for the subsequent chain migration of workers required for the industrial economy. Under the same pressures of globalization, industrial economies are being downsized and deskilled simultaneously. Sassen nearly duplicated the experiences of many in New York City's West Indies immigrant community, individuals such as Beulah Reid, who once had been a checker at the Glamor Girl lingerie factory in Trinidad. A "friend from the factory" encouraged her to come to the United States, another helped her find an apartment, and still another saw that she moved from housekeeping jobs into a clerk's job. Her path to and in the United States mirrored the networks that followed from the transnational investments.[17]

Sassen's analysis also turned attention to the continuing effects of empire and global power in the factors affecting the transnational flow of labor. As she noted, the administrative and economic networks of the former European and Japanese empires and their newer forms "under the Pax Americana . . . have not only created bridges for the flow of capital, information and high-level personnel from the center to the periphery but . . . also for the flow of migrants from the periphery to the center."[18] Although focused on the inequalities of north-to-south financial and labor exchanges, Sassen showed that transnational migratory flows are not random—nor are they simply matters of individual choice—but follow a logic inherent in the politics of globalization. In the industrialized North, they often replicated the older ties and relationships developed earlier under colonialism and reflected the country's current spheres of political influence. In this respect, she argued, developed countries have a moral and practical obligation to take responsibility for the wider structures as well as the resulting inequalities and injustices in the patterns of global labor migrations.

New and Old Claims and Challenges

A similar argument underpinned the efforts of postcolonial governments to claim a *right* to development. They continuously pressed the point in U.N. and regional bodies and in the Human Rights Commission in the late 1970s and 1980s. Their representatives commissioned the first study on development by van Boven's Human Rights Division and subsequent examinations of the problem in regional and national contexts.

Van Boven's report in 1979 was pathbreaking; it stressed the many structural obstacles to development, identified at the time as colonial rule, foreign occupation and apartheid, other forms of discrimination, and the failure to grant every nation the right to exclusive control over its natural wealth and resources. Putting human beings at the center of development objectives, it interconnected the rights of states and the people within them. Both had a right to development as a human right: individual and collective well being within states and national health required expanded opportunities for development. In 1981, the HRC's new working group further examined "the scope and contents of the right to development." Internationally, it meant a new claim of peoples' collective rights against the powerful developed countries, which profited from the global system. For its many defenders—whether U.N. member-states, human rights activists, or scholars—it stood for a third generation of "solidarity" rights in defense of the justice of Third World development. For historical and present-day reasons, poor states had a right to economic assistance; development agendas required a collective willingness to redress historic and economic wrongs. Adopting these views, the HRC formulated a Declaration on the Right to Development, passed by the General Assembly in 1986, which called on the states to make possible the requisite "positive" investments in social and economic life[19] (see Fig. 3b). The principle was claimed apart from any particular citizenship.

Two assumptions further defined the arguments. The first placed the whole issue of development in the context of the systemic interrelationship between development and underdevelopment inherited from the past. It, thus, called on industrial nations to take greater financial responsibility for the current problems of poverty and economic backwardness. The second argued that the promises of economic rights in the Universal Declaration and subsequently codified by the U.N. Covenant on Economic, Social and Cultural Rights also required people to have a right to the material bases needed to realize these principles. But the rights guaranteed by the Economic Covenant have had limited impact on state practices and the proposals on development have been "largely theoretical exercises without apparent effect on institutional arrangements."[20]

As normative visions, however, these principles capture the social ideals and aspirations of the large majority of the world's population, who want improved living and working conditions and the means to achieve them. They have been activated in global coalitions tackling the debt burden and development, including, among others, Jubilee South and the Committee for the Cancellation of Third World Debt (CADTM). They also are found in the work of migrant networks, among others the Migrants Rights International and Enlaces América, which follow the migratory paths of workers, providing NGO support, human rights legal advice, community leadership training, and high publicity about abuses in national and transnational contexts simultaneously. They continue to inform international debate at U.N. and regional world conferences and intrude into the states' round of talks over the nature and terms of trade and tariff policies set by the General Agreement on Tariffs and Trade (GATT) and, subsequently, the World Trade Organization. Thwarted at the level of implementation, ameliorative action increasingly has shifted to NGOs in national and transnational arenas.

The U.N. effort to place economic rights more centrally in the human rights agenda found an echo in NGO strategies to safeguard longstanding economic and labor rights threatened by the continuing pressures of globalization. Since 1920, the International Labour Organization had promoted common international standards on labor and employment practices. Initially, it pursued an agenda shaped by the powerful international socialist labor and trade union organizations—active as well in colonial settings—to secure improvements in conditions of labor for working people worldwide. Through ongoing negotiations between governments, employers, unions, and workers, the ILO member-states have hammered out binding agreements on labor standards, work conditions, rights of association, and antidiscrimination principles. Adding authority, many of these principles were enshrined in the domestic labor codes of the member-states. State officials appreciably acceded to international labor agreements to help regulate competition in the international market.

On the ground, NGO campaigns take place around specific violations of rights or community mobilizations for access to social services, including decent housing, emergency medical care, or provisioning of water and electricity. They combine a number of strategies, including high publicity national campaigns to bring public pressure on decision-making agencies, local demonstrations, street protests, and court challenges. Whether pursuing an activist or a legalist route—or some combination of the two—they rely on the national framework of constitutional guarantees for the specifics of the struggle. According to Blau and Moncada, "National constitutions are the key institutions that formalize what rights citizens have or can aspire to."[21] They could have added that constitutional provisions—and international human rights laws—extend many formal institutional safeguards also to foreigners and nonnationals.

Postapartheid South Africa provides an instructive example of the point. It continues the discussion first developed in Chapter 2, shedding additional light on the question of the human rights orthodoxy. The many disparate local struggles for land distribution, welfare provisions, and health services submerged in the national antiapartheid campaigns for formal democracy reemerged after 1994. These on-going struggles demonstrated both the insufficiencies of a narrow definition of freedom as solely electoral democracy and the new possibilities inherent in the state's rights conscious constitution of 1996, with its progressive Bill of Rights and activist Human Rights Commission. The HRC is charged with promoting "respect for human rights" and "securing appropriate redress where human rights have been violated."[22]

Attracting foreign investment and financing for economic growth, the postapartheid government coupled economic with political liberalism, embracing privatization and deregulation, which exacerbated wealth differentials. In the face of poverty, wealth imbalances, and a serious health crisis, especially the AIDS epidemic, that continued to marginalize the historically disadvantaged groups in the society, people's campaigns have emerged to press for greater resource allocation and economic and health benefits. Shaped by the new political context and the memory of apartheid's injustices, they now mobilize human rights language to critique the dominant power hierarchy that legitimizes its rule with reference to human rights. In microcosm, they mirror and feed into the wider global challenges lodged by the networks for economic justice against the political biases in the human rights system overall.[23]

Under the state's legal mechanisms, these South African NGOs have launched a number of campaigns for poor people's rights. Some have won important legal decisions, requiring, for example, effective implementation of emergency housing for destitute children and parents in Cape Town, as in a ruling mandated by the "benchmark" case of *Grootboom*. Similar lawsuits prevented the cutoffs of water and electricity in poor neighborhoods. There also have been political mobilizations around land rights coordinated, in one case, by the National Land Committee, an NGO, and the Landless People's Movement, a social organization of urban and rural people fighting for land reform. This network used human rights language to critique the failure of the new state to tackle the continuing injustices of social inequality. Through one highly publicized route, the groups put on mock court proceedings to illustrate the insufficiency of "the dominant human rights discourse," which had failed to defend meaningful land reform. In another coordinated campaign for land rights organized by the Land Access Movement of South Africa, the coalition announced it would not be celebrating "Human Rights Day 2003." Its publicity stated, "South Africa's 19 million poor and landless rural people" would not join what had become nothing but an opportunity "for the privileged few of our country to celebrate the rights which are not enjoyed by the majority of our people, while millions continue to suffer from landlessness, poverty, and human rights abuses."[24] To garner the public's support, in an anti-eviction campaign in Cape Town, organizers placed their understandings of human rights guarantees into the memory of the abuses of apartheid. They criticized the postapartheid government for "increasingly abandoning the 'progressive' human rights provisions of its Constitution in favor of repressive measures like apartheid-style forced removals, evictions and service cutoffs."

In postapartheid South Africa, human rights language of social justice became an effective tool for demanding change in a society shaped so profoundly by the rights values inherent in the long and arduous antiapartheid struggles. South African NGOs, too, have formed effective transnational alliances particularly in their effort to expand HIV/AIDS treatment for poor people (through domestic court challenges) and reduce the profits of pharmaceutical companies from abuse of patent laws (through alliances with international agencies and NGOs, such as the World Health Organization, Oxfam, and Doctors without Borders). They also joined with U.S. AIDS organizations to force the U.S. government to back away from its threat of sanctions against South Africa for alleged violations of patent laws by reducing the price of medicines. Assessing the wide range of evidence of people's movements in South Africa, Greenstein concluded that coalitions combining domestic mobilizations from below with court challenges and aided by international and transnational organizations offered the most successful model for critiquing and changing constrictive state social and economic policies.[25]

As a rights enforcement body, furthermore, the South African Human Rights Commission also had migrants, refugees, and asylum-seekers in its jurisdiction. It acknowledged that since 1994 the country had signed a number of international conventions "set[ting] standards for the observance of human rights, including the rights of migrants and refugees."[26] It recognized, too, the complex legal environment for migrants and refugees.

In the global economy, migrants have a number of formal legal safeguards as do refugees, which is a legal status established by the 1951 Refugee Convention and its 1967 Protocol. As job-seekers, transnational migrants have recourse to laws that antedated the human rights system itself and helped shape the list of second-generation rights proclaimed in the Universal Declaration. In addition to these older labor rights, migrant workers also explicitly are ensured the right to life and freedom from coercive hiring practices and forced labor, the *jus cogens* norms of international law affirming fundamental values binding on the governments of all states. These rights have been codified in an International Convention on the Protection of All Migrant Workers and Members of Their Families, adopted by the General Assembly on December 18, 1990. An international coalition called "December 18" has emerged to coordinate the campaign to encourage state ratification of this convention.[27] Its place in U.N. oversight is shown in Fig. 3b.

Complicating the situation, most international labor laws apply to both nationals and foreign workers alike, although some states relying on migrant labor for a fixed period and specific purpose, among them the oil-producing countries of the Gulf, have been unwilling to extend the safeguards to the foreign workers. Given the vastly different levels of global wealth, developing states also have won many exemptions from the requirements in human rights instruments to treat national and foreign labor the same. In addition, in most national economies the guest and other foreign workers have access to welfare and medical benefits as well as to pension plans for themselves and their families. It is important to note that these entitlements are deducted from wages and do not depend on citizenship. They speak of new "social contracts" that are reallocating the prerogatives that come with membership in the state.[28]

Turning legal rights and social contracts into effective safeguards, however, is a different matter. In the first place, the processes of globalization have increased the economic vulnerability of male and female labor—for the internal as well as the transnational migrants. As global capital moves production to venues it can control, it has created new, partly denationalized "industrial zones" and "global factories" in poorer countries outside the protection of labor laws and rights. Creating a coherent "Third World" response—as in the earlier shared goals of self-determination and decolonization—has proven difficult. At U.N. world conferences, for example, elites in developing countries, which have a competitive advantage in cheap labor, often ally with industrial corporate interests in the West.

A second difficulty is derived partly from the status of nonnationals as marginal groups found on the fringes of society. A report sponsored by the South African Migration Project made the point abundantly clear and it is applicable elsewhere. The authors noted that since 1994 South Africa has become a "primary node in regional migration flows" and sanctuary for some refugees fleeing wars and civil strife. The country's school and refugee acts guaranteed refugees and their children the "same basic health services and basic primary education which the inhabitants of the republic receive." Studies on the conditions for Somali refugees living in Johannesburg, however, showed that 70 percent of Somali children were not in school in 2000 and, similarly, that Somalis and other groups were denied emergency care, even though they were entitled to it. As the authors put it, "Given their tenuous status in the country . . . and their relative ignorance of their rights, many foreigners simply accept these violations. Indeed, only 1 percent of refugees who were refused health services lodged a complaint and 24 percent reported doing nothing, largely because they did not know what to do." A related study of conditions of life for immigrant communities in Australia found that female migrant blue-collar workers, often for similar reasons, rarely used the courts to protest patterns of discrimination and rights violations they faced at work.[29]

Legal Incorporation

Starting in the late 1970s, national and regional courts in many areas of the globe began to extend human rights protections to transnational migrants who fell outside the jurisdiction of national laws. The growing presence of foreigners and nonnationals in the economies and societies of nation-states was raising a host of legal issues. Responding piecemeal and incrementally, these courts made precedent-setting rulings that incorporated international human rights norms and protections into domestic law; they cross-referenced these decisions in their own rulings. Judges also mandated changes in administrative practices to accord with international human rights standards. It was an example of the "judicial tail . . . wagging the legislative dog," wrote Jacobson approvingly, although the process was neither global nor irreversible.[30]

Not all regions' legal systems accommodated such challenges, however. The Persian Gulf is a good case in point. In the mid-1970s and early 1980s, for example, the oil-producing states of the Persian Gulf imported about 3.6 million foreign workers from Arab and Asian countries. These authoritarian governments imposed strict controls over the numbers of workers, conditions of employment, housing, and access to social welfare benefits. With the exception of Kuwait, migrant workers' families were denied free medical care and education and only skilled workers could bring their families into the countries. As economist Myron Weiner notes, "These policies do more than simply establish the temporary position of the migrant workers; they institutionalize a pattern of dualism," segregating migrant groups from the rest of society, even those who have lived in the country essentially on a permanent basis.[31]

In this context of authoritarian control, domestic courts in the region offered little opportunity for redress. Other options were open, including lodging petitions with the U.N. Human Rights Commission under

Resolution 1503, which at times impacted domestic politics. This avenue occurred in a case of flagrant human rights abuses against noncitizen residents in Kuwait at the end of the first Gulf War after the defeat of Iraq and the restoration of the Kuwaiti government. In December 1992, the Lebanese-born Kuwaiti family of Ismael and Maimane Farhat filed a petition documenting the terrible abuses that their family and others had experienced at the hands of the security police in the aftermath of the war. They were represented by the Center for Constitutional Rights, a leading legal NGO in the United States active in litigation since the civil rights era of the mid-1960s. This group of progressive lawyers defends rights guaranteed in the U.S. Constitution and the Universal Declaration of Human Rights, bringing work for civil and human rights together. The organization is particularly concerned with defending those individuals and groups who have few legal protections and little access to legal resources.

The "complaint" it sent to the HRC charged the Kuwaiti government with systematic violations of the human rights of noncitizens living under its jurisdiction. As part of a vicious clampdown on foreigners said to have collaborated with Saddam Hussein's invading army, the father and son were murdered and the daughter raped. These attacks on the family were not isolated incidents. They fit into larger patterns of abuses, including "widespread summary executions; systematic torture . . . arbitrary arrests and detention without trial; hundreds of disappearances" and rape as "collective punishments" against noncitizens for reputed collaboration with the enemy. Amnesty International offered corroborating evidence as well. According to a Human Rights Watch report on Kuwait in 1995, the government's continuing fear of Iraqi intentions became an excuse for ongoing human rights violations against foreign communities, particularly the Bedouins and Palestinians. Partly because of the publicity of this particular complaint, Jaber al-Omairi, an official in the Ministry of Interior responsible for the abuses of the Farhat family, was tried and sentenced for the crimes, although later his prison time was reduced because, it was claimed, he only had been avenging Iraqi abuses.[32]

In patterns that might be indicative of future trends given the global nature of transnational migrations, courts in other regions have taken on complaints of nonnationals. At stake were many fundamental human rights principles, not only work-related issues. This intersection of migrant case law and human rights principles speaks about individuals and groups of people caught in legal limbo, languishing indefinitely in prison, unprotected and exploited in the workplace, denied citizenship because of their national origin, or facing "inhumane" and "degrading" treatment in their efforts to flee danger across borders. These human stories easily are missed in the statistical data on migration trends, levels of wealth, or abstract discussions of legal principles. Supported by community organizations and human rights legal NGOs, some of these migrants have taken their cases to court; most have not. However precedent setting, courts often ruled narrowly (as in *Matter of Kasinga*), reluctant to make radical departures in domestic law and extend their rulings to others in similar situations. Thus, the legal battles continued. Although only a number of key cases are examined in this chapter, each is considered precedent-setting and illustrative of the role of the court in defending universal human rights values also for noncitizens in national contexts.[33]

The Mariel Boat People and Unlimited Detentions in the United States

Until the late 1970s, the courts in the United States accepted only a few immigration cases, leaving matters of policy to the legislative and executive branches. They also made virtually no references to international law in their decisions on immigration. The change reflected the continuous influx of a variety of "undocumented aliens" and "unauthorized refugees," whether from Cuba or Southeast Asia or job-seeking migrants from Mexico and around the Caribbean basin. It also was a product of the professional contacts and exchanges of views that existed among the different national judges. For example, in July 1998 a delegation of U.S. Supreme Court justices headed by Sandra Day O'Connor visited the European Court and Human Rights Commission as part of a wider tour of the European court system to enhance the mutual understandings of contemporary judicial practices.[34]

Examining U.S. federal case law, Jacobson noted that between 1948 and 1994 a total of seventy-six cases cited the Universal Declaration of Human Rights; nearly 60 percent of those citations occurred after 1980 and a majority of the total (54 percent) involved immigrant and refugee status. Farooq Hassan used the phrase "the doctrine of incorporation" for the way contemporary international human rights norms have been "absorbed" into U.S. common law. As he put it, "Where domestic law is unclear or unestablished on a point which is heavily addressed by other nations, legal writers and customary international law, the United States court system [has been] willing to bridge the gap between domestic and international human rights law by adopting the essence of provisions in human rights treaties through incorporation."[35] This step is particularly noteworthy because the U.S. Senate has failed to ratify most of the existing corpus of human rights treaties. Because U.S. judges cannot rely on a specific treaty to provide relief, they have turned to the customary norms of international law, drawing on a whole host of international instruments from declarations to resolutions to binding conventions.

The landmark case in the United States for incorporating the principles of international law is *Rodriguez-Fernandez v. Wilkinson* (1981), a case concerning due process and fairness around the detention of migrants and whether the state could detain them indefinitely. In agreeing to take the case, the U.S. judges on the Tenth Circuit Court of Appeals explained their willingness to turn to international law: "Due process," they wrote, "is not a static concept, [and] it undergoes evolutionary change to take into account accepted current notions of fairness. . . . It seems proper then to consider international law principles for notions of fairness as to propriety of holding aliens in detention."[36] Hassan called the argument precedent setting. Almost in passing, he also noted that parallel legal developments were taking place in India and Pakistan as well.

Rodriguez-Fernandez addressed an issue of continuing importance. In subsequent years, however, Congress passed new immigration legislation, notably the Illegal Immigration Reform and Immigrant Responsibility Act (IIRIRA) in 1996. This law allowed the Immigration and Naturalization Service (INS) to detain "aliens" ordered deported for up to ninety days. Another provision permitted the attorney general to detain "inadmissible" aliens with no limits on the length of those detentions. Immigration rights NGOs, including the Center for Constitutional Rights, the American Civil Liberties Union (ACLU), and religious leaders, have called this law "the most diverse, divisive and draconian immigration law enacted since the Chinese Exclusion Act of 1882."[37] As a result of its passage, the related cases, including *Zadvydas v. Underdown* (1999), *Ho v. Green* (2000), and *Ma v. Reno* (2000), have been joined under the new statute. The Supreme Court granted review of *Zadvydas* and *Ma* in 2001; at the time, the lives of around 3,800 detainees were at stake.[38] All of the cases involved the indefinite detention of noncitizens because the INS was not able to return them to their home countries. A matter of grave significance for liberty, unlimited detention also emerged as one of the key contentious issues in the U.S.-led "war on terror" after the September 11, 2001, attacks on New York City and Washington, D.C. U.S. Attorney General John Ashcroft used the same provisions of the IIRIRA to detain indefinitely immigrants suspected of involvement in terrorist activities, a theme picked up again in Chapter 7. As it turned out, all these cases involved critical issues about the civil and human rights of persons in the United States—in times of peace and in times of war.

Pedro Rodriguez-Fernandez was one of about 125,000 people fleeing the port of Mariel, Cuba, and arriving in Key West, Florida, aboard the so-called Freedom Flotilla in the summer of 1980. He immediately sought refugee status, but his hearing revealed a criminal record. He was declared an "excludable" Cuban and imprisoned while the government sought to deport him back to Cuba; the Cuban government refused to accept him. The attorney general ordered his continued detention first in the federal penitentiary at Leavenworth and later in a penitentiary in Atlanta, Georgia. Rodriguez-Fernandez brought suit, claiming that his indeterminate jailing was tantamount to cruel and unusual punishment prohibited by the Eighth Amendment of the U.S. Constitution. He was not alone: any of the Mariel refugees who had not become an American citizen or a legal resident, could be detained indefinitely after finishing a jail sentence even for a minor crime. The law held that Marielitos technically "had never reached American shores—they had simply been saved from the seas." When the Supreme Court finally resolved the case in 2005, ruling that the open-ended detention of the Mariel boat people was illegal, the decision applied to 750 remaining boat people, including Rodriguez-Fernandez.[39] In the cases of Kestutis Zadvydas (born of Lithuanian parents in a German displaced persons camp in 1948), Ho (a trial that involved two Vietnamese nationals), and Kim Ho Ma (a Cambodian who left the country with his parents as a two-year-old and spent five years in refugee camps before moving to the United States), each petitioner entered the country legally but subsequently committed a crime and faced deportation following release from the state correctional facilities. As with Rodriguez-Fernandez, no country would accept them and they, too, faced indefinite jailing.

In the *Rodriguez-Fernandez* case, the court offered detailed reasoning for absorbing human rights norms into case law. Filed under domestic protections, the District Court found that the laws of the United States did not apply in the case. "Our domestic laws are designed to deter private individuals from harming one another and to protect individuals from abuse by the State. But in the case of unadmitted aliens detained on our soil, but legally deemed to be outside our borders, the machinery of domestic law utterly fails to operate to assure protection."[40] Aware that the U.S. government had ratified few international treaties, the judges turned to the established norms of international law, protecting individuals from arbitrary arrests and detention without being charged with a crime. Through a careful review of the "general practice of nations" and the "works of jurists," the judges found a universal rule of customary international law against arbitrary detention: detention without limits was a clear violation of international law. In upholding the decision, the appeal judges placed greater emphasis on domestic legal protections (due process) but also "recognized the need to remain within the ambit of international legal principles."

Subsequent decisions continued this line of interpretation. In 2001, the Supreme Court ruled on *Zadvydas et al. v. Davis*, admitting that the relevant statute of the Immigration Act had been silent about the length of detention. The majority said that because the Court interpreted the statute in order to avoid a "serious constitutional problem" (of due process and liberty), "once removal was no longer reasonably foreseeable, continued detention was no longer authorized by the state." The majority judges declared that due process applied to "all persons within the United States, including aliens, whether their presence is lawful, unlawful, temporary or permanent." They also upheld the federal courts' authority to determine whether such detention conformed to statutory intent and rejected the claim that the judicial branch had to yield to the decisions of the executive and legislative branches in these matters. For the many U.S. NGOs involved in the cases, the ruling was an "important victory," as the American Immigration Lawyers Association summed up. Another writer said it sent a "clear message to Congress and the executive branch that there [were] limits to their power to control immigration even when anti-immigration sentiment [ran] high." An ACLU lawyer, who represented Ma, felt the decision was a forceful "reminder that the constitutional right to freedom from detention applies to citizens and non-citizens alike." Subsequently, all related cases are being decided according to the *Zadvydas* ruling.[41]

However, the ruling took place after September 11, 2001, and the Court also included a "special circumstances exception" in its decision. That is, the judges claimed authority to address the limits of congressional power without entering the realm of "terrorism or other special circumstances where special arguments might be made for forms of preventive detention and for heightened deference to the judgments of the political branches with respect to national security." It left open precisely the legality of indefinite detentions under special wartime circumstances. Furthermore, after 9/11 and passage of the USA PATRIOT Act (Uniting and Strengthening America by Providing Appropriate Tools Required to Intercept and Obstruct Terrorism), the many different types of immigrants in the country have faced the greatest threats to their liberties.[42]

South Asian Migrants and Family Rights

Despite the different postwar political trajectories, the Western European states shared a similar timing with the United States concerning migrant issues. Moving piecemeal toward greater integration, the European Economic Community, which became the European Community in 1967 and the European Union in 1993 took little interest in immigration questions until the mid-1970s, leaving such matters exclusively to the sovereign states. In the community, the Council of Europe, the supranational political body with responsibility for broad issues of rights, shepherded passage of the European Convention in the early 1950s and initially set up the implementation mechanisms in three separate institutions: the European Commission of Human Rights (established in 1954), which handled individual and state complaints, including those from NGOs; the European Court of Human Rights (1959); and a Council of Ministers supervising the execution of the court's judgments. Echoing the Universal Declaration, the convention extended rights protections to "everyone" under its mantle and not just to citizens, although a number of articles specifically differentiated between citizens and aliens as, for example, Article 16, which allowed the states to "impos[e] restrictions on the political activity of aliens."

Petitioners rarely used the European Court before 1980; thereafter caseloads increased steadily.[43] The formal ending of the guest worker program in Europe in 1974 and the acknowledgment of the permanent residency of so many "temporary" workers pushed the issue of migrant labor to the forefront of social policy concerns. By 1976, the council of ministers advocated a "community approach" to the whole question of migration. It put into place a coordinated set of migration policies that underpinned the European Community's move to create a European-wide internal market without domestic borders.[44] But this easing of movement within the territory of Western Europe led to growing preoccupation with its formal external frontiers and the continuing breach of the borders by illegal migrants desperate for work. In seeking to halt migration, the Europeans constructed what is known as Fortress Europe—increasingly stringent deterrent policies for in-migration, coupled with shifting policies to deal with the integration of the immigrant communities from the former colonies and other labor-supplying areas.

The European Human Rights Convention is the final arbiter for citizens and noncitizens, defending against state discriminatory practices. After exhausting all domestic legal channels, a plaintiff within the orbit of the convention may lodge an application with the commission and, after 1998, the court. A number of high-profile immigration cases have limited the right of member governments to set immigration policies and ensured their compliance with international law. The court has ruled primarily on the basis of three articles of the European Convention: Article 3, prohibiting inhumane or degrading treatment; Article 8, granting the right to respect for family life; and Article 14, prohibiting discrimination on the basis of national and social origins, religion, or membership in a national minority. By its own count, from 1983 to 2004, the court handled sixty-seven cases dealing with matters of immigration.

The landmark case in the European Community was *East African Asians v. United Kingdom* in 1981. The case revolved around the effects of the British Commonwealth Immigrants Act of 1968. Despite its insistence on an Anglo identity, the long tradition of empire brought into the heartland sizeable numbers of colonial people; they were, remember, part of the core of the early Pan-African movement. New patterns of postwar migration in the 1950s and 1960s, notably from India, Pakistan, and the Caribbean, began to establish immigrant enclaves, raising public awareness of "others" in society. Prompted by a fear of a sudden additional influx of migrants from its former East African colonies, the law had limited entry for South Asians from Uganda, Tanzania, and Kenya. In the later nineteenth century, British imperial administrators had encouraged intercolonial migration from India to East Africa, and South Asians ended up working in the civil administration of the colony, in professional capacities as well as in small businesses.

The process of decolonization and nation-building, however, forced the exile of South Asians, from Uganda in 1972, or required that they become citizens, as in Kenya. For many, the only viable option seemed to be immigration to Great Britain. Even though they were former colonial subjects, they were barred from entry as a group by the 1968 law. Twenty-five plaintiffs subsequently brought suit against the British government. The Human Rights Court ruled in their favor. It found that the act unfairly singled out and discriminated against South Asians among the colonial peoples of the empire. Application of the legislation, the judges wrote, "constituted an interference with their human dignity because it relegated them to the status of second-class citizens and amounted to 'degrading treatment.'"[45] Although it did not rule on Article 14, the court paid particular attention to racial discrimination, which it also declared to be "degrading treatment." The court limited the sovereign prerogatives of the British Home Office to set immigration policies.

Despite the ruling, however, these "twice migrated" have faced considerable difficulties in their efforts to settle in British society.[46] Life on the ground in Great Britain has been difficult for the immigrants and their children with similar backgrounds and these quandaries are duplicated throughout Europe among so-called immigrants, many of whom, however, are second- or even third-generation born. Many, indeed, are citizens in the formal sense.

Oral history interviews from 1996 through 1997 in the town of Wellingsborough in Northamptonshire, England, captured some of the larger tensions of second-class socioeconomic status. The life histories of these South Asians showed the pervasive patterns of racial discrimination in educational and work opportunities. Men who once had been professionals ended up working in factories, and women, who had never worked, did so for the first time. Municipal social services remained inadequate and were geared toward assimilation into a presumed unitary Anglo culture, heightening the difficulties of social and cultural adjustments. As with other immigrant groups, there also were considerable intergenerational and gender tensions, particularly for the young girls who faced cultural restraints on their behavior and options, which their Anglo counterparts did not experience. The interviewees described the pervasive sense of "disillusionment" since coming to the country. Coupled with job discrimination and high levels of unemployment, these sentiments have fueled racial tensions among the whites, Asians, and Afro-Caribbeans in the community, at times spilling over into rioting and looting. Tensions reached such heights in the later 1990s that the township set up a racial equality council to address the unsettled grievances tearing apart the local community. In microcosm, the small township revealed wider patterns of resentment and hostility that followed the new migrants as they transformed the social, ethnic, and religious composition of community life.

The European Court also has used respect for family life to adjudicate the rights of transnational migrants. It supported the principle of family reunification, which guest workers seeking permanent residency had started to push for after 1974 as did citizens' groups on both sides of the Iron Curtain in the lead up to the Helsinki Accords. In an important case that drew on gender equity in matters of family life, the court ruled in *Abdulaziz et al. v. United Kingdom* (1985) that immigration legislation, which made it easier for men to bring in wives but not the reverse, was discriminatory. The ruling placed on the state "positive obligations" to protect family life over its role to establish "firm and fair" immigration control. "Immigration controls had to be exercised consistently with Convention obligations," it said, and people lawfully settled could not be deprived of the "society of their spouses."[47]

A number of other suits followed, including *Berrehab v. The Netherlands* (1988) and *Djeroud v. France* (1991). In the former case, the Dutch government refused to grant residency to a Moroccan citizen after his divorce from his Dutch wife, even though he had a child living in the Netherlands with whom he had regular contact four times a week. The court overturned the government's decision and forced a change in Dutch immigration policy to comply with its judgment. In the latter case, Mohammed Djeroud, an Algerian, had come to France at a young age with his mother and six siblings; he was convicted of theft on several occasions, served time in jail, and, finally, was deported. In a friendly decision, the court ruled that deportation "infringed on the right to respect for his private life and family." In response, the French government revoked the deportation order and issued him a ten-year residence permit.[48]

These decisions affected only a few in European societies. Although they ensured that the states' immigration policies complied with the standards of fairness in the Human Rights Convention for citizens and noncitizens, as redress for wider socioeconomic discriminations their limitations are glaring. Nonetheless, the courts have addressed head on labor and citizenship conundrums, as the case of Haitian migrant cane workers demonstrates.

Haitian Cane Workers in the Dominican Republic

Until 1978, the Inter-American Commission on Human Rights of the OAS served alone as the consultative organ to promote human rights among the member-states in the hemisphere. The commission had played an important oversight role in the crisis of disappearance in Chile and Argentina. Ratification of the Inter-American Convention in 1978 established a Court of Human Rights to enforce its principles. Less influential than its European counterpart, in a recent case the court nonetheless described its role in emblematic terms. The judges wrote, "This Court is first and foremost an autonomous juridical institution with jurisdiction both to decide any contentious cases concerning the interpretation and application of the Convention as well as ensure to the victim of a violation of the rights or freedoms guaranteed by the Convention the protection of those rights." Because its decisions were binding, it was also the "organ having the broadest enforcement powers" to ensure compliance with the principles of the convention. In addition to taking on a number of high-visibility human rights cases, the court entered into matters of migrant and citizenship rights.[49]

The Inter-American Court ruled on a potentially far-reaching case concerning migrant Haitian laborers in the Dominican Republic and Dominican-born Haitians. The plaintiffs' central thesis serves as this chapter's epigraph. The case brings together a number of vital issues in the intersection of migrant labor protections and human rights guarantees. It shows the deplorable working and living conditions of life for migrants desperate for work and the ease with which government and military personnel can evade existing labor laws and rights protections. It reveals as well that a domestic human rights network with transnational links has emerged in the Dominican Republic, determined to highlight the plight of the migrants and defend their rights in court. Finally, it demonstrates how regional law can force changes in the state's citizenship law, although on a case-by-case basis and not without controversy.

Precipitated by the "mass expulsion" of Haitian migrant workers in late 1996 and 1997, following an earlier policy of removal in 1991 that affected more than 35,000 people, twenty-eight petitioners supported by their NGO defenders brought suit against the government for many violations of the Inter-American Convention. The Dominican Republic had signed the convention in 1978 and recognized the jurisdiction of the court in 1999. Domestic laws offered no redress, the applicants asserted; they needed to have recourse to the jurisdiction and power of the Inter-American Court. Following the recommendation of the commission that looked into the case, the court issued a provisional measure in August 2000, calling for the immediate suspension of the expulsions and arranging for "expert testimony" at its headquarters in San José, Costa Rica. It opened a hearing. The Dominican government claimed it merely was exercising its "right of repatriation," an irrevocable attribute of its own sovereignty.

The collective expulsions in the 1990s revealed the long-standing antagonisms between the two nation-states intricately connected by geography, demography, and history. The successful emergence of the Dominican Republic as a sugar-exporting country after World War II reflected its access to cheap Haitian labor. An official State Sugar Council continues to recruit and organize the seasonal migration for work in the sugar—and, increasingly, coffee, rice, and cacao—harvests. The migrants live in state-run labor camps known as *bateyes* located near the cane fields.

Passage of the Inter-American Convention on human rights increasingly turned regional attention to the abuses of recruitment and the deplorable living and working conditions for Haitians in the labor camps. In the context of mounting pressure, the Inter-American Commission made two on-site visits to the Dominican Republic, in 1991 and 1997, and summarized its findings two years later in a published report. The situation on the ground, the authors wrote, was "truly a cause for concern."[50] Neither the seasonal migrants nor the more than 500,000 Haitian-born migrants working also in construction and the tourist industry received any type of identification documents. As the commissioners put it, they lived in a state of "permanent illegality," even though many had resided in the Dominican Republic for more than thirty years. Because the parents had no legal status, neither did their children; the hospitals refused to issue birth certificates to the newborn and authorities did not enter their names in the civil registry. As legal nonpersons, the migrant families had no civil protections or access to social services and they could be deported at any time. The whole situation contravened Article 11 of the Dominican Constitution, which adopts the principle of territorial citizenship. In constitutional law,

Dominicans are "all persons born in the territory of the Republic with the exception of the legitimate children of foreigners resident in the country in diplomatic representation or in transit."[51] The Dominican government claimed that Haitians—even those born in its territory—were "in transit."

The commission also found the conditions in the *bateyes* to be deplorable, with unsanitary, cramped quarters; no health services or educational opportunities, unchecked sexual exploitation of women and children; and work practices that bordered on forced labor, including payment of vouchers that were redeemable only in "company" stores. This old "truck" system of servitude has been outlawed by virtually every international labor law; working and living conditions indeed defied the principles of economic rights and justice. In the strongest language, too, the commission's report condemned the collective expulsions as a "flagrant violation of international law that shocks the conscience of all humankind."[52] The expulsions were arbitrary with no warning or chance to tell relatives or friends, and many of the expelled were owed wages at the time of their forced removal. Furthermore, those deported had not been given a hearing or any opportunity to explain their status. According to eyewitness testimony, decisions were made on the basis of a person's presumed race, indicated by darkness of skin color and mode of speaking. The military trucked those rounded up to the borders and expelled them.

The plaintiffs built the case on their right to humane treatment under the convention, including freedom of movement, residency, and nationality; the right to juridical personality; and the right to freedom from discrimination. At its first ruling in August 2000, the court made a "prima facie presumption" that the individuals "were subjected to abuse and risk." However, it did not order provisional measures and protections "for cases of unnamed groups of people" who were equally at risk. That is, the court did not extend its ruling to the many others who also faced deportation. In March 2001, the court established a Supervisory Committee comprised of commission members, government representatives, and the petitioners who represented the plaintiffs. It also gave consultative status to Dominican human rights NGOs involved in the case, most notably the Dominican Women's Human Rights Movement (Movimiento de Mujeres Dominico-Haitianas, MUDHA), acknowledging their legitimacy in defending human rights in Dominican society. This committee, which the government joined only a year later, coordinated the implementation of the provisional measures.

The provisional ruling drew the court directly into the state's right to determine citizenship. In a pioneering decision, the judges found that "many of the plaintiffs [were] entitled to Dominican citizenship according to Dominican laws" and ruled they had been living legally in the Dominican Republic at the time of deportation. It gave them citizenship, which it also extended to children born in the Dominican Republic of Haitian origin. The government has reasserted its sovereignty over citizenship in a General Migration Law of 2004, although it agreed to establish a "rose book" for the registration of children born of nonnationals. Briefs and rulings in the matter have continued.[53] The court also mandated other substantive changes in domestic laws to correspond to international standards for humane treatment at work, for ending arbitrary arrests, and for affirming family reunification, and it granted these rights to noncitizens as well. Finally, the judges ordered the government to issue bimonthly reports on the actions it was taking to comply with the new legal obligations, a ruling that the MUDHA at the time called "an important precedent and innovation."[54] The "abusive and inhuman" deportations have continued, however, although their numbers declined substantially. In response, the Dominican NGOs have not eased the pressure for greater protections. As a means to reduce the mass violations of rights, MUDHA, among others, has called for the creation of special tribunals to review each case of possible deportation.

Multinational Corporations and Forced Labor

As this Haitian case shows, migrant workers and their families faced (and continue to face) multiple violations of their rights, exploited at work, deprived of decent living conditions, and subject to arbitrary deportations at any moment. This discrimination followed their children, perpetuating vicious cycles of poverty and disadvantage. In accordance with existing international law, in its effort to safeguard the rights of distinct plaintiffs, the Inter-American Court held officials in the Dominican Republic responsible for the deplorable abuses and demanded some redress. Compliance required continuing oversight, which the court left to a committee comprised of state officials together with local and transnational NGOs. Although provisional, it represented a start—however slow and difficult—toward greater socioeconomic protection for migrants as well as for domestic workers and their families.

Operationally, however, international law only held state actors directly accountable for specific abuses or, as pushed by gender advocates, for their failure to protect persons from systematic abuses in the private sphere. Advocates and theorists since the mid-1990s increasingly have examined the law's failure to address the human rights abuses by powerful nonstate actors, including multinational corporations, which are a driving force of the world economy. With their capital mobility and financial strength, these economic actors can enter local communities and exploit the environment and labor supplies.

Through a circuitous route, and initiated by the innovative Center for Constitutional Rights, a number of high-profile lawsuits have been filed in U.S. courts against major corporations, including a suit in 1996 brought by twelve Myanmar village workers against Unocal Corporation, the oil and gas company headquartered in California, for using forced labor in its multibillion-dollar construction of a pipeline going to Thailand (*Doe v. Unocal*). The plaintiffs charged Unocal with entering into a partnership with Myanmar's brutal military rulers, knowing full well that the military would engage in "massive human rights violations" in pursuing the project. They held Unocal liable for actions by the Myanmar government during the construction phase.

The case was filed under the United States Alien Tort Claims Act, which had been adopted by the first congress in 1789, primarily to show that the new American nation had judicial provisions to ensure "justice" against a foreign complaint. The act simply read, "The district courts shall have original jurisdiction of any civil action by an alien for a tort only [for civil damages], committed in violation of the law of nations or a treaty of the United States."[55] Languishing for 190 years, the act was reactivated by lawyers in the Center for Constitutional Rights in 1980, in a case in which a victim's family (Dora Filártiga) successfully sued Américo Peña, who was living clandestinely in the United States, for the torture-killing of her brother in Asunción in 1976. At the time, Peña was police inspector under the Alfredo Stroessner dictatorship in Paraguay. In this pathfinding case, the U.S. Court of Appeals, Second Circuit, accepted federal court jurisdiction for alien tort; it ruled that the federal courts may prosecute for violations of universally accepted norms of international human rights law.[56]

This legal victory set the stage for subsequent trials in which nonnationals, who had been victims of gross violations elsewhere—torture, disappearance, genocide, forced labor—have charged their abusers in U.S. courts. The Unocal suit was the first ever to hold a multinational corporation liable for human rights violations. The suit claimed that the California-based company had engaged in "unlawful business practices" under state law. In December 2004, the parties reached a settlement. Although the terms remained confidential, it compensated the victims and provided funds for improved living conditions, health care, and education for villagers in the pipeline region. The Center for Constitutional Rights has similar cases on its international docket, including one against the Royal Dutch Petroleum Company by members of the Ogoni people in Nigeria for environmental damages and human rights violations (*Wiwa v. Royal Dutch Petroleum*) and another (*Bowoto v. Chevron*) against Chevron for the murder of local unarmed protesters in Nigeria, demonstrating against the company's failure to protect the environment.[57] In 2004, the George W. Bush administration filed a brief with the Ninth Circuit Court seeking to restrict the jurisdiction of the Alien Tort Claims Act and limit corporate liability. In June of that year, the Supreme Court, in cautious wording, upheld the statute, stating that the "door is still ajar subject to vigilant doorkeeping, and thus open to a narrow class of international norms today." These changes in the U.S. legal landscape are part of wider discussions about the role and accountability of nonstate actors in human rights abuses, as seen in Fig. 4. Future developments in international human rights law likely will include greater liability for multinational corporations.

Societal Tensions

However broad the momentum was to use the courts to obtain justice, these efforts also faced considerable societal backlash. This opposition confounded the expectations of scholars such as David Jacobson, who argued in 1996 that judicial interpretations were altering the very fabric of international relations. Pushed by transnational migrants as rights-bearing persons, sovereign authority under Jacobson's narrative was shifting to the international realm of binding law and norms, transforming the state into a bureaucratic apparatus of the human rights system. It also was rearranging the relationships among international actors. As Jacobson put it, "The state, formerly *the* actor in international relations, now becomes the forum or mechanism that binds together the nonstate associations and the set of rules that make up the international order."[58] He presented an alternative narrative about the erosion of state sovereignty, one that turned individuals and NGOs into the dynamic agents of the global community increasingly joined together on shared human rights principles and values. Although based on important legal innovations, Jacobson's assessment was premature, not only because of the fragility of legal advances and their restricted scope in practice but also because of the limitations inherent in the application of law without wide community consensus. Achievement of policy goals is not solely about courts or administrative changes. It requires public acceptance, and little domestic consensus seems to exist about legal safeguards to integrate noncitizens more fully into societies.

The age of global migrations has bred its own brand of xenophobic responses—anti-immigrant sentiments—even in countries such as South Africa with only a small proportion of nonnationals in the population. The 2005 migrant study found somewhere between 850,000 to one million foreign-born people residing in the country, representing less than

2 percent of the population. Despite the modest figures, however, the report also noted widespread hostility to foreigners. It claimed that "many South Africans perceive a foreign invasion," mirroring sentiments that have become pervasive worldwide.[59] In this context, public opinion is more willing to support draconian "containment" policies, which have ranged from stringent visa requirements to expedited deportations to detention of undocumented workers in makeshift structures to tighter border controls and surveillance. These measures, too, represent serious challenges to human rights laws and standards. If these policies have increased around the globe since the 9/11 attacks, which appreciably heightened attention everywhere to migrants and borders, they had earlier precedents.

A case in point is the collective unease that developed in response to the U.S. Supreme Court's pioneering decision in *Plyler v. Doe* (1982), which extended opportunities for free education to the children of illegal immigrants. The court was clear in intent, with potentially wide-ranging implications for law. The justices wrote, "Whatever his status under the immigration laws, an alien is a 'person' in any ordinary sense of that term." This iconic phrase by Supreme Court Justice William J. Brennan of "alien is a 'person'" also showed up in the judgments on the *Zadvydas* case. In *Plyler*, the court extended the Fourteenth Amendment's due process protections to "anyone, citizen or stranger, who is subject to the laws of a State." Thus, the judges rejected a Texas statute that withheld public funds from any school district educating children who were "not legally" admitted into the United States. The justices said at the time that the provision "impose[d] a lifetime hardship on a discrete class of children not accountable for their disabling status" and they extolled the "pivotal role" of education in "maintaining the fabric" of society and sustaining the "political and cultural heritage" of the country.

But this expansive legal argument about the inherent rights of "persons" sat uneasily with growing numbers of U.S. citizens fearful of the drain on social services and community resources. In direct response to *Plyer*, for example, the California electorate in 1994 approved Proposition 187 by a margin of 59 to 41 percent, which excluded so-called illegal aliens from public social services and barred their children from access to all levels of public education. To date, state officials and school superintendents simply have not implemented the restrictions and continue to provide education and services to noncitizen immigrants. The fundamental principle about rights for noncitizen immigrants and their children have remained highly controversial and contested. In November 2004, for example, the Arizona electorate similarly passed Proposition 200, which sought to curtail the access of "illegal" persons (in the proposition's language) to state social benefits.[60]

In the 1990s, furthermore, European societies saw a rise in avowedly antiforeign and anti-immigrant politics. These sentiments reflected tensions between old citizens and new ones, exacerbated by politicians who labeled so-called minority groups "foreign." They also expressed unease at the unmistakable rise in the numbers of undocumented workers and people seeking asylum from such human catastrophes as wars, famines, and underdevelopment. Anti-immigrant actions extended from Jean-Marie Le Pen's National Front in France, which saw the continued immigration from North Africa as a "threat" to French life to the Danish right-wing People's Party to Pim Fortuyn's crusade against Muslim immigrants for their refusal to assimilate into Dutch society.[61] These parties and politicians manipulated xenophobic sentiments, accusing foreigners of taking advantage of the region's extensive welfare provisions, depriving hardworking citizens of jobs, and bringing seemingly alien elements such as Islam into the heart of Christian Europe. So virulent were the verbal (and, at times, even physical) attacks against people from Muslim backgrounds and other asylum-seekers that human rights defenders began to speak about a threat of Islamophobia. Under this type of domestic pressure, the German government in 1993 amended its basic laws, which had provided a constitutional right of asylum. Originally written in response to the massive Nazi persecutions of its recent past, the change restricted the right of asylum in Germany.

A similar backlash by nationalist groups against the interventions of the Inter-American Court into sovereign Dominican society also threatened the safety of two of the most active advocates in the trial, Solange Pierre of the MUDHA and Father Pedro Ruquoy. A series of rulings in 2005 recognized that the two were "still at risk by reason of their participation in the [public] hearing" before the court. The court admitted they were the "targets of threats and attacks," including daily telephone calls, as those received by Pierre warning her that "people that do not speak last so much longer." Because of fears for his life, Roquoy had left the country. Many of the Haitian plaintiffs, too, were under threat and suffered "psychological problems."[62] Despite the vastly different contexts to this rise in anti-immigrant sentiments, the shared patterns of responses also reflected the prevalence of fear about the social costs of globalization. Migrants who themselves were responding to the insecurities and inequalities of the globalizing world often bore the brunt of the discontent.

*   *   *

In the face of continuing economic inequality—at the global, national, and individual levels—the struggle for economic justice faced major hurdles, although its fundamental principle continues to be a normative goal for human striving. It is, after all, about developing the human capacities and societal resources to provide the basic needs for human development and the educational and vocational tools for economic and social advancement. Unable alone to effectively challenge the large structures of the world economy, NGOs have emerged to defend—with some successes for individuals and groups—the vulnerable within it. Since the late 1970s, they have served as alternative voices in human rights struggles, determined to broaden understanding of democracy to include not just political freedoms but redistributive measures for social justice. In their defense of migrants through popular pressure and court maneuvers, NGOs have expanded the notion of who has what rights within existing political frontiers. Although highly contested, they have thrown down challenges to the very rationale underlying the nation-states.

In the early 1990s, violence broke out in many places around the globe with intensified ferocity. Some outbreaks were continuations of earlier patterns of ethnic and social tensions over power, land, and scarce resources; others were new crises, reflections of the altered geopolitical scene with the formal ending of the Cold War and its power alliances and calculations. The challenges once again mobilized—and pushed even further—the U.N. human rights machinery that had been shaped by the cases and causes examined in Part I of this book. It brought U.N.-sponsored peacekeeping missions directly into local communities, demonstrating fissures between international and local knowledge and revealing previously submerged tensions between the practices of humanitarian relief and the principles of human rights guarantees. But the post–Cold War context also permitted institutional innovations in the creation of ad hoc and permanent international criminal courts to hold individuals criminally libel for gross human rights violations. It expanded the jurisdiction of international criminal law. The growing concern with international accountability fed into and reinforced movements from below to redress historical wrongs in ways that offered distinct challenges for human rights advocacy. These are the main themes of Part III of this book.

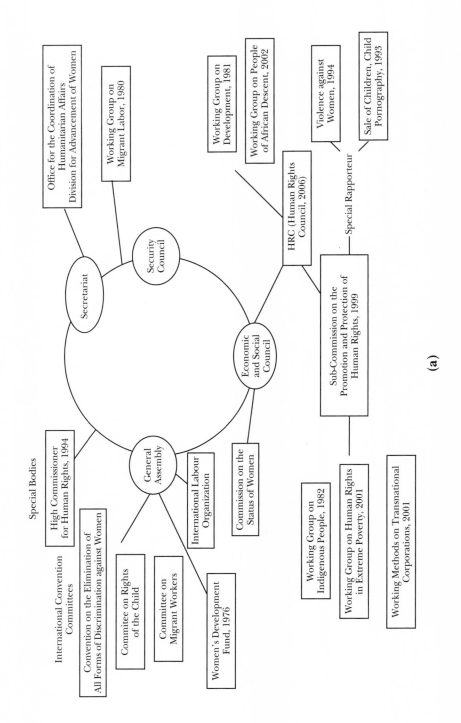

Special Bodies

International Convention Committees

Convention on the Elimination of All Forms of Discrimination against Women

Committee on Rights of the Child

Committee on Migrant Workers

Women's Development Fund, 1976

High Commissioner for Human Rights, 1994

Working Group on Indigenous People, 1982

Working Group on Human Rights in Extreme Poverty, 2001

Working Methods on Transnational Corporations, 2001

International Labour Organization

Commission on the Status of Women

General Assembly

Economic and Social Council

Security Council

Secretariat

Office for the Coordination of Humanitarian Affairs Division for Advancement of Women

Working Group on Migrant Labor, 1980

Working Group on Development, 1981

Working Group on People of African Descent, 2002

HRC (Human Rights Council, 2006)

Sub-Commission on the Promotion and Protection of Human Rights, 1999

Special Rapporteur

Violence against Women, 1994

Sale of Children, Child Pornography, 1993

(a)

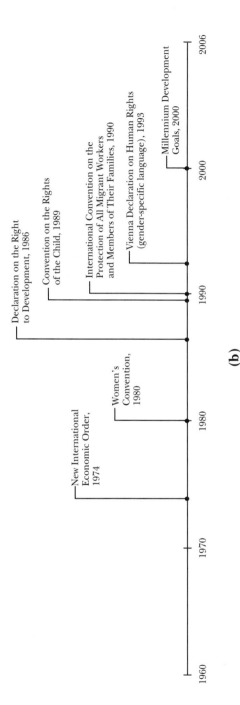

(b)

Figure 3. Major changes in U.N. promotion of gender and economic justice: (a) The chief U.N. oversight bodies responding to popular pressure for gender and economic justice. Adapted from the official U.N. Web site, www.un.org. (b) Chronology of the passage of major international resolutions and laws concerning gender and economic justice. Adapted from the official U.N. Web site, www.un.org.

Part III
Human Rights at a Crossroads: Wars, Crimes, and Priorities

In the 1990s, global human rights advocates faced a set of distinct challenges that added urgent agendas to their debates and work at the international, national, and local levels. These new developments became layered onto the existing patterns of rights advocacy and networking that continued to evolve from the past. In this sense, the decade of the 1990s emerges as an important era on its own terms for human rights history. I call it the "long" decade of the 1990s, extending roughly from 1989 to 2005. This dating moves away from a formal decade-driven chronology, as if ten years by themselves have any causative logic. It accommodates, rather, contemporaries' understanding of events after 1989 and the historians' retrospective modes of analysis. During the era international attention remained fixed on many of the problems of economic inequality, failed development programs, transnational labor migration challenges, and gender vulnerabilities addressed in Part II. The work of these transnational advocacy networks continued throughout the 1990s and into the new millennium; many of these challenges persist to this day.

A focus on continuities, however, should not mask new contexts. After all, the dramatic events of 1989, which in November brought down the Berlin Wall—once a seemingly permanent structure of a divided postwar Europe—turned the Helsinki human rights movements in Soviet-bloc countries into historical monuments. Either disbanded or transformed into ruling political parties, these movements lost their original rationale in the challenging politics of transition to democratic governance and market societies. Continuity in name—the International Helsinki

Federation, for example—belies the vastly broadened agenda of the international NGO networks subsumed under its mantle. Similarly, the election of Nelson Mandela as president of South Africa in 1994 marked the formal end of the antiapartheid movement and its wide transnational coalition of supporters. This movement now, too, has become part of the historical record; a good portion of its archives is on the Web, available for use by human rights activists, academics, and the interested lay public.[1]

Contemporaries were well aware of the political changes that seemed to be enveloping all regions of the globe, starting in the later 1980s. Subsequently, historians, too, have picked up on this particular global moment of optimism, too easily overlooked in the light of "ethnic cleansing," genocides, terrorism, and wars that also have left their painful scars on this long decade. But the early optimism was pervasive and extended far beyond the dramatic pictures of Berliners climbing the wall, which were beamed around the world nearly simultaneously; at the time, their meanings required little translation into the vernacular. It seemed as if the end of the Cold War coincided with and, indeed, promoted a wave of "people power," to borrow the slogan of the movement that had ousted the long-standing dictator of the Philippines, Ferdinand Marcos, in 1986. In the shifting geopolitical climate of the late 1980s, Soviet leaders were either unwilling or unable to enforce their authority. The Cold War political map disappeared in Eastern Europe and fourteen independent countries emerged in its stead. The Soviet Union was dissolved formally in December 1991, leaving a sovereign Russia, nine independent states from former Soviet republics, and a number of disputed territorial borders that contain seeds of future claims and conflicts, among them the small land of Transnistria, defended by Russia against Moldavia (a new republic), the territory of South Ossetia in Georgia, and the district of Nagorno-Karabakh, claimed by both Azerbaijan and Armenia, in the Caucasus region.[2]

Although the political map remained virtually unchanged in Africa, in 1992 the prominent Ghanaian historian and intellectual Adu Boahen captured this moment as many contemporaries understood it. He wrote movingly of a "powerful democratic wind . . . now raging in the continent of Africa south of the Sahara." It already had "shaken" many regions and he cataloged the push for change in West Africa (in Benin, Togo, and Ghana, among others), in Central Africa (Zaire, Mozambique, Angola, and Gabon) and in Kenya in East Africa. For Boahen, this wind followed popular movements for the restoration of multiparty democracies, although, he warned, the push also was being resisted by "some African leaders." His 1992 account of appreciable new beginnings also is echoed in Frederick Cooper's history of Africa since 1940.

Writing more broadly of democratic opposition to "dictatorship and military governments across the world, including Africa," Cooper addressed the many reasons for the similarities in "democratic experiments" on the African continent in the early 1990s. His list included the overall decline in patronage resources in the light of years of economic contraction; mounting discontent among professionals and students at blocked avenues of mobility and among workers and the urban poor at deteriorating living standards; new pressures by international financial agencies such as the World Bank, which began to link lending policies to greater governmental transparency and accountability; and a rise in the numbers of local NGOs promoting human rights and legal reforms.[3]

People in Latin and Central America also were facing the moral and practical conundrums inherent in the transitions from dictatorship to democracy. In this region, too, although following distinct time lines and strategies, democratic change was in the air. Increasingly, domestic agendas in Argentina, Brazil, Uruguay, and Chile, as well as in El Salvador, Guatemala, and Honduras began to confront the need to balance priorities: for social peace and stability, on the one hand, and for truth and justice in public reckoning for past crimes, on the other. It is no wonder that the Argentine Mothers of the Plaza de Mayo remained such inspirational figures for the human rights community in the long decade. Through their constant vigils, writings, and speech-making, they put their own histories on display, affirming the centrality of victims' narratives for any movement of healing and reconciliation.

By the early 1990s, the collective efforts to develop formal institutions to confront past crimes, such as through truth commissions, tribunals, and other legal strategies, had gathered momentum in Eastern Europe, in postapartheid South Africa, and in Latin and Central America. These societal experiments were setting new agendas for international human rights advocates and U.N. peacekeeping missions, bringing, from the grassroots levels, the complexities of transitional justice needs to the forefront of human rights debates and actions. These undertakings gave a distinctive flavor to the long decade, making the need to address historical wrongs part of present-day agendas in order to create a future that would be different from the past. In this post–Cold War climate, memory and history intruded in new ways into human rights advocacy. Figure 4 depicts the different levels of accountability that burgeoned in the long decade. As part of a continuum of responsibility, these mechanisms moved from criminal liability to truth-setting to doctrines of contingent sovereignty.

The early 1990s also seemed to hold possibilities for new forms of accommodation among Israelis and Palestinians, whose differing narratives of justice long had embroiled U.N. organs, the Human Rights Commission, and grassroots NGOs, offering a vast array of social and legal services, many under wider international and U.N. coordination. This conflict had become caught in a geopolitical stalemate, particularly with the Israeli military occupation of the West Bank and Gaza. The continuing occupation after 1967 was of vital concern to U.N. agencies. In the practice of warfare, occupations typically are for the short-run, followed by annexation or withdrawal. Furthermore, international humanitarian law (specifically, Article 49 of the Fourth Geneva Convention) forbids the victor power from settling its population on disputed, occupied territory. Yet, to increasing numbers of Israelis, the criticisms by U.N. agencies and the General Assembly resolutions were simply political, part of wider threats to the integrity of the state by neighbors bent on the destruction of Israel. Besides, they pointed to the elision of anti-Zionism with anti-Semitism particularly in the Soviet bloc countries which, in their eyes, strengthened the case for Israel as a necessary sanctuary against persecution. Relations between the state of Israel and the United Nations hit their nadir in 1975, when the General Assembly Resolution 3379 equated "Zionism with racism." For Israelis, the linkage was deeply offensive and a profound misreading of their own history. The stalemate also came from geopolitical calculations favorable to the Israeli state. Beginning with the Nixon presidency, which sought regional surrogates for American power globally, the United States became a strong ally of the state of Israel; by 1981, the U.S. government was using its veto power consistently to keep the Palestinian-Israeli conflict away from Security Council deliberations.[4]

If the early 1990s held promise for Palestinians and Israelis, it followed the events of the first intifada (1987–93), a nonviolent, mass protest movement against Israeli occupation. By then, most Palestinians in occupied land had given up the hope of "liberation" by an outside Arab force; and the government in exile in Tunisia, the Palestinian Liberation Organization (PLO), too, had changed its policies from calling for the overthrow of Israel as a Jewish state to proposing a national authority in Mandate Palestine in territories to be evacuated by the Israelis. In the uprising, however, Palestinian people took matters into their own hands. At its peak, youths demonstrated in the streets, throwing stones at the armed security forces and settlers; the Israeli state retaliated with repressive measures, including curfews, arrests, detention, and destruction of Palestinian property. But the intifada had demonstrated a strong Palestinian identity and community cohesion, which made both Palestinians and Israelis more interested in the possibility of negotiations, resulting in the Declaration of Principles (the "Oslo Accords") in 1993. Compromises secured by U.N. officials in part had facilitated bringing Israel to the negotiating table, notably, the decision by the U.N. General Assembly in November 1991 to repeal the "Zionism is racism" resolution.

The Oslo Accords established the Palestinian Authority as an interim government in the West Bank and Gaza, but they contained no agreement on the final status or end point of the negotiations. They were, indeed, interim, leaving the Jewish settlements in place; offering no guidelines for the future of Jerusalem, claimed by both societies as their capital; and bypassing the refugee question completely. Palestinian refugees had not been consulted in any phase of these negotiations. As with the length of occupation, so, too, Palestinian refugee status was anomalous in international diplomacy: international practice either imposed an exchange of population (as occurred between Greeks and Turks after World War I and as among South Asian communities in the establishment of India and Pakistan) or repatriation to facilitate a return (as encouraged by official UNHCR policies). For over four decades, neither solution could be implemented. It is no wonder, then that the Oslo Accords could not forge a just or lasting peace, although one study early in the decade compiled from community perspectives noted extensive support for the promises behind negotiation: it expressed "the strength of the yearning for peace inside both communities."[5]

The expectations for peaceful democratic change so palpable in many regions of the globe gave way to violence and civil strife. In some situations of transition, such as in Yugoslavia, international and civil wars converged in bewildering complexity after 1991 and, in 1994, genocidal murder took place in Rwanda. With the global spread of so many technologies of destruction, warfare became a deadly feature of life for civilians increasingly caught in the crossfire. International lawyer William O'Neill offered a retrospective assessment of the cycles of warfare and societal implosion breaking out in the 1990s. With considerable irony, he wrote that ending the geopolitical military and strategic balances of the Cold War made "the world increasingly safe for violent, local conflicts."[6] Even if it hints at a new geopolitical reality, the point is not quite accurate because warfare was hardly absent from the Cold War decades: there were the tragic and prolonged wars of decolonization and nation-building, internal civil strife and counterterrorist violence sponsored by Cold War antagonists, and even genocides, as took place during the rule of Pol Pot from 1976 to 1979 in Cambodia. But as O'Neill acknowledged, the end of the Cold War reduced the "value" of some geographic areas, notably parts of Africa, for powerful states calculating their interests, making local strife of limited international concern. It also raised other oil-rich regions, notably the Middle East, to prominence. The key for human rights history is not fully the extent of warfare but, rather, the changes in the international response to the outbreak of armed hostilities, in whatever form they took—whether declared wars between state armies, civil wars, or militia and guerrilla warfare.

The change came *from above*, inserting human rights into matters of war and peace. Diplomatically, the end of the Cold War had an immediate impact on international thinking. The new geopolitical context was seized on immediately for its new potential for human rights interventions. The end of Soviet authority seemed to open different possibilities for Security Council action, long stalemated in many matters of political controversy. Government representatives in the United Nations as well as agency heads envisioned a new foundation for "international order" and "global security" ensured by a timely intervention into violent situations of armed conflict, threatening the safety of civilians. In his "Agenda for Peace" in 1992, U.N. Secretary General Boutros Boutros-Ghali called for a new collective resolve to confront and contain armed conflicts and also humanitarian disasters. As a Human Rights Watch report described it the next year, the strategy called for adding human rights monitors and specialists in international humanitarian law to U.N. peacekeeping operations on the ground in an expanded effort to help rebuild shattered societies.[7]

These new operations represented a significant departure from past U.N. peacekeeping practices, which had been established in India and Pakistan in 1949 and during the Suez crisis in 1956. In the traditional U.N. model, peacekeeping missions were used in interstate conflicts to separate states and armies at the border to implement a ceasefire, exchange prisoners, or monitor disarmament. In contrast, the redesigned missions worked in the middle of fragmented societies, not at their borders, and they faced a confusing array of people with conflicting local, regional, and national ties and loyalties. One author identified twenty-five sites of armed conflict around the world in 1998, of which twenty-three were internal crises, involving extremes of violence from the clashes between government forces and militia, rebels, or criminal groups.[8] Despite the complexity of the new settings, the international mandates called for the restoration of peace and the reemergence of civil society and the rule of law—in short, for institution-building in the designated country. The ongoing implementation of these mandates in the context of intensifying civil and international strife shaped a new doctrine in the lexicon of human rights practice, known today as "humanitarian intervention." Prior to 1990, there was little precedent for such a notion or an action in the practices of international peacekeeping.

This new activism seemed to fit with the general optimism of the age, which also sustained a significant rise in the numbers of international and local NGOs throughout the world. According to Renate Bloem of the coordinating coalition of NGOs (CONGO), a dramatic rise in NGOs coincided with the ongoing processes of democratization moving unevenly around the globe. Her survey in 1993 counted 28,900 international NGOs and more than 20,000 transnational networks; nine years earlier, there had been less than half the number of international NGOs, 12,686 in total, and, in 1972, only 2,795. At the time of her report in 2001, furthermore, Bloem reported the number of NGOs in consultative status with the Economic and Social Council to be well above 2,000. The pattern was duplicated at the national level, where in the 1990s NGOs increased "sharply in numbers and popularity."[9] It is not surprising, therefore, that these dense organizational networks and horizontal ties in societies provided fertile ground for serious debate about the merits of the humanitarian doctrine as well as the efficacy of strategies to bring aid to beleaguered communities. As intermediaries between traumatized people and the international community, NGO activists on the ground negotiated for aid corridors and provided a wide range of relief as well as social and mental health services. They also heard testimonies, compelling eyewitness accounts of crimes that had been committed during war. As a result of these new channels of information, a redefinition of international criminal law—in the case of rape, for example—has reflected the victims' own experiences of the crime.

Part III assesses the complex interplay of human rights advocacy work and state power from 1989 to 2005. It focuses primarily on the new challenges that have emerged for human rights activists while also keeping in focus themes examined earlier, for they remain vital to any assessment of new departures. Specifically, it examines the fate of humanitarian intervention by following events on the ground, assessing the interaction of many different groups and organizations needed for its implementation. Recognizing the difficulty of generalizing in cases where "success" reflects the specificities of local cultures, traditions, and histories, it focuses primarily on the unfolding crises in the breakup of Yugoslavia and also on Rwanda, the paradigmatic examples that most directly helped write the doctrine of "humanitarian intervention."

Sensitivity to historical contexts was central to the original effort to pinpoint the irreducible human rights principles necessary to guide U.N.-sponsored interventions—at least for influential international NGOs. Human Rights Watch was clear on the point. No U.N. humanitarian mission, it warned in 1993, could operate as if the past did not matter, as if the missions were simply working on a "blank slate." "Abuses of the past," the group stated in no uncertain terms, "can haunt future reconstruction by triggering a cycle of revenge and by establishing a precedent of impunity for gross abuse." To address this pressing problem, the group demanded accountability, whether through "investigation and formal acknowledgment of the truth about the past [or] disciplinary measures, and prosecution of the offenders in national or international tribunals."[10] From its particular site of human rights monitoring, Human Rights Watch entered a global debate that was bringing matters of criminal justice to international attention. It led to the creation of new international tribunals to try individuals for international crimes committed in armed conflicts. These courts, however, were but one end of a much longer spectrum of measures emerging to deal with the need to redress human wrongs. This issue, too, became compelling in the long decade.

Taken together, the themes in Part III offer a number of observations that speak directly to human rights advocacy work for the twenty-first century. They show an operational gap between NGOs at the international level, which typically worked smoothly with the U.N. missions, and those at the grassroots level, even if, as the case of disappearance showed, international operations could not do without the detailed information provided by those on the ground. These divisions, arguably, reflected the contradictory perspectives of international and local advocates in confronting armed force. More to the point, the term "humanitarian" proved exceedingly malleable and difficult to harness to human rights values. Humanitarian intervention easily morphed into aggressive unilateralist war, as happened in the U.S. invasion of Iraq in March 2003. It is not surprising that in the wake of the Iraq occupation, the original doctrine has found diminished support among U.N. member-states, suspicious anyway of the use of superpower force, and among numbers of prominent NGOs fearful of coupling military force with human rights principles. The groundswell of dissatisfaction about humanitarian intervention was one major source helping push for reform of the United Nations. Sixty years later, the organization still mirrored the power balances of the immediate post–World War II era. Calls for substantive U.N. reform entered the international agenda in 2005.

Chapter 6
Ethnic Violence, Humanitarian Intervention, and Criminal Accountability in the 1990s

> I am a victim. I want justice—and it's not done by the resignation of ministers. I want to see justice done in the courts.
> —Hasan Nuhanović, BBC America, April 16, 2002

In the "long" 1990s, the societies in an increasing number of states descended into deadly armed conflict and chaos that blurred the standard operating categories of the international human rights machinery. As expressions of societal implosions, they literally bled over territorial borders. Little was familiar to Security Council members, to human rights commissioners, or to the humanitarian wing of the United Nations, although they tended to view these conflicts through familiar prisms of "ancient" ethnic hatreds and the rules of international humanitarian law. Produced by many different contexts and histories, these war-torn situations tended to be internal and international wars simultaneously, with a bewildering array of combatants, ranging from national armies to paramilitary groups to rebels and child soldiers as well as to bandits and opportunistic crime gangs. For many, violence indeed became an opportunity for unparalleled riches. In this context, the divide between military and civilian eroded as did once clear notions of friend and foe. Easily framed in ethnic and religious terms, these conflicts were equally about the maintenance of elite power and growing frustrations at the structural poverty and misallocation of resources that followed economic and social exploitation.

If the conflicts were confusing, their consequences were unambiguously large-scale human rights violations: the indiscriminate bombardment of civilian communities, the forced displacement of peoples, rape as a war aim, refugees fleeing for their lives, and the murder and deaths of so many unprotected people. Given the high, although spotty, level of media coverage of these human tragedies, one scholar involved in U.N. reform wrote in 1999 that there has been "more serious government and academic study, as well as public interest, in enforcement options over the past decade than at any other point since the Hague Peace conference a century ago."[1] However difficult to pin down with precision, the spread of human rights consciousness had produced growing public unease with the rising toll of civilian deaths and deprivations in wartime. With the mounting fear for people at risk, human rights visions again were disrupting international relations as usual.

The unfolding patterns of violence were clear, even if their root causes often remained buried beneath simplistic explanatory labels. Against the backdrop of the U.N. Security Council's preoccupation with Iraqi president Saddam Hussein's invasion of neighboring Kuwait in August 1990 and the ensuing Gulf War (in early 1991), in June of that year the Socialist Republic of Yugoslavia began to unravel as it fell into civil and international war. With the ending of socialist rule, its Serb nationalist leadership of former communists, who had been manipulating ethnic divisions as in the trial of the Belgrade Six, brazenly coined the term "ethnic cleansing" as an explanation or, rather, justification for the forced movement of peoples into ethnically homogeneous states in the Balkan region of Europe. But this "cleansing" was a mask for genocidal violence. Ethnic cleansing ever since has become an all-too-common part of the human rights vocabulary of atrocities.

In a similar pattern of implosion, Rwanda experienced a brutal genocidal conflict unleashed by the Hutu Power authorities against the Tutsi minority people between April 16 and July 14, 1994. About 800,000 Tutsi (and their supporters among the moderate Hutu people) were murdered in the three months of frenzy, which worked out to exactly "333 and a third" human beings killed per hour, according to American journalist Philip Gourevitch, who wrote a sensitive and compelling account of the tragedy. Although this slaughter, intending to kill off a group, was "unique" to the African continent, the mass killings were not, as evidenced by the anti-Igbo attacks that took place prior to the Nigerian (Biafran) Civil War of 1967 or the violence between the Hutus and Tutsis in Burundi in the early 1970s.[2] Sudan, too, has been locked in brutal civil strife for decades; tensions accelerated after 1983 between the Northern-dominated government, run as an Islamic state, and the people in the Christian south. Then, beginning in 2003, through the terrible violence committed by government-sponsored militias to quell a rebellion by the villagers in Darfur, a neglected western region of the country, the carnage shifted to conflict between so-called Arab herdsmen and African villagers. For some Western leaders, including George W. Bush, the U.S. president, this latter conflict was the first genocide of the twenty-first century.[3]

In addition, nationalist separatist tensions erupted in the province of Chechnya in the new post-Soviet Russia in 1999 that locked armies in seemingly endless battles with little regard for civilian rights or protections on either side. Similarly, success of the separatist movement in East Timor brought the wrath of the Indonesian army and its paramilitary defenders onto the civilian population in 1999, with significant loss of life. And, in the context of the disintegration of state rule in Sierra Leone in western Africa, rebel insurgency groups between 1991 and 2002 practiced inhumane tactics against their declared enemies. In one of the most brutal forms of abuse, in a terrible perversion of a government slogan calling on people to vote ("the future is in your hands"), they chopped off the hands and arms of civilians seen to be supporting the wrong side. Yet, this listing is not exhaustive; many other people faced violence by their own governments as well as by rebel groups, such as in the drug conflicts and land tensions, which, accelerating in the mid-1990s, wreaked havoc with life and liberty in Colombia, South America. These mass crimes left an indelible mark on the societies through the abuses they inflicted and the losses they caused.[4]

In the immediate post–Cold War era, U.N. officials, staff, and member-states experimented with new patterns of intervention to prevent a worsening of the crises in these violent and fragmented societies. State members of the Security Council brought together older U.N. military peacekeeping strategies and long-standing humanitarian relief commitments; they expanded the sanction and coercive prerogatives of the U.N. Charter's Chapter 7, first imposed on apartheid South Africa. Throughout the decade, these missions brought together, in various combinations, U.N.-authorized military troops, humanitarian relief agencies, and human rights agents in implementing agendas prepared from the top. The missions shifted focus from the traditional role of preserving peace between armies at territorial borders to the new agenda of deploying personnel in the middle of shattered societies partly to rebuild them. Members of these missions came into direct contact with local people in threatened communities, revealing sizeable gaps between decision-making in U.N. chambers and understanding of needs by local authorities as well as by people at risk on the ground. According to Béatrice Pouligny, based on her observations of the intervention through local eyes, "The legitimacy of any intervention, whatever it may be, whatever very generous motives it may have, is never . . . secure."[5] Taken together, these piecemeal experiments at deployment began to fashion a distinct international doctrine of "humanitarian intervention."[6]

That the Security Council packaged its military interventions in humanitarian garb first met with widespread support by prominent international leaders and activists in relief and human rights work. People displaced from or besieged in their communities because of human brutality were destitute and required immediate relief and assistance. After all, the origins of the International Red Cross and Crescent movement had combined the provisioning of medical services for wounded soldiers on the battlefield with relief for civilians made homeless by natural disasters, such as earthquakes, floods, and fires. Actual wartime practices already in the early twentieth century extended relief measures to many types of civilians brutally affected by war, from refugees to destitute and displaced populations to other vulnerable people, including women, children, and the elderly. Although embroiled in geopolitical conflicts over power and influence, the principle of collective responsibility for humanitarian crises shaped an international emergency aid community, which, after 1945, coexisted and interacted with, but was not the same as, the human rights community. Providing relief services centered on the U.N. High Commissioner for Refugees, which, as seen earlier, had been established in the 1950s to secure food, aid, and shelter for refugees fleeing across borders from human-made or natural disasters. In the 1990s, the General Assembly appointed the UNHCR as "lead agency" to coordinate relief efforts combined under the expanded U.N. field missions.

These crises also mobilized other prominent agencies, such as the International Organization for Migration (IOM), the World Food Program (WFP), and the World Health Organization (WHO). Relief was arranged as well through bilateral agreements negotiated between donor countries as those, for example, brokered by the U.S. Agency for International Development (USAID) with the Rwandan government in the early 1990s or those promoted by the European Commission Humanitarian Aid Office (ECHO), the "biggest single humanitarian funder in the world," wrote the journalist David Rieff in 2002.[7] It also activated representative NGO relief associations on the ground, such as the French-founded independent medical relief agency Doctors without Borders (Médecins Sans Frontières, or MSF), the British group OXFAM (the Oxford Committee for Famine Relief), the American-founded CARE (Cooperative for Assistance and Relief Everywhere), and the International Rescue Committee (IRC), one of the largest American NGOs, among others.

By treaty and tradition, the International Committee of the Red Cross (ICRC) was responsible for the application of binding international humanitarian law in the theaters of war, including, with the 1977 Protocol II of the Geneva Conventions, internal civil wars and strife. Although each crisis situation had its own negotiated rules among the ICRC, the host government, and other belligerents, ICRC monitors entered prisons and detention centers to ensure compliance with the Geneva Conventions. Its national branches also developed tailored strategies for the rapid delivery of the essentials of life to people displaced by war and devastated by its corollaries: famine, malnutrition, and the spread of infectious diseases. A vast array of agencies operated in the field and this listing is only the tip of the complicated relief structure known through its various and confusing acronyms. In these tragedies of mass violence unfolding in the 1990s, the boundaries between relief actions and rights protections were shown to be particularly porous and contentious.

The U.N. missions also added a decisively activist human rights component to increase compliance, sponsoring an accompanying team of on-site international specialists to monitor human rights and humanitarian law abuses. For example, negotiations around the jurisdiction of the original twenty-four-member team in El Salvador gave the monitors wide latitude. For four years, they were seen "roaming around the country, asking difficult questions, visiting prisons, writing reports, and establishing contacts with leading NGOs." The mission was "proactive" on the ground and "its findings could not be easily ignored or dismissed." Its length ensured plenty of time for serious follow-up.[8] It set precedents for other human rights missions deployed under U.N. auspices.

Inclusion of these human rights specialists was designed to overcome the limitations of Human Rights Commission procedures even though, under the continuing pressure from NGOs and victim groups, rights investigations from the center had become more comprehensive. In the early 1990s, the HRC established a number of working groups and rapporteurs to study the deteriorating human rights climate in Iraq, in the territories of disintegrating Yugoslavia, and in Rwanda, which was wracked with communal violence prior to the genocide. Despite serious warnings, for example, from the rapporteur on arbitrary executions who predicted in 1993 that Rwanda "would experience massive killings unless action was taken to curb the militias, stop the hate speech . . . and end the practice of specifying ethnicity on identity cards," no concrete preventive action was taken. In an ironic turn, at the start of the Rwandan genocide, in April 1994 the United Nations established the position of High Commissioner for Human Rights (HCHR), a proposal long pushed by leading international NGOs, human rights activists, and some member-states. Human Rights Watch had been a strong advocate of the new office, particularly in light of the creation of an undersecretary for humanitarian affairs in 1991. In its view, the undersecretary had been "given a narrow mandate that attempt[ed] to divorce humanitarian disaster from its human rights causes."[9] A separate U.N. officer for human rights would ensure a continuing flow of information not only to the secretary general but also to the Security Council as well. In the 1990s, human rights activists were pinning hopes on the sanctioning powers of the Security Council.

Despite the high expectations at the center of the humanitarian missions, their record at stopping human suffering on the ground was decidedly mixed. As a specific enforcement body deployed to keep civilians safe, they failed to prevent mass murder and carnage—what subsequently has been prosecuted as genocide, under the Genocide Convention (1948), and as flagrant violations of international humanitarian law also prohibiting crimes against humanity, war crimes, and torture. The Genocide Convention, written at the birth of the human rights regime, stood for the promise of "never again!" but its stipulations had never been applied since coming into force. Genocidal murder, furthermore, was war and as such—whether internal or international in scope—brought into operation the binding prohibitions of international humanitarian law. Although genocide and other mass crimes of violence mocked the laws, these conventions offered the legal basis to prosecute those responsible for the crimes. Yet, during the Yugoslav (1991–95) and Rwandan (1994) crises, leaders of the great power states refused to use the term "genocide," fearing its implications. The convention mandated state action to "prevent" genocide; while it set a high bar for judgment (prosecutors must establish clear "intent to destroy, in whole or in part, a national, ethnic, racial or religious group, as such"), it required individual accountability and punishment. Using or not using the term seems beside the point, as the situation in Darfur subsequently demonstrated. The violence in Darfur has been termed "genocide," but no effective or collective strategies have emerged to halt the slaughter.

Even the subsequent conflicts—shaped partly by the inability to act effectively in Bosnia and Rwanda—proved disquieting. In the related 1999 crisis in Kosovo, a province in the truncated Federal Republic of Yugoslavia, West European NATO countries and the United States (bypassing the Security Council and certain veto by Russia and China) adopted the tactic of militarized "humanitarian" intervention. NATO began a bombing campaign of Serbia, resulting in the loss of civilian life. It used military force to drive Serb troops out of the province and halt an impending human crisis following the mass displacement of Kosovar Albanians fleeing for their lives. On later reflection, it seemed to many activists a dangerous precedent to link armed military campaigns with humanitarianism, although providing humanitarian relief in war zones required security protection and access to the vulnerable victims often available only through the actions of military troops and peacekeepers. The testing of humanitarian intervention carried with it many complicated and controversial elements.

Concerns surfaced already in 1993. While still an advocate of forceful intervention, Human Rights Watch authors that year noted with unease the humanitarian "calamity" affecting the Iraqi people, "a calamity that stemmed in part from breaches of the laws of war in the allied [U.S. and British-led] bombing campaign" of the country that followed the push of Saddam Hussein's troops out of Kuwait. Quoting a WHO/UNICEF mission report, Human Rights Watch repeated the "sobering reminder" to the United Nations and member-states of the costs of military action. "The recent conflict had wrought near-apocalyptic results upon the economic infrastructure of what had been, until January 1991, a rather highly urbanized and mechanized [Iraqi] society. Now, most means of modern life support have been destroyed or rendered tenuous."[10] The report acknowledged the brutal repression by the Baathist regime of its opponents, both Kurds and Sh'ia in the late 1980s (when, it pointed out, the United Nations had been silent) and, again, after the 1991 Gulf War. These authors supported the "no fly" zones set up by the United States and Great Britain to protect the people in the north and south brutally suppressed by the government after a popular uprising in 1991, but they were critical of the sanctions imposed on Iraq by the Security Council after the invasion of Kuwait and of their renewed effort to force Saddam Hussein to dismantle his arsenal of weapons of mass destruction under U.N. inspection. For Human Rights Watch, economic sanctions severely taxed the quality of life for the Iraqi people and particularly the health of the children; they bred other forms of humanitarian dangers.

Despite misgivings and acknowledged shortcomings, the testing of humanitarian policies and strategies cohered into a doctrine, which seemed a logical end product of its own development. In his by-now classic formulation, U.N. Secretary General Kofi Annan in September 1999 affirmed the existence of a sphere of "rights beyond [territorial] borders." As he put it at the time, half a century after the founding of the United Nations, states no longer could appeal to sovereign immunities when it was clear they were abusing their own citizens. Most international NGOs at the time agreed with the need for robust international responses to mass violence and some even advanced a normative "right to assistance."[11] However, the failure of will to confront effectively the political contexts of the violence and armed conflicts constrained the operations of the humanitarian missions from the start. Building the missions meant entering the murky world of power, greed, and self-interest, as they intertwined with the compromises of state diplomacy and U.N. decision-making down through the workings of local power embedded in community, family, and gender ties and traditions.

Although these multiple pressures were duplicated elsewhere, the break-up of the former Yugoslav state and the mounting ethnic tensions in Rwanda offer particularly clear illustrations of the many conundrums inherent in the missions, which, as new forms of international mobilizations, had no firm anchor in past practices.[12] These two examples show with particular clarity positions that worked at cross purposes and the dilemmas human rights activists and humanitarian aid workers faced on the ground in such ghastly political situations. Furthermore, the specificities of the documented evidence of the violence and alleged crimes that occurred in Yugoslavia and Rwanda provided the first cases for international prosecution of international crimes under international law since the Nuremberg and Tokyo trials. Partly prodded by the victim demands for accountability in the face of such mass atrocities, the Security Council established two ad hoc international tribunals with jurisdiction to indict and try individuals charged with committing genocide, war crimes, and crimes against humanity. These ad hoc tribunals, in turn, fed the movement to universalize the applicability of international humanitarian law through the creation of the International Criminal Court (in force, 2002). Although the past never is an unambiguous prologue to the future, universalizing accountability in the international arena appears imperative for sustaining human rights work into the twenty-first century.

In a similar vein, the disturbing failures of the 1990s have led to much retrospective analysis, whether by academics or members of NGOs who had been active on the ground, or journalists later assessing their own careers. Retrospective accounts of the events in Yugoslavia and Rwanda loom large in this literature. If the undertaking has not yet added up to binding criteria that would *consistently and permanently* guide human rights actions to aid vulnerable people—establishing a shared "humanitarian threshold for intervention"—much of the analysis draws "lessons to be learned" from the previous record. It recognizes that only careful retrospective accounts from the actual decision-making prior to, during, and after these emergencies can provide possible guidance for the future. As echoed in many other publications, academics Larry Minear and Randolph C. Kent, for example, had a separate section explicitly on "lessons from Rwanda"; similarly, Thomas G. Weiss and Amir Pasic argued that Yugoslavia, although its own case, "can at least be instructive" about the possibilities of humanitarian assistance, when resources were comparatively available except the necessary political ones.[13] As it turns out, while preserving the crucial nuances that make each case unique, the crises in Yugoslavia and Rwanda together offer as compelling a story in retrospect as during the unfolding tragedies.

Ethnicization of the Conflict

From the international perspective, the crises in the Balkan region and in Rwanda were prime examples of ethnic genocide, the unbridled murder of ethnic others. This understanding shaped the U.N. missions, tragically often in self-fulfilling ways. The conflicts to be sure were ethnic in scope, but they revealed rather the politic of ethnic "othering"—the deliberate, brazen, and unabashed manipulation of ethnic identities for purposes of acquiring and strengthening political authority in the sudden power vacuums left by the ending of the Cold War. This was the case in the transition of Yugoslavia from socialist to democratic rule. In Rwanda after 1990, facing the threat of war, influential Western donor states pushed the shared power solutions at a time when the African region as a whole was becoming less central to great power interests.

Slobodan Milošević and his power entourage were determined to create an ethnically homogeneous "Greater Serbia" from the former Yugoslav territories with large Serb populations. Milošević commanded the Yugoslav army with its clandestine ties to other Serb paramilitary and militia forces throughout the territory. A similar political strategy characterized the Hutu Power leadership around President Habyarimana Juvénal (1990–94), whose base of support was in the northern provinces of Gisenyi and Ruhengeri. His mysterious death in an airplane crash April 6, 1994, marked the moment the regime unleashed its genocidal campaign, directed by Colonel Théoneste Bagosora, who then was Minister of Defense and in charge of the Rwandan army.

In approaching the conflicts, Security Council member-states, the brokers of the international diplomatic negotiations, and the influential Western media saw the mounting crises initially through the lens of a past that essentialized ethnic hatreds and animosities. In this framework, the unfolding events were manifestations of ancient and primordial enmities of group against group, seemingly defying logic or any ability to assign blame. It was tribe against tribe, "just another episode of entrenched centuries-long tribal conflict" and of "African savagery," on the one hand, and of the dark morass of "Balkan hatreds" on the other. For key leaders of the European Community, the conflict was a continuation of old "bickering by ethnic groups."[14] The appeal to ancient antagonistic divisions bred a collective passivity and, worse, contributed to the "ethnicization" of the same conflicts. At one of the earliest conferences called by the European Community to mediate the warfare breaking out in Yugoslavia in September 1991, not one representative of a nonethnic party or any defender of a new multiethnic, democratic postcommunist state was consulted.[15] The only identity officially acknowledged by those unleashing the genocide as well as by the powerful groups in the international community was an ethnic one.

Ethnic identity is not primordial but mercurial and hybrid. Ethnicity is only one of many identities (of class, occupation, gender, culture, nationality, and sexuality) that individuals and communities exhibited simultaneously. Ethnicity, writes Aimable Twagilimana, a sensitive analyst of Rwanda, is "created by specific circumstances." As such, it can be a source of community identity and integration for people sharing a language and culture; it also can be manipulated and transformed into a defining element in the political process, a xenophobic force used to exclude others for expansionist political ends or economic and financial gains or both.[16] In these latter cases, it has to work to override other tensions that divide society. Ethnic genocides were those terrible moments of state-directed violence, when one group launched a campaign of murder and annihilation against another. These moments, however, were not fully inherent in the separate groups' previous interactions or predetermined by historical developments but created politically in the particular present.

In the late 1980s, both Yugoslavia and Rwanda had ethnically complex demographic societies. As a socialist state, the Yugoslav communist leadership officially denied any political role in state affairs on ethnic grounds and, as seen, the regime was fearful of ethnic "separatism." Yet, constitutionally, it divided the state into six socialist republics based partially on distinct ethnic identities, which, perhaps unintentionally, helped transform social tensions over resources and state development programs into matters of ethnic jealousy and anger. (See Map 4 in Chapter 2.)

Reflecting the historical stretch of the Ottoman Empire over the Balkans, Bosnia-Herzegovina was the most ethnically mixed republic, with both separation and intermingling of nearly equal proportions of Serbs, Croats, and Bosnian Muslims. There were patterns of residential concentration, with a clustering of Serb communities in the west of Bosnia and in eastern Herzegovina and concentrations of Muslim populations in the center and northeast. Sarajevo, the capital city, still was known in 1990 as a multicultural center, and other large towns, such as Srebrenica, had a clear majority Muslim population residing in a larger administrative area that was heavily Serb. Political life captured these demographics. In a November 1990 multiparty election in Bosnia, for example, the Muslim Party of Democratic Action won eighty-six seats, the Party of Bosnian Serbs won seventy-two seats, and the Croatian Democratic Union received forty-four seats in the assembly. Other republics were more ethnically homogeneous. In the 1991 Croatian census, about 78 percent of the population was Catholic Croats, only 12 percent Orthodox Serbs, and 1 percent Muslim.[17] The Kosovo province in the Serb socialist republic was 90 percent ethnic Albanian.

Milošević began his power grab by seeking to centralize rule, a step resisted eventually by arms by the other presidents. Under his directions, Serb minorities, using paramilitary troops and police, began to amass separate territorial authority in Croatia (Serbian Krajina) and Bosnia (Republika Srpska) by murdering and expelling the non-Serb populations with an eye, eventually, to forming a Greater Serbia. Other leaders, most notably Franjo Tudjman of Croatia, also wanted an ethnically homogeneous state. Perhaps complicating the situation and reinforcing international acquiescence to the ethnic "solution," these divisions fell along well-known religious, cultural, and linguistic lines, which had been the basis of the implementation of self-determination in the breakup of the multinational empires immediately after World War I.

The ethnic situation in Rwanda was different but no less complex. Prior to the genocide, there were the majority Hutu people (around 80 percent of the population), the minority Tutsi people, and a small group of Ba'Twa; similar groupings were found in neighboring Burundi to the south. As Twagilimana showed, however, these were not ethnic entities by the standard definitions applied in Yugoslavia: "All three groups speak the same language . . . and share the same religious beliefs and values."[18] The overwhelming population was Catholic, with some inroads at the time by Protestant churches.

While building on indigenous social markers (between agriculturalists and cattle raisers, for example), the colonial masters of the Great Lakes territories (the Germans in the 1880s and later the Belgians) redrew Rwandan society by imposing ethnic categories and hierarchies on it, subverting local values and customs and literally drawing territorial maps with little attention to local affinities and traditions. These same practices accompanied colonial rule everywhere on the African continent—as elsewhere in the colonial world as well. After many deadly wars of pacification late in the nineteenth century, colonial administrators consolidated rule partly by a process of ethnic identity formation, through language policies and differential access to economic resources, education, wealth, and positions of authority. European colonizers reshuffled ethnic identities as they formed artificial political entities, leaving difficult legacies, which continued to distort the admittedly erratic measures taken to establish genuine democratic governance in many African countries after independence.

In Rwanda, the basis of ethnic differentiation was mythology imposed by the first German colonial masters and gradually absorbed by the society at large. At the time of conquest at the end of the nineteenth century, Rwandan kingdoms were relatively centralized and sophisticated, which confounded European assumptions of African backwardness. To compensate, early German anthropologists, linguists, and theorists explained the anomaly by creating the Tutsi as "outsiders," more European than African. These colonial groups invented what Twagilimana calls the "Hamitic Hypothesis" of Tutsi racial superiority, given their supposed origins in Egypt. In addition, the Tutsis were physically taller and lighter skinned than Hutu and Twa, proof of their superior status, according to the dominant classificatory schemes of European scientific racism at the time. During colonial rule, the Tutsis, then, were the privileged group. In time, Hutu leaders turned the myth on its head, calling the Tutsis outsiders and colonizers themselves and threats to the integrity of Rwanda—a Hutu Bantu land by origin. Twagilimana carefully documented growing ethnic polarization between the elites of the two large groups in postcolonial Rwanda, complicated by regional antagonisms between northerners and southerners over aid and development. Prior to the 1990s, the major political tensions, indeed, were regional and not ethnic. At the level of daily life, Hutu and Tutsi continued to intermarry and interact even in the face of growing elite antagonisms. A similar process of intermarriage and social intermingling also characterized many communities in Yugoslavia as, for example, in Sarajevo, Bosnia, prior to the organized disintegration of the state.

Building the Missions in Wartime

Negotiations over humanitarian mission mandates took place in the halls and chambers of the United Nations. Decision-making at the international level determined the length and strength as well as purposes of the missions, shaped by a number of long-standing principles that included consent of the parties to the deployments, the strict neutrality of the missions, and the use of force only in self-defense (the rules of engagement). Dispatched throughout the land, these new missions typically had peace-building components, which also followed standard lines, such as reasserting the rule of law and empowering civil society. Virtually no effort was made to draw on local understandings of the conflict, assess the linkages of power in local communities or the particular face of civil society, or hear from people for whom the mission was designed. From wider patterns that emerged in the decade, the "blue helmet" peacekeepers, U.N. staff, and other members of the mission generally remained distant from local people, either literally, by staying sequestered in urban centers in the better hotels ("they don't lower themselves to visit us") or securing only part of the territory or, figuratively, by bringing into play their own assumptions and prejudices about people disorganized and "debased" by violence and "incapable of planning."[19] The very people at risk were not seen as vital resources for mission purposes.

In working with the peacekeepers, similar gaps divided international NGOs and their local counterparts. Representatives of the international human rights organizations, such as Human Rights Watch, interacted more easily with the U.N. troops and other members of international agencies in the field, even though, in these armed conflicts as well as in earlier human rights tragedies, the field missions could not fully operate without the information that came from the firsthand knowledge of members of local organizations. Of course, other types of human rights advocacy work also confronted the gaps between the broad consensus that forged agreements on the international level and local realities, which they addressed, as in the example of gender, through various forms of translation. Once the mission was on the ground, information flowed more readily back to Security Council decision-makers as the appointed coordinators or army heads made urgent recommendations for modifications, depending on the shifting nature of the fighting. But the gaps in knowledge and understanding made the tasks of the mission, already forced to negotiate its place in the poorly chartered terrain between the goals of global politics and the needs of local life, more difficult.

Divided by interests, state representatives on the Security Council organized the missions for Croatia and, subsequently, Bosnia-Herzegovina in 1992. This deployment marked the onset of new possibilities in the geopolitical landscape; for decades, under tacit Cold War agreements, Europe had been off limits to U.N. military force (with one brief exception, in Cyprus). The protection forces, however, were deployed during the war, because the state members of the Security Council were not willing to use the U.N. Charter authority to impose a viable peace at the outset. Officially, their mandate included two parts, as summed up by Human Rights Watch: "to enhance the possibilities of a political settlement to the Yugoslav crisis and to ensure delivery of humanitarian assistance." To force compliance with the Security Council's call for immediate cease-fire, the U.N. also imposed economic and trade sanctions on Serbia and, borrowing the Iraqi precedent, banned military flights to safeguard humanitarian aid delivery on the ground. The missions, however, never received adequate military and material resources or political support. From the start, as Human Rights Watch put it, they were marred by "timidity, disorganization, unnecessary delay and political indecision." It is no wonder that the original contingent sent to

Croatia never met its mandate of collecting weapons from the Serb fighters or helping the displaced families return to their homes.[20]

These missions had to work under the most trying political circumstances, when the humanitarian approach became the substitute for political action and, for the length of the crisis, the situation was not labeled what it was—a genocidal violence involving mass war crimes—but rather a humanitarian crisis. The difficulty of the situation was not lost on human rights specialists and humanitarian aid workers. Rosalyn Higgins, an international legal scholar who subsequently joined the International Court at The Hague, commented bitterly, "We have chosen to respond to major unlawful violence not by stopping violence but by trying to provide relief to the suffering." Similarly frustrated, Rony Brauman, president of Doctors without Borders, noted acerbically that had Auschwitz occurred in the 1990s, it would have been called a "humanitarian crisis.[21] The point drew immediate attention to the fact that humanitarian aid cannot deal with a crisis of such magnitude nor can aid workers negotiate with a regime bent on large-scale killing.

The groups involved in carrying out the missions confronted a series of moral, political, and strategic dilemmas that defined the limits of action. They had to make quick decisions, often in the midst of confusing reports over territorial control: who would receive aid and with whom to negotiate to open the corridors for relief convoys. Already in 1992, observers counted seventeen militia forces operating in the disintegrating territories of Yugoslavia. Peacekeepers often ended up pacifying illegally conquered territories to ensure aid convoys would get through and even negotiating with vague paramilitary groups on the roads and byways to provide security, which only enhanced the suspect groups' legitimacy. In Bosnia, humanitarian aid, the focal point of the mission, became a massive racket through the levying of transit taxes and misappropriation by armed forces, which helped them partly finance their own war efforts. Each camp of belligerents had its own humanitarian aid community over which the UNHCR exercised little real control. Imposing sanctions, too, had meant quick economic gain for Romanian and Bulgarian businesses bringing in the embargoed goods.[22]

Part of the dilemma reflected the continued disagreements at the top, particularly the failure of the Security Council to define unambiguously just "how much force" the peacekeepers could deploy in the mission. They required troops to pull back from a position that could not be defended adequately and even chastised independent decision-making, as in the actions of General Philippe Morillon, who refused to leave the besieged city of Srebrenica in March 1993 until Serb forces permitted a relief convoy to enter. Secretary General Boutros-Gali publicly rebuked

Morillon for "exceeding his mandate," and shortly thereafter the French pulled him from service.[23]

If vacillation defined the top, some of the tensions also reflected the different mandates and agendas of the NGOs on the ground. They adhered to distinct modus operandi, most pronounced between the strict neutrality behind the classic humanitarian relief operations of the ICRC and, say, Human Rights Watch, an activist NGO. Over the years, neutrality and its corollary silence (public discretion) had ensured the ICRC access to prisoners of war, with no questions asked, as well as to people desperate for help, even if it meant negotiating with oppressive regimes or groups. The ICRC was not without earlier detractors, however. Doctors without Borders (MSF), the largest medical relief agency today, had been started in 1971 by French doctors in the Red Cross movement headed by Dr. Bernard Kouchner, who broke with the international agency for its failure to speak out about misery and culpability at the time of the succession crisis in Biafra during Nigeria's civil war. The watchwords of Doctors without Borders were to provide "emergency care" and to "publicly bear witness" to the plight of the populations they served: they refused to remain silent in the face of atrocities. In the 1990s, however, groups such as Human Rights Watch wanted to further redefine humanitarianism by putting human rights principles at the top of the missions' objectives. These rights activists developed their own term for the many U.N. compromises behind its own brand of neutrality, which, as they saw it, included the failure to disarm the paramilitary troops, arrest known criminals, or even safeguard forensic evidence of murder and massacre. When and where these shortcomings appeared elsewhere in the decade, they were referred to cynically as the "Bosnian disease."[24]

Catastrophes and Inadequacies

When the many contradictions of the mission collided, catastrophes mounted. The massacre of 7,800 Muslim men and boys in July 1995 in Srebrenica in eastern Bosnia by Bosnian Serb troops is one example of the tragic consequences of the missions' weaknesses. It clearly illustrated the yawning gap between the political rhetoric on high and its failure to be translated on the ground. Considered Europe's worst massacre since the end of World War II, eventually it was prosecuted as genocide. Tragically, the massacre unfolded in a declared "safe haven" zone, the first ever "safe area" established by the United Nations, and patrolled at the time by a small contingent of U.N.-authorized Dutch troops.

The city came under siege in 1992 and was provisioned through UNHCR coordination. Serb military forces surrounding the city at first

refused to open it to U.N. troops and, thus, to more aid. Under deteriorating conditions, relief agency heads tried to evacuate the sick and the
wounded, causing a mass stampede of frightened people and fueling
rumors that the UNHCR was engaged in "ethnic cleansing" as an
accomplice of Serb designs. Popular perceptions were highly volatile.
Under these dire circumstances, General Morillon had bluffed his way
into the city, pledged to remain, and, on his own authority, declared it
under U.N. protection. It was his urgent communiqués demanding
action that had convinced the Security Council to declare the city a "safe
haven," which it did on April 16, 1993. This decision, and its extension
to other cities in eastern Bosnia, "changed the geography" of the conflict. It not only concentrated resources in certain areas, which undercut
the overall mission to ensure the delivery of supplies throughout Bosnia-
Herzegovina, it also, according to firsthand accounts, seemed to have
been "a major element in the Serbs' decision to attack the Zepa and
Bihac enclaves and then to invade Srebrenica before a 'rapid reaction
force' was eventually deployed." The safe havens were used as well by
Muslim fighters to restock their supplies and materials. A summary
report in 1998 prepared by U.N. Secretary General Kofi Annan admitted
that "up to 20,000 people, overwhelmingly from the Bosnian Muslim
community, had been killed in and around the safe areas." Even at the
time, it was said that the least safe areas in Bosnia-Herzegovina were the
U.N.-declared "safe havens."[25]

In a conflict in which ethnicity mattered, Srebrenica was a Muslim
enclave in territory recognized as Bosnian Serb, located only ten miles
from the border of the Federal Republic of Yugoslavia. As in many other
parts of Bosnia, people of different backgrounds had lived together well
enough. The possibility of war seemed remote to Kadir Habivović, an
eyewitness to the massacre. He remembered the period before 1992:
"Nobody could persuade me that war would happen at all. Why?
Because [in] Srebrenica . . . the population was mixed. [It is] true that
the larger number were Muslim, much larger but there were good
neighborly relations established, so that nobody would ever have persuaded me that war could start between good people, good friends and
so on. But it happened, what happened, in Bosnia, so it happened in
Srebrenica."[26] Although friends told Kadir to leave, he remained in the
city because of family ties. "It was still possible to live normally, to an
extent," he added. "I did not feel [threatened] until the boom, the
boom of war, and the ultimatum." Laying siege to the city, troops under
the command of Ratko Mladić, the Bosnian Serb general, demanded
the inhabitants give up their weapons and leave, which they refused to
do. Habivović described the worsening conditions as the siege continued, similar to what General Morillon had found when he entered Sre-

brenica after eleven months of blockade: "stench, disease, wretched exhaustion." As Habivović told it, first food became scarce and, after that, medicines. Then, "it was total hunger," he said simply, "it was difficult, unbearable." The city doubled in size with the influx of refugees fleeing danger elsewhere.

The siege lasted three and a half years. The Dutch peacekeeping troops arrived only in early January 1995; by May, the Serb troops began shelling the city directly and targeting the Dutch base. Eye-witness Hasan Nuhanović recalled, "It was telling the people that if [the] UN cannot defend its own Observation Post, how can it defend the people." There had indeed been entreaties to the Security Council by the U.N. commander in Bosnia, General Bertrand Janvier, to either increase the protection force to adequate size or pull it so that NATO could launch decisive air strikes, but the Security Council took no action.

Dutch soldier Paul Groenewegen recalled the mounting chaos when Serb troops made their final offensive strike on the city in July 1995. The U.N. contingent, he explained, had been trying to help people. "But [at] one point, we couldn't anymore." Thousands fled into the compound. "So that was when the panic started, they didn't know what to do." Nuhanović, a refugee from a neighboring village torched in the earlier Serb offensive, similarly remembered: "There was a stream of people coming down the street . . . running, children, women, everybody and the men were running into the woods, to the woods. That was the moment when everybody separated, in fact." The Serbs began forcing the refugees at the compound, mostly either the old or sick or women and children, into buses to move them out of the city to Muslim territory. "We tried," said Groenewegen, "to interfere with [the Serbian Army] as much as possible where things weren't humane [in] how they treated the people. They didn't ask them to enter the busses, but almost kicked them into the bus."

The same policy of gender segregation took place in the city as well. Zumara Shekhomerović, a local resident, looked back at the moment. "Then we saw, from some 10 to 15 meters in front of us [that] they started separating. They were boys from 12 years of age and old men to 77 years of age." The Serb occupiers claimed they were questioning the men in a search for "Muslim war criminals." Shekhomerović continued, "When our turn came, two of our neighbors were separated in front of us. They separated many from my family and [people] from my area, I know many of those by name and surname." Then she was separated from her husband. "I never saw him again and didn't know what happened to him. I regret . . . that I didn't scream or shout for help. Maybe it would be easier to live now. I just left silently and could not speak."[27] On July 16, negotiations between the United Nations and Bosnian Serbs allowed the Dutch force to leave Srebrenica and, shortly thereafter, the first reports of the massacre seeped out of the area. The fate of most of the victims still remains unknown because Serb forces buried and reburied the bodies to hide the evidence.

Developments in Rwanda illustrated different fractures in the mobilization of humanitarian interventions. They also shed a distinctive light on civil society, not lost to academic theorists and human rights activists in the later 1990s.[28] Relying on "civil society" to strengthen the "rule of law" was a cardinal assumption in U.N. peace-building missions in the long 1990s, however. U.N. officials, staff, and advisers had been shaped by events in Eastern Europe and the Soviet Union in the aftermath of Helsinki. As Chapter 2 showed, Soviet dissidents and their western supporters (and human rights theorists) had been convinced of the progressive nature of civil society as such, understood in the early 1980s as a space of freedom between the individual and the state, which, through the free exchange of ideas, ensured tolerance, democracy, civic engagement, and pluralism.

The conflicts of the 1990s, however, complicated these inherited notions, revealing the fragility of civil society without adequate political space and commitment. In the breakup of the Yugoslav state, remember, the international community effectively marginalized the NGOs and citizens' groups defending a nonnationalist alternative to the crisis. In addition, from evidence elsewhere, these internal conflicts also undercut the simple divides between so-called civil society groups and their "warlord," or militia, opponents. Grassroots evidence from Somalia, Haiti, and El Salvador showed the many roles that local leaders and powerbrokers played. Their identities and loyalties were simultaneously multiple, so strengthening them in one capacity, in fact, reinforced clan ties and other patronage linkages.[29] The key criteria lay not in the absolute numbers of NGOs in society but in their political commitments to human rights values and democratic governance.

As Peter Uvin showed for Rwanda, in the early 1990s the NGOs simply fractured along ethnic lines under the barrage of hate propaganda put out by the government. This destruction occurred even though outside observers, notably World Bank officials and heads of development agencies, had considered Rwanda's civil society "to be highly developed—one of the most advanced cases in Africa." A 1987 World Bank report noted, for example, that "social life in the rural areas is intense and numerous forms of association give concrete shape to mutual solidarity and community actions."

Uvin identified a dense network of associations in "civil society" at the time. His list included "cooperatives, farmers' organizations, tontines [mutual credit societies] and informal associations, foreign and local development NGOs, and the Churches."[30] If his analysis suffered from tautological thinking—civil society did not exist in Rwanda, he said, because it did not function to promote tolerance, that is, it did not function as civil society—his evidence nonetheless is rich and suggestive. He showed two structural problems with the workings of civil society associations in the country: One, they were constrained by the authoritarian government, which limited their agenda to narrow development goals. And, two, development ideology continued to divorce human rights from economic growth, turning the development NGOs into self-identified nonpolitical agents for change. Thus, Uvin wrote, they did not become "vectors for challenging the multiple exclusions in Rwandese society." The warnings offered by Theo van Boven in the mid-1970s still had not been incorporated adequately into international development planning on the ground. In the middle of the human crises tearing Rwandan society apart in the early 1990s, some international aid agencies and indigenous organizations began to include seminar training in racism and human rights in their work. "A few Belgian NGOs created human rights programs"; others, such as the Concentration Council of Local Support Organizations, sponsored education in democracy and nonviolence. But, as Uvin noted caustically, it was "too little, too late."[31] In the critical years, 1990–94, Rwandan civil society could not prevent the genocide.

What ended the genocide in Rwanda was not international intervention but the military successes of the armed Rwandan Patriotic Front (RPF), a refugee army fighting the regime. In July 1994, it defeated the Hutu Power forces and overthrew the government. Most analysts agreed that every Tutsi probably would have been killed had the RPF not overwhelmed the government troops. The military victory, however, prompted a sudden stampede of refugees fleeing the war. Over 2 million people (of a total population of around 7 or 8 million before the genocide) fled across the border to Zaire (today, the Democratic Republic of Congo), creating a massive refugee crisis to which the humanitarian relief agencies responded quickly and effectively, setting up camps, providing medicines and foods, and organizing appeals for clothing, blankets, and other necessities. These agencies launched a highly successful international publicity campaign, mobilizing sympathy by effectively using TV and photographs of the children in the overcrowded camps dying from cholera and other diseases. Philip Gourevitch, writing in the middle of the crisis, offered a trenchant observation about this sudden shift in international attention. With the refugee crisis, he wrote, all international eyes were on the makeshift camps. "And with that the genocide began to be old news."[32]

In the refugee camps in Zaire and in southern Rwanda, nearly every rule of humanitarian relief was broken. Aid agency officials, for example, made no effort to differentiate between perpetrators and victims, although international humanitarian law required such distinctions. At the minimum, perpetrators needed to be separated from the innocent population. But they stayed in the camps with their military weapons, in effect terrorizing the refugee population and establishing their own hierarchy and gendered support networks with the donated goods. Humanitarian aid again became a weapon in the conflict. In response to this political situation, MSF and the American International Rescue Committee, among others, pulled out of Zaire, no longer willing to contribute to what they saw as a terror regime emerging in the camps themselves. In an interview in May 1994, Philippe Biberson, president of MSF-France, said that in Rwanda humanitarianism once again had reached a "dead end." He concluded forcefully, "one cannot halt a massacre with medicines."

The postgenocide Rwandan government headed by Paul Kagame also saw the camps as subversive enclaves, breeding grounds for a future genocidal army to launch attacks on the country, which was beginning its painful efforts of recovery from individual and collective trauma. In addition, significantly more international money poured into the camps for relief (estimated at 1 million U.S. dollars each day, for a total of more than a billion dollars) than was going into devastated Rwanda for development and stabilization projects, such as rebuilding the destroyed physical infrastructure (roads, railroads, houses, and public buildings) as well as the educational and judicial systems. Under these trying circumstances, survivors of the genocide, desperate to be heard, had only their stories to tell—ways to demonstrate their humanity through the sharing of the stories.[33]

"Beyond the Nuremberg Legacy": International Criminal Accountability

From reports by human rights activists and commanders on the ground, the mounting evidence of atrocities, beginning with the discovery of the Serb concentration camp in Omarska in northern Bosnia in 1992, forced the Security Council to take a number of unprecedented steps. It called the first-ever emergency session of the Human Rights Commission and appointed a Commission of Experts to report back on breaches of the Geneva Conventions. By calling for eyewitness and expert testimony on the "facts" on the ground, it broadened the sources for the making of new legal rules. In the same mode, members established and financed the ad hoc International War Crimes Tribunal for Yugoslavia (known by its shorthand ICTY), located in The Hague, Netherlands, with ongoing jurisdiction over events in the former Yugoslavia. The court began operations on May 25, 1992. Subsequently, the Security Council authorized the International Criminal Tribunal for Rwanda (ICTR), headquartered in Arusha, Tanzania, to investigate the crimes of the Rwandan genocide. It began operations on November 8, 1994. Not quite parallel in jurisdiction, these courts reestablished international mechanisms to hold individuals accountable for grave human rights crimes—the breaches of binding international humanitarian law and the Genocide Conventions. As with other shifts in the decade, ending the Cold War stalemates in the Security Council allowed for the testing, through lengthy judgments, and expanding of international criminal law. [34]

Initially, this move met with considerable skepticism throughout the human rights scholarly and activist community. Reflecting wide consensus, David Forsythe, an international relations expert, wrote in 1994: "Lacking the political will to act decisively to curtail abuses of prisoners and civilians, [U.N. member-states] endorsed or went along with the creation of the tribunal, a lamentable charade that constituted a 'black eye' on the international community." Ratner and Abrams, in their detailed study of accountability in international criminal law, similarly argued that the decision "was a substitute for more *assertive* measures to stop the genocides." Journalist Gourevitch, reflecting the perspectives of the new Rwandan leadership, was equally dismissive. He quoted the view of Charles Muriganda, an official who said that the tribunal was established "essentially to appease the conscience of the international community, which has failed to live up to its conventions on genocide. It wants to look as if it is doing something, which is often worse than doing nothing at all." When the tribunal refused to turn over Colonel Théoneste Bagasora to Rwanda for justice after he was captured in Cameroon, an adviser to Kagame's government said to Gourevitch, "It's a joke. . . . This tribunal is now acting as a spoiler."[35]

Time had a way of confounding assumptions, a point captured well in a BBC interview with Hasan Nuhanović on April 16, 2002, which was broadcast widely. The epigraph for this chapter is taken from this interview. Originally fleeing to Srebrenica for safety, Nuhanović was an eyewitness and a survivor; he lost both his parents and his brother in the massacre. In the full glare of the global media he felt empowered to speak as a victim and demand justice. Nuhanović was responding to the sudden resignation of the Dutch government in April that year over a damaging report about the (in)action of the U.N. Dutch peacekeepers who had failed to keep the city of Srebrenica safe. After the report's publication, Dutch Prime Minister Wim Kok gave his resignation to the queen "in the name of the victims and survivors." He accepted full responsibility for the tragedy. "The international community," Kok said, "is anonymous and cannot take responsibility. . . . I can and I do."[36] Yet, this dramatic gesture by a state leader was met with suspicion among survivors of the Srebrenica massacre. For them, justice was done only "in the courts." With these words, the dual meanings of justice converged: justice promises a just position, one that is right and moral, and it also speaks of punishment for wrongdoing.

Nuhanović was not alone. Evidence gathered widely in the field showed that people traumatized by violence and death often wanted to talk about their past, as Gourevitch sensed empirically. In many situations, the failure to stop and listen simply widened the gaps between peacekeepers and local people. Even though groups such as Human Rights Watch already in 1993 sought to put mechanisms in place to deal with the past, this side of societal reconciliation has remained the "most neglected" part in the peace process. In Cambodia, it seemed to outsiders as if no one talked about the mass killings and crimes that had occurred under the Pol Pot regime. This silence allowed many to say that Cambodians simply wanted "to forget." Drawing on anthropological evidence, Pouligny showed that if these observers had used multiple forms of evidence beyond written words—intergenerational communications, body language, children's games—they would have seen that the tragedy was "omnipresent" for the young generation, only not as written history.

The two ad hoc tribunals and also the subsequent U.N. Criminal Courts established for Sierra Leone, Cambodia, and East Timor met the expectations of many survivors of mass crimes and genocides: they wanted to bring the "facts" of the past to light and hold perpetrators "responsible" for such horrors. Similar evidence came before the women's tribunal in Vienna in 1993 from the Centre for Women War Victims in Zagreb, Croatia. Witnesses to the Yugoslav crises demanded that "those who carried out the atrocities should be tried in the places where the crimes occurred because that is the only way that innocent people can live together again."[37] These widely shared popular sentiments from different locales strengthened the work of the international tribunals—even if located far from the crimes. In these trials, the human rights community put its very principles and values on trial. It was, in effect, staging its own legal culture and demonstrating its legitimacy—indeed its right—to dispense justice. Confronted with a past full of show trials, these ad hoc courts had to demonstrate that they were something different. Figure 4 shows the prominence of the international tribunals and their national and local offshoots in the revitalized climate of accountability in the 1990s.

From timid, understaffed, and underfinanced origins, the ad hoc tri-

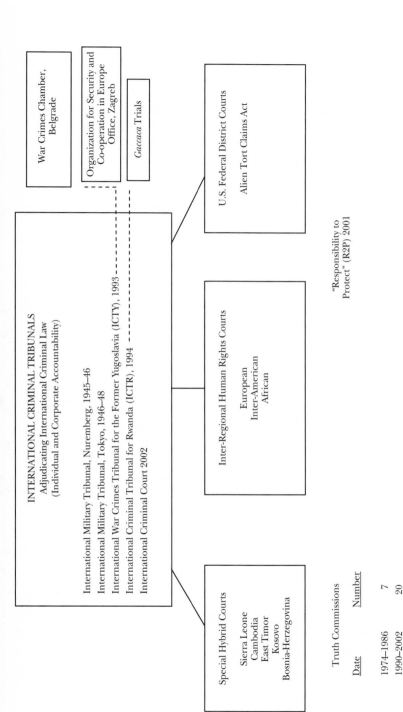

Figure 4. Levels of accountability: Growth in the 1990s. International attention to matters of legal and moral accountability surged dramatically. Adapted from the official U.N. Web sites, www.un.org/rights/ and www.un.org/law/icc/index.html. Also, the Center for Constitutional Rights, www.ccrjustice.org; the Truth Commissions, www.usip.org/library/truth/html; responsibility doctrine, www.responsibilitytoprotect.org; the European Court of Human Rights, www.echr.coe.int/echr/index.html; the Inter-American Court of Human Rights, www.oas.org/oaspage/humanrights.htm; and Gino J. Naldi, "Reparations in the Practice of the African Commission on Human and Peoples' Rights," *Leiden Journal of International Law* 14 (2001): 685–90.

bunals overcame much of the pronounced professional skepticism current at the time of their establishment.[38] In June 2004, for example, the Yugoslav Tribunal had a staff of 1,238 people from eighty-four countries; its annual budget had increased dramatically from a paltry US$276,000 at the outset to $271 million for 2004–5, reflecting its greater legitimacy. As of 2008, the date originally set by the Security Council for the conclusion of trial proceedings, the court issued ninety indictments, and many involved more than one accused. For example, an indictment from February 13, 1995, charged fifteen Serbs with having "collected and confined 3,000 Bosnian Muslims and Croat nationals" in inhumane conditions in the Omarska camp, where they "killed, raped, sexually assaulted, beat, and otherwise mistreated the prisoners." Increasingly, a growing number of accused war criminals were turning themselves in voluntarily rather than face life as fugitives. Others were pleading guilty, as did Biljana Plavšić, former leader of the Bosnian Serbs (and the only woman on trial so far at The Hague), Momir Nikolić, who admitted complicity in the Srebrenica massacre, and Miodrag Jokić, a retired Yugoslav navy commander accused of the deadly shelling of Dubrovnik in 1991. The prominent exceptions to this pattern of arrests and trials were Radovan Karadžić, former president of the Bosnian Serb Republic and Ratko Mladić, his commander. Indicated in February 1995 for genocide and crimes against humanity, Mladić is still at large (as of November 2008), protected by local communities hostile to The Hague proceedings; Karadžić was arrested in August 2008. Slobodan Milošević, charged by the Yugoslav Tribunal in May 1999 for "murder, persecution and deportation" in Kosovo, was extradited against his will to The Hague in June 2001. The court subsequently added to his indictment sixty-six counts of crimes against humanity in the Croatian war and the charge of genocide in the Bosnian war. Milošević died while still on trial. In addition, in a significant departure, the Serbian government in 2003 took the first step to establish domestic trials, and collaborated with Croatian prosecutors, to address some of the shortcomings of court proceedings held far away from Serbian daily life.[39]

The Rwanda Tribunal's staff also grew significantly, from 551 people in 1998, representing seventy-two nationalities, to a total of 872 staff in 2002–3; its budget more than tripled in the same period. As of 2004, it had completed twenty-three trials, with twenty-five pending and an additional eighteen accused awaiting trial; the staff estimated sixty to sixty-five indictments by 2008. Most of the accused were high-level military and civilian officials in the interim Hutu government, church leaders (both Roman Catholic and Protestant who sided with the Hutu Power) and influential media moguls. A large number of accused lower-level detainees also languished in Rwandan jails. In 2001, drawing on local traditions of reconciliation, officials initiated an experiment in community-based *gaccaca* courts, in which an accused was brought before local residents. If sufficient evidence emerged about complicity, the individual faced a communal court; with insufficient evidence, the person was freed. These people's courts became operational in June 2004. By inviting the traumatized community to speak out and face the accused, these local modes of justice dealt directly with the crimes almost never committed personally by distant leaders tried elsewhere but by members of the community who continued to move about, living and working among those he or she had harmed. While addressing the specificity of violence in its local context, these procedures were not immune from personal vendettas. Furthermore, to coordinate the two modes of reconciliation, the government has encouraged communication and exchange of information between local communities and the staff at the Arusha Tribunal. For example, it aired the documentary, "The Arusha Tapes," in neighborhoods undergoing the *gaccaca* trials.[40]

The proceedings of the two tribunals have had a major impact on international criminal law, as legal specialists recognize. The indictments, convictions, and written judgments accompanying the verdicts have clarified the contexts and sanction mechanisms by which individuals can be held criminally accountable for grave breaches of human rights and humanitarian law. The tribunal statutes gave the courts subject-matter jurisdiction over genocide, crimes against humanity, and war crimes. The judges also prosecuted individual cases of torture, rape, and mutilation. The Rwanda Tribunal tested specifically the applicability of Protocol II of the Geneva Conventions, which applied civilian protections to internal wars, defining the threshold of violence that activated the legal protections and their reach. Its rulings severed the original Nuremberg and Tokyo linkage to armed warfare between states, prosecuting genocide and crimes against humanity in the absence of formally declared war. In addition, the details of the convictions clarified many ambiguities in the Genocide Convention, particularly the definition of what constituted a protected "group." The main criterion remained a "stable membership determined by birth," but the rulings adopted the official classification systems of the state identity cards and the subjective perceptions of the Rwandan people. In this way, it set precedents for expanding the protections of groups under the convention. The Yugoslav Tribunal also took into account how the perpetrators defined their victims.

The formulation of subject-matter jurisdiction was a circular process with substantial input from below. In establishing authority through the Rules of Procedures and Evidence, the Security Council relied not only on international conventions and customs, the traditional schema of lawmaking, but also on general principles of "soft" law (nonbinding norms and values). It took into account the evidence of the flagrant violations of law reported back by its Commission of Experts. The international climate, too, was being shaped by eyewitness testimony gathered by women's advocacy NGOs, such as Medica Mondiale sent by the European Community to Yugoslavia in 1992 specifically to aid the women who had suffered sexual and other traumas in war. The women's tribunal also brought firsthand witnesses from the countries at war in the Balkans to the U.N. World Congress in Vienna. These women described the systematic use of violence as war strategy in the unfolding conflicts—mounting cases of rape, torture, forced pregnancy, and "different misuses" of the evidence, whether to inflame national hatreds or promote the selling of news. They showed that sexual crimes were part of a wider campaign of humiliation, intimidation, and murder, ultimately to expel what was left of whole communities. Evidence came from Sarajevo, Croatia, and women's antiwar groups in Belgrade, who offered evidence of rape "by the soldiers of the same [Serb] nationality."[41] Relating crimes to existing laws, the women's tribunal sought to raise sexual violence in wartime from its original status in international law as an outrage against personal dignity to a crime against humanity. And, indeed, the subject-matter jurisdiction of both ad hoc international courts included rape as a crime against humanity, moving well beyond the Nuremberg and Tokyo precedents.[42] Their jurisdiction had been heavily influenced by the norms and values that had been defended in human rights struggles on the ground.

The rulings also reflected the weight of evidence, setting other precedents in international law. A prime example came in the ICTR case of *Akayesu,* the first successful prosecution of rape as an act of genocide.[43] Jean Paul Akayesu had been the major of the Taba commune, responsible, as the court acknowledged, for "maintaining laws and public order." Under his watch, over 2,000 Tutsis had been killed; terrible sexual crimes also were committed. According to the evidence,

Between April 7 and the end of June, 1994, hundreds of civilians . . . sought refuge at the bureau communal. The majority of these displaced civilians were Tutsi. While seeking refuge . . . female displaced civilians were regularly taken by armed local militia and/or communal police and subjected to sexual violence, and/or beaten on or near the . . . premises. Many women were forced to endure multiple acts of sexual violence which were at times committed by more than one assailant. These acts of sexual violence were generally accompanied by explicit threats of death or bodily harm. The female displaced civilians lived in constant fear and their physical and psychological health deteriorated as a result of the sexual violence and beatings and killings.[44]

The court claimed that Akayesu "knew of," "facilitated," and "encouraged" these acts. The innovation came from the judges' criteria of rape, which changed under the weight of the women's testimonies. Listening to how the women experienced the trauma, the judges broadened the conceptual definition of rape from the physical act of "penetration" to the wider context of humiliation and coercion under which it occurred. One witness admitted that she had been physically raped. "But they were doing it in an atrocious manner, especially after having killed our brothers and our father, and these people were mocking us, they were taunting us." Drawing on witnesses' views, the court concluded that rape was "any act of a sexual nature which is committed on a person under circumstances which are coercive." It included physical force, threats, and intimidation. This landmark case, as the lawyer Navanethem Pillay showed, influenced other decisions of the court, namely *Musema*, and it impacted important cases prosecuted by the Yugoslav Tribunal as well, such as *Delalic* and *Furundžiga*.[45] Subsequently, reflecting the continuous influence of women's advocates as lawyers, heads of international NGOs, and staff of grassroots trauma centers, the International Criminal Court expanded the definition of sexual violence to include criteria such as enforced prostitution, sterilization, and forced pregnancy, which had not been part of the original jurisdiction of the ICTR or the ICTY.

Controversies over matters of scope and impartiality have not been absent from the tribunals' work. In some instances, it was a particular indictment that provoked the ire of the accused's fellow citizens. Many people in Croatia, for example, were angry that the tribunal had charged a prominent Croatian general, Janko Bobetko, as a war criminal; they felt he merely was defending his country against the Serb incursions. At the provincial level and in the Yugoslav Tribunal, furthermore, it has been difficult to hold Kosovar Albanians responsible for atrocities against Kosovar Serbs. Similarly, in Rwanda, the postgenocide government fought against allowing any of its members to be charged with rights abuses against Hutu people, whether for murder or a revenge massacre in the refugee camps. Different objectives and constraints divided tribunal prosecutors from many victims of the crimes. Seeking to be fair, the courts work in a political climate that intrudes into the efforts to determine right and wrong. For the victims, the courts' actions blur the profound moral distinctions that they insist on between themselves and the perpetrators.[46]

From the global perspective, the tribunals' jurisdiction also raised disquieting questions about the limitations of accountability. For many Security Council representatives and international NGOs, including Amnesty International and a coalition of 800 other groups, the ad hoc nature of the tribunals was itself a problem. From many different venues, growing interest in a system of universal justice encouraged U.N.

Security Council members in 1994 to call on the International Law Commission to draft statutes for a permanent International Criminal Court.

The idea had surfaced first in 1938 under the League of Nations, but it went nowhere because of the start of World War II. Many authors of the Genocide Convention also had expected establishment of a permanent court after 1948 because of the treaty's requirement of punishment; Cold War antagonisms appreciably dashed these hopes. The proposal, however, had been kept alive in the HRC's dealings with apartheid South Africa. After passage of the Apartheid Convention, commissioners appointed a Committee of Three to study the feasibility of establishing a permanent International Criminal Court to try the crime of apartheid. Although this study also went nowhere, the new geopolitical climate opening in the 1990s provided a different context. It led to an agreement on a permanent court established by treaty law and, following the precedents set by the Torture Convention, exercising universal jurisdiction. Its statute, finalized at the U.N. Diplomatic Conference of Plenipotentiaries meeting in Rome between June 15 and July 17, 1998, gave all states the right to prosecute the crimes, "regardless of any nexus the state may have with the offense, the offender, or the victim," as the lawyers Steven R. Ratner and Jason S. Abrams explained it.[47] The crimes were so egregious that state borders were no barrier to investigations and punishment.

The International Criminal Court, headquartered at The Hague, began operations on July 1, 2002. The court was given no retroactive jurisdiction and judges can only prosecute crimes committed after its formal opening. Luis Moreno Ocampo was appointed the first chief prosecutor; remember, he had been the prosecuting attorney in the initial trials of the military junta for the crimes of the dirty war in Argentina. By statute, the court was given jurisdiction "over persons for the most serious crimes of international concern" (Art. 1), which were defined as genocide, crimes against humanity, war crimes, and the crime of aggression. It works according to the principle of complementarity, meaning that the first jurisdiction stays with the national court and cases reach the International Criminal Court only if the domestic judicial system is unwilling or unable to investigate and prosecute the crime. On the one hand, in its scope, human rights scholars and activists have noted the continuing limitations of assigning responsibility only to states and individuals and not, for example, to multinational corporations (or other nonstate actors, such as armed groups and militias) colluding in such grave abuses. It confers "no legal authority" to nonstate actors in the prosecution of war crimes.[48] On the other hand, inclusion of the crime of aggression, a controversial move to be sure, has the possibility of returning international law to the values of peace, which were central to the concerns of the early architects of the U.N. Charter and the Nuremberg judgments. The statute still awaits an "acceptable definition" of aggression, so violators as yet cannot be prosecuted for the crime.

Considerable controversy has surrounded the court from its inception, particularly given the active opposition by the United States—the world's only superpower in the post-Soviet era. Fearing a "politicized" agenda, the administration of George W. Bush unsigned the treaty and, since 2002, sought bilateral agreements with states to exempt U.S. troops and peacekeepers from its jurisdiction. Yet, the court's claim to jurisdiction worldwide is its most significant attribute. It speaks of universality—the cardinal principle behind human rights as formulated in 1945—and, thus, of the applicability of international criminal law to all leaders and agents of all states, large and small. Its fate remains critical to the human rights agenda in the twenty-first century.

Lessons

As events in Yugoslavia and Rwanda have shown, the U.N. humanitarian missions operated under trying circumstances, facing conflicting interests at the top, struggles for power on the ground, and a frightened public judging by actions and results. They worked under the imperatives of humanitarianism in which beleaguered people need food, shelter, medicine, and safety. In the light of the glaring difficulties in their operations, it is no wonder that many aid workers and human rights activists, members of missions, journalists, and scholars have engaged in serious stocktaking. The authors of these reflections are not in agreement; their many different views and perspectives remain unreconciled, bequeathing an ambiguous legacy for the efforts to devise effective strategies to keep people safe in armed conflicts in the future. These retrospective accounts have adopted two major lines of analysis.

The first focused on the nature of the mission and its wider context. For these analysts, the point still centered on the term "humanitarian" and the mercurial nature of language itself, easily used by international actors for different purposes. On one end of the spectrum of views was journalist David Rieff. For him, the misuse of the term as an emotional signifier represented a veritable "crisis" in itself. From interviews with many aid workers in Bosnia, Rwanda, Kosovo, and Afghanistan after 9/11, he launched a strong critique of powerful state and U.N. leaders who, he said, had misrepresented the situation throughout the long decade. He was addressing in specific the leaders of the United States, Great Britain, and France. As Rieff saw it, they masked their own failure to act by labeling the crises "humanitarian"; seduced and assuaged their own publics (and called on them to donate) by claiming the national and international humanitarian organizations were, in fact, doing all of the necessary work; and, by the late 1990s, justified armed military warfare by calling it "humanitarian intervention," a linkage that, to Rieff, was unacceptable. As he put it, warfare brought violence and death to civilians, period, and it should never be labeled "humanitarian." If war must occur, he wrote, leaders should not use the "moral warrant of humanitarianism to justify their actions." Besides, humanitarian intervention as a so-called moral obligation carried with it the possibility of endless humanitarian wars.[49]

Jakob Kellenberger, president of the ICRC, offered a different variation on the same theme in May 2000. He, too, was concerned with the mixing of humanitarian and military aims in recent U.N. field deployments. "My point is not to criticize military intervention, which can, under extreme circumstances, become the only possibility to prevent a humanitarian situation from worsening or to create the conditions for humanitarian organizations to do their work. But we should be careful with words. Whereas an intervention can well be motivated by humanitarian reasons, 'humanitarian intervention' is a problematic expression." Although he did not reject completely the use of force for a mounting human tragedy, it was to be used only as a last resort and then called what it was—military force. The ICRC has continued to insist that strict "neutrality" and "impartiality" are essential to its work of monitoring the principles of humanitarian law and securing the necessary flows of food and relief to people at risk. This position, in turn, has found supporters among legal scholars, who seek solutions to humanitarian crises in the expansion and strengthening of international humanitarian law, particularly through the International Criminal Court's work of investigating and prosecuting crimes. They raise the question of whether the credible threat of a system of universal justice impartially applied might work as a deterrent to those thinking about violating the customary norms of international community life.[50]

Despite the skepticism from different quarters, many Western state representatives in the United Nations, high-level staff, and intergovernmental agency heads continued to adhere to the new activist principle of military interventions on moral and humanitarian grounds. So did rights activists such as Bernard Kutchner who, for a while, administered the Kosovo province when it became a U.N. protectorate in June 1999 after NATO troops pushed Serb forces back into Serbia proper. These individuals and groups still draw on the principles enunciated by Kofi Annan in 1999, although he had warned about a slippery slope to militarism. Pushed by Canadians and other parties, this position solidified into a "Responsibility to Protect" (R2P) doctrine proposed in 2001 and endorsed by world leaders at a world summit in 2005. Subsequently, it was reaffirmed by a Security Council resolution in April 2006. Figure 4 shows it in the shifting notions of responsibility emerging in the long decade. Also part of the continuing discourses over sovereignty advanced by the human rights legal revolution, it proclaimed *contingent* sovereignty dependent on state leaders' responsibility to protect people from grave harm. As doctrine, it eroded the state sovereign right to control people and borders "at all costs." The responsibility to "prevent harm" and to "rebuild" threatened communities falls to the so-called international community in cases where state leaders fail to protect their populations. Since 2001, however, this doctrine has collided with the "hard kernel" of truth about the sovereign prerogatives of states in the international arena: as an expression of power, the linkage between state sovereignty and territory remains strong. The doctrine has yet to be implemented, even when clearly oppressive and dictatorial regimes opposed urgently needed humanitarian aid.[51]

The second approach offered more pragmatic lessons. It sought to overcome the major limitations of the missions driven by the perspectives of outsiders: the Security Council, the peacekeepers, the international agencies, and the human rights monitors—each with competing mandates and little practice of coordination. As Claude Bruderlein proposed, the international community needed new theories and strategies that more effectively tapped local traditions and cultures. This group, although divided over emphasis and strategy, shared the belief that durable solutions lay in enhanced input from the locality. Its proponents wanted an approach that constructed the projects of conflict prevention, peacekeeping, and peace-building from the bottom up. The solid grounding in the specifics of the conflicts would allow a more nuanced deployment of actors to take advantage of different strengths, calling on the ICRC, for example, in cases where "neutrality" were needed and on other agencies and NGOs for more politicized actions.

For Pouligny, success required improvements in the tools of analysis brought to each crisis at every level. As she prescribed, "Everyone—not only members of the mission's analysis unit or the military intelligence cells—must have at their disposal, at all stages of their work, relevant tools of analysis to understand and monitor what is changing in the societies in which they are working." To her, this step was critical because the Security Council, in the 1990s, had encroached on the competency of the General Assembly, taking over the responsibilities for planning and executing the U.N. missions. Bruce D. Jones and Charles K. Cater also called for more attention to local cultures and traditions, "little known and less used by international actors." As they put it, members of the missions had to use the ways local communities understood war, resolved conflicts, and made amends. As the *gaccaca* courts in Rwanda showed, these traditions can complement the work of the international tribunals, operating far from local communities. Jones and Cater described the essential role of burial rituals as the vehicle for "pardon and cleansing" in Angola and Mozambique. These rites signified the transition from the "abnormalities" and atrocities of wartime into the time of peace. For more effective results, local modes of reconciliation and forgiveness needed to become a more common part of the international peace-building processes.[52]

Other analysts have proposed audacious strategies, including enhanced field roles for NGOs, more directly concerned with "nurturing and maintaining domestic mechanisms for self-protection" than international actors. Reflecting NGO perspectives and proposals, Bruderlein, for example, suggested that protection strategies should be developed first "at the field level," with the intervention of "foreign agents subjected to a series of domestic requirements." Of course, the way Rwandan society fractured in the face of ethnic hatred offers a cautionary tale for this scenario, as the author readily admits. Nonetheless, the wider point remains valid: "The default responses to early abuses against civilians should no longer be the media driven deployment of foreign observers but a process of consultation and reconciliation among local actors with the support of NGOs." Furthermore, any reform in the patterns of strategic coordination and consistency of intervention requires the political support of the U.N. member-states, as Jones and Cater understand. This means that international and national NGOs need to give more attention to educating and lobbying domestic constituencies—along the lines of the work of MADRE, committed to reeducating the American public about U.S. foreign policy. The authors point to what they call the "paradox" of their argument: "that the search for a more effective and consistent implementation of international norms and laws to protect civilians in war begins with more consistent and effective engagement in domestic politics. Just as the real test of effective protection lies at the local level, so the real political will to make this happen derives from the local level."[53] It is less a paradox than a lesson and one applicable to human rights advocacy generally.

*   *   *

The 1990s saw an outbreak of genocidal and mass violence in many parts of the globe, societal implosions that pushed U.N. interventions in new directions and at the same time confounded them. Whether "manufactured" or not, these deadly outbreaks represented patterns of violence that profoundly challenged human rights values. The armed conflicts in the era also were accompanied by mounting social tensions over the availability of scarce resources and by the refugees fleeing for their lives, and the conflicts were exacerbated by the presence of so many transnational migrants in national societies seemingly straining the welfare system and other resources. Although countered by voices of tolerance, the responses were rising tides of anger and xenophobic politics, including Islamophobia and outbreaks of anti-Semitic hatred in parts of Europe and Latin America.

To confront these expressions of hatred head on, the General Assembly called an international world conference, the World Conference against Racism (WCAR) to meet in Durban, South Africa, in late August and early September 2001. The original agenda had limited discussions to the *contemporary* manifestations of racism and xenophobia. But mounting societal concerns with handling past wrongs—from the Argentine Mothers' continuing vigils to the work of the South African Truth and Reconciliation Commission to the victims' need to speak "the facts" of their own stories—pushed the agenda in different directions. The WCAR caught the particular moment when anger at historical wrongs and deeply conflicting historical narratives intruded into an international gathering—partly on their own terms and partly as surrogates for the continuing inequalities of the world economic and political order. If its work was overshadowed by the 9/11 attacks on the United States and the ensuing U.S.-led "war on terror," the controversies played out at the conference offered valuable insights for human rights advocacy in the new millennium.

Chapter 7
September 2001 and History

Durban [the U.N.-sponsored World Conference against Racism, WCAR] tried to offer up a version of a tolerant and understanding world, but it fell far short of any utopian dream. And, a few days later, September 11 was a rude wake-up call, but not one that necessarily permanently scars the collective psyche of the world. . . . If now is not a good time for anti-racism activists to carry on the struggle, I don't know when would be better.

—William Wong, delegate, "Winter 2001–2002: Looking Back at Durban"

Over the course of the 1990s, as part of wider efforts to consider the processes of social healing and reconciliation, human rights activists around the globe increasingly began to bring issues of historical injustices into the limelight. Responding partly to the demands of victims for truth and responsibility, the debates and experiments with the institutions of "transitional justice" and peace-building models recognized the importance of addressing past grievances to move forward. This attention also accorded with people's own lived experiences, providing poignant testimony of how the personal and collective memories of traumas continued to survive in the spaces between life's knowledge and the history books that silenced it. The human rights culture not only offered a supportive context for this memory and speech but also put the issue of redress on the table. From a historian's vantage point, this heightened sensitivity to past wrongs, and the insistent claims for remedies, was one of the striking characteristics of the "long" decade.

The commitment was at the heart of the legal option emerging at the international and national levels. Through criminal proceedings, the ad hoc tribunals and the International Criminal Court spoke for ending the culture of impunity. The trials allowed for a formal accounting of past offenses and punishment for the crimes, combining two elements of justice into one process. In patterns of circular influence, these principles were mirrored in national trials and incorporated into the efforts of U.N. officials to broker peace agreements that contained mechanisms for "truth and reconciliation." Emboldened by the new attention to legal accountability, for example, U.N. and Cambodian officials in 1997 started negotiations for a tribunal of mixed domestic and international judges to try the remaining former Khmer Rouge leaders for the crimes of their regime.[1] These same values also reverberated on the ground, kept alive in the weekly vigils of the Mothers of the Plaza de Mayo and other relatives' groups in the region, who continued to demand "justice and punishment for the guilty" throughout the 1990s.

For the Mothers and for the families of the disappeared in Latin America, the legal climate only began to change in the 1990s. The causal nexus for the breakthrough was complicated. It reflected partly the dogged persistence of the Mothers' continuing interventions in public life, demanding answers. The group remained "important and influential in Latin American politics."[2] But it also reflected the growing transnational interest in these issues of justice as well as the continued political interlinking among the once tight-knit right-wing dictatorial regimes. Testing the extent of universal jurisdiction and the prosecutorial role in the post–Cold War era, judges in Spain, France, Sweden, and Italy, for example, mounted efforts to extradite and try military leaders for gross human rights abuses in Argentina and Chile, most notably forcing the detention of General Augusto Pinochet in England in 1998 (on a Spanish judge's order). This action—a shock to dictatorial leaders everywhere—also contributed new vocabulary to human rights language. Subsequently, "to be Pinocheted" implied that no present or former heads of state charged with gross human rights crimes were safe outside the sanctity of their own territorial borders.

Debates on these rulings by outside judges, in turn, reinforced the parallel domestic movements to appoint human rights judges to detain and try the officers linked to rights abuses, as was starting to take place in Argentina and Chile. An opening of an archive or a change in domestic law had repercussions in neighboring states. The Argentine Senate's revocation of amnesty on August 21, 2003, directly strengthened similar efforts at legal accountability and constitutional change in Chile. In patterns of spiraling influence, furthermore, the mounting regional pressure for full justice and accountability encouraged new debates about past abuses and necessary punishment in Peru and Brazil and also, in a different context, in Mexico. Basing its decision in part on a 2001 ruling of the Inter-American Court of Human Rights (in a case involving Peru), the Argentine Supreme Court in 2005 fully annulled the amnesty laws, paving the way for the prosecution or extradition of such notorious human rights violators as Alfredo Astiz, who had been involved in disappearing Argentines and non-nationals during the dirty wars. With this final ruling, the surviving Mothers ended their annual twenty-four-hour resistance vigil, which they had inaugurated in 1981. After twenty-five years, in the square bedecked with pictures and banners of the disappeared children and family members, they believed that the Latin American people had gained the ability to "guide" their own governments. But the Mothers also pledged to continue to demand justice and prepare the next generation to "defend human rights."[3]

The transformed climate of the 1990s also unleashed other memories of violence and grievance long submerged under Cold War constraints. For example, the 1989 Tiananmen Square massacre of students calling for democratic reforms of the Chinese political system reverberated in transnational civil society. In the words of Iris Chang, it galvanized Chinese disasporic communities to establish "webs of Internet relationships" to respond to the crisis. These links quickly brought to the surface older memories of the brutality of the Japanese military invasion of the Chinese nationalist capital in 1937, what Chang called the "Rape of Nanking." The events of this brutal occupation had been silenced through the geopolitical and trade alliances forged during the Cold War, as had the Japanese army's extensive use of Korean, Filipina, and other Asian women as sexual slaves in its wartime brothels. Only in the 1990s did these women come forward to demand apology and compensation, aided and supported by the networks of the global women's human rights movements. The haunting evidence of the brutalities of sexual violence in the civil and genocidal wars of the 1990s and in the vicious responses to the East Timor struggle for independence from Indonesia in 1998 and 1999 also linked past and present, reviving memories of widespread rapes as war policy in the region as, for example, during the Bangladesh war of independence in 1971.[4]

Surveying the "human rights horizons" in the year 2000, the lawyer Richard Falk noted this remarkable "surge" in interest in the righting of past wrongs. He commented on a new attention to *time* intruding into human rights debates, and of growing interest in the rights and responsibilities for not only the past but the future as well—protecting the environment, ensuring a food supply, and working for sustainable growth to meet the essential needs of the next generations on the globe. Falk called this imperative "intergenerational justice," a new temporal relationship linking past and future that was an essential ingredient in the work of creating "humane governance for the peoples of the world."[5]

The General Assembly's call in 1997 for a World Conference against Racism fell in the middle of these debates about historic rights and claims. The third such antiracist conference under U.N. auspices, it was the first in the new postapartheid world and the first in the new millennium as well. The site of the conference was Durban, South Africa, a place saturated with history and memory. It seemed a particularly compelling choice for the international effort to address the many faces of racism. From the international perspective, U.N. Secretary General Kofi Annan in his opening remarks credited the historical struggle with changing the meaning of South Africa "from a by-word for injustice and oppression into a beacon of enlightenment and hope, not only for a troubled continent, but for the entire world." He asked rhetorically, "Where else, my friends, could we hold this conference?" From the grassroots level, Peniel E. Joseph, an NGO delegate from the United States visiting South Africa for the first time, described his feelings of "intense euphoria" and "gratitude" and wrote about a "humbling sense of the historic struggle" that made the trip possible.[6]

To deepen the reach of the conference, the Secretary General was determined to tap a broad constituency of marginalized peoples and groups who were especially vulnerable to discrimination and exploitation. Already in his millennium statement, Annan had expressed dismay at the gaps between the work of the U.N. organs and agencies and the many impoverished and displaced people who were not represented at the United Nations. Just as Theo van Boven had widened NGO and victim access to the Secretariat and the Human Rights Commission, so, too, the WCAR organizers targeted directly the "voice of civil society" and especially the victims and the NGOs working on their behalf. They accredited nearly 1,300 NGOs not in consultative status with the ECO-SOC and over 4,000 individual NGO representatives; they also raised funds to help ensure their participation in the preparatory work and at Durban. As a social microcosm, the conference gave generally marginalized groups the world stage for a while: among them, indigenous peoples, the Dalits (or "untouchables") in Hindu caste society participating for the first time at a U.N. world conference, Afro-Caribbean migrant workers, Palestinian citizens in Israel, Roma and Sinti people, and a U.S. factory worker from Sunflower County, "a land of cotton and catfish in the heart of the Mississippi Delta."[7] The conference brought together about 18,800 people, including the official delegates from 170 states.

Given the prevailing climate of the 1990s and the several years of intensive grassroots preparation across the globe leading up to the opening celebrations on August 28, 2001, it is no surprise that when the NGO representatives arrived in South Africa they came to talk less about the future than about the "painful" past. Put another way, for many activists, a future free of racism seemed to require forthright reckoning with the horrors of the past. Renate Bloem, president of CONGO, the umbrella group of 360 international organizations spanning the globe to promote the ties between the United Nations and the NGO sector, made this observation shortly after the congress ended.[8] Delegates at the WCAR, however, had a difficult balancing act. Called on to confront contemporary forms of racist xenophobia and discrimination and hammer out a strong declaration of principles and a workable set of remedies for the new century, a groundswell of grassroots sentiments and regional state interests brought matters of historical injustices to the forefront.

As its own historical moment, then, the WCAR was a capstone event in the long 1990s, reflecting many of the particular elements that set the decade off as a distinct period in human rights history. Through its processes of negotiation, it forged a broad international consensus on the need to confront past wrongs in order to build a more tolerant future. Paragraph 106 of the declaration made the point clearly: "We emphasize that remembering the crimes or wrongs of the past, wherever and whenever they occurred, unequivocally condemning its racist tragedies and telling the truth about history are essential elements for international reconciliation and the creation of societies based on justice, equality and solidarity."[9]

This general consensus, however, fractured in the face of the specificities of historical wrongs and the concrete demands for justice. This intrusion of history and memory into the U.N. meeting played out against the many different interests and factions that divided the "international community," however important its fictional unity was for international diplomacy and public consumption. The conference itself captured its complexity, combining individuals, groups, organizations, and states with vastly different resources and power. At this historical juncture, the weight of state geopolitical interests forced media attention—and, thus, the public face of the conference internationally—onto two highly contentious issues, all but overshadowing the ongoing work of the caucuses and delegations. The one centered on African NGO and states' and African descendants' claims for reparations for the historical wrongs of the Atlantic slave trade, slavery, and colonialism. The second demonstrated that "telling the truth about history" was no easy task when multiple truths collided and the narratives were predicated on "the denial or distortion of the narratives of the others."[10] This brought the seemingly irreconcilable issue of Israeli and Palestinian claims to the forefront. Both these issues were not new to human rights advocacy but became reframed in the idioms of the decade. As its own moment, the conference told a lot about the challenges to human rights advocacy at the dawn of the twenty-first century.

Through serendipity (or the "cunning" of history), it also offered a distinctive lens on the place of human rights advocacy in the aftermath of the 9/11 attack on the United States and the ensuing American-led "war on terror." Of course, this understanding comes only with hindsight and requires a reading of the immediate post-9/11 world partly against the backdrop of the major concerns examined at the conference. As it turned out, the WCAR was positioned to address the heightened preoccupation with past wrongs boiling up in the decade and, unexpectedly, highlighted the precarious socioeconomic and legal position of those resident civilians most vulnerable to the security concerns of the "war on terror."

The Preparation Process

The General Assembly's call in 1997 to organize the world conference set in motion a well-established pattern of government and NGO responses at all levels of state and civil society. As had become customary, the preparatory operations overseen by U.N. officials interlinked government representatives and NGO members, who worked partly in tandem and partly independent of one another. The General Assembly designated the Human Rights Commission as the official Preparatory Committee and Mary Robinson, the High Commissioner for Human Rights, as the overall coordinator. Their official task was to bring all the drafts, proposals, amendments, seminar findings, and other reports together and write a draft document that would balance the multiple passions, concerns, demands, and perspectives of the many interested parties.

A series of preparatory meetings in strategic locations in 2000 and 2001 hammered out the documents, funneling upward.[11] These included NGO steering committee meetings to coordinate operations in designated geographic regions, followed by networking conferences. States and people were grouped into large regional blocs. The conference made Europe, the Americas, Africa, and Asia (including the Pacific and the Middle East) the basis for its deliberations.

The major work of debating and drafting the platform took place at regional meetings, events sequenced so, ideally, the NGOs met first, followed by the official intergovernmental regional conference a few days later. For the WCAR, these regional preparatory meetings were held in Strasbourg, France, in October 2000; in Santiago, Chile, in December 2000; in Dakar, Senegal, in January 2001; in Tehran, Iran, in February 2001; and in Kathmandu, Nepal, in April 2001, a special meeting of the Asian working groups.[12] By official guidelines, the NGOs debated their own collective proposals and a spokesperson read them to the government conference, with time allowed for individual NGOs to present "oral interventions." Negotiations over just how much time to allot for presentations often became contested matters. Although two distinct documents issued from this procedure (an NGO and an intergovernmental text), the sequential timing permitted NGO input into government drafting and deliberations.

While collaborating for the purposes of the WCAR, NGOs and government representatives had different objectives and interests as well as access to the resources of international diplomacy. These distinctions were understood at all levels of NGO participation. The NGO leadership had a definite vision for the people's forum, which they posted on their own Internet site. The forum, they announced, was a "space of its own," ideally reflecting the "needs and visions" a people wanted to channel to their governments as well as to the larger "community" of nations. A parallel statement by the International Federation of Human Rights, a Parisian network of 105 national human rights organizations from 86 countries, also advocated a distinct agenda. Determined to encourage a "constructive dialogue" favoring the exchange of ideas, the group nonetheless warned NGOs not to give up campaigning against the problems of racist abuses in their home territories. Federation officials made the point unmistakably clear. Listen to their admonition: "Several times in the course of debates in various U.N. bodies, States and some NGOs have stressed the importance of exchanging . . . good practice relating to the fight against discrimination. This approach is constructive and useful. It is vital, however, to guard against basing world conferences disproportionately on the exchange of good practice at the expense of preserving [them as] a forum for denouncing violations perpetrated by states."[13] As distinct entities, the NGOs brought to public attention the states' deviations from human rights norms and federation officials encouraged them to do so even when the problem was in their own backyard.

These views also were matched on the ground. Several Indonesian women NGO delegates attending the preparatory meetings in Tehran put out a "working report" (in English) through *ISIS-International-Manila* in April 2001. For Ester Indahyani Jusuf and Asmin Fransiska, the NGOs had to remain vigilant to ensure that the government complied with the agreements. "But if there's [a] country [that] does not want to do these documents, the U.N. cannot give punishment . . . because the system of the declaration and the plan of action is not [a binding] system, just a moral system. And, if the country did not do the thing that [it] should do, it is time that all NGOs all around the world . . . remember . . . and urge them to do that."[14] Their comments also shed light on divisions within the NGO community, angrily describing what they called the organizations "built by the government" (government NGOs, GONGOs) as opposed to "real" NGOs willing to bring real issues to the meetings and, as specified by the international agenda, present the views and "voices of the victims." In Tehran, they reported, the NGOs met several times in "closed" session to keep out the government groups "because so many meetings were ruined because of them."

Although only one report among many, the authors also showed the types of grassroots follow-up initiatives that carried the work further into local communities. Frustrated in Tehran because they had *not* been allowed to present their "oral intervention," the delegates returned home determined to strengthen the Indonesian antiracism coalitions. They subsequently sponsored several events, in one case inviting fifty NGOs to an information meeting. Many had not gone to Tehran. Wanting to do more to strengthen the coalitions and defend victims, they took steps to work more closely together. "We did not want to make the same mistakes again like Teheran," the authors wrote in describing the preparations for the next gathering in Kathmandu. They solidified alliances, sought more funding, and carefully put together all the documents they would need at the next meeting. They were determined, too, that the victims "go there to talk about what they felt."

Their experiences of political maturation were not unique. For many delegates, it was all about "the road to Durban and back," as one reporter on the Americas titled it. Describing events from the perspective of the Afro-Latino organizations, Michael Turner wrote, "As it turned out, the process of 'getting to Durban' was as important as the actual eight-day conference on the African continent." In graphic terms, he described the path for these groups: "It had a geographical axis running from Montevideo, Uruguay to Salvador, Brazil as well as from Nicaragua's Atlantic Coast to the Pacific coast of the Choco in Colombia. It was a process that generated communication between Honduran Garifunas from La Ceiba and their Garifuna relatives in South Bronx; it involved political alliances negotiated between black Venezuelan and Peruvian political representatives and advisors to the Andean regional parliament. For many Afro-Latino organizations, the road to Durban became the main event." Marilia Schüller, similarly, wrote about her "journey" to Durban and Betty Ruth Lozano, a self-described woman of African descent born in Colombia, echoed the view. Durban, said Lozano, should not be seen as a discrete event that took place in late August and early September 2001. It was, she reiterated, a "process," which started earlier and continued long after the end of the conference, involving "many encounters which have brought us face to face with our prejudices and the prejudices of others." Continuing, she noted,

When I first attended the preparatory events for the conference, I had the idea that discrimination and racism were topics that concerned only Black and Indigenous People. That was the idea I took with me to the preparatory conference for the Americas. But there we met other groups of people, like the Rome people, of whom I had only a distant notion. . . . I thought the Roma were in Europe and they were something different. So it came as a shock . . . to find that the representative of the Rome people at the conference in Chile was a Columbian.

William Wong, from whose retrospective account the epigraph for this chapter is taken, also forged new connections in Santiago, where, he realized, the plight of Asians as a minority group had been overlooked because governments in the hemisphere typically did not see the Asian community as a "vulnerable minority group." However, Wong's NGO, the National Asian Pacific American Legal Consortium (NAPALC), had worked closely with African Americans "for a long time," and the Canadian Asians, too, "were able to talk across racial and ethnic lines." They even approached Asian NGOs in Singapore and India, although, he noted, drawing attention to the situation of Asian minorities was not "popular" with many Asian governments. Despite the hurdles and with support from other coalitions, Wong and his colleagues persuaded the United Nations to recognize Asians and Asian descendants as a formal caucus at Durban. Wong, too, had complicated the binary notions of race.[15]

From the participants' viewpoint—not only the historian's—Durban had a wider logic. It solidified new advocacy networks and taught important lessons in transnational negotiation to take to future conferences. It established promising organizational linkages, as the alliance forged between Afro-Latinos and the African and African Descendants Caucus at the steering committee meeting in Geneva in June 2001. Post-Durban-related conferences in Barbados and Johannesburg continued the pattern.

For some groups, it meant new roles in interregional discussions of discrimination and economic development. Under the impact of Durban, for example, the Inter-American Commission on Human Rights examined for the first time the economic vulnerabilities and land claims of Afro-Latinos and the Human Rights Commission established the first Working Group on People of African Descent (see Fig. 3a). At its initial meeting in November 2002, among other tasks, it set new development goals, calling for closer ties to international development agencies to design "special projects" and "investments" in health, education, housing, and electricity for these vulnerable minority communities. Furthermore, in the case of Brazil, "the largest country in which Latinos of African heritage constitute a sizeable percentage of the population," the lead-up to Durban brought community activists involved in development projects into dialogue with government authorities in the Foreign Ministry and Ministry of Justice and some joined the official delegation to Durban. Subsequently, they continued to work with the government as well as with the bilateral and multilateral donor agencies (the Inter-American Development Bank and the World Bank, for example) to establish priorities more geared to the needs of specific communities. For example, they proposed a "racial report card" to assess in detail the policy impact on criteria such as "gender equity" and "benefits for children." The immediate effect enhanced community input in development planning, although it remained unclear whether these substantive changes would be sustained in the long run.[16]

These initiatives reflected the formal efforts of organizers and activists to incorporate the perspectives of marginalized groups into the planning stages. For Theo van Boven, who attended Durban as an "independent advisor" in the Dutch delegation and a "resource person" for the NGO forum, the prominence of the victims' perspectives was the defining characteristic of the conference. Forty-four different thematic and geographical caucuses were accredited at the WCAR. Some delegates were skeptical of the whole undertaking. Pauline Muchina, from Kenya, noted that "many African people and African NGOs had heard little about the WCAR. This lack of information . . . was not restricted to Africa. For many people around the world, the conference was seen as having little to do with their daily lives. This information gap is typical . . . creating room for doubts about whether the outcomes of such meetings have any real impact in the world."[17] Seen as a dynamic process, however, its effects radiated into civil society, broadening coalitions, empowering advocates to ask new questions, and incorporating newer constituencies into the human rights and development agendas.

Stories and Analyses

For many participants, the centerpiece of the NGO forum was a special session titled *Voices* held each day during the conference. Featuring twenty-one personal stories of hardship and pain—and of the necessity to struggle for change—it highlighted the distinctively human side of rights tragedies in the victims' own words. The commitment to capture the victims' experiences had been an essential ingredient in the preparatory work. The African networking meeting in Botswana said it well, but similar sentiments were expressed in the other regional NGO documents. In preparing their accounts, NGOs in Botswana laid forceful claim to the "right" to their "own interpretation and historical truth."[18] They were going to present their own history through their own eyes.

The choice of voices seemingly reflected a patchwork approach, designed not for precise comparative or analytical purposes but as a catalog of the specific challenges for the global antiracism movements. It gave ample testimony to the continuing forms of group discriminations in contemporary society. These voices found their way into the final conference document, although its structure—tightly divided into terse, numbered paragraphs—hardly did justice to the passionate convictions and moving details behind the stories. *Voices* also became its own publication through the support of the South African Human Rights Commission and the U.S.-based global International Human Rights Law Group. These stories at the time served as important illustrations of many of the wider discussions about group vulnerabilities at the conference. As their own "truth," however, they also played a subversive role, complicating notions advanced by leaders, regional blocs, and caucuses elsewhere.

A good example was the situation in South Africa, a "beacon of light" as Kofi Annan had proclaimed, but a country also facing continuing tensions over land ownership and poverty in the face of its hard-won democratic rights and legal equality norms. The story of Griffiths Molefe, eighty-four years old at the time of his recounting, offered ample testimony to the persistence of racial injustice and its accompanying poverty in contemporary South Africa. A farm worker since 1925 (Molefe began work at the age of seven), he had been "herd man looking after cattle" for a series of white farmers and worked for the last one for forty years. Evicted from the land in 1998, in the past four years he had been living in a "tent and shack" alongside the road where he was dropped. The eviction had been preceded by other harassments. In his words, the farmer "took all my livestock and later denied it"; the farmer's children "hurled stones into the house, breaking windowpanes and damaging some of my belongings. I reported the matter to the police and . . . the police did nothing to help me."[19] Molefe's was not an isolated case; concern with the systemic nature of discrimination sparked the continuing community actions against poverty and privatization across the country. The Landless People's Movement and Jubilee 2000, the South African branch of the global network fighting the crippling effects of international debt, staged a series of protests outside the halls of the WCAR. Even though the conference gave ample space to the alternative human rights advocacy networks challenging the socioeconomic hierarchies that often took racial forms, protesters knew they were arrayed against powerful states defending the existing world economic order. The WCAR reflected the many layers of outsiders in human rights struggles.

The detailed focus on people's lives did not operate in isolation. The WCAR had been called to address the nature of racism in the postapartheid world, where the "scourges" of racist discriminations and intolerances had not been eradicated.[20] It generated a large volume of documents, drawing on a range of expertise, from academic scholars at five U.N.-sponsored expert seminars to trained professionals long in the field to U.N. staff to heads of intergovernment and government agencies and to the activists on the ground. From many sides, organizers and participants grappled with finding the most useful conceptual rubrics and analytical tools to guide future actions and strategies. The conference was as much about analysis as narratives.

The documents produced by the activists, government officials, and academics were varied and complex. As the European NGOs meeting in Strasbourg acknowledged, they were dealing with "cross-cutting themes" that no longer could be examined in isolation. Without homogenizing the distinct regional and national patterns, participants sought adequate tools to assess the global contexts. A broad consensus agreed that, for a coordinated agenda, contemporary racism was understood best as an institutional and a structural problem, aggravated by the ongoing pressures of neoliberal globalization. The debates and discussions tended to look at the structural patterns of domination, whether in the law and its enforcement, landholding and property relations, or employment or education. Attention turned to the ways that state and institutional power enforced social disadvantages.[21] The key marker in this analysis became the differential access among citizens as well as between citizens and nonnationals to available resources, such as clean water, public health services, education, and decent housing. Report after report indicated a clear linkage between poverty, minority status, and racist practices. Put another way, the groups most vulnerable to institutional racism were disproportionately poor and minority. The documents showed, too, that these patterns were global in scope.

Seen in this light, the individual tales of hardship and vulnerability stood for larger trends in the global structures of domination and discrimination. The conference deliberations stressed the interplay of narrative and analysis. It linked, for example, the particular vulnerability of racial and ethnic minorities to exploitation by criminal trafficking networks as well as to systemic outbreaks of hatred and violence in national societies. The voices of women reflected many interconnections: an Afro-Brazilian domestic worker, a poor black woman in a catfish factory in the U.S. south, the widow of a murdered Dalit activist, an Afro-Colombian woman displaced through the pressures of global development, aggravated by civil war and drug trafficking. The narratives drew attention to women's multiple identities—to gender, labor, minority status, and region—or, in the language of the conference, the "intersectionality" of the many social variables at play in human identity. Ameliorative agendas had to confront the challenges of "double" or even "multiple" discriminations. From the rich data based on concrete information, the

WCAR targeted specific redress for groups of people with particular vulnerabilities.[22]

In the context of institutional racism, the situation of victims was not isolated. The disabilities of Palestinian status in Israel could be examined in relation to those of the Roma and Sinti peoples in Eastern Europe suffering long-standing social and legal stigmas perpetuated in postcommunist societies, the Dalits in India, and the indigenous Americans. The special session gave prominent voice, for example, to Willy Weisz, confronting the rise of anti-Semitism in the xenophobic and racist politics in Austria and elsewhere. As Weisz explained, "We have learned from the experiences of our parents and grandparents in the 1930s and 1940s. . . . So, I understood . . . that anti-Semitism must be fought by reacting whenever we are made aware of spoken or written prejudices, not only when actions are threatening." It heard from Ashid Ali, a young Bangladeshi-born man and schoolteacher in England. Living in Oldham, the site of the "worst race riots in decades," he described the patterns of segregation in British society. Session organizers also invited Ibrahim Abu Sbeih, a Palestinian citizen living in an "unrecognized" village in the Negev in Israel. Because of its status, the village lacked economic infrastructure and such basic municipal services as "water, electricity, health services, schools, streets, communication." It also had disproportionately high levels of illiteracy and unemployment. A parallel meeting took up the issue of the rise of Islamophobia, which grassroots and transnational human rights NGOs earlier had identified as a serious problem of societal prejudice emerging in Europe, exacerbated by anti-immigrant politics as well as by government policies and media coverage.[23] By making the *Voices* document available, these juxtaposed narratives seemed to work well together. In reality, the effort to affirm shared experiences proved explosive for some, challenging preconceived interests among state and caucus blocs unwilling to listen to the narratives of the other.

Those who attended the WCAR entered the world of international diplomacy, with its play of geopolitical interests, power, and posturing. Behind the analysis and narratives lay high stakes, particularly because organizers had set the practical agenda of identifying the victims of racist discriminations, assessing the current levels of protection, and proposing new "remedies, recourses, redress, compensation and other measures." Proposals included concrete claims with financial consequences. They brought increased scrutiny of domestic relations from abroad and challenges to states' projected identities. The WCAR was wracked with tension, much of it crisscrossing the obvious divides between civil society and state representatives.

For some groups and caucuses, participation drew international attention to their plight. This was true for the Korean women who had been enslaved by the Japanese military in World War II. They were among the many NGO groups demanding justice and carrying banners reminding the world of their past lives. They called for restitution for the crimes from the Japanese government. For Roma and Sinti people, attendance was an opportunity to strengthen their networks, develop transatlantic ties, and gain the goodwill of other coalitions for future actions and campaigns. Participation, however, was only one among many strategies for change, which included legal challenges in domestic courts as well as in the European Human Rights Court.[24]

Other caucuses had precise aims. For example, indigenous people's coalitions had been pursuing a number of strategies to defend their lands and resources. Excluded from the start from international law, which did not recognize indigenous treaty-making sovereignty or their territorial claims, they also were not included in the principle of self-determination enacted in the anticolonial struggles in the 1950s and 1960s. Although the Human Rights Sub-Commission in 1982 established a working group to address indigenous rights, native peoples launched separate national struggles with some successes, such as First Nation peoples in Canada and also aboriginals in Australia once that country adhered to the Convention on the Elimination of All Forms of Racial Discrimination in 1975. Living under continuing threats of losing their land, resources, community cohesion, and way of life, coalition leaders at the WCAR were determined to secure their own standing in international law. Human rights "universalism" had failed to safeguard the fundamental basis of indigenous life in territorial integrity. Cooperation at the conference was designed to secure international avenues of redress beyond the states. The Final Declaration, however, affirmed indigenous rights consistent only with the principles of sovereignty and the territorial integrity of the states. It warned explicitly that use of the term "indigenous peoples" in the Declaration and Programme of Action "cannot be construed as having any implication as to rights under international law" (Arts. 23 and 24). This declaration was a "setback" for tribal members seeking legal status equal to the states in international law, observed George Shepherd. A large global anti-racist network promoting indigenous and minority rights, IMADR, also called the official state position "unsatisfactory." At this juncture, however, government representatives still remained "the gatekeepers within the U.N. system" for self-determination.[25]

The Dalits had more success, according to their own objectives. The Indian government failed to keep caste off the international agenda. Dalit advocates had argued that caste discriminations were forms of racism tied inexorably to birth and they limited individual life chances.

True to its global agenda, the WCAR expanded the discussion to all countries with sizeable Hindu populations and similar social hierarchies. Given the historic South Asian diaspora, participants identified twelve other Asian countries that organized society along caste lines and argued that the caste designation aptly described the situation also of the Burakumin peoples of Japan, the Osu of Nigeria's Igbo people, and certain groups in Senegal and Mauritania. Tensions had surfaced already at the preparatory meetings. In response, the Asia-Pacific NGO conference had "strongly condemned" the governments of both India and Japan for opposing the effort to include caste-based discriminations on the conference agenda. The final document only offered a set of generalizations deploring caste discriminations and, sustaining the U.N. principle of good practice, failed to implicate any state government in the abuse. But, true to the conference's spiraling effects, the Human Rights Commission subsequently took up the issue of caste discriminations, which also became part of monitoring the Convention on the Elimination of All Forms of Racial Discrimination.[26] Negotiations at the WCAR expanded official U.N. implementation measures.

Of the many disagreements, two proved intractable at the time. The one concerned the explicit call for reparations for the long-term damages done by the slave trade, slavery, and colonialism; the other was the language used to describe the state of Israel in its dealings with the Palestinians. Both issues had appeared earlier at the regional preparatory meetings; in the light of the hostilities by Western states, many in the media already declared the WCAR "dead on arrival." Despite the efforts of U.N. leaders not to let the conflicts "derail" (the word is Kofi Annan's) the conference, the United States and Israel walked out of the meeting on September 3, 2001.[27] As became clear in retrospect, each country did so for its own reasons beyond the manifest ones. Neither was going to be tied to the principles of international law and cooperation under U.N. auspices.

No one had expected it to be easy. Mary Robinson was clear on the point. "Asking people to face up to the problems of racism in their midst is not always welcome," she said pointedly in her opening address. For van Boven, the withdrawal was "an ill-advised step"; while admitting that the conference had not been earth-shaking, he noted wryly that the documents produced by the world gathering "undoubtedly deserve detailed analysis." The overwhelming majority of NGO delegations, too, reacted negatively to the walk-out. Many blamed the international media as did Marilia Schüller, World Council of Churches delegate, who said, "The fact that the mass media focused only on some particular sections of the NGO Forum document was disrespectful to all other peoples addressing a vast number of issues significant to themselves as victims of racism." Reflecting widespread sentiments, Betty Lozano believed as well that the U.S. and Israeli withdrawal was "seized upon" by the communications media to declare the conference a "failure." Perhaps the most pointed criticism came from a South African Bishop, Mvumelwano Danadala. Addressing the continuous need to embody the values of democratic tolerance, he said, "We cannot dialogue simply when it is likely to favour us."[28]

Reparations and Economic Justice

For many civil society groups brought into the WCAR process as well as for many regional state representatives, confronting contemporary racism inexorably meant dealing with the "terrible wrongs" of the past. Past and present merged together in a systematic focus on the lasting damages of the historical tragedies of the slave trade, slavery, and colonialism. Within this framework, a study of racism had to understand its roots and its continuing legacy into the present in order to plan for a future no longer bound by the past. As already expressed at an OAU (Organization of African Unity) meeting in Abuja, Nigeria, in 1993, the harm caused by slavery and colonialism "is not a thing of the past, but is painfully manifest in the damaged lives of contemporary Africans from Harlem to Harare, in the damaged economies of the black world from Guinea to Guyana, from Somalia to Suriname." These sentiments drew on long traditions of Pan-African mobilizations.[29]

At the WCAR, the movement to name, address, and redress the legacies of past wrongs was spearheaded by African state representatives in the U.N. African Group, although they never fully spoke with one voice. They were strengthened by a wide range of NGOs, including many African American civil rights groups, such as the National Association for the Advancement of Colored People (NAACP), and members of the Black Congressional Caucus. Their ranks specifically included the Durban 400 coalition, which had been organized to lobby the case for reparations at the conference: among its prominent members were the International Secretariat of the December 12th Movement, which had been collaborating in the work of the Human Rights Commission since 1989, and N'COBRA (the National Coalition of Blacks for Reparations in America). They also had the active support of organizations such as the World Council of Churches and the Jamaican Reparations movement. The case for the historical perspective also showed up in the *Voices* session. In describing the structural limitations on her own life chances as a poor Afro-Brazilian domestic worker, Creuza Maria de Oliveira offered this powerful statement to the audience:

First of all, I would like to remind you about colonization and slavery in America before speaking of discrimination and racial prejudice in Brazil. This system treated black people as "things," oppressed through the total absence of human rights. The Brazilian society structured and developed itself because of the work of black slaves. Brazil received about 4.5 million enslaved Africans. . . . Currently, slavery is illegal but descendents of African slaves continue to be oppressed by the lack of opportunity in all aspects: economic, cultural, social and educational.[30]

Members of the Asian and American regional meetings also brought to the conference vivid understandings of how their regions' history had been distorted by colonial exploitation of land, resources, and people. In this U.N. forum, furthermore, the Europeans were not absent from the discussion. The forty-one member-states of the Council of Europe acknowledged the "suffering" caused by slavery and colonialism but proposed no redress. The European NGOs went further, bridging the regional divisions and allying with many non-Western states and peoples on this issue. The 250 NGOs at Strasbourg went on record for apology and reparations.[31]

Here, the European NGO delegates followed the lead of the Dakar document, which framed the debates for the purposes of the conference. Written as a global statement, the document was hammered out by forty-four of fifty-two states invited to the regional meeting, with NGO input. It mapped the historical case carefully. The unprecedented uprooting (what historians today call the "forced" migration) of peoples from Africa by the slave trade and the New World institution of chattel slavery—a hereditary status passed on from generation to generation—lay at the root of contemporary racism. As a result of the specifics of the slave trade, blackness was equated with slavery and subordination, helping construct racial identities rooted in a hierarchy of privilege and oppression that followed a color line shading from white to brown to black. The Santiago preparatory meeting also stressed the importance of writing this *full* history of racism; it was "essential to build[ing] societies based on justice, equality and solidarity."[32]

The Dakar document stated that this history had to be called what it always was, a "crime against humanity," a legal category that knew no statute of limitation. Already in 1998, the government of Senegal, chairing the African Group, had brought a similar resolution to the Human Rights Commission, although it simply languished at the time. Furthermore, the multiplying effects of the trade on the African continent itself—wars, social and generational disruptions, and hierarchal rule—thwarted alternative social and political developments, trends subsequently exacerbated by the impact of nineteenth-century colonization. Acknowledging that not all of Africa's present social, political, and economic difficulties were caused by "foreign factors and historic events," the Dakar document nonetheless sought to show how past injustices continued to reverberate in the present.[33] It linked slave and colonial status to contemporary structural and institutional disadvantage.

To redress the egregious wrongs of the past and take steps toward global healing, the draft drew three distinct modes of contemporary justice together: acknowledgment, apology, and reparation. It asked for an unambiguous acknowledgment that slavery, colonialism, and apartheid were among the "most serious and massive institutionalized forms of human rights violations." It demanded an "explicit apology by the former colonial Powers or their successor [states] for these human rights violations" and asked that it be inserted into the Final Declaration. It laid claim to "adequate reparation" for the communities of victims of the crimes, "regardless of when or by whom they were committed." Directly addressing the international "community of states" through U.N. auspices, it drew on the principles behind the "right to development" and the outright repudiation of the international debt—as having long been paid off through the exploitation of slave labor as well as of colonial peoples and their natural resources. Seeing the contemporary economic order as unjust and unfair—structured on the backs of slavery and colonialism—it tailored the argument to wholesale compensation for the devastations of the past. In the plans of actions and remedies, the proposal sought an International Compensation Scheme for the victims and a separate Development Reparations Fund to promote economic growth and support broad educational and social programs in countries marred by colonialism.[34] It expected the funds to come from the implicated states, private corporations, and institutions, which had benefited from slavery and colonialism.

At the WCAR, African governments and NGOs translated as an international cause an agenda that had been percolating in transnational dialogue throughout the African diaspora. The WCAR, then, represented a particular moment in a long and complicated process of recovery, which historian Anne Bailey called "re-memory" and "re-dress"; both stood in close relationship to one another.[35] It harked back to earlier Pan-African movements of remapping global connections and rewriting world narratives and remembered the great expectations for the redress of the crimes of slavery and segregation brought to the newly founded United Nations by U.S. civil rights leadersin the early 1950s. It reflected recent efforts, partly under U.N. auspices, to anchor collective memory in memorials of the slave trade and the slave plantation system—through UNESCO-designated heritage sites. The opening to the public of slave forts in Ghana, such as Fort Prinzenstein or Cape Coast Castle, for example, drew many visitors from the African diaspora looking for their own roots. The origins of these projects, however, lay in the 1970s, with the formation of the African Descendants Association, a collaborative effort of African-American and African groups to preserve a shared and painful past. Memorial sites, too, have opened in the New World. As Bailey showed, the Jamaica Memory Bank sponsored an exhibit on slavery in Montego Bay in late 2001 to "intense" public interest. Some people were drawn to the macabre—the brutal forms of torture used to break the will of the slaves—and others, she noted, "made comparisons with the economic disparities of today, 'saying it is the same thing going on.'" Her oral interviews among Ghana's Ewe population showed little popular resonance with the notion of reparation but captured a profound sense that their communities had been "deeply affected by the slave trade." As a consequence, "some talked about the need for development monies," Bailey added.[36]

The Dakar demand for "reparation" also was anchored in human rights legal developments in Africa in the 1990s, specifically in the evolution of the work of the African Commission on Human and Peoples' Rights, founded in 1987, and the African Human Rights Court, operating since 1998. The proposal, then, was partially the product of the changing climate in the long 1990s. Through its decision-making, the commission, for example, called for "reparations" of human rights abuses specifically in Malawi and Rwanda; demanded "restitution" of liberty for detainees in Nigeria; and recognized the principle of "compensatory damages." The new court's statute included provisions for remedies as well. Article 27 says: "If the Court finds that there has been a violation of a human or peoples' right, it shall make appropriate orders to remedy the violation, including the payment of fair compensation or reparation." The improving legal climate for human rights in the Africana regional system brought the principle of redress to the forefront of the judicial and political communities.[37]

Two serious obstacles limited the outcome at the WCAR, however. One was the incomplete nature of the proposal for full historical reconciliation as outlined, disrupted already by the *Voices* on display. Session organizers included Mariama Oumarou, a black Tuareg from Niger born into slavery. She told about her early youth in the "home of Igdas, a white Tuareg who was my master and the master of my mother Nola and my grandmother, Amina" and of the drudgery of her work. Later, she was sold to a man in Nigeria, ostensibly as a "fifth" wife, but really as slave and sexual object.[38] Full reparation, then, required a more extensive process than the Dakar proposal, an accounting of "African agency in the Atlantic slave trade," of internal diasporas and still fragmented histories, and of the problems of contemporary slavery (acknowledged in the Durban Declaration and Programme of Action).

In addition to the need for apology "on both sides" for the crimes, Bailey suggested truth commissions in Africa for healing, which would hear testimonies of communities that enslaved and of enslaved communities and accommodate the vastly different historical experiences in the tragedy. The WCAR was a moment of heightened international recognition of the general need to attend to history's wrongs. Its wider project of "re-memory" and "re-dress" remained valid for ongoing reconciliation, developing momentum, however, in national dialogues and more manageable settings. Some delegates had anticipated that the effects of the WCAR debates indeed would "set the basis for a higher level of activity in . . . national venues."[39]

The second obstacle lay in the geopolitical realm of state power. The United States and many European states opposed any form of compensation or formal apology that might imply legal liability. More precisely, of the European nations, Great Britain and Spain remained adamantly opposed while Germany and France favored an apology as its own repair and the start of a new dialogue. The tensions all but disrupted the first Preparatory Committee meeting in Geneva in early May 2000, which was forced to put the demand for "compensation" in brackets to highlight the serious disagreements. In Santiago, Chile, Michael Southwick, the U.S. representative, supported by the Canadian, voiced serious concerns over several paragraphs in the final draft document, particularly the language calling the slave trade a "crime against humanity" (par. 4) and all references to reparations. Both representatives said it was "inappropriate to apply a modern concept of international law to acts which took place centuries ago." At a hearing before the Subcommittee on International Operations and Human Rights of the U.S. House of Representatives, Acting Assistant Secretary for International Organization Affairs William B. Wood spelled out the U.S. government's position more clearly. Wood noted there was no consensus for reparation in the United States. He pointed to the legal uncertainties as well as to the practical hurdles in handling restitution for a centuries-old injustice. Striking at the heart of the matter, he questioned whether the effort to handle historical wrongs would "eliminate" racism in the contemporary world. And that was the point for the George W. Bush administration at the time. Quoting Secretary of State Colin Powell, Wood said the WCAR should not become "mired in the past." Such a preoccupation would "detract" from the main purpose of the conference, which was to develop a positive agenda and set of practical initiatives to combat racism in the future.[40] A highly revealing statement, it drew attention to how the powerful rarely admitted the need to deal with past wrongs. Confident in their position, the past to them appeared irrelevant.

In the light of great power opposition, many African leaders, much to the chagrin of the supportive NGO community, traded in the Dakar package for assurances of future debt relief, economic investments, and development programs. The Durban Plan became part of the U.N. Millennium Development Goals, which had earmarked seven-tenths of a percent of the GNP of richer countries for aid and assistance to the impoverished nations of the world; although, as of 2005, the signatory states had not met their promises. With this understanding, a compromise statement was brokered by South Africa. By then, the U.S. delegation had walked out; the George W. Bush administration had sent only low-level representation in the first place. The Final Document declared slavery and the slave trade "appalling tragedies . . . a crime against humanity and should always have been so." It fell short of requiring apology and restitution. Economic justice required a greater willingness to account for past practices than most governments were prepared to make at the WCAR.

Conflicting Claims for Justice

Palestinian people confronted a similar denial of history and context in their struggle for human rights and self-determination. At least an effort to restrict the perspectives in the debate defined the public voice of much of the leadership of Israel and the United States in their increasingly strong bilateral alliance after 1981. And, for most Palestinian leaders on the ground, the United States held the key in international diplomacy to a negotiated settlement of the conflict. At its base, a struggle over land and place in the former Mandate Palestine, it also was about deeply conflicting historical narratives of the same time and space—of sanctuary from persecution for Israelis, on the one hand, and of displacement, exile, and occupation for Palestinians, on the other. The need to confront and, ultimately, reconcile these different narratives remains an essential ingredient in any search for a just solution.

In more than sixty years, the conflict had produced seven regional wars, countless deaths, and huge suffering and pain. Bursting out (figuratively) at the WCAR, it was never on the periphery of international concerns; for decades, it had elicited varying levels of intense interest from people and states around the world. Particularly after 1967 and the occupation, the situation on the ground became important for human rights advocacy work, by organizations that emerged independently in the two societies, by affiliated NGOs providing legal aid and social and welfare services as part of larger transnational networks, and by many NGOs working across the divides with members of *both* societies for peace and reconciliation. Yet, solutions have proved exceedingly difficult to achieve, a continuing reminder of the obstacles to large-scale political and social change in a hostile geopolitical environment.

Many of these NGOs and delegates attended the WCAR. The groups included, to mention only a few, B'tselem: Israeli Information Center for Human Rights in the Occupied Territories, an Israeli-based NGO determined to create dialogue favorable to change in Israel, and the Rabbis for Human Rights (RHR), founded in 1988 to bring military abuses to the attention of the Israeli public. There were members of Al Haq, a Palestinian Legal and Human Rights Organization, the Palestinian Center for the Protection of Human Rights and the Environment, and the Ta'ayush, newly allied in 2000, which promoted "partnerships" of Jewish and Palestinian citizens of Israel. These organizations brought alternatives for a peaceful solution to the deadly conflict, based on international humanitarian law and the human rights principles of full equality, democracy, and coexistence. Take away the protections of law, confessed the head of the Palestinian Center for Human Rights in an interview unrelated to the conference, and "you take away the credibility within Palestinian society of all the human rights organizations, the peace activists, and the people working to build a healthy civil society here."[41] Many on the ground saw their work as fundamental to ending the cycles of violence and retribution that had wracked both societies for decades. They brought the human rights mechanisms of reconciliation to the conflict and were committed to preserving the foundations of community and social cohesion.

This position found unequivocal support among delegate members of the World Council of Churches and the Quaker Friends societies. In many ways, the position, also affirmed by the organizers of the *Voices* session, determined that this U.N. forum give ample space for the victims to speak about their own experiences—and to be heard. Yet, despite the long tradition and "rich experience" of working for peace and organizing joint actions, many groups felt betrayed by the events from above, consistently bypassed in the numerous and difficult phases of diplomatic negotiations. These sentiments were reminiscent indeed of the drowning out of alternative societal views in the Bosnian crisis. At the WCAR, the peace perspectives, under assault from below, also were overshadowed by the tensions, which took up much of the public energy of the conference.[42]

As many delegates at the conference understood it, the WCAR was profoundly shaped by "current world affairs." It was, Marilia Schüller wrote in her summary of the proceedings, convened at a time when the "situation in the Middle East was at the forefront of people's minds." By this, she meant the Israel-Palestine conflict. The preparatory work and formal opening of the conference coincided with the outbreak of the second intifada in September 2000, with graphic images broadcast around the world of suicide bombers targeting Israeli civilians and the Israeli security forces shooting unarmed protestors, demolishing houses, and engaging in extrajudicial killings. The "intensity of the violence" caught observers ill-prepared; despite pleas for international engagement, it quickly settled into a "deadly routine."[43]

For those on the ground, the situation had deteriorated under the Oslo process. Between 1997 and 2002, the pace of Israeli settlement-building in the West Bank and East Jerusalem grew at its fastest rate ever, and for average Palestinians in the territories, life became even more insecure through the construction of roadblocks and barriers around Palestinian towns and villages, preventing ease of movement and further fragmenting society. Highways and byways were built for Israeli settlers or those with formal papers to move around freely and, eventually, in 2002 the Israeli government began to build a security wall on confiscated Arab land. Working against the damages of occupation, human rights organizations also had become disillusioned with the new Palestinian Authority and Yassir Arafat; its leadership, many believed at the time, was antidemocratic and corrupt, arbitrarily imprisoning its critics and, seemingly, unwilling to declare the settlements illegal in international law. In this climate, groups such as Hamas, the Islamic Resistance Movement formed in 1988, and Islamic Jihad found societal support for their tactics of violence.

Never a simple relationship, the government, citizens in Israel proper, and settlers also accepted violence as a necessary tactic for order, control, and security. By official accounts, government forces were determined to "break the will" of Palestinians to impose a solution and settlers, many intransigent about their right to biblical lands, resorted to acts of violence against Palestinian villagers nearby. Many saw themselves as the front line in the struggle against terrorism. Addressing an audience in the post-9/11 world, one settler near Nablus made the case that long had been at the basis of settler identity. "I am pessimistic," she said. "There is no end in view. The whole western world must face up to the problem of terrorism everywhere. We are a microcosm of that. We can't negotiate!" Furthermore, the bombings "traumatized" average Israeli citizens and—as most scholarly experts and peace activists have recognized—helped solidify the widely held view in Israel that there was no effective partner for negotiation.[44]

The WCAR met in the middle of this deteriorating situation on the ground. Reflecting its profound anger, frustration, and mistrust, it also was a clear mirror of the competing narratives of past and present in the region. Participants from the Middle East, specifically Iran and the Arab countries, also used their recent experiences with colonialism to make sense of the patterns and practices of contemporary racism. Their documents reflected the shared region-wide narrative of colonial domination. They also had a region-specific history of Israel as a Western outpost, which inflicted on Arab people military defeats, conquests, and occupation. At the very moment that Asians, Africans, and Middle Easterners were beginning to break free of colonial domination, the nation-state of Israel was established in a territory that overwhelmingly had been Arab and Muslim for centuries. From the perspective of the neighboring states and peoples, Israel was a colonial state imposed by the Western powers at a moment in history that was initiating decolonization. Because of these conflicts, Israel never had been included in the Asian grouping for U.N. purposes.

From the start of the human rights era, different characterizations of historical moments collided in this Palestinian region. They surfaced as deep emotional wounds at the WCAR. One centered on the year 1948 itself. From their very moment of Israel's emergence, the citizens of the new Israel saw 1948 as a historic year, the fulfillment of two thousand years of exile and persecution; the state offered the right of return and sanctuary for all Jewish people, everywhere. Soon in Palestinian historical consciousness, by contrast, 1948 became a "catastrophe" (Nakba), as the Palestinian preparatory group titled its report filed in Geneva. Israel, furthermore, had never acknowledged Palestinian "losses" of land, homes, and livelihood as its Arab people became disbursed into refugee camps throughout the region and, after 1967, under increasingly harsh and profoundly antidemocratic rule of occupation.[45]

As in the case of crimes and reparations, the choice of language became the flashpoint of debates, matched at the time by real bullets on the ground. Tensions centered on the words used to describe these sharply contrasting historical experiences. The legitimate need to start to hear contrasting views, which the U.N. conference offered, became lost in the din of words that each side found deeply offensive—a return, for example, to the "Zionism as racism" equation (which the U.N. had repudiated), the label "apartheid" for the Israeli state, and one-sided condemnations of violence perpetrated by a people (Palestinians) but not a state (Israel). Many in the Jewish caucus also believed fully that the debates were nothing but efforts to "delegitimize" the state of Israel.[46]

In this climate, the Jewish caucus joined the United States and Israel in walking out, although critics of the U.S. decision in specific noted that the timing came right after the major international session on reparations. Those representatives were followed by a number of high-level international NGO delegations. Most NGOs, individual delegates, and state representatives opposed the decision. However difficult the international climate was, world gatherings were singular opportunities to grapple with different perspectives and agendas. Thus, for example, eighty-one NGOs from thirty-five mostly Eastern and Central European states issued an official joint statement after the walkout, decrying the "intolerant" and "disrespectful" language in the sections on Israel and the "distortions" in the statements on anti-Semitism. The same group nonetheless laid out the many ways the preparatory processes and conference deliberations had established a "solid foundation" for the future. Its statement stressed the innovative topics under discussion, the ways new groups had been incorporated into human rights discourses, and the efforts at reform of criminal law to safeguard minority rights, now more firmly anchored in the U.N. agenda.[47]

The conference, however, had been unable to preserve diplomatic "good practices" that sustained dialogue even between enemies. It had addressed as global problems the renewed outbreaks of anti-Semitism and the spread of Islamophobia and anti-Arab sentiments. Even before 9/11, many NGOs and government representatives were well aware that Arabs and Muslims were being singled out as objects of suspicion and fear simply because of their heritage and not because of any concrete actions on their part. They also drew on deep regional concerns in Europe and Latin America with the revival of anti-Semitic hostilities and, as a direct consequence, led to the first international commemoration of the memory of the Holocaust on the sixtieth anniversary of the liberation of Auschwitz in January 2005.

In the final effort to reach international agreement, the South African delegation, this time supported by the Europeans, brokered a compromise statement during an extended day of negotiations. It took out the offending paragraphs about Israel in a vote of fifty-one to thirty-eight. Led by Syria and Pakistan, all fifteen Middle Eastern states that had helped draft the original paragraphs voted as a cohesive bloc against the compromise. When states with Muslim majority populations were included, two-thirds of the states that had attended the Asian preparatory conference in Tehran opposed the settlement. Of course, the diplomatic partnerships of the region were more complex as many regional states also allied with the United States for their own specific needs. The vote was a compromise struck at an international gathering. But it represented an international agreement without the involvement of the two major sets of antagonists—Israel and the Arab and Muslim world.[48]

No solution as yet has been reached on the decades-long conflict between Israelis and Palestinians; extremists still exist on both sides. However, new perspectives have emerged that, with international guidance demanded "by virtually all Palestinians and many Jewish Israelis," might sustain more positive dialogue. For example, the pending fortieth anniversary of the 1967 war prompted some Israeli scholars and commentators to question its legacy in the long "quagmire" of occupation and settlement. At its root lay the definition of Israel as Jewish state and refuge for all Jews. This made annexation of Arab people out of the question in 1967, but it also highlighted, more clearly in retrospect, a fundamental contradiction brought to the WCAR through the voice of Abu Sbeih. He turned attention to the state institutions and practices that allowed an increasingly slim Jewish majority to rule over a subordinate Palestinian people. Gershom Gorenberg extended the point when he wrote, "To keep the West Bank will require Israel either to cease being democratic or cease being a Jewish state. Not only settlers but national leaders have eroded the rule of law in pursuit of what they considered a patriotic goal."[49]

The WCAR, furthermore, brought to international attention for the first time new coalitions of NGOs, promoting a common agenda for Palestinian citizens of Israel, those in the territories, and the refugees. Coordinated by Ittijah, a network of Palestinian NGOs in Israel, an alliance was formed with the two other groups for inter-Palestinian advocacy in Cyprus in 2000. Bringing together previously disparate voices, these types of NGOs can integrate into the resolution process the fuller spectrum of Palestinian views and include all the people who have such high stakes in a just solution. Recent interviews with refugees, furthermore, showed shifting views on the ground. For many, to be sure, justice remained only in a "right of return" to their original homeland in present-day Israel. But for others, justice entailed returning to a viable Palestinian state. One leader of a refugee camp in Lebanon explained to the Friends Working Group, "I believe that many people here would be satisfied to re-settle in the new Palestinian state rather than in Israel. . . . They would regard it as a true exercise of their right of return . . . a peace with sovereignty and dignity.[50] Furthermore, the experiences with military offenses have revealed the limitations of a technologically superior military force in battle with society. Israel's military has not proven adequate either for the security that most Israelis want or for the suppression of the full spectrum of opposition tactics, which Palestinians use against the brutalities and daily humiliations of occupation. The weight of this evidence has convinced human rights activists on the ground that the preconditions for an equitable solution remain with the U.N. resolutions on the conflict—from their recognition of the state of Israel to their rejection of the settlement policy. They require the full implementation of fundamental human rights norms as well as the binding principles of international humanitarian law, as codified in the Geneva Conventions and reaffirmed by the statutes of the International Criminal Court.[51]

Human Rights and the "War on Terror"

Three days after the end of the WCAR, agents of al Qaeda launched the vicious attack on the World Trade Center in New York City and the Pentagon in Washington, D.C., turning commercial airliners into terrifying weapons. The initial global response was near uniform condemnation of the deadly terrorist attacks. They were an extreme manifestation of the hatred, intolerance, and xenophobic actions that the WCAR had been called to address. For a time, much of the world stood behind the United States. But that unity soon was tested by disagreements among government leaders, international human rights NGOs, and world public opinion over the course and conduct of the ensuing "war on terror" led by the George W. Bush administration. For many delegates, as William Wong expressed it, the numerous innovative deliberations and findings of the conference "got buried as though [they] lay beneath the crumbling World Trade Center towers."[52]

For the Bush administration and its military coalition allies as well as a sizeable segment of U.S. public opinion, 9/11 was a watershed event, transforming the basis of international politics. Inaugurating a "different kind" of war and struggle, it was said to demand new responses, aggressive strategies, and the right of military preemption. Domestically, it meant forceful assertion of executive power to act decisively with little congressional or judicial oversight. These policies of the sole superpower set the "war on terror" as the dominant international agenda item in the early twenty-first century.[53] In the initial aftermath of 9/11, too, many human rights activists and military lawyers feared for the human rights project itself.

In response to 9/11, there has been a general broadening of governmental surveillance powers in many parts of the globe; this includes provisions to ease the conditions for arrest of foreign suspects and target immigrant communities, specifically those of Middle Eastern and Arab backgrounds. Many Western governments, often without adequate justification, focused on Arab and Muslim communities, including immigrant groups, as subversive and dangerous to the global order. The U.S. attorney general used the Supreme Court's *Zadvydas* decision, as Chapter 5 indicated, to detain "suspected terrorists" based on the "special circumstances" clause of the ruling. Immediately after the attacks, the government rounded up and detained twelve hundred immigrants, including hundreds from Arab and Muslim communities of the Middle East and South Asia. Many of the inmates languished for months in jail without access to lawyers or families. The Justice Department ruled that the attorney general had "personal responsibility" to make a detailed assessment of each case for due process principles against national security considerations. It allowed for the detention of immigrants for long periods with no charge. Most of these detainees eventually were deported for minor visa infractions. Assistant Federal Defender Luis A. Ortiz of Philadelphia drew attention to a pattern of response that was common in other countries as well. He noted simply, "The rights of immigrants seem to be most compromised in times of crisis."[54]

The USA PATRIOT Act, signed by President Bush on October 26, 2001, furthermore, increased governmental authority to track communications and tighten border controls and it established new crimes and penalties with regard to terrorism. It also allowed the government to detain indefinitely in undisclosed locations foreigners who were certified by the attorney general as posing a security risk. In addition, in the international arena, the White House legal staff and the Justice Department, bypassing the normal channels of bureaucratic vetting, argued against the applicability of many of the provisions of the Geneva Conventions (including those limiting torture) to the "war on terror." They established a policy of unlimited detentions for so-called "unlawful enemy combatants," who were picked up from Afghanistan and, also, from other theaters far from the battlefield. A dubious legal category, the designation deprived detainees of the rights to prisoner-of-war status guaranteed by the Geneva Conventions. Eventually, most were transferred to the U.S. naval base prison in Guantánamo Bay, Cuba.[55] Government officials set up other detention camps from Abu Ghraib in Iraq to Bagram Air Base in Afghanistan and significantly expanded the U.S. policy of what they called "rendition," sending accused terrorists for interrogation to countries known routinely to use torture. In response to the terrorist attack and future threats, the U.S. government instituted a set of extrajudicial procedures outside the U.S. criminal law system and in defiance of the principles of international humanitarian law.

These forms of security measures reinforced a language of terrorism that discussed terror only as acts of destruction and violence and was unwilling to look at any of the root causes or contexts that gave rise to them. The initial response to 9/11 was to declare a "war" on terrorism until every single terrorist cell and group throughout the globe was rooted out and ultimately defeated. Most so-called "terrorist" experts— not those in the new field of counterterrorism called up by 9/11— forcefully questioned this wisdom. Offering insights from the decade-long British struggle in Northern Ireland, Louise Richardson, for example, argued for a different approach. A declaration of real "war," she wrote, was "doomed to failure." In the British case, she said:

The resolution of the problem and the end of the terrorist campaign of the IRA [Irish Republican Army] . . . was brought about only by years of painstaking negotiation and engagement of the grievances that fueled the support for terrorists. The fact that 30,000 British soldiers supported by thousands more local security forces could not defeat a few hundred members of the IRA would certainly suggest that the American military operating thousands of miles from home, in an alien culture, and often without the support of reliable local security forces, is unlikely to defeat every terrorist group of global reach.[56]

The U.S. position on terrorism was not new. It was well entrenched among government elites protecting their own power and authority. It even branded many of the human rights partisans who ultimately resorted to armed force as terrorists by their government opponents. The same rhetoric became the dominant U.S.-Israeli governmental framework for dealing with the Palestinian suicide bombers during the second intifada. Yet the Palestinian issue was not solely one of violence; it represented a persistent, early twentieth-century conflict carried into the next century. Despite increasing recognition of the need for a two-state solution, it has remained mired in the concerns of the more powerful Israeli state, which have overridden the objectives of the Palestinians to obtain their own basis for self-determination.

Backed by military action starting in November 2001 in Afghanistan and followed by the U.S.-led invasion of Iraq in March 2003, the "war on terror" may have been the single most visible feature of international political developments in the early years of the twenty-first century. Yet, from the start, it was challenged by rights advocates around the globe who drew on more than half a century of developments in international norms and laws and on the civil liberties protections in distinct national contexts.[57] Furthermore, William Wong's comments in the epigraph showed, too, that antiracist groups active at the WCAR were determined to continue their work in this post-9/11 climate.

The defense of rights has been sustained by legal rulings in national and regional settings and by programmatic guidelines from intergovernmental bodies. Reflecting this context was a crucial U.S. Supreme Court decision in June 2004 dealing with the legality of unlimited detentions in times of war. As Justice Sandra Day O'Connor put it for the majority, "As critical as the Government's interest may be in detaining those who actually pose an immediate threat to the national security of the United States during ongoing international conflict, history and common sense teach us that an unchecked system of detention carries the potential to become a means for oppression and abuse of others who do not present that sort of threat."[58] Addressing, in this case, the constitutional issues surrounding the indefinite detention of a U.S. citizen, Yaser Esam Hamdi, the majority opinion upheld the petitioner's right to due process and to "contest the factual basis for that detention before a neutral decision maker." The Court saw its prime task "in these difficult times" to effect a balance between the individual's legitimate right to liberty and the government's equally "weighty" and "sensitive" interests in national security as a necessary "underpinning of the 'war on terror.'"[59] In the majority view, the key point was to find an equitable balance between liberty and security. The majority, thus, rejected the central argument of the Bush administration's case, which claimed broad exclusive executive branch exercise of powers in wartime. Administration officials had claimed for wartime wide presidential authority to detain citizens without due process or judicial protections. The Court majority feared that such broad powers, unchecked by judicial review, ultimately would undermine the very values the country "holds dear." Justice David H. Souter makes the point sharply in his written opinion. Recalling Justice Robert H. Jackson's observations, he wrote, "the President is not Commander in Chief of the country, only of the military."[60] In subsequent challenges, the courts have ruled consistently against the broadest claims to executive power by Bush administration officials.

In a parallel case decided the same day concerning the indefinite detention of the approximately 654 aliens at the Guantánamo prison (the case was brought by fourteen prisoners), the majority held that there is "nothing" in U.S. case law that "categorically excludes aliens detained in military custody outside the United States from the 'privilege of litigation.'"[61] In effect, it extended due process as well as the international norms of humane treatment to alien detainees in U.S.-run territory. In this respect, the Court continued the process of extending legal guarantees to noncitizens, even in times of war and emergencies. In a strikingly similar finding, nine Law Lords of the House of Lords on December 16, 2004, ruled against the major provisions of the British government's antiterror strategy enacted in the wake of 9/11. In a "powerfully worded, ground breaking decision," the majority (8 to 1) also found that unlimited detention was "draconian" and "unjustifiable," even in the face of possible terror attacks, and violated the fundamental freedoms guaranteed in the European Convention on Human Rights.[62] Unlike their American counterparts, British authorities were using their criminal law statutes to pursue alleged terrorists.

The Bush administration has been slow to carry out the courts' orders. Officials continued to insist in this type of war on executive right to detain suspects without formal charges or trials. Forced to work with Congress, government officials proposed military commissions to determine the status of the so-called "enemy combatants," but rights advocates have argued that these provisions unduly limited the rights of the defendants and their lawyers. In June 2008, the Supreme Court rejected the Military Commission Acts, delivering the third legal blow to one cornerstone of the Bush administration's "war on terror" policies. The issue of detention and rights still is unsettled in U.S. practice and law.[63] So, too, is the reach of international humanitarian law. The army's recently revised military manual of conduct has fully complied with the protections of the Geneva Conventions. Pushing their position, however, government authorities have authorized separate CIA interrogation sites to gather information from suspects using harsh techniques that strain the customary protections of Common Article 3 of the Geneva Conventions. Human rights advocates in the twenty-first century face an important question: Will leaders of a state as powerful as the United States be held accountable, through commissions of inquiry and trials, for grave breaches of international humanitarian law? If not, the human rights system of law will continue to be partially and arbitrarily applied.

Other areas of the globe have addressed similar issues. For example, OAS members adopted collective measures to combat terrorism after 9/11, agreeing in June 2002 to an Inter-American Convention against Terrorism. In response, the Inter-American Commission on Human Rights prepared an elaborate study to guide the integration of human rights norms into policy agendas; it is titled "Report on Terrorism and Human Rights." The commissioners assessed the relevant human rights and humanitarian laws for three distinct contexts of counterterrorist planning: during times of peace, during declared states of emergency, and during armed conflict. They stressed the nonderogable obligations on state officials preparing antiterror structures: provisions must safeguard humane treatment, ensure personal liberty and security, guarantee the right to a fair trial and freedom of expression, and defend the principle of nondiscrimination as a central tenet of international human rights law. "The very object and purpose of the anti-terrorist initiatives in democratic society is to protect democratic institutions, human rights and the rule of law, not to undermine them," the authors warned.[64]

From transnational arenas of judicial, political, and civil society, rights defenders have sought to temper state authority and control in the development and implementation phases of antiterrorism measures. Even in times of crisis, they say, echoing the position of the U.S. Supreme Court and the Inter-American Commission, governments must not subvert the fundamental principles at the basis of democratic societies. Many made the additional point that broad-based, global antiracist politics were necessary to root out the ideological and social preconditions that breed terrorist violence. As Aaron Rhodes, executive director of the International Helsinki Federation noted simply, "Terrorism reveals how dangerous racism is."[65] With this statement, he joined a chorus of voices that has looked to the contexts for such extremist behavior. Rhodes pointed to the need for a worldwide campaign against the patterns of arrogance, discrimination, and racism that have helped to support Jihadist recruitment and programs.

Although it is too early to write about the outcome of these transnational strategies with any certainty, even for the immediate future, the mobilizations around the WCAR provided many of the underpinnings for rights advocacy challenged by security calculations. The conference opened a debate that became even more compelling. Much hard work across the globe had gone into the preparation for the world meeting; similar work continued after its conclusion. Lessons from face-to-face community organizing on the ground—from providing legal aid and shelters for migrants to rewriting training manuals for lawyers and judges that strengthen minority rights to ensuring equitable resource allocation for development to monitoring the Internet for hate speech—had set the agenda for the WCAR. The conference's work centered on the groups most vulnerable to racist discriminations in the exercise of their fundamental human and civil rights: ethnic, religious, and national minorities; immigrant communities; nonnationals; and people under occupation. Not surprisingly, many of these same groups have come under direct suspicion after 9/11. The conference debates are continuing beyond the specific legal challenges to the "war on terror." With its focus on the vulnerable across the globe, this U.N. forum, with its follow-up plans of action, is still helping to direct the efforts to combat poverty and food deprivation, migration and inclusion, and democratic governance at work beneath the more visible "war on terror."

Conclusion
Making a Difference

So many people don't think that one person can make a difference.
But really, it has to start somewhere, so let it start with me.
—Patsy Ruth Oliver, environmentalist and activist

The lead up to the war in Iraq in early 2003 brought into sharp relief the tension between the human rights politics of international law and multilateral cooperation and the world of great power politics, based on separate calculations of national interests and defense. It seemed to pit two alternative visions of international relations against one another; the crisis over Iraq embroiled virtually the whole world. The weekend of February 14–16, 2003, saw mass global protest movements against the impending U.S. invasion of Iraq under the George W. Bush administration's announced preemptive war doctrine. In 600 cities in nearly every region of the world, over six million people joined the large gatherings in public venues. The communications revolution of the Internet synchronized the event; the global media captured it in detail. The size of the demonstrations took even the organizers by surprise. Some journalists began to speak of world public opinion as a "second superpower" arrayed against the first.[1]

The protests were a grassroots groundswell of public opposition to the war and, arguably, a defense of the values at the heart of human rights advocacy. Those in the crowds ranged from long-term peace activists to human rights defenders to members of antiglobalization coalitions to ordinary people, many of whom had never before participated in demonstrations. That February, public sentiment burst out to defend the role of the United Nations as the arbiter of the grave matter of war and peace.

A parallel drama unfolded at the United Nations, shaped in good measure by international human rights legal practices. Emboldened partly by public opposition to the war, a majority of the Security Council member-states refused to give the U.S. government the imprimatur it demanded. At stake at the time were Iraq's alleged arsenal of weapons of mass destruction and the role of the U.N. inspectors in the peaceful disarmament of the country. The Security Council became a court-like setting for the presentation and evaluation of the evidence for a secret, dangerous weapons' program given by U.S. Secretary of State Colin Powell. Expectations about international law, the weight of evidence, and the burden of proof had compelled the particular courtroom style of the confrontation. Even the superpower was forced to play.

War broke out precisely thirty-one days after the dramatic February events, also revealing the obvious: state military force and international public opinion are two distinct forms of power in the international arena. Public opinion could not stop an administration already predetermined to go to war, if need be even unilaterally. Shortly after the invasion, the United Nations sanctioned the military action with resolutions that supported the U.S. goals of occupation and regime change in Iraq. A significant crystallizing moment in the early twenty-first century, the war raised the stakes about the catalysts for political change in the international arena. Which actions matter in global politics?

Both in the lead up to and in the immediate aftermath of war and occupation, the debate remained focused primarily on the present. It centered on the decisive nature of political change ("democratic" or "regime" change) brought from *outside* through the exercise of military power by the United States. This view highlighted the weakness of the United Nations. Despite all of its repeated resolutions in the 1990s, the Security Council had not been able to force compliance by the government of Saddam Hussein. Only great powers make things happen in the global community.

Yet, the focus on the external sources of change overlooked the local and indigenous movements for democratic reform and human rights principles bringing their own understandings, definitions, and sense of timing to the reform effort. The links to foreign occupiers tainted some of the domestic participants in the continuing democratic struggle. The U.S.-led invasion certainly mattered, but it left the interregional relationships among states in enormous uncertainty. It exacerbated and created sectarian divisions, challenged existing alliances, produced complicating electoral victories, and led to a refugee crisis of tragic proportions that also has threatened to destabilize at least several neighbors of Iraq.

Arguments about change from the immediate present are always inconclusive. Informed public debate requires historical perspective that would bring more critical questioning to the political decisions.

Specifically, in the 1980s, the United States was a strong ally of the Iraq of Saddam Hussein and a significant supplier of the chemical and biological weapons used in its deadly war with Iran (1980–88)—and against its own Kurdish and Shi'a citizens. But in the 1980s, the United States and the United Nations had offered "hardly a squeak" of protest against the regime's dictatorial policies, as the Human Rights Watch report from 1993 pointedly noted. By contrast, in the 1990s, there was a "180-degree turn" in the treatment of Iraqi human rights abuses. The international position shifted "from lassitude to forthright condemnation in the strongest possible terms" as a result of *new* political strategies among the Western powers, and particularly the United States, in the first Gulf War.[2] A longer time horizon in this bilateral context shows unmistakably that the so-called project of "democracy" was arbitrary and cynical. For decades, the United States had been one of the major supporters of authoritarian regimes in the Middle East (from Egypt to Jordan to Saudi Arabia) and, thus, part of the reason for the stagnant political developments in the region. Whatever the official rhetoric, the project of "democracy" aimed to support a predetermined great power agenda.

The high geopolitical drama in 2003 also brings into bold relief the central challenges at the heart of this book. A historical study of the origins, development, and impact of human rights advocacy since 1945, it sets the inquiry against the shifting geopolitical world of state power and interests emerging simultaneously. Developing within the context of early twentieth-century transnational societal linkages for a new domestic and international order, by the 1940s human rights vocabulary had become a widely shared vernacular for change. A timely people's intervention—supported by many state representatives—inserted human rights principles into the new Charter of the United Nations at its founding conference in San Francisco in 1945. It also secured a formal place for human rights advocacy in U.N. organs, commissions, and affiliated agencies. At the same time, the societal mobilizations for change and reform continued along their own trajectories and many participants subsequently embraced human rights principles as vital for their cause.

Concentrating on a sixty-year time frame and with a wide geographical swath, this study has looked directly at the points of intersection of these appreciably distinct arenas of operation. As its prime illustrations, it has used the rich details of the human dramas in different struggles for human rights causes around the globe. The book has argued, furthermore, that these examples—from the transnational antiapartheid movements to the Mothers' mobilizations to gender struggles as well as those for economic justice and migrant and minority rights—captured many of the major lines of development of human rights advocacy over the past sixty years.[3] Hardly predetermined, these outcomes grew from contentious historical confrontations. Furthermore, the study has placed these sixty years in a broader historical framework, showing continuities from the early twentieth century and pointing out implications for future advocacy work.

At many levels of analysis, this book has interconnected human rights mobilizations on the ground with the parallel and complementary mobilizations of states, U.N. organs, and intergovernmental agencies. It also has kept in sight the vast array of antagonistic forces that stood in the way of change, whether in defense of state sovereign rights, cultural autonomy, or local power constellations. To provide an assessment of the historical impact of rights advocacy in the international arena, attention has focused on the specific contexts that drew U.N. oversight to injustices and violations in society; the role of local organizations and U.N. staff as well as survivors and family members in making public their specific stories and personal tragedies; the critical reciprocities between international laws and norms emerging in local struggles; and the many political, cultural, and structural impediments to the realization of the human rights values of equality, justice, and security. In addition, the study has followed the historical evolution of a distinct transnational civil society through the separate and overlapping activities of NGO advocacy networks, showing when and how they came to play such an active role in human rights advocacy. As it turned out, effective NGO advocacy in international circles involved its own difficult struggle. Finally, it also has drawn attention to individual and group courage and actions—to human agency—in the movements for human rights. Under the tragic circumstances of systemic abuse and through a widening circulation of information, activists have invented, transported, and retranslated mechanisms for the strategic defense of rights. The cumulative impact of these individual choices has challenged domestic and foreign policies, widening consciousness of global interdependencies. Individual decisions have made a difference in global politics, as the epigraph to this chapter asserts so clearly.[4]

This book blends historical methodologies with readings in political science and case studies of international relations theory. Its approach has a logic inherent in the history of its subject matter. The analytical effort to link local and global contexts found its parallel in the historical unfolding of human rights movements. Their arena became transnational, crisscrossing territorial borders and developing vertical ties to state and international decision-makers as well as to the victims on the ground. Testifying to the breadth of interconnections, activists have described these personal and institutional linkages as a form of globalization from below. Coined, perhaps, as an alternative to the dictates of neoliberal economic globalization from above, it speaks of strengthening societies and of sustaining community life. It also points to media and communication channels that circulate alternative information, to the ongoing work of "translation" on the ground, to coordinated campaigns, and to local activists' regular attendance at regional and world conferences. These characteristics slowly emerged piecemeal even before the communications revolution of the 1980s, tested already in the alliances of states and peoples against the system of apartheid. In this development, the United Nations played an important role, providing organizational coherence, coordination, and a central location for the many disparate activists and their allies establishing the new patterns of transnational advocacy. As this book shows and as the 2003 Iraq debate again brought into the open, in dealing with threats to "international peace and security" the United Nations is not more than the sum of its five veto-holding great power members on the Security Council.[5] It cannot act in the face of veto. As this study also shows, the United Nations is the one intergovernmental body that demands ethical standards in the conduct of states toward their own people and residents and also toward other states and persons made stateless. In addition, its lawmaking capabilities can provide universal accountability to the human rights norms and rules of the international order.

New Perspectives from History

As part of a global dialogue on human rights in the early twenty-first century, this study also has engaged in a forthright discussion of the contributions that historians make to the debates. In a field largely dominated by political scientists and international relations theorists, it brings to the forefront of discussion sensitivity to the importance of time and place. Shaping an advocacy and monitoring system after 1945, human rights discourses were historical constructs in their specificity, products of a confluence of events that brought particular causes and claims to international attention. As it turned out, this system also provided a context for new theoretical departures and challenges.

Theme driven, my study follows a chronology over sixty years that is not linear but overlapping and interconnected. In addition to overcoming much of the presentist bias in the literature, the approach opens new interpretations—or new ways of analyzing known material. Shunning a standard Cold War explanation, Part I nonetheless describes the emergence of an "orthodoxy" in human rights thinking, organizing, and monitoring. When seen from below, it reflected a set of historical contingencies and people's mobilizations that pushed U.N. oversight and monitoring to confront the flagrant expressions of state repression of its own citizens: in legally enforced racial segregation (apartheid), in concentrated state power that suppressed personal freedoms, and in the enforced disappearance of alleged enemies of the state. The processes of embracing human rights norms varied and their contents differed, but they offered extraordinary organizational unity, reinforcing ongoing local activism, which, in circular fashion, fed into the human rights movements. For the victims, it meant a vehicle for empowerment and immediate resonance abroad. Encroaching on sovereign prerogatives in these confrontations, U.N. "interventions" established important precedents for limiting the domestic jurisdiction protections of international law when state actors systematically abused their political authority. In the 1970s, the discursive field of the orthodoxy became increasingly linked to market forces, setting up interpretive and strategic confrontations with other human rights advocates determined to meet people's basic economic and social needs. This conflict, however, should not detract from the importance of democratic transparency and humane governance for a life of dignity.

Part II shows how the limitations of orthodox thinking and monitoring began to influence the historical development of human rights advocacy. Drawing on much longer traditions of transnational actions for women's rights, labor protections, and the principles of economic justice, in the later 1970s these mobilizations became part of human rights networks as critics of the orthodoxy; guided by established human rights norms, they moved to deepen them. Put slightly differently, in the course of their work for change on the ground, many activists became aware of the limitations of the existing human rights doctrines to address the abuses and violations they confronted every day. As implemented, the system hardly was universal.

Through shared contexts of confronting the challenges of economic development, women's groups found renewed vigor in gender analysis. In a complicated pattern that brought leaders of developing countries, activists, and scholars together, the advocates for socioeconomic justice and the right to development drew sustenance from the economic principles of the Universal Declaration of Human Rights. Both groups established dense webs of global networks and coalitions, which often worked in tandem, as seen at the WCAR. Both contributed innovative thinking to human rights principles, broadening their coverage in practice to include, among others, battered women and other victims of gender violence, the noncitizen detainees, and transnational labor migrants. They shifted attention to new sites of violation, from public arenas to the private spheres of family life and customary norms, and expanded accountability to nonstate actors, including multinational corporations. Although legal justice had been part of orthodox concerns, the new activists have used the judicial system to challenge public authorities and restructure state power. Combining the pressures of social protests with court trials, they have achieved concrete gains in resource allocation and equity principles—even if limited to specific individuals and groups and challenged by shifting levels of societal opposition.

Through its thematic approach, Part III argues that the "long" 1990s represented a distinct era in human rights history with a logical end point in 2005. Of course, the designation did not preclude continuities; the work of the many advocacy networks formed earlier proceeded apace. After all, adoption of gender as an official lawmaking category occurred first in 1993 at the Vienna World Conference. Developments in the decade, too, offered a different perspective on the orthodoxy. As seen in the example of postapartheid South Africa, its constitution, with expansive human rights protections won in struggle, provided a new context for poor people's ongoing efforts to secure basic needs, including social services and health provisions. Similar challenges opened in the former socialist countries of Europe.

The WCAR drew vital energy from the grassroots activists already involved in a host of community development and gender projects, rejoined at this moment through their shared efforts to confront racial and other systemic patterns of discrimination around the globe. Through its dynamic preparatory processes extending beyond the meeting, this conference at the cusp of the twenty-first century brought to international attention the particular vulnerabilities of members of poor, migrant, and minority communities worldwide. In the "war on terror" following the 9/11 attack on the United States, many of these same groups saw their rights threatened and eroded. The WCAR had made the point of ongoing relevance, showing the insufficiencies of human rights agendas, which did not address the tragic consequences of the erosion of local community ties and solidarities in the face of neoliberal economic and political policies.

The long decade of the 1990s also offered its own unique challenges. If, from the perspective of human rights, the Cold War was one historical phase in the clash of great power interests, its specific antagonisms had been important for U.N. business. The demise of the Soviet system opened new possibilities for unprecedented steps in Security Council activism. Expressed by the many U.N. missions that by 1999 had established the new doctrine of "humanitarian intervention," it further eroded the inviolability of domestic jurisdiction by demanding "responsible sovereignty." Entering uncharted and highly complicated terrains of armed conflict and civil strife, these missions had decidedly mixed outcomes, providing little guidance for future actions. For many activists in human rights and humanitarian work, the subsequent U.S.-led invasion of Iraq in 2003 strained the doctrine further. At the same time, attention to transitional justice and the peace-building phases of the missions, coupled with ongoing pressures by victims and survivors of earlier tragedies, pushed the issue of apology and redress to the forefront of human rights debates. This agenda showed that the realities of global interdependencies, whether in technological advances or environmental degradation, needed a deeper sense of global community, one that acknowledged vastly different historical experiences of winners and losers. Reconciling these many narratives remains vital for global justice—at the national and international levels as well as in interregional contexts—even if the WCAR could not reach viable compromises.

The Security Council embarked on a new activist agenda in the 1990s, expanding its charter role of safeguarding "international peace and security." For the first time in its history, the council even countenanced discussion of the *security* implications of global climate change and food shortages. Mounting concern with these expansive claims and actions led to a movement for reform of the United Nations. In late 2004, after almost sixty years of operation, the United Nations needed, in the words of the U.N. leaders, "another San Francisco moment" to reinvigorate collective values and confront the wider global threats and challenges of the twenty-first century. Reform began in 2005.[6] In setting an important agenda for the future, these efforts marked a concluding moment in the historical developments of the bedrock international institution for human rights. It serves, then, as an ending point for this study.

The reforms brought the first institutional change in the human rights organs established by the U.N. Charter, replacing the Human Rights Commission with a smaller Human Rights Council. Its members are chosen by a two-thirds vote in the General Assembly. This change, however, was just a tweaking of the system. More fundamental for future rights advocacy were debates about the composition of the Security Council and its vetoing members. The Security Council represented the weight of the past, perpetuating the geopolitical constellation of power as it existed in 1945. Many states and blocs had an interest in change, but for contradictory reasons. For example, leaders of weaker states, fearful of interventions, wanted vetoing members from developing countries; current economic powerhouses, such as Germany, Japan, and Brazil, expected entry to reflect new regional economic realities; still others favored a more central role for Middle Eastern states in global decision-making.

Changing the institutional basis of world power is daunting. So, too, is the related movement for fundamental reform of the international rules of trade and finance, which favor the rich, industrialized nations. The increasingly tragic consequences of failed development programs stalk human rights agendas, whether in local empowerment efforts to free women from gender violence or movements to secure adequate food and fresh water or broaden access to education and culture. The push for international reform of governance and finances intersects with the wider human rights goals of fair representation, just structures of society, and equitable and sustained development.[7] Human rights advocacy is central to their success as, for example, in encouraging a more consistent role for civil society groups (tested around the WCAR) in the financial negotiations over loans, which still take place largely between the International Monetary Fund and the governments alone. It also requires the "paradoxical" results of greater domestic public involvement to develop universally applied criteria for any future multilateral missions to protect people at risk. The same mechanism is needed as well to ensure full compliance with the principles of international humanitarian law.

Universal accountability for international human rights and humanitarian law is vital for the future, produced by the historical developments of international law since 1945. That year set the stage for a legal revolution, proclaiming a universal system of rights in treaty law for all human beings, everywhere. What this legal coverage meant in practice was determined largely in struggle, by a slow and an uneven process of incorporating individuals and groups under its mantle and balancing conflicting claims. International jurists have worked to bridge the emerging gaps between changing community norms and the reach of the law, responding to the accumulation of evidence of egregious wrongs given to the U.N. human rights commissions, committees, and working groups, including, recently, eyewitness testimonies at hearings and court trials. The response has been a continuous development of international law as seen in the operation of major conventions—among them, the two covenants (in force 1976), the Elimination of All Forms of Racial Discrimination (in force 1969), the so-called Women's Convention (in force 1981), the Convention against Torture (in force 1987), and the Protection of the Rights of Migrant Workers and their Families (in force 2003). It also expanded subject-matter jurisdiction beyond the Nuremberg and Tokyo precedents for the ad hoc criminal tribunals and the statutes of the permanent International Criminal Court. According to Steven R. Ratner and Jason S. Abrams, the ICC statute was significant because it "shed light on community expectations of individual responsibility."[8] It reflected the continuing exchanges between law formulation, on the one hand, and the work of victims, survivors, and NGO activists who help articulate community understanding of accountability for crimes and violations, on the other.

The consensual process of lawmaking and the input from victims on the ground address a fundamental challenge of many cultural critics who see international law as a totalizing force and new form of Western imperialism. As Sally Merry has argued persuasively, lawmaking in human rights contexts differs from the practices in colonial settings, despite "some obvious parallels" in the use of "introduced law" to rearrange gender and social power, challenge old ways of doing things, and redirect state administrative regulations and services. Human rights law is produced by "consensual deliberation," through a dynamic process of consultation, negotiation, and decision-making—even in the context of the global inequalities of power. It is not a "fixed or coerced system" determined by one outside authority. Other analysts, notably Jack Donnelly, reinforced the point by pointing to the "overlapping" (not complete) political consensus derived from wide participation in and near universal adherence to human rights treaty laws and international customary norms. These principles have been adopted and adapted by local activists and the NGOs to guide their own campaigns for change, which in daily operation remain sensitive to local cultures and traditions. In the work of the Ethiopian women's self-help organization, grassroots activists sustained and defended local traditions even as they sought to transform harmful practices.[9] Although derived from consensus, human rights laws and norms have not been universally applied. From its historical vantage point, this study has argued that the future viability of human rights as an international legal system in good measure rests with the solution to this major challenge.

People Matter

Human rights advocacy is about people who make a difference, some in the limelight and others in less visible but vitally important ways. If neither universal nor equal in its protection, the system worked by human intervention, drawing together a range of activists from the founders of local NGOs to distraught family members, many of whom straddled the line between victim and activist, to frontline activists providing food and other necessities to beleaguered communities in war-torn areas. It inspired average citizens to demand divestment, and it relied on judges offering witness protection programs, the U.N. staff challenging bureaucratic routines, and others—who simply were outraged by the particular wrongs—willing to ask the tough questions and get involved. In the face of grave injustices, it is about individual and group empowerment: the conviction to stand up to the coercive apparatus of a military dictatorship even if under attack, the willingness to go before the global media and demand to be heard, the performance of marriage ceremonies symbolizing new relationships between wife and husband. Many of these stories are in this book. Many others are not, but they nonetheless may be serving as local inspirations and, in the future, may become part of other transnational examinations of rights struggles, whether through micro-histories, longitudinal studies of changes in one locality, or approaches similar to this one, which interconnects international institutions and legal developments with local rights movements.

Under human rights purviews, people also mattered to international decision-makers in new ways. Standing between the victims and the U.N. bureaucracy, Theo van Boven reflected wider sentiments when he advocated new criteria to assess economic development. Moving from mere numbers and aggregate statistics of growth, he put human welfare at the center of development, measured concretely by people's access to education, housing, food, health care, and leisure time. As he said categorically in 1981, development had to be given "practical meaning" for human life—for the satisfaction of material and nonmaterial needs—otherwise it would remain simply a "high sounding slogan."[10] Increasingly as well, the timely publication of individual memoirs and submerged histories has impacted diplomacy, affecting interstate relations with demands for acknowledgment, apology, and compensation. With their focus on human suffering, community displacement, and grave injustices, these stories have complicated the older narratives of war and nation-building. It also seems clear that in the international wars of the early twenty-first century—in Afghanistan, in Iraq, and between Israel and Lebanon, for example—public concern from many venues increasingly has made the indiscriminate killing of civilians indefensible. It is a striking sentiment that has forced, for example, U.S. and NATO commanders on the ground to address the concerns rather than mask the deaths by using such military terms as "collateral damage." Although it has not disrupted war-making, it has brought the taking of innocent lives to new international attention.

Consolidated in the second half of the twentieth century, the human rights project entered history's large pantheon of visions for human betterment. Scaled down in operation, it differed from the grand schemes of socialist equality rooted in the inexorable laws of history, from the Manichean struggles for racialist utopias, and from religious futures sanctioned by God's plans. Some analysts place human rights under the notion of progress, although the designation is difficult to reconcile with its own historical record. Rooted in struggle rather than in one universal, moral Truth, rights gains can be lost. Propelled by the genocidal wars, brutalities, and the Holocaust of mid-century, human rights principles offered alternatives to war and destruction in an agreed-on set of universal criteria for human dignity, fundamental justice, equality, and security.

Through a widening process of global circulation and translation, these criteria set standards for people to evaluate their own opportunities, the situation of neighbors, and the plight of distant others. They brought new critiques to the exercise of power in state actions, the conduct of war, and multinational corporate investments. Internationally agreed on through processes of renegotiation and intracultural exchanges, the vision of equality, justice, and peace guides the day-to-day work toward the goals. This profound vision, rooted in concrete human actions, is the project's strength, captured well by a Spanish immigrant-rights activist facing the pressure of African labor migrants desperate for work. As he said, "When you measure the volume of people we can hire against the needs of their countries, it's a drop in the ocean. . . . But, we have to keep working, drop by drop."[11] This commitment sustains human rights advocacy at every level, bringing moral conscience to power politics and raising the bar toward a higher standard of acceptable behavior in national and global politics. If the past is prologue, human rights laws, institutions, and advocacy will realize their protective and transformative potential when strengthened by dynamic and popular support from below. If the past is guide, it will require a greater sense of urgency among domestic publics everywhere to ensure the universal applicability of its laws and norms developed over the past sixty years.

Notes

Introduction

1. For the statistics, see Karen Hagemann and Stefanie Schüler-Springorum, eds., *Home/Front: The Military, War and Gender in Twentieth Century Germany* (Oxford: Berg, 2002), 18.

2. John P. Humphrey, *Human Rights and the United Nations: A Great Adventure* (Dobbs Ferry, N.Y.: Transnational Publishers, 1984), 10, 23.

3. Mary Midgley, "Towards an Ethic of Global Responsibility," in *Human Rights in Global Politics*, ed. Tim Dunne and Nicholas J. Wheeler (Cambridge: Cambridge University Press, 1999), 160–61.

4. The poles themselves are more fluid. A defense of the state is at times argued on moral grounds. Richard A. Falk, *Human Rights Horizons: The Pursuit of Justice in a Globalizing World* (New York: Routledge, 2000), 226–29.

5. Mark Mazower argues that this human rights "revolution" also represented a shift from minority (group) guarantees to individual rights. Based heavily on Anglophone evidence and leadership perspectives, the argument is less about group versus individual rights than about an important recognition of tensions within rights visions that push distinct priorities at precise moments of time. Mark Mazower, "The Strange Triumph of Human Rights, 1933–1950," *Historical Journal* 47 (May 2004): 379–98.

6. See Thomas Blom Hansen and Finn Stepputat, *Sovereign Bodies: Citizens, Migrants, and States in the Postcolonial World* (Princeton, N.J.: Princeton University Press, 2005), 11–20, for a focused discussion of political community as constituted by the "state of exception."

7. Patricia Hyndman, "Cultural Legitimacy in the Formulation and Implementation of Human Rights Law and Policy in Australia," in *Human Rights in Cross-Cultural Perspectives: A Quest for Consensus*, ed. Abdullahi Ahmed An-Na'im (Philadelphia: University of Pennsylvania Press, 1992), 310.

8. Often used synonymously with "international," "transnational" more appropriately refers to a circulation of ideas, movements, and contacts among people in different societies and not to the international level of state and intergovernmental interactions.

9. D. J. Ravindran, "In Pursuit of Human Dignity," in *A Human Rights Message*, Ministry of Foreign Affairs, Sweden (Borås: Centraltryckeriet, 1998), 127–31. The collection was published to commemorate the fiftieth anniversary of the passage of the Universal Declaration of Human Rights.

10. Ibid., 128, 129, 131.

11. For a good summary of the debates, see Jack L. Goldsmith and Eric A.

Posner, *The Limits of International Law* (Oxford: Oxford University Press, 2005), 14–17.

12. Among his many publications, see Jack Donnelly, *Universal Human Rights in Theory and Practice*, 2nd ed. (Ithaca, N.Y.: Cornell University Press, 2003), 11–16.

13. Falk, too, is a prolific scholar; for his take on human rights, see *Human Rights Horizons*.

14. Among others, see Audie Klotz, *Norms in International Relations: The Struggle against Apartheid* (Ithaca, N.Y.: Cornell University Press, 1995), and Margaret E. Keck and Kathryn Sikkink, *Activists Beyond Borders: Advocacy Networks in*

15. Akira Iriye, *Global Community: The Role of InternaInternational Politics* (Ithaca, N.Y.: Cornell University Press, 1998).

15. Akira Iriye, *Global Community: The Role of International Organizations in the Making of the Contemporary World* (Berkeley: University of California Press, 2002).16. Micheline R. Ishay, ed., *The Human Rights Reader: Major Political Essays, Speeches, and Documents from the Bible to the Present* (New York: Routledge, 1997). For the historical meanings of such terms as "liberty," "privilege," and "freedom" over time, see Orlando Patterson, "Freedom, Slavery, and the Modern Construction of Rights," in *Historical Change and Human Rights: The Oxford Amnesty Lectures, 1994*, ed. Olwen Huften (New York: Oxford University Press, 1995), 132–78.

17. Jan Herman Burgers, "The Road to San Francisco: The Revival of the Human Rights Idea in the Twentieth Century," *Human Rights Quarterly* 14.4 (November 1992): 447–77. Paul Gordon Lauren, *The Evolution of International Human Rights: Visions Seen* (Philadelphia: University of Pennsylvania Press, 1998).

18. The recently deceased American historian Kenneth Cmiel has brought historical precision to the debates. See, in particular, his "The Recent History of Human Rights," *American Historical Review* 109.1 (February 2004): 117–35.

19. For a theoretical defense of a new social history, which claims social agency within existing linguistic, political, and economic structures, see Pierre Bourdieu, *The Field of Cultural Production: Essays on Art and Literature* (New York: Columbia University Press, 1993). For a spirited discussion of old and new social and cultural history, see "AHR Forum: Geoff Eley's A Crooked Line," *American Historical Review* 113.2 (April 2008): 391–437. Human rights language, of course, also is available to those who defend existing power hierarchies and global inequalities.

20. The expression comes from law professor George Abi-Saab as found in Celina Romany, "State Responsibility Goes Private: A Feminist Critique of the Public/Private Distinction in International Human Rights Law," in *Human Rights of Women: National and International Perspectives*, ed. Rebecca J. Cook (Philadelphia: University of Pennsylvania Press, 1994), 89. Also, Lawrence M. Friedman, *A History of American Law*, 2nd ed. (New York: Simon & Schuster, 1985), 17, who speaks of law as a living system.

21. Midgley, "Towards an Ethic," 179.

Chapter 1. Raising the Bar, 1900–1949

1. Among others, see Jack Donnelly, *Universal Human Rights in Theory and Practice*, 2nd ed. (Ithaca, N.Y.: Cornell University Press, 2003), 128.

2. In Johannes Morsink, *The Universal Declaration of Human Rights: Origins, Drafting and Intent* (Philadelphia: University of Pennsylvania Press, 1999), 38.

3. For an older but highly valuable study of the law of nations until the mid-

twentieth century, see Arthur Nussbaum, *A Concise History of the Law of Nations* (New York: Macmillan Company, 1950), 191–99.

4. For a compelling analysis in the case of Pan-Africanism, see Tiffany Ruby Patterson and Robin D. G. Kelley, "Unfinished Migrations: Reflections on the African Diaspora and the Making of the Modern World," *African Studies Review* 43.1 (April 2000): 11–45. This understanding also means questioning in which contexts the unifying rubrics used by contemporaries (from diaspora to class identities to sex to colonial subject) remain useful for historical analysis. The same scrutiny applies, of course, to human rights identities.

5. Akira Iriye, *Global Community: The Role of International Organizations in the Making of the Contemporary World* (Berkeley: University of California Press, 2002), 10.

6. Marilyn J. Boxer and Jean H. Quataert, *Connecting Spheres: European Women in a Globalizing World, 1500 to the Present*, 2nd ed. (New York: Oxford University Press, 2000), 215.

7. Alexander Walters, Henry B. Brown, H. Sylvester Williams, and W. E. Burghardt Du Bois, "Address to the Nations of the World by the Races Congress in London, 1900," retrieved August 30, 2006, from http://www.etext.org/Politics/MIM/countries/panafrican/pan1900.html.

8. Kevin Repp, "The Metropole as Colony: Visions of Greater Berlin in Late Imperial Germany," paper presented at the 2002 meeting of the American Historical Association, San Francisco, and Frederick Cooper and Ann Laura Stoler, eds., *Tensions of Empire: Colonial Cultures in a Bourgeois World* (Berkeley: University of California Press, 1997). Also, Jean H. Quataert, *Staging Philanthropy: Patriotic Women and the National Imagination in Dynastic Germany, 1813–1916* (Ann Arbor: University of Michigan Press, 2001), 239–40.

9. Prasenjit Duara, "The Discourse of Civilization and Pan-Asianism," *Journal of World History* 12.1 (Spring 2001): 99–130, and H. Glenn Penny, "Productive Knowledge: Transnational Narratives of 'Indianness' in Nineteenth Century Germany," paper presented at the annual meeting of the German Studies Association, Pittsburgh, September 28–October 1, 2006. Discourses circulating in the imperial culture linked definitions of civilization to colonization itself, stressing the benefits and rights colonialism brought to humanity.

10. International Institute of Social History (hereafter IISH), Amsterdam, Deuxième International, Supplément, Période 1889–1914, Les Congrès, No. 339, Colonies and Dependencies, Report to the International Socialist Congress held at Amsterdam, August 14–20, 1904, by H. M. Hyndman, London, 1904, and No. 421, Documentation, reprinted from India, September 2, 1904.

11. IISH, Amsterdam, Women's Organizations, War, Peace, League of Nations, "Women's International League for Peace and Freedom, 1915–1938: A Venture in Internationalism," Geneva, July 1938; The Women's Library, 5/ICW/3, International Council of Women and 2/IAW/C/1, International Women's Suffrage Alliance, "Reports." Also, Leila Rupp, *Worlds of Women: The Making of an International Women's Movement* (Princeton, N.J.: Princeton University Press, 1997).

12. The Women's Library, International Women's Suffrage Alliance, "Report of the Seventh Congress, Budapest, Hungary, June 15–21, 1913" (Manchester, n.d.), 87–88. Palestine, arguably, was singled out because of its biblical importance.

13. Rebecca Karl, *Staging the World: Chinese Nationalism at the Turn of the Twentieth Century* (Durham, N.C.: Duke University Press, 2002), 167–69; Duara, "The Discourse"; and Walters et al., "Address, 1900."

14. For references to the diverse roles of Roy and Padmore, see Patterson and Kelley, "Unfinished Migrations." For Terrell, see Kathryn Kish Sklar, Anja Schüler, and Susan Strasser, eds., *Social Justice Feminists in the United States and Germany: A Dialogue in Documents, 1885–1933* (Ithaca, N.Y.: Cornell University Press, 1998), 114–19.

15. As did Chinese students at the 1903 Osaka, Japan, exhibit on the "races of man." See Karl, *Staging*, 111, and, for African American protests, see "African-American Women and the 1893 Chicago World's Fair, 1893," Women and Social Movements in the United States, 1600–2000, path: documents, retrieved June 30, 2005, from http://womhist.binghamton.edu/.

16. Iriye, *Global Community*, 15.

17. Ibid., 14–17.

18. The Women's Library, 5/ICW/1/7–11, Conferences, Address of the president of the ICW by Mrs. May Wright Sewall, delivered at the opening of its Third Quinquennial in Berlin, June 8, 1904, 8.

19. Walters et al, "Address, 1900."

20. I provide here evidence taken from the publications of activists in social movements, which includes just a limited range of source materials. Obviously, there were extraordinary writers such as W. E. B. Du Bois, whose searing critique of racism and theoretical perspectives on capitalism drew truly global connections at all turns around the sources and victims of oppression. My interest is in the practical language of struggle on the ground in its particular historical context; this perspective shows change over time in the use of language, not continuity.

21. Karl, *Staging*, 62, and Yukiko Sumi Barnett, "India in Asia: 'kawa Shûnei's Pan-Asian Thought and His Idea of India in Early Twentieth Century Japan," *Journal of the Oxford University Society* 1 (2004): 1–23.

22. For humanitarian sentiments eliciting wide public responses, see, among others, the influential exposé on the cost of war published during the Boer War, 1899–1902 by the feminist activist Emily Hobhouse, *The Brunt of the War and Where It Fell* (London: Methuen & Co., 1902). Red Cross appeals for humanitarian relief in kind and money also were an increasingly common sight on the street corners of Europe's cities in the early twentieth century. For these sources, see Archives du Comité international de la Croix-Rouge, Archives Comité et Secretariat jusqu'en 1918, Groupe AF (Ancien Fonds), 1863–1914, Geneva. The AF contains materials prior to 1918.

23. Typical of this teleologically driven literature is Paul Gordon Lauren, *The Evolution of International Human Rights: Visions Seen* (Philadelphia: University of Pennsylvania Press, 1998).

24. The Women's Library, 2/IAW/1/C/4, International Woman Suffrage Alliance, *Report of the Ninth Congress, Rome, Italy, May 12–19, 1923* (Dresden, n.d.). The same congress identified women's causes with visions of human solidarity, ranked "superior" to (in the original) racial or national solidarity (71). Also, Walters et al., "Address, 1900."

25. Socialists not only proclaimed these principles but enacted them in coordinated demonstrations on May 1 (International Workers' Day) and, after 1911, International Women's Day. For a telling example from the German case, see *Die Gleichheit*, January 22, 1912, "Aus der Bewegung" proclaiming, "Whoever raises the red flag, struggles for *Menschenrechte*." Although I do not want to reduce human rights deployment to matters of pragmatism, its specific use early in the twentieth century often reflected such calculations. Jack Donnelley

reaches a similar conclusion, with different evidence, in *Universal Human Rights*, 12.

26. The work at The Hague was followed closely by members of transnational movements. For a "global" demonstration in defense of the work, see Margarethe Leonore Selenka, ed., *The International Demonstration of Women for the Peace-Conference of May 15, 1899*, trans. Emily Darby (Munich: A. Schupp, 1900), 1, 17–29. See also Irwin Abrams, "The Emergence of the International Law Societies," *Review of Politics* 19.3 (July 1957): 361–80.

27. Some eighteenth-century European positivists called the existing "law of nations" (international law) European public law. Through the unequal treaty system, it was extended to countries in East Asia in the mid-nineteenth century and later was broadened to more "universal" status through multilateral agreements. Recent Third World scholars have noted its biases, stressing many fundamental norms of law governing the acquisition of territory or compensation for property interests, which served colonial patterns of appropriation. Admitted to the "advantages" of European law through the Treaty of Paris in 1856, the Ottoman Empire nonetheless negotiated international recognition of the Islamic crescent by first demanding its de facto use in 1878 at the outset of armed hostilities. Similar patterns of negotiation characterized new human rights lawmaking after 1945. For these developments, see Nussbaum, *A Concise History*, 165–67, 188–90, and Hilary Charlesworth and Christine Chinkin, *The Boundaries of International Law: A Feminist Analysis* (Manchester: Juris Publishing, 2000), 36–38.

28. The term "NGO" was not used at the time; it has become part of international vocabulary only since the human rights era and gathered widespread currency, starting in the 1970s.

29. A. Pearce Higgins, *The Hague Peace Conferences and Other International Conferences Concerning the Laws and Usages of War: Texts of Conventions with Commentaries* (Cambridge: Cambridge University Press, 1909), 51, 75.

30. Geoffrey Best, *Humanity in Warfare: The Modern History of the International Law of Armed Conflicts* (London: Weidenfeld and Nicolson, 1980).

31. They drew here on the 1868 "St. Petersburg Declaration Renouncing the Use, in Time of War, of Explosive Projectiles Under 400 Grammes Weight," found in Adam Roberts and Richard Guelff, eds., *Documents on the Laws of War* (Oxford: Clarendon Press, 1989), 30–31.

32. Best, *Humanity in Warfare*, 163–66, and Roberts and Guelff, *Documents*, 4, 44.

33. The Geneva Conventions were implemented between belligerent armies (British and Boer) in the southern African colonial war. In addition, medical corps also accompanied Europe's colonial troops, helping to expand the training of medical volunteers back home, increasingly used by national Red Cross associations before World War I.

34. Hannah Arendt, *The Origins of Totalitarianism* (1951; rpt., Cleveland, Ohio: World Publishing Company, 1951), 123, and Jean H. Quataert, *The Gendering of Human Rights in the International System of Law in the Twentieth Century*, American Historical Association Series in Global and Comparative History (Washington, D.C.: American Historical Association, 2006). For more specific details, see, among others, Hugh Thomas, *Cuba or the Pursuit of Freedom* (1971; updated ed., New York: Da Capo Press, 1998), 328–38; S. B. Spies, "Women and the War," in *The South African War: The Anglo-Boer War 1899–1902*, ed. Peter Warwick (Essex: Longman, 1980), 165–66, 174; and Horst Drechsler, *"Let Us Die Fighting": The Struggle of the Herero and Nama against German Imperialism (1884–1915)*, trans. Bernd Zöllner (London: Zed Press, 1980), 151–60, 213.

35. Vahakn N. Dadrian, "Genocide as a Problem of National and International Law: The World War I Armenian Case and Its Contemporary Legal Ramifications," *Yale Journal of International Law* 14.5 (Summer 1989): 262, and Donald Bloxham, *The Great Game of Genocide: Imperialism, Nationalism, and the Destruction of the Ottoman Armenians* (Oxford: Oxford University Press, 2005), 162–69. For the German case, which included 1,700 trials of lesser figures for war crimes in Leipzig between 1921 and 1927, see David Grimm Choberka, "War Crimes Trials in Weimar Germany," review H-German, February 2005, retrieved October 30, 2006, from http://www.h-net.org/reviews/showrev.cgi?path = 656911170 54184.

36. In the interwar years, leaders in colonial states such as France, with its universalist rhetoric, spoke of the progressive role of labor in colonial settings for teaching the modern values of hard work. At the same time, French authorities refused to sign ILO covenants banning forced labor. It is difficult to square imperialist rule with any genuine tradition of rights. For such an effort, see Alice L. Conklin, "Colonialism and Human Rights, A Contradiction in Terms? The Case of France and West Africa, 1895–1914," *American Historical Review* 103.2 (April 1998): 419–12.

37. Carol Miller, "Geneva—the Key to Equality: Inter-war Feminists and the League of Nations," *Women's History Review* 3 (1994): 219–45, and Iriye, *Global Community*, 21. Iriye catalogs a steady advance in transnational organizing in the 1920s and 1930s. In 1920, there were 79 new international NGOs compared to a decade earlier; ten years later, the total stood at 375, a gain of 296 over the decade.

38. IISH, Second International, War, Peace, Arbitration and the League of Nations, No. 250, Les Résolutions de la Conférence internationale ouvrière et socialiste de Berne, 2–10 Février 1919, and International Informationcentre and Archives for the Women's Movement (IIAV), Amsterdam, Women's Organizations, War, Peace, League of Nations, "Women's International League for Peace and Freedom." Documents on the first Pan-African Congress are from the Web-based collection, W. E. B. Du Bois, "The Pan-African Movement."

39. Mark Mazower, "The Strange Triumph of Human Rights, 1933–1950," *Historical Journal* 47.2 (June 2004): 379–98; Susan Pedersen, "The Meaning of the Mandates System," *Geschichte und Gesellschaft* 32.4 (2006): 560–82; idem, "Back to the League of Nations," *American Historical Review* 112.4 (October 2007): 1091–117; and Michael D. Callahan, *Mandates and Empire: The League of Nations and Africa, 1914–1931* (Brighton: Sussex Academic Press, 1999).

40. For the intellectual heritage of liberal imperialism, see John Stuart Mill, *Considerations on Representative Government* (1861), particularly Chapter 18, "Of the Government of Dependencies by a Free State," excerpts in Micheline R Ishay, ed., *The Human Rights Reader: Major Political Essays, Speeches, and Documents From the Bible to the Present* (New York: Routledge, 1997), 287–90.

41. Pedersen, "The Meaning of the Mandates," 581–82.

42. Carole Fink, *Defending the Rights of Others: The Great Powers, the Jews, and International Minority Protection, 1878–1938* (Cambridge: Cambridge University Press, 2004). An example of the Polish Minority Treaty (1919) is in Ishay, *The Human Rights Reader*, 307–11.

43. Mazower, "The Strange Triumph," 379. As my book shows, the post–World War II human rights era embraced minority protections through its broad antidiscrimination principles, increasingly reinforced by analysis that linked minority status to poverty and social disadvantage. Human rights princi-

ples in practice also had to balance women's claims against other time-honored group protections, such as religious rights.

44. Among the important figures were the Chilean jurist Alejandro Alverez, cofounder of the American Institute of International Law; the Russian émigré A. N. Mandelstam, who settled in Paris after the Bolshevik Revolution; and the Greek expatriot A. F. Frangulis, founder of the International Diplomatic Academy in Paris. See Burgers, "The Road," 450–51.

45. These were the traditional definitions of international cooperation outlined by the high contracting parties in the Covenant of the League of Nations.

46. H. G. Wells, "The Rights of the World Citizen: Two Stages in Their Formulation," in *Human Rights and World Order: Two Discourses to the H. G. Wells Society*, ed. James Dilloway (Nottingham: The H. G. Wells Society, 1998), 29–34. W. Warren Wagar, my recently deceased colleague, encouraged my reading of this text.

47. John P. Humphrey, *Human Rights and the United Nations: A Great Adventure* (Dobbs Ferry, N.Y.: Transnational Publishers, 1984). Humphrey prepared the original draft of the Universal Declaration of Human Rights, commenting on the sources he consulted.

48. Helle Kanger, *Human Rights in the U.N. Declaration* (Stockholm: Almqvist & Wiksell, 1986), 12–13, and Elizabeth Thompson, *Colonial Citizens: Republican Rights, Paternal Privilege, and Gender in French Syria and Lebanon* (New York: Columbia University Press, 2000), 231–32, for Free French efforts to win over the Levant.

49. In Burgers, "The Road," 474.

50. For more details on responses, see Lauren, *The Evolution*, 172–84, and Kenneth Cmiel, "Human Rights, Freedom of Information, and the Origins of Third-World Solidarity," in *Truth Claims: Representation and Human Rights*, ed. Mark Philip Bradley and Patrice Petro (New Brunswick, N.J.: Rutgers University Press, 2002), 108–9.

51. The Indonesian 1945 constitution, retrieved June 10, 2007 from the Web site of UCLA, Center for East Asian Studies, http://www.isop.ucla.edu/eas/doc uments/indonesia-const.htm. Similar language was included in the new constitutions of other postcolonial countries; language, of course, does not say anything about implementation. For the Vietnam example, see Odd Arne Westad, *The Global Cold War: Third World Interventions and the Making of Our Times* (Cambridge: Cambridge University Press, 2005), 89.

52. Humphrey, *Human Rights*, 13, and Kirsten Sellars, *The Rise and Rise of Human Rights* (Phoenix Mill, U.K.: Sutton Publishing, 2002), 2–4, 8. It is all too easy to point to hypocrisy in a study of human rights, particularly in the context of geopolitics. My purpose is to uncover the shortcomings and the failures of the past, including cynicism and hypocrisy, in order to advocate for a different future.

53. The point is reinforced by Mary Midgley, who writes somewhat wryly that "academics" had been "startled" by the way human rights notions were picked up by ordinary people to say something that they "find very important." Mary Midgley, "Towards an Ethic of Global Responsibility," in *Human Rights in Global Politics*, ed. Tim Dunne and Nicholas J. Wheeler (Cambridge: Cambridge University Press, 1999), 160. For the first reassessment since the end of the Cold War of the Soviet role in shaping international criminal law, see Francine Hirsch, "The Soviets at Nuremberg: International Law, Propaganda, and the Making of the Postwar Order," *American Historical Review* 113.3 (June 2008): 701–30.

54. George F. Kennan, *The Other Balkan Wars: A 1913 Carnegie Endowment Inquiry in Retrospect with a New Introduction and Reflections on the Present Conflict* (Washington, D.C.: Carnegie Endowment for International Peace, 1993), 15. Kennan was the architect of the U.S. containment policy at the opening of the Cold War.

55. For reformulations of the "laws of war," see Fritz Kalshoven, *Constraints on the Waging of War* (Geneva: Martinus Nijhoff, 1987). An effort to write a convention guaranteeing freedom of information worldwide also was part of the same process of legal negotiations. By 1952, it foundered on insurmountable tensions between Western countries and new postcolonial nations over the proper balance between rights and responsibilities in matters of press freedoms. See, Cmiel, "Human Rights, Freedom of Information."

56. For the activism of the General Assembly, see 44(1), December 8, 1946, Resolution Adopted on the Treatment of Indians in the Union; 56(1), December 11, 1946, Political Rights of Women; 65(1), December 14, 1946, Future Status of South West Africa. United Nations Documentation, Research Guide. Resolutions adopted by the General Assembly, path: earlier sessions, first (1946) onward, retrieved November 8, 2006, from http://www.un.org/Depts/dhl/res guide/gares1.htm. The cable sent by Dr. A. B. Xuma is found in the ANC Historical Documents collection online, retrieved November 8, 2006 from http://www.anc.org.za/ancdocs/history/cable.html.

57. U.N. General Assembly, 106 S-1, May 15, 1947, Special Committee on Palestine, Resolutions adopted on Reports of the General Committee.

58. Du Bois, "An Appeal to the World: A Statement on the Denial of Human Rights to Minorities in the Case of the Citizens of the United States of America," in *W. E. B. Du Bois Reader*, ed. Eric Sundquist (New York: Oxford University Press, 1996), 459–60. Also, William L. Patterson, ed., *We Charge Genocide: The Historic Petition to the United Nations for Relief from a Crime of the United States Government against the Negro People* (New York: Civil Rights Congress, 1951), 195. Richard Falk argues, for example, that human rights issues were "deemed marginal" in the aftermath of World War II. In the immediate postwar period, though, they helped shift the focus of transnational advocacy. Richard Falk, *Human Rights Horizons: The Pursuit of Justice in a Globalizing World* (New York: Routledge, 2000), 37.

59. Francesca Miller, *Latin American Women and the Search for Social Justice* (Hanover, N.H.: University Press of New England, 1991), 198, and her essay "Feminisms and Transnationalisms," *Gender and History* 10.3 (November 1998): 571. Latin American political elites at the time were Iberians (and, hence, Western) and did not incorporate indigenous values into their policies and perspectives.

60. In 1994, this council ended its work when it oversaw the independence of Palau, an island republic in the Pacific Ocean, and no longer exists as a permanent body.

61. In Dominic McGoldrick, *The Human Rights Committee: Its Role in the Development of the International Covenant on Civil and Political Rights* (Oxford: Clarendon Press, 1991), 4.

62. Patterson, *We Charge Genocide*, 29.

63. The breakthrough case in 1971 arose from a decision to declare illegal the annexation of German South-West Africa by South Africa.

64. In Iriye, *Global Community*, 92.

65. In Morsink, *The Universal Declaration*, 12, and, for summary details of the

drafting phases, 4–12. I want to thank Elizabeth Thompson for helping me identify this delegate.

66. Bhikhu Parekh, "Non-ethnocentric Universalism," in *Human Rights in Global Politics,* ed. Dunne and Wheeler, 140, and, for the appeal to "history," Michael Ignatieff, *Human Rights as Politics and Idolatry* (Princeton, N.J.: Princeton University Press, 2001), 55. For the role of conscience among early positivists in natural law theory, see Nussbaum, *A Concise History,* 119–25.

67. For example, the early Western feminist Mary Wollstonecraft, a critic of liberal state-building at the end of the eighteenth century, called the failure to accord women full citizenship rights during the French Revolution an affront to their inherent dignity. Mary Wollstonecraft, *A Vindication of the Rights of Woman,* ed. Carol H. Poston (New York: W. W. Norton, 1975), 9, 33, 45. The notion also was part of early radical and socialist critiques of the capitalist order upheld by natural rights. Still to be written is a global genealogy of the multiple meanings of dignity in these HRC debates.

68. M. Glen Johnson and Janvsz Symonides, *The Universal Declaration of Human Rights: A History of Its Creation and Implementation* (Paris: UNESCO Publishers, 1998), 32.

69. "On the Jewish Question," in Ishay, *Human Rights Reader,* 189–99, quotation from 196.

70. Morsink, *The Universal Declaration,* 247. The emphasis on rights *and* duties is found in the American Declaration of the Rights and Duties of Man, OAS, Res. 30, 1948.

71. For a summary of these debates, see Donnelly, *Universal Human Rights,* 27–33, and Morsink, *The Universal Declaration,* 227, 230.

72. As found in Humphrey, *Human Rights,* 73.

73. ILO treaties include the Freedom of Association and Protection of the Rights to Organize Convention (No. 87) 68 U.N.T.S., in force July 5, 1950. The Commission on the Status of Women wrote the Convention on Nationality of Married Women, 309, U.N.T.S. 65, in force August 11, 1958. These treaties are available through the University of Minnesota, Human Rights Library, path: International Human Rights Instruments, alphabetized topic list, retrieved November 25, 2006, from http://www1.umn.edu/humanrts/instree/ainstlsa2 .html.

Part I. An Emerging Human Rights Orthodoxy

1. Howard Tolley Jr., *The U.N. Commission on Human Rights* (Boulder, Colo.: Westview Press, 1987), 18.

2. J. E. S. Fawcett, "Human Rights and Domestic Jurisdiction," in *The International Protection of Human Rights,* ed. Evan Luard (New York: Praeger, 1967), 288–89.

3. For a thorough assessment of the "Cold War," a term not used officially by the Soviet Union and Third World states, see Odd Arne Westad, *The Global Cold War: Third World Interventions and the Making of Our Times* (Cambridge: Cambridge University Press, 2005).

4. For an interesting and a highly informative study of the social tensions around debates over citizenship in the case of Mandate Lebanon and Syria, see Elizabeth Thompson, *Colonial Citizens: Republican Rights, Paternal Privilege, and Gender in French Syria and Lebanon* (New York: Columbia University Press, 2000).

5. Tony Judt, *Postwar: A History of Europe since 1945* (New York: Penguin,

2005), 27, and Mark Mazower, "The Strange Triumph of Human Rights, 1933–1950," *Historical Journal* 47.2 (June 2004): 379–98, for details on Eastern European leaders' hostility toward minority protections.

6. For one poignant account, see Urvashi Butalia, *The Other Side of Silence: Voices from the Partition of India* (Durham, N.C.: Duke University Press, 2000).

7. Westad, *The Global Cold War,* 9, and Tolley, *The U.N. Commission,* 146, who notes U.N. inaction in the case of Kurds, Tibetans, the Naga people of India, West Irians, and the Germans of Southern Tyrol.

8. Crawford Young, "The Dialectics of Cultural Pluralism: Concept and Reality," in *The Rising Tide of Cultural Pluralism: The Nation-State at Bay?* ed. Crawford Young (Madison: University of Wisconsin Press, 1993), 3, makes the point that only in the 1960s did academics begin comparative research on the ethnic identities, complicating the nation-state system.

9. For an accessible study of much of this literature, see Frederick Cooper, *Africa since 1940: The Past of the Present* (Cambridge: Cambridge University Press, 2002).

Chapter 2. Cold War Politics and Human Rights Publics

1. Henry Steiner and Philip Alston, *International Human Rights in Context: Law, Politics, Morals,* 2nd ed. (Oxford: Oxford University Press, 2000), 589. The epigraph to this chapter also makes the point.

2. In assessing human rights historiography, Cmiel distinguishes between research on theory and research on advocacy. Kenneth Cmiel, "The Recent History of Human Rights," *American Historical Review* 109.1 (February 2004): 126

3. C. Clyde Ferguson, "The United States, the United Nations and the Struggle Against Racial Apartheid," in *The Dynamics of Human Rights in U.S. Foreign Policy,* ed. Natalie Kaufman Hevener (New Brunswick, N.J.: Transaction Books, 1981), 203, 207.

4. The apartheid laws gave whites a virtual monopoly over political, economic, and social life, backed by extensive police and military powers. Ronald W. Walters, *Pan Africanism in the African Diaspora: An Analysis of Modern Afrocentric Political Movements* (Detroit, Mich.: Wayne State University Press, 1993), 216. Although the overall numbers of people increased over the decades after 1948, the racial proportions reflected in the 1990 census were similar to those seen in earlier years.

5. Frederick Cooper, *Africa since 1940: The Past of the Present* (Cambridge: Cambridge University Press, 2002), 134. The statistics are in R. B. Ballinger, "UN Action on Human Rights in South Africa," in *The International Protection of Human Rights,* ed. Evan Luard (New York: Praeger, 1967), 269–70.

6. Soon after the war ended, human rights became a language of diplomatic censure. Evan Luard, "Promotion of Human Rights by UN Political Bodies," in Luard, *The International Protection,* 143, for the example of North African states and France in the 1950s.

7. U.N. General Asssembly, Resolution 1514 (15), December 14, 1960. For an abbreviated text and other relevant U.N. documents, see Steiner and Alston, *International Human Rights,* 1265–68. Even if independence did not overcome the legacy of colonial rule or ensure successful economic development, it is important to mark the moments of significant break with the past. The resolution, however, did not permit ethnic claims to disrupt "national unity" or the "territorial integrity" of the new nation.

8. Audie Klotz, *Norms in International Relations: The Struggle against Apartheid* (Ithaca, N.Y.: Cornell University Press, 1995), 40, argues that in the 1940s and 1950s support for racial equality grew within the context of the postwar human rights agenda. The reverse is probably more nearly correct.

9. These details are drawn from ANC documents on the Web: Youth League Manifesto, 1944; ANC Annual Conference Resolution, December 14–17, 1946; ANC Youth League Basic Policy Document, 1948. See Historical Documents, Part I, 1912–1960, retrieved May 25, 2007, from http://www.anc.org.za/anc docs/history/.

10. The charter is in Tim J. Jucker, *Opposition in South Africa: The Leadership of Z. K. Matthews, Nelson Mandela and Stephen Biko* (Westport, Conn.: Praeger, 1995), 85–86.

11. Hilda Bernstein, *For Their Triumphs and for Their Tears: Women in Apartheid South Africa* (London: International Defense and Aid Fund for Southern Africa, 1985), 106, recognizes the many different parallel campaigns going on simultaneously.

12. Govan Mbeki, *South Africa: The Peasants' Revolt,* found in the ANC Historical Documents, Part I, path: Selected Documents.

13. Ballinger, "UN Action," 254–55.

14. Carol Lazar, *Women of South Africa: Their Fight for Freedom,* photographs by Peter Magubane and introduction by Nadine Gordimer (Boston: Little, Brown, 1993), 229.

15. J. D. B. Miller, "South Africa's Departure," *Journal of Commonwealth Political Studies* 1 (November 1961): 73. In December 1961, Nyerère became president of the new independent republic of Tanzania. Klotz, *Norms,* challenges traditional international relations theory by showing how human rights values drove these states' actions, often against their (rational) economic interests.

16. *U.S. Participation in the UN: Report by the President to the Congress for the Year 1965* (Washington, D.C.: Department of State, 1967), 203–5, quote at 204.

17. In particular, William Korey, "The U.N.'s Double Standard on Human Rights," at the Hearing before the Subcommittee on International Organizations of the Committee on International Relations, House of Representatives, Ninety-Fifth Congress, First Session, May 19, 1977 (Washington, D.C.: Committee on International Relations, 1977), 33. Also, Leonard Garment to the HRC, *U.S. Participation in the UN: Report by the President to the Congress for the Year 1976* (Washington, D.C.: U.S. Government Printing Office, 1977), 212–13.

18. In studies that use compliance criteria at the international level to organize the arguments, the historical breakthrough for NGOs is largely obscured. Howard Tolley, *The U.N. Commission on Human Rights* (Boulder, Colo.: Westview Press, 1987), 64–70.

19. Akira Iriye, *Global Community: The Role of International Organizations in the Making of the Contemporary World* (Berkeley: University of California Press, 2002), 46.

20. Ballinger, "UN Action," 274–75.

21. In George M. Fredrickson, *Black Liberation: A Comparative History of Black Ideologies in the United States and South Africa* (New York: Oxford University Press, 1995), 267.

22. Cooper, *Africa since 1940,* 7, 146.

23. Gladys Tsolo, "Azania (South Africa): My Experience in the National Liberation Struggle," and "Interview with Ms. Gladys Tsolo of Azania," November 1, 1978, in *National Liberation and Women's Liberation,* ed. Maria Mies and

Rhoda Reddock (The Hague: Institute of Social Studies, n.d.), 96–111. Tsolo joined the Pan-Africanist Congress in East Germany and thus uses "Azania" (the land of the blacks), its term for the territory of South Africa.

24. In the interview, Tsolo did not talk about human rights, which is not surprising, perhaps, because rights language was more common among political elites localizing the idea. It is as important for the human rights era as earlier not to homogenize and flatten language.

25. Tsolo, "Azania," 103–4.

26. "The Demands of the Women of South Africa for the Withdrawal of Passes for Women and the Repeal of the Pass Laws," petition presented to the prime minister, Pretoria, August 9, 1956, Historical Documents, Part I. Also, Lazar, *Women*, 70, and Vakani Makhasikazi Collective (Johannesburg), *South African Women on the Move* (London: Zed Books, 1985), 227–29.

27. Young-Sun Hong, "Transparent Man on Transnational Display: Exhibiting East Germanness in the Third World," paper presented at the Twenty-seventh Annual Conference of the German Studies Association, September 18–21, 2003, New Orleans, Louisiana.

28. Tsolo, "Azania," 106.

29. Ibid., 111.

30. M. Glen Johnson and Janvsz Symonides, *The Universal Declaration of Human Rights: A History of Its Creation and Implementation* (Paris: UNESCO Publishers, 1998), 86–88.

31. Americans for South African Resistance (AFAR). George M. Hauser, "American Supporters of the Defiance Campaign," before the U.N. Special Committee against Apartheid, June 25, 1982, ANC documents, retrieved April 2004 from http://www.anc.org/za/ancdocs/history.

32. Fredrickson, *Black Liberation*, 252–53, 273.

33. For a firsthand account of opposition in the Soviet Union, see Ludmilla Alexeyeva, *Soviet Dissent: Contemporary Movements for National, Religious, and Human Rights*, trans. Carol Pearce and John Glad (Middletown, Conn.: Wesleyan University Press, 1985), 269, who places the origins of the human rights movement in Soviet Russia at a 1965 demonstration in Moscow's Pushkin Square. See also, Padraic Kenney, *A Carnival of Revolution: Central Europe 1989* (Princeton, N.J.: Princeton University Press, 2002), 9.

34. Andrei Sakharov, *Memoirs* (New York: Knopf, 1990), 314–16.

35. For the broader shift in climate, see Tony Judt, *Postwar: A History of Europe since 1945* (New York: Penguin, 2005), 313–18 and 422–49, and Odd Arne Westad, *The Global Cold War: Third World Interventions and the Making of Our Times* (Cambridge: Cambridge University Press, 2005), 96–97, for the convergence of views between North and South. The connection is found also in documents at the International Institute for Social History (hereafter, IISH), Amsterdam, Belgrade Six, UBA/CSD vrz 28/1/2, Press, *Gegenstimmen*, Nr. 18/5 (Winter 1984).

36. Egon Larsen, *A Flame in Barbed Wire: The Story of Amnesty International* (New York: W. W. Norton, 1979), 10, 119; for a more thorough historical account, see Tom Buchanan, "'The Truth Will Set You Free': The Making of Amnesty International," *Journal of Contemporary History* 37.4 (2002): 584, 592, 595. Its early relations to the British government were troubled. See as well Tom Buchanan, "Amnesty International in Crisis, 1966–7," *Twentieth Century British History* 15.3 (2004): 267–89, and Kirsten Sellars, *The Rise and Rise of Human Rights* (Phoenix Mill, U.K.: Sutton Press, 2002), 97–113.

37. Luard, "Promotion of Human Rights," 157.

38. "Introduction: The Anti-Apartheid Movement and the U.N," ANC documents, retrieved July 22, 2005, from http://www.anc.org.za/ancdocs/history/aam/aamhist.html, and Kader and Louise Asmal, "Anti-Apartheid Movements in Western Europe," retrieved July 22, 2005 from http://www.anc.org/za/anc docs/history/aam/kader12.html. Also, William Korey, *NGOs and the Universal Declaration of Human Rights: "A Curious Grapevine"* (New York: St. Martin's Press, 1998), 95–97.

39. In Fredrickson, *Black Liberation,* 267.

40. Vakani Collective, *South African Women,* 228–29.

41. "Free Nelson Mandela: An Account of the Campaign to Free Nelson Mandela and All Other Political Prisoners in South Africa," ANC documents, retrieved July 22, 2005, from http://www.anc.orz.za/ancdocs/history/aam/pris oner.html.

42. Klotz, *Norms,* 93–111, and U.S. Library of Congress statistics, retrieved July 22, 2005, from http://countrystudies.us/south-africa/84.htm.

43. ANC Historical Documents Archive, path: Selected Documents, 1985–1990, "ANC Call to the People," retrieved June 2, 2007, from http://www.anc .org.za/ancdocs/history/ungovern.html.

44. The full text is in Mary Frances Dominick, ed., *Human Rights and the Helsinki Accord: A Five Year Road to Madrid* (Nashville, Tenn.: William S. Hein & Co., 1981, rpt. for Transnational Legal Studies Program, Vanderbilt University School of Law), 335–402, quote at 336–37.

45. Vojin Dimitrijević, "The Place of Helsinki on the Long Road to Human Rights," in Dominick, *Human Rights,* 19. Innovations in law included a declaration (1966) and convention (1973) making apartheid a crime against humanity and, after 1975, the arms embargo, which was imposed by the Security Council in 1977. International lawyers agree that the techniques developed by the General Assembly and Security Council to deal with human rights violations were forged on "the anvil of the South African apartheid system." See Steiner and Alston, *International Human Rights,* 649.

46. Virginia A. Leary, "The Right of the Individual to Know and Act upon His Rights and Duties: Monitoring Groups and the Helsinki Final Act," in Dominick, *Human Rights,* 133.

47. Quotes from Leary, "The Right," 135–36 and Judt, *Postwar,* 434.

48. Kenney, *A Carnival,* 10.

49. For a succinct summary of contemporary views, see Judt, *Postwar,* 566–76, quote at 567.

50. From Roger Errera, "Charter 77 in Czechoslovakia and the International Protection of Human Rights," in Dominick, *Human Rights,* 172–74.

51. Larson, *A Flame,* 139–45.

52. For a typical approach, see *Violations of the Helsinki Accords: August 1983– September 1984. A Helsinki Watch Report, October 1984* (New York: Helsinki Watch, 1984).

53. Arthur J. Goldberg, "Human Rights and the Belgrade Meeting," in Dominick, *Human Rights,* 76–77, and Dante B. Fascell, "The CSCE Follow-Up Mechanism from Belgrade to Madrid," in Dominick, *Human Rights,* 110.

54. An archive of this trial is at the International Institute for Social History in Amsterdam, Holland, itself a major repository for materials on the history of international organizing. IISH, Amsterdam, UBA/CSD, Belgrade Six, 1984–85, Vladimir Mijanović, Milan Nikolić, and other Yugoslav intellectuals tried in Bel-

grade for illegal meetings and attempts at subversion of the state. For the quote, see 28.1/2, translated typescript from *Vrij Nederland,* Amsterdam, June 10, 1984.

55. IISH, UBA/CSD, 28.1/3 (support), Helsinki Watch Urgent Action, May 25, 1984.

56. Human Rights Watch, *Under Orders: War Crimes in Kosovo* (New York: Human Rights Watch, 2001), 17–27.

57. "Final Word of Milan Nikolic," (typescript), UBA/CSD, 28.2/1, No. 61, Belgrade, February 1, 1985 (estimated date), and 28.2, *Gegenstimmen,* No. 18.5 (Winter 1984): 1–27.

58. Ibid., 28.1/2, TAZ, June 6, 1984.

59. Ibid., 28/5, No. 22, Vladimir Mijanovic, "An Appeal to the Public"; the archive has articles from the *New York Times, Time* magazine, the *Washington Post, Le Monde,* the CSCE (Commission on Security and Cooperation in Europe) *News Release, Samizdat 84, Bulletin der Sozialistischen OstEuropakomites,* and many other publications.

60. Ibid., 28.1/3 (International Support), June 1984 to February 1985.

61. Ibid., 28.1 / 2 (press) clipping, the *Washington Post,* February 4, 1985; 28.1/3, Press release no. 64/85, Petra Kelly, "The Greens Will Continue to Follow the Trial of Belgrade Intellectuals."

62. Judt, *Postwar,* 606, 631.

63. Margaret E. Keck and Kathryn Sikkink, *Activists beyond Borders: Advocacy Networks in International Politics* (Ithaca, N.Y.: Cornell University Press, 1998), 28, and Audie Klotz, *Norms,* 3.

64. Since 1974, "human rights represents the fastest growing field of interest" for the independent Norwegian Nobel (Selection) Committee. See Geir Lundestad, "The Nobel Peace Prize, 1901–2000," retrieved June 3, 2007, from http://nobelprize.org/peace/articles/lundestad-review/index.html, and the Nobel Prize Internet Archive, from http://almaz.com/nobel/peace/prize.html.

65. Among other sources, see Jack Donnelly, "The Social Construction of International Human Rights," in *Human Rights in Global Politics,* ed. Tim Dunne and Nicholas J. Wheeler (Cambridge: Cambridge University Press, 1999), 77.

66. Tolley, *The U.N. Commission,* 176, in the case of Chile in 1978.

Chapter 3. Mothers' Courage and U.N. Monitoring of Disappearance, 1973–83

1. Howard Tolley, *The U.N. Commission on Human Rights* (Boulder, Colo.: Westview Press, 1987), 15, 33, 56–57.

2. Margaret E. Keck and Kathryn Sikkink, *Activists beyond Borders: Advocacy Networks in International Politics* (Ithaca, N.Y.: Cornell University Press, 1998), 88, 90. The quote from Johan Galtung is in Akira Iriye, *Global Community: The Role of International Organizations in the Making of the Contemporary World* (Berkeley: University of California Press, 2002), 133 and 129 (for the statistics).

3. A graphic example is General Heriberto Justo Auel, member of the Argentine military junta, whose retrospective view is in Eric Stener Carlson, *I Remember Julia: Voices of the Disappeared* (Philadelphia: Temple University Press, 1996), 147–50, a highly informative collection of firsthand accounts of disappearance.

4. *Disappeared! Technique of Terror: A Report for the Independent Commission on International Humanitarian Issues* (London: Zed Books, 1986), 31–47, which has a "new face of terror" as one of its chapter titles.

5. The Mothers are extremely well known in the human rights literature, and I have drawn on a range of sources for this section. For the general's quotes, see Iain Guest, *Behind the Disappearances: Argentina's Dirty War Against Human Rights and the United Nations* (Philadelphia: University of Pennsylvania Press, 1990), 21. Also Marguerite Guzman Bouvard, *Revolutionizing Motherhood: The Mothers of the Plaza de Mayo* (Wilmington, Del.: Scholarly Resources, 1994).

6. His statement is found in Carlson, *I Remember Julia*, 179.

7. These recollections were gathered by Bouvard, *Revolutionizing Motherhood*, 8, 72, 103.

8. Guest, *Behind the Disappearances*, 53, and Bouvard, *Revolutionizing Motherhood*, 65.

9. Carlson, *I Remember Julia*, 104–10.

10. Ibid., 9.

11. Bouvard, *Revolutionizing Motherhood*, 87.

12. Theo van Boven, *People Matter: Views on International Human Rights Policy*, collected and introduced by Hans Thoolen (Amsterdam: Meulenhoff, 1982), 6.

13. Geneva Convention Relative to the Protection of Civilian Persons in Time of War, August 12, 1949, in *Documents on the Laws of War*, ed. Adam Roberts and Richard Guelff, 2nd ed. (Oxford: Clarendon Press, 1989), 288, and Charles D. Smith, *Palestine and the Arab-Israeli Conflict: A History with Documents*, 6th ed. (Boston: Bedford/St. Martin's, 2007), 306–12.

14. Guest, *Behind the Disappearances*, Appendix 5, 439–41, and Tolley, *The U.N. Commission*, 61–82.

15. Guest, *Behind the Disappearances*, 442–44.

16. In Carlson, *I Remember Julia*, 74.

17. Dr. Esther Saavedra, in ibid., 47–48.

18. Guest, *Behind the Disappearances*, 214.

19. In Carlson, *I Remember Julia*, 30.

20. *Disappeared!*, 93, and van Boven, *People Matter*, 5, 8, 96.

21. In Carlson, *I Remember Julia*, 91.

22. Human Rights Watch, *Under Orders: War Crimes in Kosovo* (New York: Human Rights Watch, 2001), vi.

23. Guest, *Behind the Disappearances*, 101, and Bouvard, *Revolutionizing Motherhood*, 33. The company was Burson-Marsteller, a global public relations firm.

24. Guest, *Behind the Disappearances*, 97–98, 477–78, note 29.

25. Van Boven, *People Matter*, 6, 114, and Tolley, *The U.N. Commission*, 61, 98, 102–3.

26. "The Broadening and Deepening of the Human Rights Programme, Address at the opening of the Third Committee of the General Assembly at its Thirty-sixth Session," New York, September 23, 1981, in van Boven, *People Matter*, 29.

27. For the vivid details on this shift in operations, see David Kramer and David Weissbrodt, "The 1980 U.N. Commission on Human Rights and the Disappeared," Symposium: International Organization, *Human Rights Quarterly* 3.1 (February 1981): 18–33.

28. Tolley, *The U.N. Commission*, 104–6.

29. *Disappeared!*, 43.

30. Ibid., 46–47.

31. Keck and Sikkink, *Activists beyond Borders*, 88, 92. For U.S. policy, see Kenneth Cmiel, "The Emergence of Human Rights Politics in the United States," *Journal of American History* 86.3 (December 1999): 1, 235.

32. Bouvard, *Revolutionizing Motherhood*, 118, for Galtieri's role. "Word for Word: The 'Dirty War,'" *New York Times*, August 25, 2002, A10, reports on the declassification of 4,677 documents on human rights abuses in Argentina from U.S. archives.

33. "Brazil Opens Files on Region's Abuses in Age of Dictators," *New York Times*, June 9, 2000, A10.

34. Declaration on the Protection of All Persons from Enforced Disappearance, GAA/Res.47/113, December 18, 1992, with references to earlier resolutions, and Convention for the Protection of All Persons from Enforced Disappearance, adopted December 20, 2006 (not yet in force), retrieved June 14, 2007, from http://www.disappearances.org/mainfile.php/undoc/115/. The relatives' transnational organization (FEDEFAM) in the early 1980s wrote a first draft of this convention, which it submitted to the HRC, see *Disappeared!*, 36.

35. Margorie Agosin, "A Visit to the Mothers of the Plaza de Mayo," *Human Rights Quarterly* 9.3 (August 1987): 428.

36. In Keck and Sikkink, *Activists beyond Borders*, 96, and, for the Chile and Guatemala groups, Agosin, "A Visit," 429. For access to the Web site of the Committee of Relatives of Victims of Human Rights Violations in El Salvador ("Marianella Garcia Villas"), see Human Rights Internet, Canadian Partner Directory, retrieved July 23, 2005, from http://www.hri.ca/partners/directory.shtml.

37. The reports are found on the official Web site of the Inter-American Commission on Human Rights, retrieved June 3, 2004, from http://www.cidh.oas.org/countryrep/Chile74end/chap.16.htm and http://www.cidh.oas.org/countryrep/Argentina80eng/conclusions.htm .

38. Presentation speech, Oslo, Norway, December 10, 1977, retrieved June 15, 2007, from http://nobelprize.org/nobel_prizes/peace/laureates/1977/press.html.

39. Amnesty International, *Torture in the Eighties* (1984), excerpts in Richard Pierre Claude and Burns H. Weston, *Human Rights in the World Community: Issues and Actions*, 2nd ed. (Philadelphia: University of Pennsylvania Press, 1992), 79–90, quote at 79.

40. Guest, *Behind the Disappearances*, 342–43; Steven R. Ratner and Jason S. Abrams, *Accountability for Human Rights Atrocities in International Law: Beyond the Nuremberg Legacy*, 2nd ed. (Oxford: Oxford University Press, 2001), 364–65; Tolley, *The U.N. Commission*, 136–38.

41. These details are in Bouvard, *Revolutionizing Motherhood*, 255–57.

42. Guest, *Behind the Disappearances*, 151, 211, and Keck and Sekkink, *Activists beyond Borders*, 105.

43. Van Boven, *People Matter*, 10.

44. Of course, social memory is always multiple, complicated, and contradictory, which adds to the difficulties of political transitions. In another study, I have looked at the politics of memory in the context of nationalism; see Jean H. Quataert, *Staging Philanthropy: Patriotic Women and the National Imagination in Dynastic Germany, 1813–1916* (Ann Arbor: University of Michigan Press, 2001), chapter 6.

45. Carlson, *I Remember Julia*, 159–63. Because of his reputation for fairness and independence, in 2003 Ocampo was chosen to become the first chief prosecutor of the newly formed International Criminal Court.

46. "Truth Commission Digital Collection," United States Institute of Peace, retrieved June 16, 2007, from http://www.usip.org/library/truth.html. For a

critical account of the compromises in the establishment and operation of the South African model, see Richard A. Wilson, "Justice and Legitimacy in the South African Transition," in *The Politics of Memory: Transitional Justice in Democratizing Societies*, ed. Alexandra Barahona de Brito et al. (Oxford: Oxford University Press, 2001), 190–217.

47. Jacqueline Pitanguy, "Using Power to Transform," in *Look at the World Through Women's Eyes: Plenary Speeches from the NGO Forum on Women, Beijing '95*, ed. Eva Friedlander (New York: Women's Inc., 1996), 111–13; Asunción Lavrin, "Latin American Alternatives," Forum: International Feminisms, *Gender and History*, special issue 10.3 (November 1998): 523–27, including feminist critiques of the Mothers, and Mary E. John, "Feminisms and Internationalisms: A Response from India," in ibid., 546.

48. "Juana Beatrice Gutiérrez and the Mothers of East Los Angeles," in *Women Reshaping Human Rights: How Extraordinary Activists Are Changing the World*, ed. Marguerite Bouvard (Wilmington, Del.: Scholarly Resources, 1996), 179–97, and "Timeline," MADRE: Demanding Human Rights for Women and Families Around the World, retrieved June 16, 2007, from http://www.madre.org/press/timeline.html.

Part II. The Debate Continues

1. Ran Greenstein, "Socioeconomic Rights, Radical Democracy, and Power: South Africa as a Case Study," in *From the Margins of Globalization: Critical Perspectives on Human Rights*, ed. Neve Gordon (Lanham, Md.: Lexington Books, 2004), 121.

2. Elizabeth Thompson, *Colonial Citizens: Republican Rights, Paternal Privilege and Gender in French Syria and Lebanon* (New York: Columbia University Press, 2000), 260. The point is reinforced by Frederick Cooper who describes the increasing masculinization of public space in the new African independent nations, Cooper, *Africa since 1940: The Past of the Present* (Cambridge: Cambridge University Press, 2002), 125–27. This gender pact notwithstanding, repeated tension between secular nationalist and religious movements in the Middle East and elsewhere also have framed the agendas of the women's groups that became part of an emerging movement to define women's rights as human rights.

3. Odd Arne Westad, *The Global Cold War: Third World Interventions and the Making of Our Times* (Cambridge: Cambridge University Press, 2005), 75–77.

4. Howard Tolley Jr., *The U.N. Commission on Human Rights* (Boulder, Colo.: Westview Press, 1987), 38. Also, Adu Boahen, "Human Rights, Democracy and Economic Development," in *Africa in the Twentieth Century: The Adu Boahen Reader*, ed. Toyin Falola (Trenton, N.J.: African World Press, 2004), 462.

5. For information on this work, see Margaret Snyder, *Transforming Development: Women, Poverty and Politics* (London: IT Publications, 1995).

6. For the shift, see Tolley, *The U.N. Commission*, 87, 91, 99, and Henry J. Steiner and Philip Alston, "Comments on International Solidarity and the Rights to Development," in *International Human Rights in Context: Law, Politics, Morals*, 2nd ed., ed. Henry J. Steiner and Philip Alston (Oxford: Oxford University Press, 2000), 1319–20, which anchors the debate in its immediate historical context.

7. For an example of unfavorable conditions adversely affecting the poor, see Larry Rohter, "Brazil Collides with the I.M.F. over a Plan to Aid the Poor," in Steiner and Alston, *International Human Rights*, 1346–48, and Judith Blau and

Alberto Moncada, *Human Rights: Beyond the Liberal Vision* (Lanham, Md.: Rowman & Littlefield, 2005), who offer a systematic critique of the dominant neoliberal policies of powerful international financial institutions, using human rights criteria of social needs as their point of reference.

8. Blau and Moncada, *Human Rights*, offer an excellent summary of the different positions at stake.

Chapter 4. The Gender Factor since the 1970s

1. Diane Taylor, "Alicia Partnoy: A Portrait," in *The Politics of Motherhood: Activist Voices from Left to Right*, ed. Alexis Jetter, Annelise Orleck, and Diana Taylor (Hanover, N.H.: University Press of New England, 1997), 199.

2. This is another critical fault line in rights claims. For a detailed analysis of diverse lawyers' approaches to these contradictions, including concern with the feminist erosion of public and private spheres seen as a foundational norm in international legal traditions, see Karen Engle, "International Human Rights and Feminism," *Michigan Journal of International Law* 13 (1992): 525–31.

3. Glenn Ramsey, "Erotic Friendship, Gender Inversion, and Human Rights in the German Movement for Homosexual Reform, 1897–1933" (Ph.D. diss., Binghamton University, 2004), and John C. Fout, ed., *Forbidden History: The State, Society, and the Regulation of Sexuality in Modern Europe* (Chicago: University of Chicago Press, 1990).

4. Laura Reanda, "The Commission on the Status of Women," in *The United Nations and Human Rights: A Critical Appraisal*, ed. Philip Alston (Oxford: Clarendon Press, 1992), 267–303, and John P. Humphrey, *Human Rights and the United Nations: A Great Adventure* (Dobbs Ferry, N.Y.: Transnational Publishers, 1984), 19, who reminisces about the controversy to establish a separate women's commission. Also, John R. Mathiason, "The Long March to Beijing: The United Nations and the Women's Revolution, vol. 1, The Vienna Period," 19–20, retrieved June 22, 2007, from http://www.intlmgt.com/longmarch/Long %20March%202006.pdf. I thank the author for making his full manuscript available to me.

5. Margaret Snyder, *Transforming Development: Women, Poverty and Politics* (London: Intermediate Technology Publications, 1995), 9.

6. Mathiason, "The Long March," 28–29

7. Snyder, *Transforming Development*, 10.

8. In ibid., 11, 13.

9. Miriam Cooke, *Women Claim Islam: Creating Islamic Feminism through Literature* (New York: Routledge, 2001), vii, adding that "Arab women, historically invisible, are part of the trend."

10. Avronne S. Fraser, *The U.N. Decade for Women: Documents and Dialogue* (Boulder, Colo.: Westview Press, 1987).

11. Ibid., 66–67.

12. Snyder, *Transforming Development*, 49.

13. Fraser, *The U.N. Decade*, 17, 58, 78, 147; *Report of the World Conference to Review and Appraise the Achievements of the United Nations Decade for Women: Equality, Development, and Peace, Nairobi, 15–26 July 1985* (New York: United Nations, 1986), 93–94; Eva Friedlander, ed., *Look at the World Through Women's Eyes: Plenary Speeches from the NGO Forum on Women, Beijing '95* (New York: Women, Ink, 1996), xvii, 3–6.

14. Fraser, *The U.N. Decade*, 210.

15. The U.S. signed the convention in 1980 but still has not ratified it. The country reports are available on the Web, from http://www.un.org/women watch/daw/cedaw/reports.htm.

16. Rebecca J. Cook, "State Accountability under the Convention on the Elimination of All Forms of Discrimination Against Women," in *Human Rights of Women: National and International Perspectives*, ed. Rebecca J. Cook (Philadelphia: University of Pennsylvania Press, 1994), 235.

17. Fran P. Hosken, *The Hosken Report: Genital and Sexual Mutilation of Females*, 3rd rev. ed. (Lexington, Mass.: Women's International Network News, 1982).

18. Similar changes were also taking place among feminist international lawyers in the mid-1980s. For a recollection of growing dissatisfaction with the dominant lines of jurisprudence, see Engle, "International Human Rights," 601. See also, Rhonda Copelon, "Intimate Terror: Understanding Domestic Violence as Torture," in Cook, *Human Rights*, 116–52. The focus on torture arguably reflects the heightened international attention on the abuse through the Argentine Mothers' mobilizations at the time.

19. Found in Elisabeth Friedman, "Women's Human Rights: The Emergence of a Movement," in *Women's Rights, Human Rights: International Feminist Perspectives*, ed. Julia Stone Peters and Andrea Wolper (New York: Routledge, 1995), 31.

20. Howard Tolley, *The U.N. Commission on Human Rights* (Boulder, Colo.: Westview Press, 1987), 176.

21. Radhika Coomaraswamy, "Reinventing International Law: Women's Rights as Human Rights in the International Community," in *Debating Human Rights: Critical Essays from the United States and Asia*, ed. Peter Van Ness (London: Routledge, 1999), 174.

22. Cooke, *Women Claim*, xi, and "The Rise of Conservatism and Its Various Forms—Strategies," Sunera Thobani, moderator, in *Look at the World* (Beijing), 147–57. Also, Jean H. Quataert, *The Gendering of Human Rights in the International Systems of Law in the Twentieth Century* (Washington, D.C.: American Historical Association, 2006), 35–38.

23. Sally Engle Merry, *Human Rights and Gender Violence: Translating International Law into Local Justice* (Chicago: University of Chicago Press, 2006), 135–37.

24. Information on MADRE philosophy, operations, and programs is found on the Web at http://madre.org/index.html, path: programs, where we work.

25. The so-called generations of rights are denoted chronologically. This book's organization, however, discusses gender mobilizations before those for economic rights and, thus, I address the third generation in the next chapter.

26. Coomaraswamy, "Reinventing," 178.

27. Copelon, "Intimate Terror," 121–23, 135, and Celina Romany, "State Responsibility Goes Private: A Feminist Critique of the Public/Private Distinction in International Human Rights Law," in Cook, *Human Rights*, 85–115.

28. Kenneth Roth, "Domestic Violence as an International Human Rights Issue," in Cook, *Human Rights*, 327–29.

29. *The Human Rights Watch Global Report on Women's Human Rights* (New York: Human Rights Watch, 1995). Amnesty International's current campaigns (2007) include a "stop violence against women" mobilization, retrieved June 26, 2007, from http://www.amnesty.org/campaign/.

30. Full details of the global campaign are in Charlotte Bunch and Niamh Reilly, *Demanding Accountability: The Global Campaign and Vienna Tribunal for Women's Human Rights* (New York: Center for Women's Global Leadership, 1994).

31. Ibid., 23, 78–79.

32. "The Vienna Tribunal," VHS, by Gerry Rogers (Women Make Movies, 1994).

33. For a cultural relativist defense, see Chris Brown, "Universal Human Rights: A Critique," in *Human Rights in Global Politics*, ed. Tim Dunne and Nicholas J. Wheeler (Cambridge: Cambridge University Press, 1999), 103–27, and, for a critique, see Ken Booth, "Three Tyrannies," in ibid., 36, for the quote.

34. As found in the essay by Radhika Coomaraswamy, "To Bellow Like a Cow: Women, Ethnicity, and the Discourse of Rights," in Cook, *Human Rights*, 43–45.

35. Insook Kwon, "'The New Women's Movement' in 1920s Korea: Rethinking the Relationship between Imperialism and Women," *Gender and History* 10.3 (November 1998): 381–405; Mary E. John, "Feminisms and Internationalisms: A Response from India," in ibid., 539–48; and Florence Butegwa, "Using the African Charter on Human and People's Rights to Secure Women's Access to Land in Africa," in Cook, *Human Rights*, 495–514.

36. For a short discussion of the Asian values debate, see Quataert, *The Gendering*, 36–38. It also is not surprising that governments, too, have attached the largest number of reservations to the Women's Convention than to any other international human rights treaty, although the picture is not static. The reservations are at the U.N. Web site "Declarations, Reservations and Objections to CEDAW," retrieved October 30, 2005, from http://www.un.org/womenwatch/daw/cedaw/reservations-country.htm. For a legal assessment, see Rebecca Cook, "State Accountability," 228–56.

37. Nahid Toubia, *Female Genital Mutilation: A Call for Global Action* (New York: Women, Ink, 1995), 7. The full name of the organization is Research, Action and Information Network for the Bodily Integrity of Women.

38. For defenders of the practice, the term "mutilation" carries harsh connotations, expressing a powerful global consensus and shutting out alternative views. For a positive assessment of this ceremony based on ethnographic evidence from Africa, see Richard A. Shweder, "What about 'Female Genital Mutilation'? And Why Understanding Culture Matters in the First Place," *Daedalus* 129.4 (Fall 2000): 209–33. I use the term "mutilation" or "cutting" as the particular activists in the local setting use it, recognizing that words matter.

39. "Body Literacy in Eastern Africa," retrieved June 8, 2004, from http://www.womankind.org.uk/four%20literacies/bodylit/eafricapf.h tml. (This site no longer exists.) See the WOMANKIND Worldwide Web site at http://www.womankind.org.uk/faqs.html.

40. Toubia, *Female*, 21. The ceremonial cutting is much more radical than male circumcision, with which it often is compared. In its most intrusive form, infibulation, much of the girl's vagina is cut away. In its mildest form, the clitoris is still removed, and debate exists on its effects on women's sexual feelings.

41. Despite claims that the practice is based on Islam, its adoption did not follow the spread of Islam. There are many Islamic countries where FGM is not practiced as, for example, in Saudi Arabia, Turkey, and Pakistan. It also is found among Christians in Egypt and Ethiopia and was prevalent among certain tribes of Ethiopian Jews, including the Falashas (although since going to Israel, the practice seems to have died out). Anika Rahman and Nahid Toubia, *Female Genital Mutilation: A Guide to Laws and Policies Worldwide* (London: Zed Books, 2001), 6, and Toubia, *Female*, 31–34.

42. Rahman and Toubia, *Female*, 20–31, and Henry J. Steiner and Philip Alston, *International Human Rights in Context: Law, Politics, Morals* (Oxford: Oxford University Press, 2000), 409–25. For the ban on FGM, see BBC News, "New Call to Ban Female Mutilation," September 19, 2004, retrieved June 3, 2008, from http://news.bbc.co.uk/2/hi/africa/3669762.stm.

43. Mark Lacey, "Genital Cutting Shows Signs of Losing Favor in Africa," *New York Times*, June 8, 2004, A3. An interview with Jessica Neuwirth, who helped found Equality Now in 1992, is in *Women Reshaping Human Rights: How Extraordinary Activists Are Changing the World*, ed. Marguerite Guzman Bouvard (Wilmington, Del.: Scholarly Resources, 1996), 235–54. Equality Now connects several thousand individuals and groups in sixty-five countries to support action.

44. "Body Literacy in Eastern Africa," WOMANKIND Website that no longer exists.

45. Herbert S. Lewis, "Ethnicity in Ethiopia: The View from Below (and from the South, East, and West)," in *The Rising Tide of Cultural Pluralism: The Nation-State at Bay?*, ed. Crawford Young (Madison: University of Wisconsin Press, 1993), 158–78, and Lovise Aalen, "Ethnic Federalism and Self-Determination for Nationalities in a Non-Democratic State: The Case of Ethiopia," *International Journal on Minority and Group Rights* 13.2–3 (2006): 243–61. For detailed information on Kembata, a site run by a diasporic community in the United States, "Kambata Development Network," retrieved June 4, 2008, from http://www.kdneth.org/. Note that the spelling of Kembata varies in the literature.

46. Shweder, "What about 'Female Genital Mutilation'?" 5 (online), and M. Gebre-Medhin and K. Missailidis, "Female Genital Mutilation in Eastern Ethiopia," *Lancet* 356.9224 (July 8, 2000): 137–38.

47. Atango Chesoni and Grace Githaiga, "Enhancing Ethiopian Women's Access to and Control over Land: The Second Workshop," in *Women and Land in Africa: Culture, Religion and Realizing Women's Rights*, ed. L. Muthoni Wanyeki (London: Zed Books, 2003), 340–74, report. See also "Profile: Bogaletch Gebre," *Lancet* (British edition) 369.9579 (June 2007): 2,071.

48. The Web site of the KMG is http://www.kmgselfhelp.org (hereafter, KMG), path: how we started.

49. KMG, path: Eradication of FGM and Environment.

50. Ibid., path: comments about KMG's work.

51. Merry, *Human Rights*, 193.

52. For Fauziya Kassindja's case, see her memoir, written with Layli Miller Bashir, *Do They Hear You When You Cry* (New York: Delacorte, 1998). Note that the official title of the case misspells her name. Also, for an overview on gender-based asylum cases, see Center for American Progress, path: International Women's Day 2007, retrieved July 1, 2007, from http://www.americanprogress.org/.

53. Council of Europe, European Court of Human Rights, *Survey of Activities, 2002*, Registrar of the European Court of Human Rights (Provisional Version), 15, 31, and press releases issued by the Registrar of the European Court of Human Rights, Chamber Judgments Concerning Austria, France, Germany, and the United Kingdom, retrieved June 12, 2003, from www.echr.coe.int/Eng/Edocs/2002 Survey.

54. *Lawrence and Garner v. Texas*, No. 02-102, Westlaw, 539 U.S. 558, 123 S. Ct. 2472, 9, and "In a Momentous Term, Justices Remake the Law, and the Court," *New York Times*, July 1, 2003, A1, 18.

Chapter 5. Citizenship, Socioeconomic Rights, and the Courts in the Age of Transnational Migrations

1. Both quotes are found in Theo van Boven, *People Matter: Views on International Human Rights Policy* (Amsterdam: Meulenhoff, 1982), 25–26, 174.

2. Howard Tolley, *The U.N. Commission on Human Rights* (Boulder, Colo.: Westview Press, 1987), 142–44.

3. Ibid., 153.

4. Margaret Snyder, *Transforming Development: Women, Poverty and Politics* (London: Intermediate Technology Publications, 1995), 23, and Judith Blau and Alberto Moncada, *Human Rights: Beyond the Liberal Vision* (Lanham, Md.: Rowman & Littlefield, 2005), 90–91.

5. In Charlotte Bunch and Niamh Reilly, *Demanding Accountability: The Global Campaign and Vienna Tribunal for Women's Human Rights* (New Brunswick, N.J.: Center for Women's Global Leadership, 1994), 71, and Blau and Moncada, *Human Rights*, 95.

6. See, for example, Myron Weiner, *The Global Migration Crisis: Challenge to States and to Human Rights* (New York: Longman, 1995), 123.

7. "Economic, Social and Cultural Rights," retrieved July 6, 2007, from http://www.hrw.org/doc/?t=esc, and "Twenty Years of Women Recreating the World," retrieved July 6, 2007, from http://madre.org/articles/int/fall03nl.html.

8. Inter-American Court of Human Rights, Series E, Provisional Measures, *Case of Haitians and Haitian-Origin Dominicans in the Republic* (Dominican Republic), 12.271, retrieved December 16, 2004, from http://www.corteidh.or.cr/index_ing.html, path: jurisprudence, provisional measures.

9. Although globalization may be deterritorializing citizenship for more privileged mobile economic groups, it is not doing the same for the unskilled and "illegal" migrant, for whom the nation-state appears as "hard" as ever. Thomas Blom Hansen and Finn Stepputat, "Introduction," in *Sovereign Bodies: Citizens, Migrants, and States in the Postcolonial World*, ed. Thomas Blom Hansen and Finn Stepputat (Princeton, N.J.: Princeton University Press, 2005), 34.

10. Van Boven, *People Matter*, 176.

11. For a sophisticated analysis of the contradictions of globalization, see Saskia Sassen, *Globalization and Its Discontents: Essays on the New Mobility of People and Money* (New York: New Press, 1998).

12. In Johannes Morsink, *The Universal Declaration of Human Rights: Origins, Drafting and Intent* (Philadelphia: University of Pennsylvania Press, 1999), 81.

13. Benny Morris, *The Birth of the Palestinian Refugee Problem, 1947–1949* (Cambridge: Cambridge University Press, 1987), 1, 142–54. December 11, 1948, one day after proclaiming the Universal Declaration, the General Assembly Resolution 194 (III) affirmed the right of the refugees to return to their homes. Also, International Quaker Working Party on Israel and Palestine, *When the Rain Returns: Toward Justice and Reconciliation in Palestine and Israel* ([Philadelphia]: American Friends Service Committee, 2004), 115.

14. David Jacobson, *Rights across Borders: Immigration and the Decline of Citizenship* (Baltimore: Johns Hopkins University Press, 1996), 14.

15. Data collected by the U.N. Department of Economic and Social Affairs in preparation for a General Assembly meeting on migration and development. U.N. International Migration and Development, press release, September 12, 2005; for refugee statistics, see UNHCR, retrieved June 25, 2007 from http://www.unhcr.org/statistics.html, path: 2006 global trends.

16. Felicia Mello, "Coming to America," *The Nation*, June 25, 2007, 14–24, quote at 14.

17. "In Brooklyn Woman's Past, a Story of Caribbean Striving," *New York Times*, June 28, 2003, A1, B2.

18. Sassen, *Globalization*, xxxvi, note 12.

19. "Declaration on the Right to Development," General Assembly Resolution 41/128, December 1986, and Blau and Moncada, *Human Rights*, 55–56.

20. Tolley, *The U.N. Commission*, 216.

21. Blau and Moncada, *Human Rights*, 138.

22. Ran Greenstein, "Socioeconomic Rights, Radical Democracy, and Power: South Africa as a Case Study," in *From the Margins of Globalization: Critical Perspectives on Human Rights*, ed. Neve Gordon (Lanham, Md.: Lexington Books, 2004).

23. Gillian Hart, *Disabling Globalization: Places of Power in Post-Apartheid South Africa* (Berkeley: University of California Press, 2002), and Greenstein, "Socioeconomic Rights," 93. I draw heavily on Greenstein's article for this analysis.

24. Greenstein, "Socioeconomic Rights," 102, 104–5.

25. Ibid., 98, for his overall assessment, and 114–20 for details on the HIV/AIDS campaigns.

26. "Lindela: At the Crossroads for Detention and Repatriation: An Assessment of the Conditions of Detention by the South African Human Rights Commission," Johannesburg, December 2000, retrieved June 25, 2007, from http://www.queensu.ca/samp/migrationresources/xenophobia/reports/ sahrc1.pdf

27. Each of these organizations has a Web site. The Migrant Rights convention is found at http://www.migrantsrights.org/Int_Conv_Prot_Rights_Mig Workers_Fam_1999_En.htm.

28. Richard Lewis Siegel, *Employment and Human Rights: The International Dimension* (Philadelphia: University of Pennsylvania Press, 1994), and Jacobson, *Rights*, 63.

29. Loren Landau, "Migration, Urbanisation and Sustainable Livelihoods in South Africa," Migration Policy Brief No. 15 (2005), retrieved July 17, 2007, from the Queen's University Web site, http://www.queensu.ca/search/. Also, Patricia Hyndman, "Cultural Legitimacy in the Formulation and Implementation of Human Rights Law and Policy in Australia," in *Human Rights in Cross-Cultural Perspectives: A Quest for Consensus*, ed. Abdullahi Ahmed An-Na'im (Philadelphia: University of Pennsylvania Press, 1992), 320.

30. Jacobson, *Rights*, 14.

31. Weiner, *The Global Migration Crisis*, 81.

32. *Farhat v. Kuwait*, A petition filed with the United Nations Commission on Human Rights Pursuant to Resolution 1503, December 13, 1992, retrieved July 17, 2007, from Project Diana, online human rights archive, http://www.yale.edu/lawweb/avalon/diana/farhat/farhat.htm. The Center for Constitutional Rights also has a site, at http://www.ccr-y.org/v2/about/mission_vision.asp.

33. The United States ratified the International Covenant on Civil and Political Rights (one of the very few international treaties to which it has acceded), for example, but only on the condition that it was not "self-executing and did not itself create obligations enforceable in federal courts." Explained by the majority in *Sosa v. Alvarez-Machain*, Nos. 03-339, 03-485, Westlaw, 124, S. Ct. 2739, 25, decided June 29, 2004.

34. "U.S. Supreme Court Delegation to Visit European Court and Commis-

sion of Human Rights," *Human Rights News* 488 (July 9, 1998), press release, retrieved December 9, 2004, from http://www.echr.coe.int/.

35. Jacobson, *Rights,* 97, and Sassen, *Globalization,* 13. Also, Farooq Hassan, "The Doctrine of Incorporation: New Vistas for the Enforcement of International Human Rights?" *Human Rights Quarterly* 5 (1983): 69, 84.

36. *Rodriguez-Fernandez v. Wilkinson,* No. 81-1238, Westlaw, 654 F.2d 1382.

37. Megan Peitzke, "The Fate of 'Unremovable' Aliens Before and After September 11, 2001: The Supreme Court's Presumptive Six-Month Limit to Post-Removal-Period Detention," *Pepperdine Law Review* 30 (May 2003): 2.

38. *Ma v. Reno,* 99-35976, U.S. Court of Appeals for the Ninth Circuit. Also "Supreme Court Bars Government from Holding Aliens in Detention Indefinitely If Removal Is Not Foreseeable," *Zadvydas v. Davis,* 121 S. Ct. 2491 (2001), Poverty Law Library, Detention Case List, and *Ma v. Ashcroft,* July 27, 2001, OOC. D.O.S. 6360, on remand from the U.S. Supreme Court. Similar cases are pending in Nevada and the central, eastern, and southern districts of California.

39. Mirta Ojito "The Long Voyage from Mariel Ends," *New York Times,* January 16, 2005, Week in Review, 3.

40. As found in Hassan, "The Doctrine," 71.

41. Peitzke, "The Fate," 11–12, for NGO responses.

42. Ibid., 12–15, for the threats since 9/11.

43. "The European Convention and Its Protocols," retrieved December 22, 2004, from http://www.echr.coe.int/.

44. Jacobson, *Rights,* 91.

45. Council of Europe, European Court of Human Rights, *East African Asians v. United Kingdom* 3, E.H.R.R. 76 (1981), retrieved June 12, 2003, from Public Interest Law Initiative, http://www.pili.org/resources/discrimination/coe.htm, path: European Court of Human Rights Case Law. This judgment also shows the fluidity of protections for individuals and groups under the human rights rubric.

46. Emma Crewe and Uma Kothari, "Gujurati Migrants' Search for Modernity in Britain," in *Gender and Migration,* ed. Caroline Sweetman (Oxford: Oxfam, 1998), 13–20, interviews in Wellingborough with people in communities of South Gujarati, who either moved directly to Great Britain from India or, as "twice migrated," arrived through East Africa. Of similar background, they are not the same individuals as the plaintiffs.

47. *Abdulaziz, Cabales, and Balkandali v. United Kingdom,* Series A, No 94, 15/198/71/107–109, decided May 28, 1985, A, 59, 60.

48. *Berrehab v. The Netherlands,* 3/1987/126/177, decided June 21, 1988, and *Djeroud v. France,* 34/1990/225/289, decided January 23, 1991. For an overview of the immigration cases, European Court of Human Rights, retrieved December 28, 2004, from http://www.echr.coe.int/Eng/Judgments.htm, path: Search the Case-Law-HUDOC.

49. "The Right to Information on Consular Assistance." Also, Inter-American Court of Human Rights, provisional measures, *Case of Helen Mack-Chang vs. Guatemala,* concerning the disappearance of Myrna Mack, 2002, as found at http://www.corteidh.or.cr/medidas.cfm.

50. The Inter-American Commission on Human Rights, Organization of American States, "Report on the Situation of Human Rights in the Dominican Republic," OEA/Ser. L/V/II.104, October 7, 1999, 14, retrieved December 19, 2004, from http://www.cidh.oas.org/pais.eng.htm, path: Country Reports, Dominican Republic 1999.

51. Ibid., 10–13, path: status of permanent illegality.

52. Ibid., 15.

53. For follow-up briefs and rulings, "Order of the Inter-American Court of Human Rights of February 2, 2006," path: Jurisprudence, by country (Dominican Republic), Provisional Matters February 2, 2006, retrieved July 18, 2007, from http://www.corteidh.or.cr/index.cfm.

54. The NGO National Coalition for Haitian Rights, court decisions, retrieved August 9, 2004, from http://www.nchr.org/hrp/dr/report_cases.htm.

55. In Steven R. Ratner and Jason S. Abrams, *Accountability for Human Rights Atrocities in International Law: Beyond the Nuremberg Legacy*, 2nd ed. (Oxford: Oxford University Press, 2001), 395.

56. The original case is *Filartiga v. Pena-Irala*, No. 191, Docket 79-6090, decided June 30, 1980, Westlaw 630 F.2d 876; the recent case, *Sosa v. Alvarez-Machain*, 22. The court ruled against the petitioner but nonetheless upheld the federal jurisdiction of the Alien Tort Claims Aact. Also, Richard Alan White, *Breaking Silence: The Case that Changed the Face of Human Rights* (Washington, D.C.: Georgetown University Press, 2004).

57. A detailed explanation of the *Wiwa* case is at the center's Web site, retrieved November 19, 2008 from www.ccrjustice.org, path, our cases, no. 45.

58. Jacobson, *Rights*, 119.

59. Landau, "Migration," 4.

60. *Plyler v. Doe*, 457 U.S. 202 (1982), 457 U.S. 202, retrieved December 31, 2004, from http://www.tourolaw.edu/patch/Plyler/. Interestingly, the plaintiffs based their case on international law; the judges, however, ruled on the Fourteenth Amendment. See also Jacobson, *Rights*, 104–5, for discussion of the debates around Proposition 187. For the Arizona proposition, see *Arizona Republic*, online print edition, retrieved December 23, 2004, from http://www.azcentral.com/.

61. For a broad overview, see Rey Koslowski, *Migrants and Citizens: Demographic Change in the European State System* (Ithaca, N.Y.: Cornell University Press, 2000).

62. The MUDHA is a partner in the Minority Rights Group International advocacy coalition on rights and development. Solange Pierre, "Court Victory for Expelled Haitians," retrieved August 4, 2004, from http://www.minorityrights.org.

Part III. Human Rights at a Crossroads

1. Historical Documents, Part I: ANC Documents; Part II: World Against Apartheid and International Solidarity with the Liberation Struggle; and Part III: Biographies, retrieved July 14, 2007, from http://www.anc.org.za/ancdocs/history/.

2. For details on the extraordinary changes at the political level in Europe, see Tony Judt, *Postwar: A History of Europe Since 1945* (New York: Penguin Books, 2005), 637–57. Following a similar trend, widespread popular discontent overthrew the Indonesian strongman, Mohamed Suharto, in 1998.

3. Toyin Falola, ed., *Africa in the Twentieth Century: The Adu Boahen Reader* (Trenton, N.J.: Africa World Press, 2004), 461, and Frederick Cooper, *Africa Since 1940: The Past of the Present* (Cambridge: Cambridge University Press, 2002), 181.

4. For a sensitive account of the conflict that adopts the perspective of

Israeli-Palestinian groups working for peace between the two societies, see International Quaker Working Party on Israel and Palestine, *When the Rain Returns: Toward Justice and Reconciliation in Palestine and Israel* ([Philadelphia]: American Friends Service Committee, 2004). The authors show that as late as March 1980, the United States accepted Security Council Resolution 465, which condemned Israeli settlement policy as a "flagrant violation of the Fourth Geneva Convention" (197).

5. Ibid., 85.

6. William G. O'Neill, "Gaining Compliance without Force: Human Rights Field Operations," in *Civilians in War*, ed. Simon Chesterman (Boulder, Colo.: Lynne Rienner, 2001), 98.

7. *The Lost Agenda: Human Rights and UN Field Operations* (New York: Human Rights Watch, 1993), 1.

8. Claude Bruderlein, "The End of Innocence: Humanitarian Protection in the Twenty-First Century," in Chesterton, *Civilians in War*, 221–22.

9. Renate Bloem, "The Role of NGOs in the Age of a Democratic Civil Society," September 28, 2001, Address to the Conference of NGOs, retrieved May 15, 2007, from http://www.globalpolicy.org/ngos/role/policymk/select/2001/0927co ngo.htm. India, for example, had about 1 million NGOs and Brazil, 210,000, according to her data. For the earlier figures, see Akira Iriye, *Global Community: The Role of International Organizations in the Making of the Contemporary World* (Berkeley: University of California Press, 2002), 129. Similar grassroots developments are taking place in China, even in the face of restrictions on association, independent politics, and human rights advocacy. Howard French, "Citizens' Groups Take Root Across China," *New York Times*, February 15, 2007, A8.

10. *The Lost Agenda*, 10.

Chapter 6. Ethnic Violence, Humanitarian Intervention, and Criminal Accountability in the 1990s

1. Edward C. Luck, "The Enforcement of Humanitarian Norms and the Politics of Ambivalence," in *Civilians in War*, ed. Simon Chesterman (Boulder, Colo.: Lynne Rienner, 2001), 198.

2. For the statistics, see Philip Gourevitch, *We Wish to Inform You That Tomorrow We Will Be Killed with Our Families: Stories from Rwanda* (New York: Farrar Straus and Giroux, 1998), 133; for the wider African picture, see Frederick Cooper, *Africa since 1940: The Past of the Present* (Cambridge: Cambridge University Press, 2002), 191–92. For a critical account of the ethnic cleansing that "evokes genocide," see René Lemarchand, *Burundi: Ethnocide as Discourse and Practice* (Cambridge: Cambridge University Press, 1994), xi.

3. Scott Strauss, "Darfur and the Genocide Debate," *Foreign Affairs* 84.1 (January/February 2005): 123–33.

4. Konrad H. Jarausch and Michael Geyer, *Shattered Pasts: Reconstructing German Histories* (Princeton, N.J.: Princeton University Press, 2003), 115.

5. Béatrice Pouligny, *Peace Operations Seen from Below: UN Missions and Local People* (Bloomfield, Conn.: Kumarian, 2006), 180.

6. Some historians recently have used the term "humanitarian intervention" for the nineteenth-century Concert of Europe policies protecting minorities (Christians) in the Ottoman Empire. These treaties more properly resemble the "unequal treaty system" imposed by the imperialist powers on China and Japan at the time. For an early but careful assessment of European public law,

see Arthur Nussbaum, *A Concise History of the Law of Nations* (New York: Macmillan Company, 1950). In its universal reach, the 1990s doctrine of humanitarian intervention was new to the international scene.

7. David Rieff, *A Bed for the Night: Humanitarianism in Crisis* (New York: Simon & Schuster, 2002), 247.

8. William G. O'Neill, "Gaining Compliance Without Force: Human Rights Field Operations," in *Civilians in War*, ed. Simon Chesterman (Boulder, Colo.: Lynne Rienner, 2001), 99.

9. Ibid., 96, for the Rwandan report. See also *The Lost Agenda: Human Rights and UN Field Operations* (New York: Human Rights Watch, 1993), 8.

10. *The Lost Agenda*, 156–57.

11. Among other examples, the following NGOs favored the NATO bombing campaign in 1999: Human Rights Watch (earlier it had called the situation in Rwanda a "political" problem), MSF, ICR, CARE, the Sphere Project, formed by a coalition of humanitarian agencies in 1997, which advocated the "right to assistance," and also U.S. InterAction (the American Council for Voluntary International Action). Rieff, *A Bed*, 208–12, and Barbara Crossette, "U.N. Chief Wants Faster Action to Avoid Slaughter in Civil Wars," *New York Times*, September 21, 1999, A1, 12.

12. Here I am not offering a full account of the political details of each crisis; many excellent studies do just that. Among others, Peter Uvin, *Aiding Violence: The Development Enterprise in Rwanda* (West Hartford, Conn.: Kumarian Press, 1998), has an excellent summary of political events. Also, Thomas G. Weiss and Amir Pasic, "Dealing with the Displacement and Suffering Caused by Yugoslavia's Wars," in *The Forsaken People: Case Studies of the Internally Displaced*, ed. Roberta Cohen and Francis M. Deng (Washington, D.C.: Brookings Institution Press, 1998), and *Under Orders: War Crimes in Kosovo* (New York: Human Rights Watch, 2001).

13. Larry Minear and Randolph C. Kent, "Rwanda's Internally Displaced: A Conundrum within a Conundrum," in Cohen and Deng, *The Forsaken People*, 88–89; Weiss and Pasic, "Dealing," in Cohen and Deng, *The Forsaken People*, 207; and Strauss, "Darfur."

14. Aimable Twagilimana, *The Debris of Ham: Ethnicity, Regionalism, and the 1994 Rwandan Genocide* (Lanham, Md.: University Press of America, 2003), 170; Rieff, *A Bed*, 131; and *The Lost Agenda*, 100.

15. Gourevitch, *We Wish*, 212–13, quoting Susan Woodward.

16. Twagilimana, *The Debris*, 11, 33–34, 45.

17. The precise ethnic mapping is too complex to duplicate here, but I have indicated the main contours of the particular ethnicities at work in postcommunist Yugoslavia. Here I draw on Weiss and Pasic, "Dealing," 183–91, and documents on the indictments in Norman Cigar and Paul Williams, eds., *Indictment at the Hague: The Milosevic Regime and Crimes of the Balkan Wars* (New York: New York University Press, 2002).

18. Twagilimana, *The Debris*, 11.

19. Pouligny, *Peace Operations*, 33, 43, from her observations on the ground.

20. *The Lost Agenda*, 85–95.

21. Higgins quote in Weiss and Pasic, "Dealing," 199; for Brauman, see Rieff, *A Bed*, 166.

22. Pouligny, *Peace Operations*, 203–4, and *The Lost Agenda*, 91–92.

23. *The Lost Agenda*, 97–98.

24. Steven Erlanger, "Aide Takes Stock of U.N. in Kosovo," *New York Times*,

July 17, 2000, A4, and the Doctors without Borders Web site at http://www.doct orswithoutborders.org.

25. Pouligny, *Peace Operations*, 127, and Cigar and Williams, *Indictment*, 181–91.

26. "Srebrenica: A Cry from the Grave," PBS, path: Eyewitness Accounts, retrieved July 29, 2007, from http://www.pbs.org/wnet/cryfromthegrave/eye witnesses/kadir.html.

27. Ibid., path: Eyewitness Accounts, Paul Groenewegen, Hasan Nuhanovic, Zumra Shekhomerovic.

28. Uvin, *Aiding Violence*, and Mary Kaldor, "Transnational Civil Society," in *Human Rights in Global Politics*, ed. Tim Dunne and Nicholas J. Wheeler (Cambridge: Cambridge University Press, 1999).

29. Pouligny, *Peace Operations*, 67–87, has an informative section on indigenous "civil society."

30. Uvin, *Aiding Violence*, 163–67.

31. Ibid., 174–78.

32. Gourevitch, *We Wish*, 163.

33. It is no wonder that Gourevitch subtitled his account "Stories from Rwanda." For the financial costs, see ibid., 270, 315, and, for the Biberson quote, see Rieff, *A Bed*, 167.

34. Weiss and Pasic, "Dealing," 201. My subdivision title comes from Steven R. Ratner and Jason S. Abrams, *Accountability for Human Rights Atrocities in International Law: Beyond the Nuremberg Legacy*, 2nd ed. (Oxford: Oxford University Press, 2001). For the sources of law, see Hilary Charlesworth and Christine Chinkin, *The Boundaries of International Law: A Feminist Analysis* (Manchester, U.K.: Juris Publishing, 1988), 62–63.

35. In Weiss and Pasic, "Dealing," 201; Ratner and Abrams, *Accountability*, 191, italics in the original; Gourevitch, *We Wish*, 253.

36. For the investigation that led to the resignations, see "Report Blames Dutch Leaders, U.N. for Massacres in Bosnia," *Press and Sun-Bulletin* (Binghamton, New York), April 11, 2002, A3.

37. Pouligny, *Peace Operations*, 260, 262, and the summary views of Slavica Kušić are in Charlotte Bunch and Niamh Reilly, *Demanding Accountability: The Global Campaign and Vienna Tribunal for Women's Human Rights* (New Brunswick, N.J.: Center for Women's Global Leadership, 1994), 40.

38. For these details, I used the official Web sites of both tribunals: for Rwanda, http://www.ictr.org, and for Yugoslavia, http://www.un.org/icty/. In addition, press release, SC/8252, "Brief: Security Council on Progress towards Concluding Trials by 2008, November 11, 2004."

39. An official Bosnian Serb commission report in November 2004 on the massacre at Srebrenica admitted the killings had been fully planned, *New York Times*, November 9, 2004, A4.

40. For details on the *gaccaca* (the spelling varies) courts: AI Rwanda, "Gacaca: A Question of Justice," December 17, 2002, retrieved July 31, 2007, from the Amnesty International Web site, library, AI index, AFR 47/007/2002. Only in 2007, furthermore, did the parliament end capital punishment, setting the stage for the extradition to Rwanda of suspects from Europe, West Africa, and North America. The international tribunals had made ending the death penalty a precondition for transferring accused suspects to the national judiciary, *New York Times*, July 28, 2007, A6.

41. Bunch and Reilly, *Demanding Accountability*, 37, 39.

42. The tribunals' statutes and those of the International Criminal Court show how human rights struggles impacted international law. For example, crimes against humanity (Art. 7) include deportation or forcible transfer of populations (ethnic cleansing), torture, rape and sexual slavery, enforced disappearance, and apartheid. For the full text, see Ratner and Abrams, *Accountability*, 376–77.

43. ICTR, path: "cases Akayesu, Jean Paul, completed (ICTR-96–4)," and Navanethem Pillay, "Sexual Violence in Times of Conflict: The Jurisprudence of the International Criminal Tribunal for Rwanda," in Chesterman, *Civilians in War*, 165–76. Antiapartheid lawyer Pillay was cofounder with Jessica Neuwirth of the U.S. NGO Equality Now. For her work as a lawyer, see "Navi Speaks," in *Women Reshaping Human Rights: How Extraordinary Activists Are Changing the World*, ed. Marguerite Guzman Bouvard (Wilmington, Del.: Scholarly Resources, 1996), 140–56. In July 2008, the General Assembly confirmed Pillay's appointment as UN High Commissioner for Human Rights.

44. ICTR, path: "Akayesu," 12A.

45. For eyewitness testimony and the case's wider impact, see Pillay, "Sexual Violence," 172, 174.

46. "Croatia Protects a General Charged with War Crimes," *New York Times*, December 3, 2002, A10, and "Unsolved Crimes Add to Plight of Serbs in Kosovo," *New York Times*, August 28, 2003, A3.

47. Howard Tolley, *The U.N. Commission on Human Rights* (Boulder, Colo.: Westview Press, 1987), 124, and Ratner and Abrams, *Accountability*, 161.

48. Claude Bruderlein, "The End of Innocence: Humanitarian Protection in the Twenty-First Century," in Chesterman, *Civilians in War*, 223–24.

49. Rieff, *A Bed*, 218.

50. Kellenberger is in Roberts, "Humanitarian Issues," 189, and Bruderlein, "The End," 225–28, on "reasserting" and "expanding" humanitarian law.

51. The U.S. invasion of Iraq in March 2003 eroded the legitimacy of the doctrine as its supporters admit on the official R2P Web site. See www.responsibilitytoprotect.org/index.php and, for the "hard kernel" quote, Thomas Blom Hansen and Finn Stepputat, eds., *Sovereign Bodies: Citizens, Migrants, and States in the Postcolonial World* (Princeton, N.J.: Princeton University Press, 2005), 1.

52. For these views in the order they were presented, see Claude Bruderlein, "The End," 228–30; Pouligny, *Peace Operations*, 273; and Bruce D. Jones and Charles K. Cater, "From Chaos to Coherence? Toward a Regime for Protecting Civilians in War," in Chesterman, *Civilians in War*, 244–45. In dealing with atrocities committed by local groups in Uganda, Luis Moreno Ocampo, after meeting with community leaders, agreed to "integrate peace talks, and international court investigation and traditional justice and reconciliation processes." See "Victims of Ugandan Atrocities Choose the Path of Forgiveness," *New York Times*, April 18, 2005, A1, 8.

53. Jones and Cater, "From Chaos," 260–61, and, for the previous quote, Bruderlein, "The End," 232.

Chapter 7. September 2001 and History

1. Steven R. Ratner and Jason S. Abrams, *Accountability for Human Rights Atrocities in International Law: Beyond the Nuremberg Legacy* (Oxford: Oxford University Press, 2001), 324–28, address the legal case for prosecution in Cambodia.

2. Marjorie Agosin, "A Visit to the Mothers of the Plaza de Mayo," *Human Rights Quarterly* 9.3 (August 1987): 434.

3. "Argentina's Mothers Pass on a Legacy of Defending Human Rights, *Toward Freedom,* March 9, 2006, retrieved August 6, 2007, from http://toward freedom.com/home/content/view/769/1/. The Mothers have maintained their weekly vigils in the plaza. Also, "Long after Guerrilla War, Survivors Demand Justice from Brazil's Government," *New York Times,* March 28, 2004, A14; "Chile's Leader Presses Rights Issues Softly but Successfully, ibid., September 7, 2003, A3; and "Wide Net in Argentine Torture Case," ibid., September 11, 2000, A6. These articles show reciprocal influences, although each example is a distinct case of "transitional justice" struggles for truth and accountability.

4. Iris Chang, *The Rape of Nanking: The Forgotten Holocaust of World War II* (New York: Penguin Books, 1997), 9; Dai Sil Kim-Gibson, *Silence Broken: Korean Comfort Women* (Parkersburg, Iowa: Mid-Prairie Books, 1999); and Yoshimi Yoshiaki, *Comfort Women: Sexual Slavery in the Japanese Military during World War II,* trans. Suzanne O'Brien (New York: Columbia University Press, 1995). The Korean women's movement pushed the Japanese government to acknowledge the military's involvement in the brothels in 1992. However, the government's failure to take responsibility through full apology and compensation remains a highly contested issue to this day.

5. Richard Falk, *Human Rights Horizons: The Pursuit of Justice in a Globalizing World* (New York: Routledge, 2000), 194, 199.

6. Kofi Annan's opening address, retrieved December 9, 2004, from http://www.racism.gov.za/substance/speeches/unopen.htm, and Peniel E. Joseph, retrieved December 9, 2004, from http://www.greens.org/s-r/27/27-25.html.

7. Sarah White, worker at Delta Pride, retrieved August 7, 2007, from http://www.globalrights.org/site/DocServer/voicesreport.pdf?docID=197.

8. Retrieved August 7, 2007, from http://www.ngocongo.org/index.php? what=resources&g=10, path: WCAR.

9. The official U.N. Web site for the WCAR (henceforth, WCAR site) is http://www.un.org/WCAR/, path: Durban Declaration and Programme of Action, final document retrieved December 9, 2004 from http://www.unhchr.ch/html/racism/02-documents-cnt.html.

10. Quoted from Hanan Ashrawi, a prominent Palestinian political figure and an advocate for a just reconciliation, in *When the Rain Returns: Toward Justice and Reconciliation in Palestine and Israel* ([Philadelphia]: American Friends Service Committee, 2004), viii.

11. These meetings took place in Poland, Costa Rica, Sri Lanka, Senegal, Botswana, Ecuador, and Jordan.

12. WCAR site, path: reports, resolutions, decisions and general documents, reports from the regional meetings, retrieved December 9, 2004, from http://www.unhchr.ch/html/racism/02-documents-cnt.html. The special networking meeting of the Asia-Pacific NGOs in Kathmandu, Nepal, originally was to have met prior to the second session of the Preparatory Committee to channel its recommendations to the Geneva body, but, to the dismay of many, it met after the session.

13. "The Objectives Declared by the World Conference," materials submitted by NGOs, retrieved December 9, 2004, from http://www.hri.ca/racism/Sub mitted/Theme/FIDHenglish.shtml.

14. "Working Report of Prepcom WCAR in Tehran," Jakarta, March 23, 2001, distributed by *ISIS-International-Manila.*

15. Drawn from J. Michael Turner, "The Road to Durban—and Back," *NACLA Report on the Americas* 35 (May–June 2002). The comments of Schüller

and Lozano are in the World Council of Churches Report on the WCAR, "Making a Fresh Start," 3–6 and 10–12, retrieved August 9, 2007, from http://www.oikoumene.org/fileadmin/files/wcc-main/2006pdfs/durban report.pdf. Wong was a regular correspondent sending many reports on the WCAR to AntiRacismNet. The epigraph to this chapter is found in his piece "Winter 2001–2002: Looking Back on Durban—Commentary," January 1, 2002, AntiRacismNet archive, courtesy Cambio, Winter 2001–2.

16. Turner, "The Road." For a wider context, see "Former Slave Havens in Brazil Gaining Rights," *New York Times*, January 23, 2001, A1, 4.

17. Pauline Muchina, "An African Perspective," WCC Report, 7, and Theo van Boven, "World Conference against Racism: An Historical Event?" WCAR site, path: NGO Documents and Other Materials.

18. WCAR site, Major NGO documents, "Draft Declaration of the Botswana Consultative Meeting," Gaborone, Botswana, January 8–12, 2001, 2.

19. Griffiths Aaron Molefe, *Voices*, 104–7.

20. WCAR site, Final Report, 7–8 (A/CONF.189/12).

21. WCAR site, "Report of the European NGO Forum for the WCAR," Strasbourg, France, October 10, 2000, and similar points are in NGO forum "Final Declaration," September 3, 2001, par. 48, 222.

22. WCAR site, Final Document, par. 180–85.

23. Willy Weisz, Ashid Ali, and Ibrahim Abu Sbeih, *Voices*, 40–43, 61–64, 88–91. See also Haifaa Jawad and Tansin Benn, eds., *Muslim Women in the United Kingdom and Beyond: Experiences and Images* (Leiden: Brill, 2003), for discussion of a scathing British report (the Runnymede Trust report in 1997) on the rise of anti-Muslim sentiments.

24. Yoshiaki, *Comfort Women*, 4, and WCAR site, path: NGO documents, articles, analyses, statements, Anna Cewenakova, European Roma Rights Center, Institutionalized Racism and Roma.

25. WCAR site, NGO documents, path: articles, analyses, and statements, George W. Shepherd, A New World Agenda for the 21st Century: The World Conference against Racism and Xenophobia in Durban, South Africa. See also major NGO documents, "IMADR Post-WCAR Statement," and Falk, *Human Rights*, 152, writing about a different context.

26. WCAR site, "Declaration and Plan of Action," Kathmandu, Nepal, April 27–29, 2001 (A/CONF.189/PC.2/9), and, on caste issues, among other sources, see Human Rights Watch, *World Report 2002: Racial Discrimination and Related Intolerances* (New York: Human Rights Watch, 2002).

27. Annan made his plea on August 29, 2001, at the outset of the conference; see "Daily Updates," Day 2, August 29, 2001.

28. Mary Robinson's opening address retrieved December 9, 2004, from http://www.racism.gov.za/substance/speeches/index.html; van Boven, "World Conference," and delegate responses are in World Council of Churches "Report," 5, 11, 19. The U.S. mainstream press gave very little attention to the preparation phases but publicized the controversies. Media responses also are in the WCAR site, path: Articles, Analyses and Statements on Durban, theme, general.

29. Jullyette Ukabiala, "Slave Trade 'A Crime against Humanity,'" *Africa Recovery* 15.3 (October 2001): 5.

30. Creuza Maria de Oliveira, *Voices*, 45.

31. "Declaration," Santiago, and "Report of the European NGO Forum for the WCAR," Strasbourg, October 10, 2000.

32. "Report of the Regional Conference for Africa," Dakar, January 22–24, 2001 (A/CONF.189/PC.2/8), 12, and "Declaration," Santiago (emphasis added). For a historical account, see Robin Blackburn, *The Making of New World Slavery: From the Baroque to the Modern, 1492–1800* (London: Verso, 1997).

33. "Report," Dakar, par. 9–11. The arguments also are found in the NGO networking meeting in Gabarone, "Draft Declaration."

34. "Report," Dakar, par.16–18, 20, and B, par. 2 and 3. It explicitly used as precedent the bilateral agreements between West Germany and Israel that secured reparations for many Jewish Holocaust survivors and families.

35. Anne C. Bailey, *African Voices of the Atlantic Slave Trade: Beyond the Silence and the Shame* (Boston: Beacon Press, 2005), 217.

36. Ibid., 9, 19, 224.

37. Gino J. Naldi, "Reparations in the Practice of the African Commission on Human and Peoples' Rights," *Leiden Journal of International Law* 14 (2001): 685–90.

38. Mariama Oumarou, *Voices*, 36–39.

39. Bailey, *African Voices*, 226–29, and, for a firsthand account, see Roger Wareham, "The Popularization of the International Demand for Reparations for African People," in *Should America Pay? Slavery and the Raging Debate on Reparations*, ed. Raymond A. Windbush (New York: Amistad, HarperCollins, 2003), 235. In the United States, the movement for apology for slavery and the slave trade is gaining momentum, emerging, as a recent article in my local paper noted, from fringe group to "sophisticated, mainstream movement" of significance for the twenty-first century: *Press & Sun-Bulletin* (Binghamton, N.Y.), July 19, 2006, A4.

40. The government report, which passed unanimously, together with the objections (Annex V) were sent to Geneva, "Declaration," Santiago, 52–53, and William B. Wood, Acting Assistant Secretary for International Organization Affairs, U.S. Department of State, "The UN World Conference against Racism," oral testimony before the House International Relations Committee, Subcommittee on International Operations and Human Rights, Washington, D.C., July 31, 2001, retrieved December 13, 2004, from http://www.state.gov/p/io/rls/rm/2001/5514.htm.

41. In *When the Rain Returns*, 41.

42. Ibid., 232–41, including a listing of peace organizations. Also, Anna Baltzer, *Witness in Palestine: Journal of a Jewish American Woman in the Occupied Territories* (Boulder, Colo.: Paradigm Publishers, 2006), 214–15, for other human rights groups working across the divides.

43. Schüller, "The Journey to Durban," 5; Charles D. Smith, *Palestine and the Arab-Israeli Conflict: A History with Documents*, 6th ed. (Boston: Bedford/St. Martins, 2007), 513; and *When the Rain Returns*, 46.

44. For the settler quote, see *When the Rain Returns*, 30, and Smith, *Palestine*, 500.

45. WCAR site, path: NGO documents, Palestinian NGO position paper, "Ending the Ongoing Nakba."

46. "Declaration," Kathmandu, par. 189 and 21, respectively, and also par. 83, which decries the "racist policies of the Israeli state." The NGO Amman meeting reiterated the discredited U.N. resolution, saying that Zionism has not "abandoned its racist policies" and similar sentiments also are found in the NGO Final Document, par. 160–65 on "Palestinians and Palestine," including

labeling Israeli state actions a "crime against humanity" (par. 162). See also WCAR site, NGO Documents, path: Articles, Analyses, and Statements, David Matas (B'nai B'rith Canada), "Civil Society Smashes Up," and Sybil Kessler, "Hard Lessons: From the Battleground of Durban to a Distressed NYC" and "Daily Updates," Day 2, August 29, 2001.

47. "Joint Statement by Eastern and Central European NGO Caucus and Other Members of the NGO Forum of the World Conference against Racism," endorsed September 8, 2001, retrieved March 3, 2004, from http://www.hri.ca/racism/major/europe.shtml, and "Jewish Caucus Walks Out of NGO Forum against Racism," retrieved March 3, 2004, from http://www.hri.ca/racism/major/jewishcaucus.shtml.

48. WCAR site, Major NGO documents, Tehran, "Draft Declaration," 23, Annex II, list of attendance.

49. *When the Rain Returns*, 54. Also, Gershom Gorenberg, "Israel's Tragedy Foretold," *New York Times*, March 10, 2006, A21, and Tom Segev, "What If Israel Had Turned Back?" *New York Times*, June 5, 2007, A23. Specialists in the field also make the point. See William L. Cleveland, *A History of the Modern Middle East*, 3rd ed. (Boulder, Colo.: Westview Press, 2004), 345.

50. Information on Ittijah, which has consultative status in the United Nations, is at its Web site, http://www.ittijah.org/about/about01.html, and Palestinian refugee views, *When the Rain Returns*, 119–20.

51. Article 8 (War Crimes), viii, has made illegal "the transfer, directly or indirectly, by the Occupying Power of parts of its own civilian population into the territory it occupies." The full statute of the International Criminal Court is in Ratner and Abrams, *Accountability*, 378.

52. William Wong, "Winter 2001–2002," and also van Boven, "World Conference."

53. Although a large body of literature debating these global strategies exists, my own argument focuses on assessing the human rights crisis in the immediate post-9/11 climate in the light of the historical developments of human rights and the issues of group vulnerability raised at the WCAR.

54. Luis A. Ortiz, "The U.S. Patriot Act: 'Where Were the Patriots?'" internal memo for the federal defender's office for the Eastern District of Pennsylvania (Philadelphia, n.d.), 8. I thank Felicia Sarner, a federal defender in the office, for giving me a copy of this memo. Also, Megan Peitzke, "The Fate of 'Unremovable' Aliens Before and After September 11, 2001: The Supreme Court's Presumptive Six-Month Limit to Post-Removal-Period Detention," *Pepperdine Law Review* 30 (May 2003): 13.

55. "After the Terror Attacks, a Secret and Speedy Rewriting of Military Law," *New York Times*, October 24, 2004, A1, 12–13, and Seymour M. Hersh, *Chain of Command: The Road from 9/11 to Abu Ghraib* (New York: HarperCollins, 2004).

56. Louise Richardson, *What Terrorists Want: Understanding the Enemy, Containing the Threat* (New York: Random House, 2006), xxii, 188.

57. Among others, the Inter-American Commission on Human Rights, "Report on Terrorism and Human Rights," OAE/Ser.L/v/11.116, October 22, 2003, retrieved November 11, 2004, from http://www.cidh.org/Terrorism/Eng/toc.htm.

58. *Hamdi v. Rumsfeld*, No. 03-6696, decided June 28, 2004, Westlaw, 124 S. Ct. 2633, 13.

59. Ibid., 3, 7, 11–12.

60. Ibid., 22–23.

61. *Rasul v. Bush*, Nos. 03-334, 03-343, decided June 28, 2004, Westlaw, 124 S. Ct. 2686, 12.

62. "British Court Says Detentions Violate Rights," *New York Times*, December 17, 2004, A1, 17.

63. Before this book went to press, the U.S. Supreme Court again ruled for detainee rights. The majority said, "The laws and Constitution are designed to survive, and remain in force, in extraordinary times." *New York Times*, June 12, 2008, A1, 22.

64. "Report," Executive Summary, OEA/Ser.L/v/11.116, October 22, 2002, par. 2, retrieved March 6, 2004, from http://www.cidh.oas.org/Terrorism/Eng/exe.htm.

65. Aaron Rhodes, "Combating Racism while Fighting Terrorism," paper presented at Workshop I, All Different, All Equal: ECRI (European Commission against Racism and Intolerance), Ten Years of Combating Racism, Strasbourg, 18 March 2004, retrieved December 9, 2004, from http://www.coe.int/t/E/human_rights/ecri.

Conclusion

1. Geoffrey Nunberg, "As Google Goes, So Goes the Nation," *New York Times*, Week in Review, May 18, 2003, referring to Patrick E. Tyler, "Threats and Responses: News Analysis—A New Power in the Streets."

2. *The Lost Agenda: Human Rights and U.N. Field Operations* (New York: Human Rights Watch, 1993), 135–36.

3. Concentrating on specific moments and contexts in the linkages between global and local change, I have largely omitted other human rights themes and perspectives. See, for example, Burns H. Weston, ed., *Child Labor and Human Rights: Making Children Matter* (Boulder, Colo.: Lynne Rienner, 2005).

4. I have taken the epigraph from Alexis Jetter, Annelise Orleck, and Diana Taylor, eds., *The Politics of Motherhood: Activist Voices from Left to Right* (Hanover, N.H.: University Press of New England, 1997).

5. In the lead up to the Iraq war, the Bush administration used the U.N.'s reputed failure to act (or, as officials called it, the "international community's" failures) as a justification for its own unilateral military action.

6. "U.N. Is Transforming Itself, But into What Is Unclear," *New York Times*, February 28, 2005, A3, and "Terror in the Weather Forecast," ibid., April 24, 2007, A25.

7. Soren Ambrose, "Multilateral Debt: The Unbearable Burden," *Foreign Policy in Focus* 6.37 (November 2001): 6.

8. Steven R. Ratner and Jason Abrams, *Accountability for Human Rights Atrocities in International Law: Beyond the Nuremberg Legacy*, 2nd ed. (Oxford: Oxford University Press, 2001), 50.

9. Sally Engle Merry, *Human Rights and Gender Violence: Translating International Law into Local Justice* (Chicago: University of Chicago Press, 2006), 225–27, and Jack Donnelly, *Universal Human Rights in Theory and Practice*, 2nd ed. (Ithaca, N.Y.: Cornell University Press, 2003), 40.

10. Theo van Boven, *People Matter: Views on International Human Rights Policy* (Amsterdam: Meulenhoff, 1982), 71, 173. I have taken my subtitle for this chapter from van Boven's collection.

11. "To Curb Illegal Migrants, Spain Offers a Legal Route," *New York Times*, August 11, 2007, A3.

Index